'E

The social life of
Britain's five-year-olds

Routledge Education Books

Advisory editor: John Eggleston
Professor of Education
University of Keele

The social life of Britain's five-year-olds

A report of the Child Health and Education Study

(Albert . Francis)

A.F. Osborn, N.R. Butler and A.C. Morris

Routledge & Kegan Paul
London, Boston, Melbourne and Henley

First published in 1984
by Routledge & Kegan Paul plc

39 Store Street, London WC1E 7DD, England

9 Park Street, Boston, Mass. 02108, USA

464 St Kilda Road,
Melbourne, Victoria 3004, Australia

Broadway House, Newtown Road,
Henley-on-Thames, Oxon RG9 1EN, England

Set in Press Roman 10 pt by Columns of Reading
and printed in Great Britain by
St Edmundsbury Press Ltd
Bury St Edmunds, Suffolk

Library of Congress Cataloging in Publication Data

Osborn, A.F. (Albert Francis), 1939-

The social life of Britain's five-year-olds.
Bibliography: p.
Includes index.
1. Children—Great Britain—Social conditions—
Longitudinal studies. 2. Socially handicapped children—
Great Britain—Longitudinal studies. 3. Social adjustment
—Longitudinal studies. 4. Children of the mentally ill—
Longitudinal studies. I. Butler, Neville R. II. Morris,
A.C. (Anthony Charles), 1950- . III. Title.
HQ792.G7083 1984   305.2'33'0941   83-23029

British Library CIP available

ISBN 0-7100-9618-6

Contents

v

Contents

Contents

Figures

Figures

Tables

Child Health and Education Study

This was a national longitudinal study of children born during the week 5-11 April 1970 in England, Scotland and Wales.

The children in this survey were originally subjects of the British Births survey carried out in 1970 under the auspices of the National Birthday Trust Fund and the Royal College of Obstetricians and Gynaecologists.

The 1975 follow-up survey was carried out by the Department of Child Health, University of Bristol, under the directorship of Professor Neville Butler and with the collaboration of the Health Visitors' Association.

The Director

Professor Neville Butler, MD, FRCP, FRCOG, DCH is Professor of Child Health at the University of Bristol, consultant to the World Health Organisation and to the Pan-American Health Organisation. His work with British child development studies began in 1958 when he was Director of the Perinatal Mortality Survey.

Principal Research Officers

Medical – Dr. Sue Dowling, MB, BS, MSc (Soc Med), MFCM
Social – Albert Osborn, BA
Computing – Brian Howlett, BSc, BA, FSS, MBCS

Research Associate

Statistics – Anthony Morris, BA, MSc

Dr. Sue Dowling is currently lecturer in Community Medicine at the University of Bristol.

Preface

This book is about social inequality in Britain and the way this affects the lives of five-year-old children. At this age children reach the end of what is widely accepted to be the most significant period of their lives; a time when growth and development takes place at a faster rate than at any other time. It is well known that poverty in these formative years can effectively restrict children's normal rate of physical and cognitive growth so that they fail to achieve their full potential. Thus the effects of social inequality in the preschool years can result in wide disparities in cognitive ability between children who have achieved the same chronological age. This is especially important at the age of five, when children in Britain are legally required to enter full-time education, because those who are from socially disadvantaged homes will be less able to learn from their school experience than their more advantaged peers.

For these reasons a national survey was carried out to examine many aspects of social and family inequality and to obtain information on two major subjects of special relevance to the under-fives; uptake of preschool education and day care services, and maternal employment. We explore various aspects of inequality by using data from the Child Health and Education Study which carried out a survey in 1975 of the social circumstances, general development, health and use of preschool educational and health services of 13,135 children aged five years in England, Scotland and Wales. All these children were born during the week 5-11 April 1970 and at that time were subjects of the British Births survey (Chamberlain et al., 1975; Chamberlain et al., 1978).

This is the third national longitudinal study of child development based on one week of births that has been undertaken in Britain; the first was the National Survey of Health and Development which began in 1946 (Douglas and Blomfield, 1948) and the second was the National Child Development Study (Davie et al., 1972) which started in 1958 as the Perinatal Mortality Survey (Butler and Bonham, 1963). These surveys enable us to compare the social life of children in 1975 with that of two earlier cohorts of children over a total span of twenty-four years.

Over the whole of this period and to the present day there have been three broad issues of special concern to all responsible for the well-being of children under five; the family, preschool education and day care provision and the employment of mothers. We have organised this book around these three issues with social inequality recurring as a common theme.

In Part 1 — The families — we first examine the concept and extent of social inequality in our sample of children and compare the social circumstances of our cohort with those of the children in the earlier cohort studies. We then look at family disruption and describe how loss of a parent can result in downward social mobility. This is followed by an analysis of the division of labour in the home and the extent to which the father had taken part in domestic and child care activities. Finally, we compare these different social and family factors in their effects on the children's cognitive development and behavioural adjustment and depression in the mothers.

In Part 2 — Preschool education and day care — we discuss the pattern of entry to infant schools in Britain and how this was related to children's uptake of preschool educational services. Next we show the different social and family factors that influenced the type of preschool experience the child had, and whether or not the mother herself helped in any way at the preschool institution her child attended. Lastly, we examine the association between attendance at a preschool institution and the child's cognitive ability and behavioural adjustment.

In Part 3 — Mothers in paid employment — we consider the social and family factors that influenced the likelihood that a mother obtained paid employment and the extent and nature of her work. The attitudes of employed and non-employed mothers towards maternal employment are contrasted and the reasons why mothers went out to work are reported. The arrangements made by the mothers for the care of their children while they were at work are described. We conclude with an analysis of the association between maternal employment and the child's cognitive ability and behaviour and depression in the mother.

In Part 4 — Research methods — we describe how the survey was carried out, trace rates and possible sources of bias due to non-response. Detailed explanations are given of the tests and assessments used and our methods of analysis.

It is not possible to summarise succinctly the conclusions of our research in one paragraph. At the end of every chapter, however, there is a short summary of our main findings and conclusions. To help the reader locate specific topics of interest, the table of contents includes headings of subsections as well as titles of chapters.

Authors' note

Whilst this book was in the press, the tragic death was announced of Brian Jackson, typically during an event when he was raising money for children. In recognition of Brian's widely acclaimed work in promoting the wellbeing of children, this book is dedicated to him.

Acknowledgements

This book is the result of the collaborative work of a great many people throughout the preparation and execution of the survey, the coding and data processing of the data gathered, and the computer analysis to produce the final results that are published here. None of this would have been possible, however, were it not for the generous financial support received from the Medical Research Council, Social Science Research Council, National Birthday Trust Fund, Action Research for the Crippled Child, the Leverhulme Trust, and many other independent Trusts.

In this nation-wide survey we were grateful for the willing cooperation of Area Nurses (Child Health) of the (then) Area Health Authorities in England and Wales, Nursing Officers in the Scottish Health Boards, and their health visitors who helped to trace the study children and carried out the survey. We were also grateful for the collaboration of the Health Visitors' Association who were cosponsors of the study. We should like to mention the valuable assistance of the National Health Service Central Register and Family Practitioner Committees in England and Wales, and the Administrators of Primary Care in Scotland who also cooperated with their colleagues in the Health Authorities/Boards in locating the children's whereabouts.

We should like to thank the administrative and secretarial staff of the Child Health and Education Study who, at various stages of the work, have responded cheerfully to the demands placed upon them. Special mention should be made of Maureen Fraser, Jenny Heck, Mary Horwood, Geraldine Ringham and Jane Tily. The huge amount of clerical work involved in the administration of the survey and the coding of the questionnaire data called for enormous patience and fortitude. We were fortunate in finding these qualities in Sylvia Zair, who supervised the coding processes, and our principal clerical and coding staff; Jean Burbridge, Gwen Craddock, Mary Larnach, Pam

Lyons, James Parsons, Britta Pendry, Mary Probert and Sheila Taylor. Acknowledgement is also due to Mary Haslum and Alan Carpenter who devised and supervised the coding of the Test Booklet data.

The authors warmly thank their colleagues in the Department of Child Health Research Unit for their comments and constructive criticisms on earlier drafts of the chapters in this book. Special thanks are due to Marilyn Osborn for her contribution to the discussion in the chapters concerned with mothers in paid employment, and to Margaret Adams who helped to smooth many of the rough edges of the text.

We are also grateful to the Medical Research Council National Survey of Health and Development (1946 cohort) based in the Department of Community Health, University of Bristol, for providing data from the National Survey, and the National Children's Bureau for providing data from the National Child Development Study (1958 cohort) for the comparisons with results from our own survey presented in Chapter 2.

Finally, we wish to thank all the mothers and children who have taken part and shown such an interest in the study. This book is about them and for them in the hope that by learning from their lives it might be possible to build a better world for children in the future.

Prologue

In the week which began on Sunday 5 April 1970, 16,333 children were born in England, Wales and Scotland. This book is a broad study of what happened to them during their first five years of life.

Much else happened in that week. On the Sunday President Nixon told Vice President Agnew not to go to the baseball match because his casting vote was needed to appoint a controversial judge to the Supreme Court. In Europe, the Foreign Secretary, Michael Stewart, flew to Ankara with 1,200 pounds of dried soup for victims of the Turkish earthquake; and bombs exploded in the Crumlin Road, Belfast. On Monday there was rain, sleet and some snow right across the British Isles and much of the continent. A referee was killed by lightning after he ruled that a match should go on despite a violent thunderstorm, and Count Karl-Maria von Sprett, the German ambassador, was murdered in Guatemala. On Tuesday the papers carried photographs of daffodils in the ruins of Lesnes Abbey at Woolwich; and a pair of ospreys returned to their traditional eyrie at Loch Garten on Speyside. Wednesday brought the coldest April night since records began; and the 'Brotherhood of Father Christmas and Union of Santa Claus' was fined £10 for obstructing the pavement outside Selfridges in Oxford Street. Sir Adrian Boult gave a triumphal performance of the Brahms D Major symphony at the Royal Festival Hall; and the next day brought a conservative victory in the Greater London Council election and an Oscar for film star John Wayne in Hollywood. On Friday the spaceship Apollo 13 set off on course for the moon, and Paul McCartney admitted that the Beatles had broken up. The last day of the week brought the Cup Final at Wembley between Chelsea and Leeds United. For the first time ever at that stadium it ended in a draw and the silver trophy lay unclaimed in the Royal Box.

All the kaleidoscopic quality of life during the first five years of these children's lives stands out of reach of this report. Yet the statistics and discussions which follow, although they grasp only part of the larger reality, serve to show how out of the great variety the pattern of life for some children is distinctly different from that of other children. This book is concerned, then, with the structures within which the lives of the children are organised. I hope it will not be forgotten, however, that behind every number and statistic lies an individual child. Certainly that is how their parents — the chief source of information — always saw it.

It is not possible to tell the human story of over 16,000 unique and individual boys and girls. That too lies outside the scope of the study, but in following the data this should perhaps be remembered. Perhaps it helps, just for a moment, to hear the voices of some of the mothers remembering what, to them, was the most important moment of that week.

'Dawn came at 4.30 on the Sunday morning. It didn't take long, it was just like a bad period pain. Somehow I knew she was going to be a boy and when she popped out I was a bit surprised — as if there'd been a mistake. But all I wanted to do was go to sleep and let them get on with it.

'Dawn frightened me to death when I got her home. I thought I'd drop her on the floor and she'd break like a piece of jelly. And then the little perisher worried me because she wouldn't cry. I think I'd got my brother's baby at the back of my mind — that was a cot death — and it sort of shook me. So I wondered if there was anything wrong with Dawn. And a lot later it turned out that there was. It was either her liver or her kidneys, and she had to go into a special unit. She's alright now — a little blond bundle of mischief she is.'

On Monday it was Mrs Shapiro's turn: 'I didn't know much about it — it was a caesar, and now I can't have any more. Not that my husband minds. You have to do it quick, that caesar. No time for husband's permission, he was off at work. So I woke up to Lucy. She was really beautiful. Not wrinkled at all. I don't know — I'd been so distressed — she was like a shock. You see, she worked. I couldn't believe that. But all the little pieces, eyes, legs, wee-wee. Complete set like Lego.

'Later I wasn't the world's best mum. You know, cross at night when she wouldn't sleep, and then cross in the morning when she wouldn't wake up. I *hated* being mummy — cross — all — the — time. But you learn. Slowly you learn to enjoy them. Lucy is a miracle. Those first five years — we've done nothing I could tell you about. We've just had a quietly exciting life.'

Wednesday brought Jeremy's introduction to the world. 'Well, he just sort of popped out. It was a bit quick, but do you know only a few minutes before my husband popped out too — to get the bread from the shop. I think he must have known he was coming; I didn't.

But last time when we had Anthony in the hospital he just passed out. Search me why, but I think fathers are like that.

'This time I had him at home. Mind you, I thought it would be a girl. I think a woman always knows, and when the midwife came — I had this one at home — we played records, and she chose that Rolf Harris one: "Two little boys had two little toys".

'But it wasn't like I expected. He *was* a boy. Still, I wouldn't like those modern things when you know in advance: takes all the fun out of it. I enjoyed having Jeremy, really enjoyed it. The doctor arrived too late, but we gave him a cup of tea. I think he'd had a harder day than me, and I'd got Jeremy — but I felt he needed a bit of cheering up.'

These are three voices from 16,000. But though the researchers are conscious of the individual nature of each child, family and experience, this survey must deal in general trends over time. All the children were surveyed at birth, under the auspices of the National Birthday Trust Fund, so this study is built on existing foundations and allows the reader the very rare opportunity of following a large group of children through their first five years.

This, then, is a national longitudinal study, and that produces its own challenges and dilemmas. First of all, it has required a multi-disciplinary approach. The research team has consisted of social scientists, many different specialisms in medical practice, and statisticians. Secondly, the study has drawn on the voluntary help and expertise of very large numbers of colleagues in the three countries. Thirdly, there is the sheer scale of the data collection. By the end of 1977, close to a quarter of a million computer cards had been punched and put onto magnetic tape. All this takes huge amounts of time and by the time the report is available the children have of course grown older. It is always about their yesterdays.

Lastly, research of this nature is costly and it is not easy to find financial sponsorship, however vital the work, for the reels of time involved.

So longitudinal studies on this scale are unusual. Nonetheless they are, in my view, worth the considerable price that they claim — on imagination, on time, on resources. Normal surveys take a representative slice of human life: much as a geologist drives a bore deep into the earth. What emerges is an illuminating but necessarily static picture. A longitudinal study adds something else, it brings in the third dimension — time. Like the difference between a still and a moving film, it can — at its best — give us a glimpse of the movement of ordinary life. The authors do not pretend that they have fully realised this potentiality, only that it is latent in the method.

Lastly, there has been the dilemma of organising this vast amount of information in some logical and coherent form. By itself it is, of course, meaningless. One is faced either with the working of the Second Law of Thermodynamics or Sean O'Casey's observation that the 'whole world is in a terrible state of chassis'. Naturally the best statistical techniques have been used to elicit order and significance out of these great Alps of data. However that itself must be preceded by the formulation of questions.

The authors have taken a universal question; what gives one child born in this week a better life-chance than another born in the same week? They have then tried to pursue why some children are at risk, developmentally delayed or behaviourally deviant — and other children are not. They have not, in the research, been judgmental. Instead they have inquired into inequality in provision or in families' aspirations or in their demands. They have described regional differences, and those between town and country, inequalities between the sexes or between majority and minority groups. They have looked at environmental factors and at the many different and subtle forms of family life; one-parent, large family, rooted, mobile, prospering or struggling. Simultaneously they have searched, again without offering a verdict within the evidence, for patterns which positively show forms of equality in life chances or universality in the provision of services.

Whether the authors have asked the right questions of the data, the reader will judge. All they are concerned to do in this book is to show the extent and nature of social inequality in their sample of five-year-olds and to point to some of the possible consequences of this for their progress through life. I hope, however, that our study will be more than just an interesting historical record, and that it can provide the basis for finding ways of improving the lives of future generations of children.

Brian Jackson
Department of Child Health
University of Bristol

Part C

The Principles

Part One

The families

Introduction

The first five years of life are unique. Not only is this period critical for a child's future development and life chances, but it is also the only time when the crucial concerns surrounding his or her health, education and socialisation are left almost entirely to people who, for the most part, have no special training in these vital spheres. These people are, of course, the child's parents. Oddly enough, considering the great store set by professionalism and expertise today, society expects parents to be endowed with both ability and resources for meeting every personal and economic need of their child. This expectation persists despite the fact that such resources, as we know only too well, are never evenly distributed. Some children, for example, do not have two parents; for others their parents may be very young, inexperienced, poorly educated, in poor health, emotionally unstable, immature or have inadequate financial means for supporting a family and limited scope for making a living. To the extent that parental skills, educational, social and economic resources are distributed unequally among families, so some children start life with greater chances of healthy development and successful achievement in later life than others less fortunate. In the first chapter we describe the home circumstances of the children in the study, pointing up the familial, social and economic factors which created increased opportunities for some and curtailed the lives of others. This theme of inequality will be elaborated in subsequent chapters which deal with the social circumstances of children in Britain today.

In order to place the findings in this study within a historical context we have made comparisons between them and those relating to other households in the 1970s and compared our children with previous generations of children over a twenty-five-year period (Chapter 2). This has been achieved by using such sources as the 1971 General Household Survey and the 1946 and 1958 birth cohort studies (Douglas and

Blomfield, 1958; Davie *et al.*, 1972). These comparisons reveal how the material conditions of the life of young children have gradually changed over the years, compared with those of the population of Britain at large.

Since our study is national in scope it can be said to be truly representative of Britain as a whole. At the same time it is important to recognise that there are substantial variations in the socioeconomic and demographic characteristics of Wales, Scotland and different regions of England which have resulted from their individual histories of industrial and cultural development. Some of these regional variations are described in the chapters which follow so that the significance of the national figures for individual regions may be more readily appreciated.

Chapter 1

Social inequality

Social inequality continues to be a central concern of western democracy notwithstanding the growth in prosperity since the war years and the development of the welfare state in Britain. Despite social reforms aimed at reducing inequality, poverty persists and, depending on the criteria used, has been shown to affect at least seven percent and possibly as much as twenty-five percent of households in the United Kingdom (Townsend, 1979, Chapter 7). Poverty not only reduces the quality of life in material terms, it also influences family relationships, cultural activities and child rearing practices and increases the risk of ill-health (Black Report, 1981; Coffield *et al.*, 1980).

An even greater problem is that poverty tends to be transmitted from one generation to the next in the same families. It is as if some children inherit the poverty of their parents in the way that others inherit their parents' wealth. This intergenerational continuity of poverty gave rise to the cycle of deprivation thesis which received wide publicity in the speeches of Sir Keith Joseph during the early 1970s. A key element of this thesis was the notion of inadequate parenting which was itself caused by poverty and educational failure in the early lives of the parents, and led in turn to increased risk of school failure, poor employment prospects and poverty in the next generation. An alternative argument is that intergenerational continuity of poverty is a consequence of social structural factors; in particular the class system (Berthoud, 1976 and 1981, Rutter and Madge, 1976). For a variety of reasons children from low social classes are unlikely to achieve professional status whereas children of professionals are likely to attain occupations of similar status to their fathers (Goldthorpe, 1980).

The extent of poverty in Britain and its implications for the socialisation process in the early years made socioeconomic inequality a key factor in our study of this sample of five-year-olds. In particular we wanted to identify those families who suffered a multiplicity of

5

deprivations, the importance of which has been expressed frequently by others (Holman, 1978, pp. 35-43; Rutter and Madge, 1976, pp. 248-52; Wedge and Prosser, 1973), and also to identify relatively advantaged families. This latter point is important since comparisons of the most disadvantaged with the average is only half the picture in a society in which there is also a relatively privileged sector. With these objectives in mind we devised an index of socioeconomic inequality which we considered to be particularly relevant to child development issues.

Rationale of the Social Index

Our point of departure was taken from previous research which has shown associations between social conditions and child development. One such study was the National Child Development Study (Davie *et al*., 1972) which showed marked variation in school attainment and social adjustment related to a number of social and housing factors (ibid., p. 54). Social class, overcrowding, availability of household amenities and housing tenure were each independently associated with the reading ability of seven-year-olds after adjusting for the effects of all the other variables. Although conducting an analysis which 'separates out' the independent effect of each variable, the authors were careful to avoid the trap of asserting causal inference:

> It would, of course, be naive to assume a direct causal relationship between, say, lack of hot water in the household and children's reading attainment. But poor housing conditions may well lead to a poor standard of physical health; depression and irritability in a parent; and may produce a feeling of 'distance' from the more privileged sections of society (with which the school may be identified). (ibid., p. 57)

Whilst one might argue about the specific explanations offered for the association between housing conditions and attainment, the general point is correct. The measures of housing — crowding, amenities and tenure — represent, so to speak, some configuration of factors which actually impinges on the child in different ways so as to accelerate or retard his or her rate of development. In other words, the association between housing conditions and measures of attainment in children is attributed to socialisation processes going on within the home. The relationship between a father's occupation and his child's school attainment is frequently described as the 'social class effect' with little thought given to what this might mean in this context. We suggest that occupational status is indicative of the same types of socialisation processes that have been associated with different housing conditions: a view which is supported by the widely documented association of housing differences with social class (Reid, 1981). Furthermore, there is substantial evidence that different socialisation patterns prevail within different social classes (Kohn, 1969; Newson, 1970 and 1978) and it is safe to assume that such differences would be found between families living at either end of a spectrum of housing standards. On the basis of this evidence we would contend that measures of social class and housing standards together with other factors such as parental education and the character of the neighbourhood environment are all essentially indicators of what may be regarded as one socioeconomic dimension. Ultimately it is of little interest that low social class, lack of a bathroom or hot water and overcrowded housing each has a separate effect on, say, reading ability, if our final conclusion is the familiar and global acknowledgement that poor children perform less well than their better-off peers. For these reasons we suggest that all the different social and housing indices should be combined in a single index.

A further reason for taking this approach to measuring social inequality is that social indicators are notoriously vague. For example, in families where the fathers were all in unskilled manual occupations (social class V), few people would be surprised to find tremendous variation within this group in standard of living, life style, educational values and cultural attitudes (Askham, 1969). Greater group homogeneity might be achieved within the sample if, instead of the simplistic and broad social class variable based only on father's occupation, several interrelated factors were used that would distinguish families who are conspicuously disadvantaged from those who enjoy a high degree of advantage. Between these two extremes would be families at different levels of advantage or disadvantage. What we are proposing is a stratification model in which families would be ranked according to the social and material resources at their command, and which permits the identification of the most vulnerable children in social terms, i.e. those in families experiencing multiple deprivations.

We have attempted to put the model into operation by scoring eight socioeconomic items using the scheme given in Table 18.4 (Chapter 18) and summing the scores to produce a Social Index score. Items selected for the Social Index were limited to those which suggested unequivocal advantage or disadvantage. These were occupational status of father, educational qualifications of parents, type of neighbourhood in which family lived, level of crowding, type of accommodation, housing tenure, bathroom availability and car ownership. Further details of these items and the method of scoring are given in Chapter 18. Variables which provide only *indirect* indication of social disadvantage were not used in this index. Large families and one-parent families, for example,

7

are often associated with poor socioeconomic position or low social class, yet in favourable economic circumstances these factors do not in themselves imply disadvantage. Indeed, one of the objectives of Chapter 3 is to investigate the social circumstances of children in one-parent families compared with children living with both their parents.

The Social Index scores were distributed between four and sixteen (see Table 18.5). Low scores were achieved by families who were relatively advantaged in terms of the Social Index items and high scores by families who were disadvantaged in many respects. Only 387 (2.9 percent) families achieved the lowest possible score. In all these families the father would have been in an occupation with professional status (social class I), one or both parents would have a degree or equivalent qualification, they would live in owner-occupied accommodation in a well-to-do neighbourhood and run a car. None of these families would be living in overcrowded conditions or lack a bathroom. Families with a Social Index score of 5 (N = 868, 6.6 percent) were on the whole very similar to those with the minimum score. The main difference concerned their neighbourhood of residence which was likely to be rated as an average urban or rural area, rather than well-to-do. In terms of the father's occupation, the parents' education and housing, Social Index 4 and 5 families were practically the same. These two groups, therefore, are combined in tabular analysis using the Social Index in the chapters which follow, and have been defined as the 'most advantaged' families.

The mean Social Index score was 8.2 (standard deviation = 2.0) and a score of 8 or 9 was achieved by the 'average' family which comprised 36.8 percent of the sample. To achieve these scores, a family would have been advantaged in one or two respects such as the parents having at least minimal educational qualifications or owning the house they lived in, or living in a well-to-do neighbourhood, or owning a car. But they would not have been advantaged in all these ways.

Families which we have defined as being 'most disadvantaged' had Social Index scores of 11 or more (N = 1,479; 11.3 percent). These typically had none of the advantages we have mentioned above, and in addition suffered at least one disadvantage such as living in a poor urban neighbourhood, living in privately rented furnished accommodation, living in overcrowded conditions, lacking a bathroom or living in rooms. A family suffering *all* these disadvantages would obtain a Social Index score of 17. In fact no family scored the maximum, but five scored 16 and sixty-nine scored 14 or more.

Two other groups complete the socioeconomic hierarchy defined by the Social Index. These were families who scored 6 or 7, and those who scored 10. The first of these groups were the 27 percent who fell between the 'most advantaged' and 'average' Social Index groups, and therefore have been defined as 'advantaged'. The 15.3 percent of families who scored 10 came between the 'average' and 'most disadvantaged' groups and thus were deemed 'disadvantaged' in that they either lacked all the positive characteristics in terms of education, housing or neighbourhood, or else any advantages they may have had were offset by disadvantages.

Case studies

Assessing our families in terms of the items comprising the Social Index we uncovered wide divisions in the standard and quality of life from the most advantaged to the most disadvantaged groups. The contrast in social circumstances of these two groups at the extreme ends of the spectrum can best be illustrated by two case studies presented below. These cases were randomly selected from families living in a large city in the English midlands with Social Index scores in the 'most advantaged' or 'most disadvantaged' groups. The profiles are drawn entirely from the information recorded on the questionnaires for these cases. To increase anonymity, however, certain details not connected with the Social Index have been altered.

1 A 'most advantaged' family (Social Index score 4). In this family the study child had one sister who was older than her by two years. The parents were buying a ten-roomed detached house in a well-to-do neighbourhood where the houses were well-spaced and generally well-maintained. Multi-occupation in this neighbourhood was rare and most families had higher than average incomes. In the home there was no lack of household amenities such as bathroom, indoor lavatory or hot water supply. The family had a garden where the children could play. Domestic equipment included a washing machine, spin drier, refrigerator and telephone. The family could enjoy watching television programmes in colour. They also ran a car. The health visitor who carried out the interview with the mother was of the opinion that the standard of furniture and equipment in the home was luxurious. Both parents were in their thirties. The father had degree level qualifications and was practising as a solicitor. The mother, with education to 'O' level, had worked in an office for the previous two years for ten hours a week. This she did mainly to earn money for extras, such as savings, holidays, household appliances, luxuries and the car.

The family obtained a low, i.e. 'most advantaged' Social Index score because of the father's degree level qualifications and professional status, and because they were owner-occupiers of a house in a well-to-do neighbourhood and also ran a car. However, there were additional material advantages. For example they were buying a detached house

9

which was larger than average, and there was no lack of amenities or equipment. The father's profession as a solicitor probably brought in a higher than average income and some fringe benefits; for example, conveyancing when they bought their present home. In addition, the mother could add to the family income by doing a secretarial job for 2½ hours a day whilst the children were at school. This, then, is the kind of situation we are describing when we refer to the 'most advantaged' families in the study, of whom there were 9.6 percent in the sample.

Elsewhere in the same city was another family whose circumstances were in sharp contrast with those of the family we have just described.

2 A 'most disadvantaged' family (Social Index score 15). This Asian family lived in a part of the city in which houses were closely packed together, many were in poor state of repair, multi-occupation was common, and most families were likely to have had low incomes. The two parents and three children occupied privately rented furnished accommodation which was shared with another family. They had two rooms of their own, but the kitchen, bathroom, indoor lavatory, hot water supply and garden were shared. A telephone was available, however, and the family had the use of a car.

Neither parent had any educational qualifications, having left school at fifteen, and the father did unskilled manual work in a factory that made motor cycles. The mother did not go out to work herself. The opportunity for the mother to seek employment would have been severely limited, however, as the study child's two younger siblings were born within little more than two years of her own birth. The mother herself was only twenty years old when the study child was born. The family had lived in the same accommodation since the time of the study child's birth.

The family had a high, i.e. 'most disadvantaged' Social Index score because they were living in overcrowded conditions in privately rented furnished rooms in a poor neighbourhood, and the father was an unskilled manual worker. They were, however, disadvantaged in other respects also. In particular they lacked complete independence because they were sharing accommodation with another household (in fact it might have been more than one other household). Some of the difficulties probably stemmed from the fact that the mother herself was only twenty years old when the study child was born, and she had two more children before she was even twenty-three (Butler and Sloman, 1980). The father's job was likely to be low paid and insecure, so that with the heavy family responsibilities there would have been little opportunity to obtain better accommodation. The mother, with three children to care for in very stressful circumstances, would also have been unable to go out to work to supplement the family income, even had she wanted to.

These two case studies are a cogent illustration of how two children growing up in different parts of the same city were exposed to vastly different home and social environments. Moreover, these inequalities extend beyond the home. The more fortunate of these two children was enrolled in a playgroup from the age of three and then transferred to an independent fee-paying preparatory school at four and a half. The other child also attended playgroup, but not until the age of four and a half, and then did not enter infant school until nearly five and a half years of age. This comparison highlights the advantage accruing to the child in the socially advantaged family in that their good financial position allowed them to exercise choice over the type of education most suited to their child (i.e. a private school) which gained a year's start over the girl from the disadvantaged home. This extra educational advantage was added to the many other advantages we listed for the child from the advantaged home.

To reinforce this picture of what disadvantage can mean in plain factual terms, we are giving thumbnail sketches of five other families from the most disadvantaged Social Index group in the study which will illustrate the different kinds of adverse life situations that children in such families are likely to have experienced.

1 South West England (Social Index score 11). The parents of this child were divorced in the month after her birth. The father left taking one of the older sisters with him whilst leaving the mother to care for the new baby and two children aged six and three. The study child had a severe hearing defect and attended school for the deaf from the age of two and a half. Her elder brother was totally deaf. At the age of one year the study child was taken into care of the Local Authority and lived with foster parents for seven months. When the study child was five, the mother and three children were living in a privately rented furnished flat consisting of two rooms, kitchen, bathroom and indoor toilet.

2 South West England (Social Index score 13). This family lived in a caravan on a site which the health visitor thought was of poor standard. The fact that they lived in a caravan inevitably meant that the family of two parents and three children were severely overcrowded. The three children slept in one room, and the study child shared a bed with one other. The conditions were very poor, with no hot water supply, indoor lavatory or bathroom, although the caravan did have a small kitchen. The outside toilets were shared by others on the site. They had the use of a washing machine, but it was not clear if this was part of the camp

11

facilities. The family did, however, run a car or van. The father had qualifications equivalent to G.C.E. 'O' level, but was employed as a labourer repairing roads and digging trenches. The mother was only seventeen years old when she had her first child, having left school at age fifteen.

3 Industrial area of South Wales (Social Index score 14). This family shared the home of the father's parents. The mother was eighteen when the study child was born and the father was nineteen. A second child was born three years later. The father's sister was also still living at home. Fortunately the house was large enough to accommodate both families as it consisted of seven rooms and a large kitchen. The study child's family had the use of two rooms on an upper floor, but perhaps were able to share living rooms with the grandparents. However, there was no bathroom or hot water supply and the only lavatory was outside. The house was privately rented, unfurnished, in an average urban neighbourhood. The father was a builder's labourer, and both parents left school at fifteen without educational qualifications.

The health visitor who interviewed the mother thought that the domestic situation of the family was provoking behavioural problems in the study child:

'He is rather undisciplined and difficult to control, owing to the fact that they are living in the home of his father's parents with an unmarried sister there as well. Thus there are three adult women and two adult men to go to when there is any question of discipline.'

4 Large city in Scotland (Social Index score 14). The study child in this family was the fourth of six daughters. The mother had her first child when she was nineteen. In the same year, the father became unemployed at age twenty-one and was still unemployed ten years later at the time of the study child's fifth birthday. His last job was labouring for a metal contractor. The mother also was not employed, and had not had a job outside the home since the study child was born. Both parents left school at fifteen and had no educational qualifications.

This large family of two parents and six children was living in a four-roomed council flat with sole use of kitchen, bathroom, indoor lavatory and hot water supply. A garden or yard was shared with other households. There was a lack of basic domestic equipment available to a majority of British families such as refrigerator, washing machine, spin drier, telephone or car. They did have a television, but it didn't work.

The health visitor who carried out the survey with this family recorded that furniture and equipment were of a very low standard and that the flat was chaotic. She also made the following observations:

'This child was born at home in extremely poor social circumstances. The family lived in overcrowded, dirty conditions in condemned property. (The study child) had an infection of her umbilical cord and eyes in the first week of life. At five months of age she had gastroenteritis requiring hospital admission. The child had not been immunised against any infectious diseases. At present the family live in a pre-war slum clearance housing scheme and home circumstances remain poor. The father has been unemployed for ten years and both parents drink excessively. The N.S.P.C.C. have visited this family.'

5 Large city in Scotland (Social Index score 16). Both parents in this family had left school at age fourteen without educational qualifications. The father worked as a builder's labourer and the mother had the study child and three subsequent children before the former was five. Two older children had been previously adopted. This family comprising two parents and four children under five lived in grossly overcrowded conditions in a tenement flat, which appeared to consist of a large kitchen (i.e. 6 feet or more wide) and one other room. The study child shared a bed with two of her younger siblings in one room while the other three members of the family slept in the kitchen. There was no bathroom or hot water supply, and the only lavatory was outside and shared by other households. The family did not have such basic items of equipment as refrigerator, washing machine or spin drier, nor did they have access to either a telephone or car. There was, however, a black and white television set.

These case studies are presented with the intention of providing a picture of the kinds of situation we are talking about when we define children or their families as belonging to the 'most disadvantaged' Social Index group. Such vignettes, no matter how vividly they portray a family's circumstances, can only be illustrative and contribute little to our understanding of the factors that determine the way in which social and economic resources are distributed throughout the different segments of the social hierarchy we have defined. Among the different disadvantaged families we have looked at young parents, many children, poor housing, and a conspicuous lack of household equipment and amenities appear to predominate. In order to get a clearer idea of these crucial social distinctions and their origins we propose now to discuss the variation between our five designated Social Index groups, in terms of the family composition and characteristics, housing conditions, domestic equipment and social amenities at their disposal. In doing this we are shifting the emphasis away from the particular characteristics and plight of individual familes to an examination of the ways in which the socially disadvantaged differ as a group from other social groups in the hierarchy.

Group variation

Differences in family characteristics between the five Social Index groups are shown in Table 1.1.

Age of parents

The proportion of mothers under twenty-five years old when the study child was five was nearly 15 percent among the disadvantaged and most disadvantaged families whereas in the most advantaged group it was only 1 percent. The proportion of disadvantaged fathers under twenty-five was smaller than that for the mothers but the differences between our Social Index groups followed the same pattern. This finding is partly explained by the fact that parents in the older age groups were further on in their life cycle and were therefore more likely to have achieved a better economic status and higher standard of living than the younger parents. Another, and possibly more important, reason is that parents who started their family young did so before they had a chance to become economically viable and so were unable to reach a reasonably high standard of living while bringing up dependent children. In addition there is an increased likelihood of pregnancy among teenagers who themselves came from disadvantaged home backgrounds.

Family size

The proportion of children in large families, i.e. with four or more children, increased considerably with increasing level of disadvantage. Thus, only 8.2 percent of most advantaged families had four or more children compared with as many as 36.1 percent of most disadvantaged families. From this it can be seen that if we consider all the siblings of the study children in this sample in addition to the study children themselves, the proportion of all these children who were growing up in poor social circumstances would be greater than the proportion of poor families. In point of fact the proportion of children of all ages in families in the most disadvantaged group was 14.4 percent compared with 11.3 percent of study children. What is more, it was the families with least resources who needed to distribute what resources they had more thinly.

Ethnic group

There were only 1.3 percent of children in the sample whose parents were of West Indian origin, but this proportion increased to 4.7 percent in the most disadvantaged Social Index group. Similarly, 5.1 percent of the children in the most disadvantaged group were Asian (Indian or Pakistani), although only two percent of the total sample were Asian. These groups were correspondingly under-represented in the socially advantaged categories with only one out of 174 West Indian families and nine out of 257 Asian families in this sample having a Social Index score which placed them in the most advantaged group.

Housing

Slum clearance powers and legislation aimed at protecting tenants which has made private letting of property a less attractive business proposition, has resulted in a decline in privately rented accommodation. Thus the housing of low income families has become more the function of local authorities (Holman, 1978). Council housing is also becoming the sector accounting for the largest number of deprived dwellings (Townsend, 1979, Chapter 13).

This concentration of socially disadvantaged families in local authority housing is confirmed in our study in which more than two thirds of disadvantaged and most disadvantaged families were council tenants (Table 1.2(a)). At the same time, although privately rented accommodation is on the decline, it is still more likely to be occupied by disadvantaged social groups. Table 1.2(b) indicates that only 0.2 percent of the most advantaged families were in privately rented accommodation, compared with 18.1 percent of the most disadvantaged families. This difference is partly, though not entirely, due to the fact that living in privately rented furnished accommodation contributes to the Social Index score. However, this affects only one percent of the total sample (Table 18.4) and the figures in Table 1.2(b) include families in both furnished and unfurnished privately rented accommodation (6.3 percent of the total sample).

The most disadvantaged children were more likely to live in accommodation above ground floor level (18.1 percent) where the opportunity for outdoor play was much more limited whereas this applied to less than one percent of the most advantaged children. As many as 28.1 percent of most disadvantaged families had accommodation consisting of no more than three rooms (excluding any kitchen or bathroom), but only 1.4 percent of the most advantaged families lived in such small accommodation.

The families

Household amenities

Analysis of the availability of household amenities shown in Table 1.3 shows just the same kind of trends across the Social Index groups as in the previous table. With increasing levels of social disadvantage there was a greater chance that the families in question would share with another household or lack altogether such basic amenities as a bathroom, kitchen, indoor lavatory, hot water supply or garden. As many as 23.4 percent of the most disadvantaged children did not have their own garden or yard where they could play. One in five (20.2 percent) of the most disadvantaged families did not have sole use of an indoor lavatory although many of these had sole use of an outside toilet instead (13 percent of the most disadvantaged group). However, there remained 7.1 percent who shared either an indoor or outdoor toilet with at least one other household whereas only four (0.3 percent) of the most advantaged families shared toilet facilities.

Domestic equipment

Table 1.4 shows how a number of selected items of domestic equipment or facilities were distributed between the five Social Index groups. Television is a major source of education, information and news, as well as entertainment, and was available to all but one and a half percent of the children in the study. Also there was practically no difference in the proportion of families lacking television across the Social Index groups. Differences were found, however, in the proportion of families who had colour television. Colour television costs more to buy or rent and carries a higher licence fee, and for these reasons might be assumed to be an index of affluence. There is some support for this assumption in Table 1.4 in that 58.7 percent of the most advantaged families had colour television compared with 30.2 percent of the most disadvantaged. This conforms to the downward trend one might expect but there are also two further points which are interesting. First, two in five (39.5 percent) of the most advantaged families had only a black and white set – a fact that suggests that for these at least, watching television in colour did not figure very highly in their scale of values. Secondly, at the other end of the social scale we found as many as 30.2 percent of the most disadvantaged families had colour television, notwithstanding their otherwise poor socioeconomic circumstances. This suggests that television played a very important part in the lives of this group in that they were prepared to pay out what might have been a sizeable proportion of their income in order to have the benefit of colour. On the other hand it might well have been the only

16

entertainment they could afford.

Very few homes are without a refrigerator, yet one in four (25.6 percent) of the most disadvantaged families in our sample lack this essential commodity. The distribution of washing machines were very similar to that of refrigerators, and again one in four (25.3 percent) of the most disadvantaged families did the family wash by hand or went to a launderette. Nearly all (98.8 percent) of the most advantaged families owned a car or a van, but the proportion declined rapidly throughout the social scale to only 29.6 percent of the disadvantaged and 15.3 percent of the most disadvantaged families. Part of the explanation for this difference, however, is that car ownership is a contributory factor in the Social Index (Table 18.4). Of the most advantaged families, 92.9 percent had a telephone, compared with only 22 percent of the most disadvantaged group. Whereas car ownership has remained relatively stable over the second half of the 1970s, availability of a telephone among lower socioeconomic groups has been rapidly increasing (*OPCS General Household Survey: 1981*, London: HSMO, p. 7).

Health visitor assessments

We have so far been discussing some of the more 'objective' indices of social difference. An alternative and more subjective approach is provided by the observations of the health visitors carrying out interviews for the study who were asked to make three types of assessment of the conditions of the child's home. These were the quality of the furniture and equipment of the home, whether the home was tidy or not and the kind of relationship the family had with their neighbours. (See question H1 in the Home Interview Questionnaire reproduced in the Appendix.) These assessments were based on similar questions in a Schools Council enquiry carried out by Professor Chazan in Swansea (Chazan *et al.*, 1971).

The results obtained are presented in Table 1.5 and they reveal a marked reluctance on the part of the health visitors to apply the extreme categories of the five-point ratings used. Thus only 4.4 percent of the homes were described as having furniture and equipment of low or very low standard. However, this assessment applied to as many as 19 percent of the most disadvantaged families. Another 20.9 percent of the most disadvantaged group had homes the health visitors thought were well-equipped or luxurious, but four times this proportion (88.1 percent) of the most advantaged families had well-equipped or luxurious homes. In line with the objective indices described in earlier tables, the health visitor's evaluation of the homes showed the marked disparities in quality of life between the Social Index groups.

The tidiness of the home partly reflects the ability of family members to maintain some degree of order. At the same time it must be recognised that not all families value tidiness, and some believe that a bit of muddle makes a house more homely. There is, however, a third factor, for a house with insufficient space to store belongings will inevitably appear untidy to an outsider. It is therefore no surprise to find that 18.3 percent of most disadvantaged homes were dubbed untidy or chaotic compared with only 1.7 percent of the most advantaged homes.

The third assessment made by health visitors interviewing these families concerned how well they got on with their neighbours. This was a difficult assessment to make and in as many as 12.6 percent of the families the health visitors were unable to express an opinion about their relationship with neighbours. Where an opinion was given, however, the familiar trend across the Social Index groups appeared yet again. Families in the most disadvantaged category were less likely to get on well with their neighbours (41.4 percent) whereas among the most advantaged 76.6 percent were on good terms with their neighbours. Conversely only 2 percent of the most advantaged families did not mix or were on bad terms with their neighbours, against 14.3 percent of the most disadvantaged group.

These results do not support the idea of a cohesive working class community. In fact families living in more densely populated areas of poor housing, where they were probably living in close proximity with others in similar circumstances, were less likely to be mutually supportive than more well-to-do families. Of course, being on good terms might simply mean not having open rows with the neighbours, or living in harmony without getting in each other's way. However it is interpreted, health visitors were clearly of the opinion that socially advantaged families were more fully integrated into the neighbourhood environment than were the disadvantaged families.

In brief, the health visitor's assessment of the home environment and the family's relationships with neighbours suggests that the disadvantaged group experienced a greater degree and variety of stress in their homes and family life than did the socially advantaged whose homes were orderly and who generally maintained a congenial relationship with their neighbours.

Regional variation

The patterns of social inequality we have described above refer to Britain as a whole. Some regions of the country do not conform to this general picture, however, because their unique social history and industrial development have created within them different social and

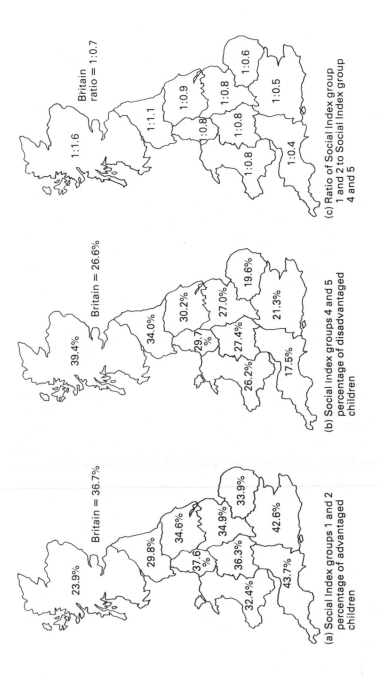

Figure 1.1 Social Index group by region and country

(a) Social Index groups 1 and 2 percentage of advantaged children

Britain = 36.7%

23.9%

29.8%

34.6%

37.6%

34.9%

36.3%

33.9%

32.4%

43.7%

42.6%

(b) Social Index groups 4 and 5 percentage of disadvantaged children

Britain = 26.6%

39.4%

34.0%

30.2%

29.7%

27.0%

27.4%

19.6%

26.2%

21.3%

17.5%

(c) Ratio of Social Index group 1 and 2 to Social Index group 4 and 5

Britain ratio = 1:0.7

1:1.6

1:1.1

1:0.9

1:0.8

1:0.8

1:0.6

1:0.8

1:0.8

1:0.5

1:0.8

1:0.4

occupational structures. The mining communities of the North of England and South Wales differ in important ways from the predominantly rural populations of East Anglia and South West England. The government and service industries of London and the South East attract people with professional and managerial skills whereas the manufacturing industries of the Midlands demand skilled and semi-skilled manual workers. Such economic and industrial variations result in some regions being relatively more affluent than others.

The maps presented in Figure 1.1 show the extent of variation in the proportions of advantaged and disadvantaged families between Wales, Scotland and the eight regions of England in terms of the Social Index. The proportion of the whole sample who were socially advantaged (Social Index groups 1 and 2) was 36.7 percent, but map (a) shows that this proportion varied from a minimum of 23.9 percent in Scotland to a maximum of 43.7 percent in the South West of England. The proportion of socially advantaged families in Wales (32.4 percent) was somewhat lower than for the whole of Britain. Conversely the proportion of socially disadvantaged children (Social Index groups 4 and 5) shown in map (b) was smallest in the South West of England (17.5 percent) and greatest in Scotland (39.4 percent).

These figures suggest that the ratio of advantaged to disadvantaged families was greatest in the south and became progressively smaller moving northwards. To explore this further the balance between the advantaged and disadvantaged sectors within regions is represented in Figure 1.1(c) as the ratio of the number of children in Social Index groups 1 and 2 to those in Social Index groups 4 and 5. These ratios confirm that the regions with the most favourable social balance were the South West (ratio = 1:0.4) and South East (ratio = 1:0.5). Moving northwards the ratio became progressively more unfavourable until in the North region of England the number of disadvantaged families exceeded the number of advantaged families (ratio = 1:1.1) and Scotland had the most unfavourable ratio of all (ratio = 1:1.6).

The social structure in terms of the balance between the relatively well-off and poorer sections has important implications for the needs of populations in different regions and for the delivery of services. Authorities in areas where there are more socially disadvantaged than advantaged families would have smaller incomes to provide services to meet the needs of disadvantaged families. In contrast, areas with low levels of social need, i.e. where there are more advantaged than disadvantaged families, would have higher incomes as well as less demand on Local Authority services. In these terms Scotland, the North of England and Yorkshire and Humberside were the parts of Britain that were most seriously affected by the imbalance between the socially disadvantaged and advantaged sectors.

Summary

The extent of poverty in Britain and the process of intergenerational continuity of deprivation makes essential the study of social inequality in this sample of five-year-olds. We are concerned in particular with the possible effects of social inequalities and family differences on children's ability and behavioural adjustment. For this purpose we have devised a model of socioeconomic inequality which assumes a social hierarchy within which some families are advantaged in many respects whilst others are disadvantaged in a number of ways. We have operationalised this model as a Social Index which is composed of eight variables relating to occupation, educational status, and housing factors. The Social Index is put forward as an alternative means of establishing socioeconomic status instead of a single variable of father's occupation which is the currently accepted indicator of a family's social class. To demonstrate the use of this new instrument we have described a number of case studies: two reflect the marked contrast between children and their families located at the extreme ends of the advantage-disadvantage spectrum and six others illustrate the variety and complex mesh of problems encountered in socially disadvantaged families.

The lesson to be learned from these case studies is that social disadvantage assumes a variety of guises and cannot be attributed to either low status occupation, lack of education, poor housing or low income alone; rather it must be viewed as an accumulation of disadvantages and multiple problems that, interacting together, imposes such concentrated stress on these parents and their children.

Marked differences in family and housing factors were found across the five Social Index groups. Disadvantaged parents were likely to be younger and have more children than their socially advantaged counterparts, and a greater proportion of West Indian and Asian families were identified in the most disadvantaged group. Disadvantaged families were more likely to live in rented accommodation, above ground floor level and in accommodation that was cramped for space and lacked the household amenities enjoyed by better-off families. Colour television, refrigerator, washing machine, telephone and car were much more commonly found in socially advantaged than disadvantaged homes and the reports from the health visitors carrying out the interviews indicated a greater likelihood that the homes of the disadvantaged contained poor quality furniture and equipment and appeared untidy. There was also less chance of the disadvantaged group being on good terms with their neighbours in contrast to the advantaged sector who on the whole maintained good relationships with the households in their vicinity.

In every respect the socially disadvantaged families as a group were conspicuously worse off than the socially advantaged families. The wide disparities in their housing and the associated living conditions, compounded by the greater number of children, that characterise the disadvantaged families evokes a level of stress and turmoil in which it is difficult to imagine a child surviving, let alone thriving. But about one in ten of our sample was in fact growing up in just these adverse and unpropitious conditions.

Chapter 2

Social change

Economic growth in Britain in the 1950s and 1960s resulted in many improvements in material conditions of life (Toland, 1979). Yet notwithstanding the real increase in the nation's wealth during that epoch there are still marked inequalities in the distribution of income and resources (Townsend, 1979). At the same time as these economic changes have been taking place the social structure of Britain has evolved so that the size of the service sector, the professional and managerial occupational groups, has steadily increased with a corresponding decline in the semi-skilled and unskilled manual occupational groups (Goldthorpe, 1980, Chapter 2). These economic and social trends together with a number of social reforms that profoundly affect family life (for example, changes in the law affecting divorce and abortion) have brought about substantial changes in the lives of children that carry important implications for their health and development. In this chapter we investigate the impact of social change on the lives of three generations of young children over a period of twenty-five years. Two kinds of questions will be asked: (a) how has social change affected the lives of children and their parents compared with the wider population in Britain?, and (b) has economic growth resulted in a reduction in social class differences in the standard of living of young children? These questions are important in view of the significance of the material environment for young children not only in terms of quality of life, but also insofar as such factors have profound implications for a child's health, education and social development.

To explore these issues, comparisons will be made between the CHES (1975) survey and two earlier birth cohort studies, namely the Medical Research Council's National Survey of Health and Development (1946 Cohort, Douglas and Blomfield, 1958) and the National Child Development Study (1958 Cohort, Davie et al., 1972), data from the 1951 and 1971 censuses and other sources.

Social class

The social class structure of the NSHD families in 1950 was very similar to that of all households in the 1951 census although there were somewhat fewer children with fathers in social class II occupations and more in social class III compared with census households (Table 2.1). During the two decades between then and the 1971 census there was an increase in the proportion of households in social classes I and II and a corresponding decrease in social classes IV and V in line with the trend described by Goldthorpe (1980). This trend was even more marked in families with young children, however, so that only 18.1 percent of children in the CHES sample had fathers in social class IV or V occupations in 1975 compared with 28.4 percent of NSHD children in 1950. The corresponding increase in children with social class I and II fathers was from 18.7 percent in 1951 to 26.5 percent in 1975 so that there was a greater proportion of children than households in these social classes in the 1970s whereas the reverse was the case in the 1950s. This upward shift in the social class structure appears to have progressed at a faster rate in families with young children than in households in general — a fact that can only partly be explained by the longer intervening period (i.e. twenty-five rather than twenty years) during which social mobility could progress. The results suggest that men with family responsibilities had become more ambitious in recent years or that men without good occupational prospects were less likely to marry and start a family in the 1970s than was the case in the immediate post-war years.

The proportion of fatherless children between the 1946 and 1970 cohorts was due mainly to the exclusion of illegitimate births from the former, although the incidence of one-parent families had also risen during this period (National Council for One-Parent Families, 1980).

Education of parents

Education has both intrinsic and extrinsic value to parents and their children. Its intrinsic value lies in the acquisition of knowledge itself which in enriching the life and thoughts of the parents can widen the world of the child. However, this essential and original purpose of education is often of secondary importance to its extrinsic value of providing the means to increased occupational opportunity. Yet this too is of vital significance to children in that the material conditions of their lives are almost entirely dependent on the parents' occupational prospects which in turn hinge to a considerable degree on their educational attainments.

One of the most important social reforms that has clearly affected the educational opportunities of the parents in these successive birth cohorts was the 1944 Education Act which introduced universal secondary education and raised the minimum school leaving age from fourteen to fifteen. Prior to this Act the elementary system provided a basic compulsory education for all children up to age fourteen whilst entry to grammar school depended on the financial resources of the parents or on a child winning a scholarship. This system did not effectively provide all children with an education commensurate with their abilities.

At that time more than half the gifted children did not get beyond the elementary school, and one child in five was given a standard of education for which he was unsuited; a standard more often too low than too high. (Douglas, 1964, p. 14)

The reforms resulting from the 1944 Act meant that all children continued their education one year longer than hitherto, selection for grammar school was based on a common entry examination at age eleven or shortly after and the secondary modern school curriculum was more geared to the occupational and industrial needs of the society than was the elementary education received by eleven- to fourteen-year-olds prior to the Act. As a result of these changes the age at which parents of children in the 1946 cohort left school does not carry the same educational connotations as for parents of CHES children because the former were subject to the elementary and grammar education systems which preceded the 1944 Act whereas the latter experienced the post-1944 system of primary and secondary education. Of the parents of the NCDS cohort of children about half would have been subject to the pre-1944 system. The raising of the school leaving age to 16 in 1973 would not have affected the educational career of even the youngest parents in CHES.

These changes in the educational system mean that the definition of what can be regarded as 'receiving education beyond a minimal level' is different for each of the three cohorts. In the NSHD 28 percent of the mothers received more than elementary education compared with 32 percent of fathers. About a quarter of the parents of children in the NCDS received education beyond minimum school leaving age. Amongst the CHES parents 35 percent of mothers and fathers had continued their full-time education past the age of fifteen. The small difference between mothers and fathers of children in the NSHD who had more than minimal education was not evident in either the NCDS or CHES results. This suggests that the changes in the educational system resulted in greater equality between the sexes in terms of this minimal level of

25

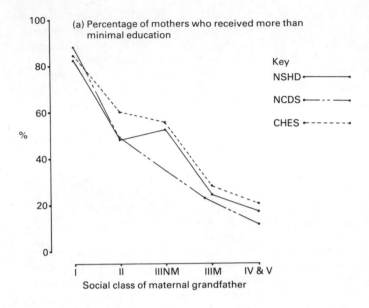

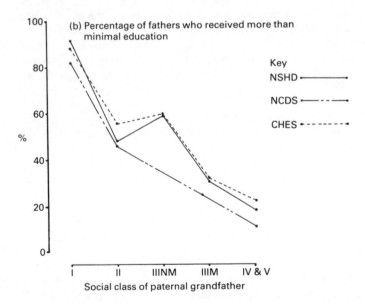

Figure 2.1 Proportion of parents who received more than minimal education by social class of origin in three cohorts

26

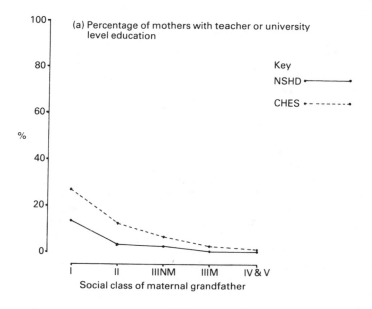

(a) Percentage of mothers with teacher or university level education

Key
NSHD
CHES

%

Social class of maternal grandfather

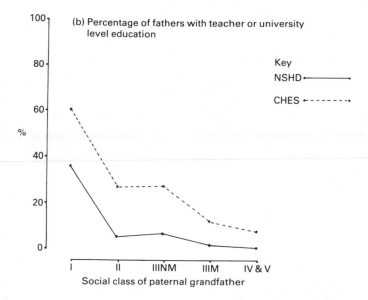

(b) Percentage of fathers with teacher or university level education

Key
NSHD
CHES

%

Social class of paternal grandfather

Figure 2.2 Proportion of parents with teacher training or university level education by social class of origin in two cohorts

27

education.

The social origins of the parents greatly influenced the likelihood of their receiving more than minimal education. In Figure 2.1 we show the proportion of mothers and fathers in each of the three cohort studies who received more than minimal education, as defined above, according to the social class of their own fathers at the time they left school. The distances between the lines are of little interest because of the different definition of minimum education applicable to each cohort. What is important in these diagrams is the steep decline in educational opportunity from social class I to social class IV and V in every cohort. If the social class difference in educational experience had decreased over the years the lines would have become more horizontal. Instead the slope of all three lines was much the same for both mothers and fathers. This suggests that over the twenty-five-year period represented by these figures (about 1935 to 1960) there was little change in the degree to which social background determined whether or not a child received more than minimal education.

The Oxford Social Mobility Survey (Halsey *et al.*, 1980) showed similar trends related to grammer schools entry over the period from about 1930 to 1950. Between these years the proportion of sons from service class backgrounds who entered grammar schools rose from 27 percent to 36 percent, an increase of 9 percent, whilst working class entrants to grammar schools rose by the same amount from 6 percent to 15 percent (ibid., Table 12.1). Thus new grammar school places were distributed equally between the social class groups rather than increasing the proportion assigned to working class children which would have had the effect of reducing the social class difference in entry to selective schools. In short, educational selection procedures were still discriminating in favour of children from service class backgrounds.

Selection plays an even greater part in access to institutions of higher education and Figure 2.2 shows that the social class difference in the proportion of parents with teacher training or university education actually widened between the 1946 and 1970 birth cohorts. Also at all social class levels differential access to higher education between fathers and mothers increased over this period.

Housing tenure

Successive governments in Great Britain have given high priority to improving housing conditions and to increasing opportunity for home ownership across a wider segment of society than hitherto. Since the Second World War a substantial number of rented dwellings in the private sector have been demolished under slum clearance powers, with

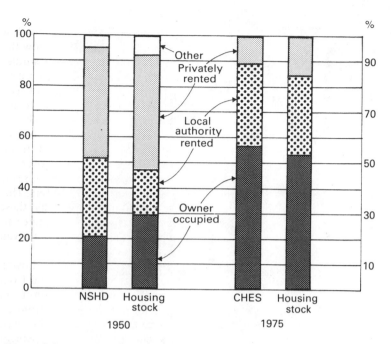

Figure 2.3 Changes in housing tenure between 1950 and 1975
Source for data on housing stock: Butler and Sloman, 1980

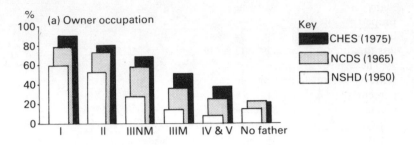

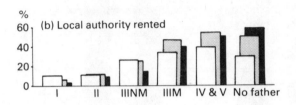

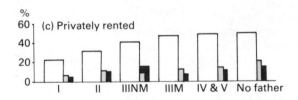

Figure 2.4 Changes in social class differences in tenure between 1950 and 1975

many of the incumbent households being rehoused in local authority property. 'The housing of households with low incomes has with time become more and more the function of local authorities and less and less the function of the private rented sector.' (Holmans, 1978, p. 19).

These measures have led to a decline in the proportion of private rented housing stock available from 45 percent in 1950 to less than 16 percent in 1975 (Figure 2.3). This decline in private renting was even greater in regard to families with young children. In 1950 the figure for families in such accommodation was 43.8 percent compared with 10.2 percent in 1975. Conversely the incidence of home ownership increased more rapidly than average for families with children over the same period – from 20.8 percent in 1950 to 56.4 percent in 1975 whereas the proportions of the housing stock which was owner occupied rose from 29 percent to 53 percent.

Thus while families with young children in 1950 were less likely than the average household to be owner-occupiers, the position had reversed by 1975 so that a greater proportion of young children than expected were living in houses that were owned or being bought by their parents. There was also an increase in the proportion of housing stock rented from local authorities – from 18 percent in 1950 to 31 percent in 1975 – but this change was notably less for families with young children which in 1950 represented 30.8 percent and in 1975 32.3 percent. The increasing share of local authority housing occupied by older, childless households (Holmans, 1978, p. 17) suggests that expansion in this sector has been sufficient to accommodate about the same proportions of families with young children over this period whilst the older generation of tenants stayed on as their children left home when they were grown up.

These results suggest that the rate of increase in owner occupation between 1950 and 1975 has been faster for families with young children than households generally. To what extent, however, has the expansion of the owner-occupier sector reduced the social class difference in this type of tenure? An analysis of housing tenure by social class for the three birth cohorts is given in Figure 2.4. This indicates that the social class difference in owner occupation has remained much the same over the twenty-five-year period. Owner occupation in social class I increased from 60 percent in 1950, to 80 percent in 1965 and 90 percent in 1975. In contrast the proportion of social class IV and V families in owner occupation was only 7 percent in 1950 and increased to 24 percent in 1965 and 38 percent in 1975. Figure 2.4 shows that the new housing stock which became available for purchase between 1950 and 1975 was taken up in much the same proportion by all social classes in these cohorts. The fact that there was such gross inequality in owner occupation in 1950 does not seem to have resulted in different rates of house purchase between social classes so as to bring about a more equitable distribution of home ownership. This reflects the inequalities in income and job security which are still associated with occupations of different status upon which the possibility of buying one's home depends.

The proportion of fatherless families in owner occupation increased by only 8 percent between 1950 and 1965 (14 percent to 23 percent) compared with about 20 percent in other families. There was no increase between 1965 and 1975 in the proportion of fatherless families who owned their own homes whilst for other families there was an increase of about 10 percent during this period. The lack of a male breadwinner in these families is clearly a major reason for their reduced likelihood of becoming home owners. A second reason is the often transient nature of the one-parent family status due to remarriage or reconciliation. These factors probably also account for the increased likelihood of fatherless families to be in local authority housing where they might be given priority (Figure 2.4(b)). The proportion of this group who rented from the local authority doubled from 29 percent in the NSHD (1950) cohort to 58 percent in the CHES (1975) cohort.

The social class trend in the proportion of families in local authority accommodation was opposite to that found for owner occupation. Declining social class was associated with increased likelihood of renting from the council. Figure 2.4(b) shows that this trend increased between 1950 and 1975 because of the decline of local authority tenants in the non-manual classes and the increase in this tenure in the manual classes. The reduction in the proportion of manual workers' families in local authority housing between 1965 and 1975 only marginally affected the widening social class difference in this type of tenure.

Figure 2.4(c) shows that the social class difference in the proportion of children in privately rented housing in 1950 was much reduced by 1965 with little further change by 1975. However, analysis of tenure by Social Index group described in Chapter 1 (Table 1.2) showed marked social variation in the percentage of children in privately rented accommodation and reveals the limitation of using occupation only as an index of social class. A higher than average proportion of fatherless families rented privately in all these cohort studies which further illustrates the continuing dependence on the private sector of families with special difficulties.

Thus the general picture is one in which the earlier tripartite system of tenure-owner occupation, private renting and council renting has largely been replaced by a bipartite system consisting of owner occupation and local authority renting with only a small private renting sector. The decline of the private sector from being the major provider of domestic accommodation to the least significant coupled with the growth of home ownership among those families who can afford it, has resulted in an important change in the social composition of local authority tenants as our results (described above) show. This change probably owes itself to the policy followed by local authority housing departments of giving priority to families who are most in need of being housed; however praiseworthy and even practical this policy may be it carries the risk that council estates may become social ghettos fostering a high level of delinquency and other social pathologies which are not the optimal environment in which to raise young children.

Household amenities

As housing expectations change and improve over the years new social indicators evolve to measure acceptable standards. This makes valid comparisons between housing conditions over a twenty-five-year period very difficult. For example the 1951 census, enquiring about piped water and indoor plumbing, revealed that 13 percent of households shared their cold water supply with other households and that 5 percent did not have water piped to their homes at all. Likewise as many as 8 percent of all households had no lavatory either inside or outside of their homes which was connected to a sewer, septic tank or cesspool. In the intervening years housing standards had so improved that it was no longer necessary to check whether these basic amenities were available in the 1970s.

However, some indicators have remained which can be used to compare the pattern of change in home conditions that specifically affect children with that for all households. Crowding, expressed as the ratio of the total number of adults and children living in the same household to the number of living rooms and bedrooms available, is one such measure of housing adequacy. Although differences in definitions of rooms between the studies will have affected the overall estimate of crowding this does not invalidate comparisons between cohort studies and census data or social class comparisons because the same method was used for calculating room density in birth cohort and census at each stage. In 1951 the proportion of households in Great Britain who were living in overcrowded conditions (over 1.5 persons per room) was 6.9 percent. Among families with young children, however, 23.3 percent in Britain as a whole were living in overcrowded conditions (Figure 2.5). Although this striking difference can be partly explained by the fact that households containing children were more likely to be overcrowded than households in general (in which are included single person households) it is nevertheless clear that children were more inadequately housed than were households generally in the 1950s.

Key
Children in birth cohorts
All households

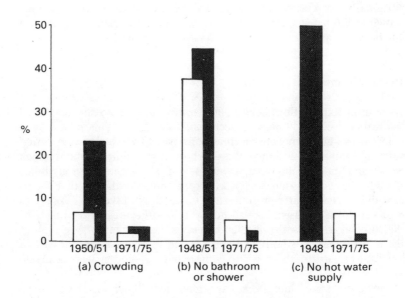

Figure 2.5 Changes in crowding and availability of amenities between 1948 and 1975

Sources of information

	Households	Birth cohorts
(a) Crowding	Census (1951)	NSHD (1950)
	Census (1971)	CHES (1975)
(b) No bathroom or shower	Census (1951)	NSHD (1948)
	GHS (1975)	CHES (1975)
(c) No hot water supply	No information	NSHD (1948)
	Census (1971)	CHES (1975)

Between the 1950s and 1970s the proportion of families with young children living in overcrowded housing reduced at a faster rate than did households in general so that by the later date 3.5 percent of the CHES cohort compared with 1.8 percent of households were in overcrowded accommodation.

In 1948 44.5 percent of families with children did not have a fixed bath or shower compared with 37.6 percent of households in the 1951 census (Figure 2.5(b)). By 1975, however, the position had reversed so that fewer families in the CHES study lacked a bathroom (2.5 percent) than did households (5 percent). Also only 1.6 percent of CHES (1975) families had no hot water supply compared with 6.5 percent of census (1971) households. In 1948 nearly half the NSHD families had no hot water supply which demonstrates the considerable improvement in the availability of this amenity although no comparative information was available for households in the 1950s.

The changing pattern of tenure, particularly the decline in privately rented accommodation, might be expected to have produced a reduction in social class differences in housing quality. Comparisons between the three cohorts in terms of social class differences in the proportion of children in overcrowded housing and lacking certain household amenities are shown in Figure 2.6. Marked inequalities between social class groups in crowding, lacking a bathroom and lacking a hot water supply were present in the NSHD sample in 1948 and 1950. Access to a garden or yard, however, was much the same for all social classes. The proportion of social class I families in the NSHD who were disadvantaged in these ways was so small that there was little scope for improvement. At the other end of the social scale the opposite was the case. As many as 35 percent of social class IV and V NSHD families were living in overcrowded accommodation, 58 percent lacked a bathroom or shower and 62 percent had no hot water supply. By the time of the NCDS survey in 1965 the social class difference in availability of bathroom and hot water supply had reduced markedly but the reduction in overcrowding was not so pronounced. In the CHES (1975) survey crowding, lack of bathroom and lack of hot water supply was virtually eliminated in the non-manual classes whilst in social class IV and V 7 percent were in overcrowded accommodation, 2 percent had no bathroom or shower and 3 percent had no hot water supply. Thus over the twenty-five-year period covered by these studies the improvements in housing standards have resulted in a reduction in the social class differences observed in 1948/50. However, as we have shown in Chapter 1, marked inequalities still existed in the 1970s and the social change described in this chapter can only hint at the degree of inequality that must have prevailed in the post-war years.

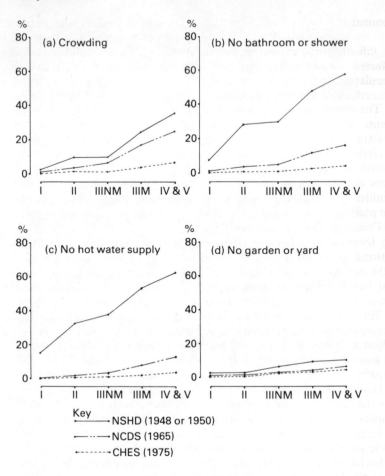

Figure 2.6 Changes in social class differences in housing conditions between 1948 and 1975

Summary

In this chapter we have attempted to show how social change has affected the lives of young children (a) compared with the wider population, and (b) in reducing social class differences in parental education, housing and amenities.

The twenty-five-year period from 1950 to 1975 saw marked improvements in housing conditions throughout Britain together with an upward shift in the social class structure with increased proportion of professional and managerial classes and a corresponding decline in the semi-skilled and unskilled classes. On the whole these changes were more marked in families with young children and whereas in 1950 such families were generally worse off than the wider population, by 1975 the position had reversed.

Comparisons of social class differences in parental education, housing tenure and availability of household amenities between the three national birth cohort studies (NSHD — 1946 birth cohort; NCDS — 1958 birth cohort; and CHES — 1970 birth cohort) suggested that there had been a reduction in social inequality in terms of some of these factors but not others over the period reviewed.

The social class difference in the proportion of parents who had received more than minimal education was as great in the 1970 birth cohort as in the 1946 birth cohort. When we considered the proportion of parents who had had higher education, the social class gap had actually widened.

Home ownership increased between 1950 and 1975 but the increase was the same in all social classes so that the same degree of inequality remained. The decline in privately rented accommodation and increase in local authority tenures has resulted in a greater proportion of the lower social classes being housed by the local authority.

Social class differences in crowding and availability of household amenities (bathroom or shower, hot water supply) were so great in the 1946 birth cohort that general improvements in these housing standards inevitably reduced social inequality because hardly any social class I or II families were overcrowded or lacked these amenities in 1950. By 1975 the social class differences in crowding and lack of amenities remained but were much reduced.

Chapter 3

Disrupted families

In the two preceding chapters we have described the various social and economic inequalities that our research findings have revealed within this sample of five-year-old children and their families. Assessed according to our Social Index the families of low socioeconomic status in our study were found to have a greater chance of being deprived of adequate housing accommodation and household equipment than their better-off peers, and the overall quality and standard of their life styles and the resources at their disposal were markedly inferior by any criterion to that of families in the average and superior economic echelons.

In this coming chapter we turn to examine an even more fundamental source of deprivation for young children — namely the loss or absence of parents. For this sample of children born in 1970 the likelihood of divorce and separation of their parents has increased, following the Divorce Law Reform Act of 1969 and the Matrimonial Causes Act of 1973, both of which has made dissolution of marriage much easier (Leete, 1979, p. 9). We do not suggest that this new legislation has in itself increased the risk of family disruption as many children in earlier generations have been experiencing the emotional strain of an incompatible marriage, but these troubles may now be more apparent with the increased ease and social acceptance of divorce. Indeed the Acts may simply have endorsed the already apparent social demand for easier divorce reflected in increasing divorce rates which doubled during the previous decade (Gibson, 1974). In 1972 8 percent of all families with dependent children were headed by a single parent on account of illegitimacy, the death of a parent or divorce and separation. By 1976 this proportion had increased to 10 percent and to 12 percent by 1980 (OPCS Monitor, 1982, Ref. GHS 82/1).

Since the emergence of the discipline of psychology and the understanding it has given us of child development, there has been a general consensus of opinion that a stable family life in early childhood is of crucial importance to the child's emotional and intellectual wellbeing. This article of faith prevails even though there is a good deal of controversy on what constitutes the 'optimal family' from the child's perspective (compare for example Hughes *et al.*, 1980, Chapter 2; Pringle, 1980(a); Oakley, 1981). Neither is the need to try to ensure that every child is properly cared for in the early years negated by the argument that later ill effects of early deprivation can be avoided if the proper steps are taken as suggested by Clarke and Clarke (1976), notwithstanding the important therapeutic implications of their findings. The loss of a parent through death, divorce or any other reason may be distressful and confusing to a young child, and even if he or she acquires a 'substitute' parent in place of the one that is lost there may be difficulty in establishing a relationship between him or her and the new parent figure (Burgoyne *et al.*, 1981). For the child in a one-parent family, moreover, there is not only an emotional gap in his or her life caused by the loss of one parent which the majority of other children with two parents do not experience, there are also profound economic and social considerations when one parent has to provide the family income in addition to fulfilling the important roles of parent and homekeeper. This chapter will focus on the socioeconomic circumstances of the children in the study who had experienced some form of family disruption compared with those who were living with both natural parents at age five most of whom would have been in a relatively stable family situation since their birth.

Our classification of types of family is described in detail in Chapter 18 where it can be seen that 90 percent of this sample were living with both natural parents at age five. 2.7 percent were in step-families, 0.7 percent had been adopted by both parents, 5.7 percent were in one-parent families and 0.5 percent were living with neither natural parent. The one-parent families were subdivided into two groups depending on whether or not there were other adults living in the same household who might provide some support for the single parent. One-parent families in households where there were other adults were defined as 'supported' one-parent families, and lone parent families where the parent was the only adult.

Patterns of family change

To obtain some idea of the changes in parental circumstances that can occur during the first five years of life a comparison was made between marital status of the mother at the time of the child's birth, and the type of family in which they found themselves when the child was five (Table 3.1). For various reasons described in Chapter 16 children in atypical families were slightly under-represented in the 1975 survey. Thus the proportion of mothers in the five-year follow-up study who were unmarried when their child was born is smaller than the figure obtained for the complete sample in the birth survey (5.4 percent as against 7.5 percent, Table 3.1).

Nearly all (97.7 percent) of the mothers in families in which both natural parents were present when the child was five, had been married at the time of the child's birth. It is also possible that at least some of the mothers who reported that they were unmarried when their child was born were at that time living with the child's natural father. Thus the majority of children with both natural parents at five were likely to have enjoyed a relatively stable parental situation over the whole period. We recognise that not all these children had had perfect lives and that some couples stay together 'for the sake of the children' even though the marriage has all but broken down. This type of situation is not the norm, however, and will not seriously affect our assumption of general stability in families with both natural parents.

Among the families of children who at five no longer lived with both natural parents a substantial number of the mothers were married at the time of the child's birth. This group of previously married mothers comprised 61.1 percent of supported single mothers, 75.5 percent of lone mothers and 63.9 percent of mothers in step-families, and they represent families where specific changes in parental situations occurred during the five year period. Looked at another way some 6.1 percent (N = 776) of the total sample at five had started life with both natural parents but had lost one of them in the intervening period. A small proportion of the whole sample (3.4 percent, N = 428) were not with both natural parents either at birth or at five years. Where children had lost both their natural parents by the age of five there is a strong likelihood that at their birth their natural mothers were not married; of those who had been adopted by five 73.5 percent were illegitimate, as were 38.3 percent of those who lived with grandparents or foster parents.

Age of child

We have suggested that a substantial minority of children experienced fundamental changes in their family composition between birth and five. But the implications of these changes for children at age five would depend to a considerable degree on how recently they had taken place. Children who had lost a parent just prior to our survey might be expected to be more affected by this recent change in circumstances than those who had lived with the same substitute parent(s) for most of his or her preschool life. Also, children who lose a parent with whom they had formed a strong attachment will experience a greater sense of loss than those who never knew their parents.

In Table 3.2 we show the children's age when the current (1975) family situation began. This table includes only those children who were not living with both natural parents at age five and shows that more than half (58.3 percent) the adopted children were placed soon after their birth whereas over a third (39.4 percent) of children with lone parents had been in this situation for no more than two years. However, there was substantial variation in the age at which the different types of family situation had begun and, with the exception of adopted children, the pattern over the five-year period was much the same for all types of family.

Reason for loss of parents

Of the 1,270 children who were no longer living with both natural parents, the great majority (80.9 percent) were still with their natural mother, i.e. had lost their natural father, and only 85 (6.7 percent) had lost their natural mother (Table 3.3). The remaining 12.4 percent had lost both parents and were nearly all adopted, fostered or living with grandparents. Thus most children in disrupted family situations remained with their mother rather than their father. This is partly explained by the fact that a quarter (24.2 percent) of the mothers of this sub-sample of children had been single at the time of the birth and would automatically assume responsibility for their child's upbringing unless they placed them for adoption. It also reflects the widespread belief that the mother-child relationship is of especial importance for young children and should be preserved wherever possible (Pringle, 1980(a); Rutter, 1972).

Whether this viewpoint is a product of the traditional social and economic division of labour that firmly vests the early child-care role in the mother or whether it stems from a belief in the biological tie between mother and child is a much debated point (Rossi, 1977); with increasing equality between the sexes the proportion of single fathers may also increase but at present single parenthood is an almost exclusively female prerogative and there is little sign of change in the imbalance. Between 1972 and 1980 the proportion of families with children of all ages headed by mothers increased from 7.1 percent to 10.7 percent whilst those headed by fathers increased from 1.2 percent to 1.5 percent (OPCS Monitor, 1982, Ref. GHS 82/1). Thus not only are there fewer one-parent fathers, the rate of growth of this type of family set-up has been markedly slower than in one-parent families headed by mothers.

That mothers are favoured in obtaining custody of children under five is highlighted in our study by the fact that only 23.5 percent of the children were deprived of their mother through divorce or separation compared with 37 percent of children who lost their fathers for this reason. Loss of one or both parents was due to death in the case of 7.3 percent of children and again this cause accounted for the loss of the mother more frequently than of the father (14.1 percent and 7.4 percent respectively), even though mortality was higher for the latter.

Over a third (37.2 percent) of the illegitimate children in the total sample were living with both natural parents when followed-up at five years of age. However, Table 3.4 suggests that illegitimacy was more likely to result in a child being adopted or going to live with grand-parents or in a foster home at age five than to be in a one-parent or step-family. The latter types of family situation were more likely to be a result of divorce or separation. Gibson (1974) has observed that, '. . . for some three-quarters of all divorcing couples, divorce is a tem-porary condition between the dissolution of an unhappy first marriage and the formation of a more hopeful second marriage.' (p. 90)

This tendency for remarriage following divorce is reflected in our study in the higher than average proportion of children in step-families at age five (43.4 percent) whose parents had divorced or separated. In contrast to this there is less likelihood that a surviving partner will remarry after the death of a spouse, as illustrated by Table 3.4 which indicates that only 2.2 percent of the children in step-families had lost the original parent through death whereas in single-parent families over 10 percent had done so.

We fully recognise that in presenting these statistics we cannot catch the ebb and flow of family life, or map the tensions and crises that all parents face at one time or another in their task of bringing up their children. Our purpose has simply been to paint a broad picture of the major changes and life events which have impinged on this group of children during the first five years of their lives. We have shown that of the great majority of five-year-olds as many as nine out of ten had been cared for by their two natural parents from birth and though this does not entirely exclude the possibility of domestic intrafamily upheavals or even brief temporary separations, in general it does infer a degree of permanence and security of family background in the preschool phase.

Such stability was denied to many of the one in ten children who by their fifth birthday had lost one or both natural parents through death, divorce or marital separation or had been in a one-parent family throughout their first five years. There were certain to have been emotional consequences for the children and parents in this study who experienced family disruption. However, there were also social and economic implications in terms of the characteristics of the parents most likely to be vulnerable to family disruption and also in terms of the consequences of such disruption for housing opportunities and quality of life. It is these contrasts that the remainder of this chapter examines.

Family characteristics

There were differences in parental age, ethnic group, parental level of education and father's occupation between disrupted families and those who were intact when the study child was five. These differences are summarised in Table 3.5.

Age of parents

Table 3.5(a) and (b) shows the proportion of children whose parents were under twenty-five years old when the five-year follow-up survey took place. The twenty-five-year cut-off point was chosen in view of the social and developmental vulnerability of children born to teenage mothers (Wadsworth *et al.*, in press). At this young age parents have had less time to become established in a home of their own and their income is likely to be low which adds to the difficulties the parents might experience due to their social immaturity. As expected the average age of fathers in the sample was higher than that of mothers and only 2.8 percent of the former were under twenty-five compared with as many as 8.6 percent of the latter. In disrupted families, however, the proportion of young mothers was substantially greater, being 13.7 percent of lone mothers, up to 27 percent of supported one-parent mothers and mothers in step-families. This increased probability of young mothers in disrupted families was not apparent in fathers except for those in step-families where 18.7 percent were under twenty-five. Instead, one-parent fathers tended to be older than the average father of a five-year-old; 12.9 percent of supported and 19.4 percent of lone one-parent fathers were under thirty compared with 26 percent of fathers in intact families. This age difference between one-parent mothers and fathers conforms with the patterns found in other studies (Ferri, 1976; Leete, 1978, p. 8).

Couples who adopt usually take this step only after several years of infertility, and adoption agencies also emphasise the need for maturity in prospective parents. It is of no surprise therefore that only one percent of adoptive mothers and no adoptive fathers were younger than twenty-five. Indeed the majority of adoptive mothers (68 percent)

43

were over thirty-five compared with only a quarter of the other mothers in the sample who were this age.

Parents' education and social class

Increased educational opportunity in the 1960s and 1970s has resulted in a decline in the proportions of unqualified men and women over the years (OPCS Monitor, 1982, Ref. GHS 82/1). Nevertheless, more than half (55.7 percent) of the mothers and just under half (48.2 percent) of the fathers in our sample had no formal qualifications or vocational training. Also there were marked inequalities in educational level between parents in different types of family. A somewhat higher proportion of parents in one-parent families and step-families had no educational qualifications compared with intact families. This difference was particularly large for lone fathers, among whom 73.5 percent were unqualified compared with 47.8 percent of fathers from families having both natural parents. Adoptive parents were the least likely to be unqualified whereas in 'other' types of families a high proportion of substitute mothers (78.2 percent) had no qualifications. This is probably because the grandmothers or foster mothers who serve as parents in these families completed their education in an era of much more limited educational opportunity.

A higher than average proportion of fathers in atypical family situations were in manual occupations – this is related to the relatively higher rates of divorce in the lower social class groups (Gibson, 1974). Adoptive fathers were less likely to be manual workers – a fact which reflects criteria of selectivity applied by adoption agencies.

Family size

Only 10.2 percent of the children in the sample had no siblings living at home, but the proportion was higher in atypical families with as many as 36.8 percent of the children in supported one-parent families being the only child. These were likely to be the children of young unmarried women who were still living in their own parents' home. In contrast, a higher proportion of lone parents had four or more children (21 percent) than average (16.5 percent) in spite of the difficult problems they must face in meeting the needs of a large family without other adult support. This deviates from the results found in NCDS follow-up of eleven-year-olds (Ferri, 1976, Table A6.3) in which 31 percent of two-parent families had four or more children compared with 29 percent of lone mothers.

Ethnic group of parents

Although West Indian parents made up only 1.3 percent of the total cohort studied, they accounted for 5.4 percent of the lone-parent group; in contrast to this a lower than average proportion of Asian children had experienced any form of family disruption during their first five years of life. This contrast probably reflects the different cultural mores and religious beliefs that regulate these two ethnic minorities.

Perhaps the most important lesson to be culled from these statistics is the wide diversity of family circumstances which characterise the now familiar concept of the single-parent family. We can, for example, envisage from these data the young unmarried mother who returns to her parents' home to bring up the new baby that has arrived without the benefit of a legal father. Although this solution may offer her and the new arrival a secure start it nevertheless contains many potential stresses which may persuade the young mother to opt for marriage as an alternative but with someone who is not the child's father. Other figures highlight the young unmarried mothers who make a deliberate decision to cope on their own, also the less fortunate ones for whom this is not a choice but relentless necessity. A breakdown in marriage, which is a more frequent cause of family disruption, may lead to one parent having to assume responsibility for several children or, in the event of remarriage or cohabiting, there will be a change in the parent figure for the child. Looked at from this angle we can see that many different events and circumstances culminated in the variety of family situations that came to light through our survey.

Housing conditions

Tenure

Within the total study cohort more than half the families owned or were in the process of purchasing the house they lived in, compared with less than a third of disrupted families. Table 3.6 shows that over half the step-families and single-parent families were in accommodation rented from the local authority whereas only 30 percent of children with both natural parents were local authority tenants. Notwithstanding the decline in privately rented accommodation (see Chapter 2) which has resulted in only 6.2 percent of our sample being private tenants, this proportion was as high as 11.8 percent in step-families and 13 percent and 14.3 percent respectively in supported and lone single-parent families (Table 3.6).

Size and level of accommodation

Single-parent families were frequently accommodated in council flats and as many as 21.7 percent of lone parents and their children lived above ground floor level. This compared with only 6 percent of children with both natural parents. The difficulties associated with coping with children above ground level cannot be emphasised enough. The problems of stairs or lifts to negotiate with push chairs, prams and shopping and the fear of allowing a young child out on his or her own without supervision means that mother and children may spend more time in the confines of the home than they might wish with all the tensions that this produces. This was frequently exacerbated by the fact that a third of lone parents lived in small accommodation of no more than three rooms (excluding any bathroom or kitchen). This compared with only 12.7 percent of children living with both natural parents in small accommodation.

2.8 percent of lone parents and their children were living in what would officially be regarded as 'overcrowded' conditions; i.e. with a persons to room ratio greater than 3 to 2. This was despite the fact that there was only one adult person in the household. Supported one-parent families, however, were more likely to be overcrowded (7.5 percent compared with an average of 3.5 percent) because they were sharing accommodation with others.

The general import of the results summarised in Table 3.6 is that children in families which experienced some kind of discontinuity of parent figures, particularly children with lone parents, were more likely to be poorly housed than children living with both natural parents.

Housing amenities and equipment

Accommodation which did not provide householders with sole use of such amenities as kitchen, bathroom, indoor lavatory or hot water supply would be considered seriously inadequate in view of the fact that fewer than four percent of the families in this study either shared or did not have them (Table 3.7). However, as with our previous indices of housing, there was a greater likelihood that one-parent and step-families would lack these amenities or share them with other households. This applied particularly in regard to supported one-parent families who, by definition, often shared accommodation with other families. Ten or eleven percent of these families shared or lacked a bathroom, indoor lavatory or hot water supply. Children in disrupted families were also less likely to have access to a garden where they could play and those with lone parents were most affected by this constraint; nearly a quarter of the latter had no garden or yard compared with 6.3 percent of children with both natural parents.

Domestic equipment and facilities

The poor quality of life of many lone parents compared with that of the average family is further illustrated in Table 3.8 which shows that the proportion of lone parents having the use of the equipment and facilities listed was lower for every item than for other types of family. In general the pattern of results in this table is similar to the earlier analyses of housing and amenities in that step-families and one-parent families were less likely than intact or adoptive families to have the use of television, refrigerator, washing machine, car or telephone.

Colour television costs more to buy or hire than does black and white television, also the licence fee is higher. Thus ownership of colour television might be used as an indicator of affluence. Over half the families in the study owned or rented colour television but this increased to 62.5 percent in adoptive families. Predictably, only 28.6 percent of lone parents had colour television. Indeed as many as 4 percent of lone parents had no television at all compared with an average of the whole sample of 1.5 percent who lacked a television set. Similar inequalities were found between the different types of family with respect to ownership of refrigerator, washing machine and telephone. Lack of such appliances clearly makes life more difficult and the families most in need of these time- and labour-saving amenities were the very ones who were most likely not to have them. The resource of which the lone parent was most likely to be deprived was a car or van. This was the one item where there was a substantial difference in ownership between lone parents (20.9 percent), supported one-parent families (36.1 percent) and step-families (59.8 percent).

These analyses of housing, amenities and domestic equipment show a consistent picture in which disrupted families were most likely to be deprived of the minimal standards of living enjoyed by intact families. The families who were most vulnerable were the single parents who lived alone with their children. This group were disadvantaged in every respect — housing, amenities and domestic equipment. Supported single parents were somewhat better off because many of them shared accommodation with other families, for example, their own parents, and thus often had access to their household resources. However, multi-occupation could hardly be put forward as a permanent solution to the problems of single parentness unless the independence of the lone parent could be preserved.

Subjective assessment of the home environment

An alternative method of assessing the home environment, was through health visitors who were asked to give an opinion concerning:

a) the quality of furniture and equipment in the home,
b) the tidiness of the home, and
c) the relationship of the family with the neighbours.

This was done using the three scales in question H1 of the Home Interview Questionnaire reproduced in the appendix. The results are summarised in Table 3.9.

The health visitors' assessments of the quality of furniture and equipment produced results that conformed to the same pattern as the 'objective' indices of housing and amenities discussed earlier. Higher proportions of step-families (9.3 percent) and one-parent families, particularly lone parents (14.2 percent), were in accommodation thought by the health visitor to be of poor standard. This compared with only 3.7 percent of families with both natural parents. None of the adoptive families was thought to have furniture or equipment of low standard; on the contrary 73.7 percent of these families' homes were judged to be well-equipped or luxurious as against 29.5 percent of lone parents.

It might be argued that untidiness need not be a result of poor housing. However, cramped accommodation and lack of storage space may well result in clothes and toys being stacked in corners of rooms or left lying about. Moreover there is little motivation to spend time keeping tidy accommodation which is inherently inadequate and inevitably appears shabby. Thus it is no surprise to discover that the homes of disrupted families whom, as we have described, tend to live in the worst types of accommodation were more likely to be described as untidy or chaotic by the health visitor. Lone parents are particularly vulnerable as they have no one to help with housework or maintenance.

Finally, we found that the very families who might need most help and support, i.e. the one-parent families, were those who according to the health visitors, were most likely to not mix or be on bad terms with their neighbours. This applied to 14 percent of lone parents compared with 5 percent of families with both natural parents. The majority (62 to 66 percent) of intact and adoptive families were on good terms with their neighbours whereas this was considered to be true of only 42 percent to 45 percent of disrupted families.

Our discussion of housing conditions and standard of living has so far been limited to the situation existing at the time of the child's fifth birthday, with no attempt to consider whether the poor social circumstances of disrupted families were a cause or consequence of family change. In short, was socioeconomic disadvantage a factor in provoking the break-up of families? Or, conversely, did the break-up of a family result in downward social mobility? These questions are to be considered next.

Social mobility

Studies of social mobility have conventionally depended on classifications of male occupations as a measure of socioeconomic status. Whilst there are sound theoretical reasons for this the consequent dilemma of how to decide the social status of families without an employed male head has resulted in mobility studies being restricted to men, (e.g. Goldthorpe, 1980). Studies which have been specifically concerned with one-parent families, which are more often than not headed by women, have experienced difficulty in assigning a social position to such families (e.g. Ferri, 1976). These problems derive entirely from the exclusive use of occupation as an index of social status.

The Social Index, which we describe in detail in Chapters 1 and 18, is a stratification measure which, because it does not depend only on the occupation of the father, provides a social ranking for all families including one-parent families headed by a woman. A comparison of mean Social Index scores for our six types of family is presented in Figure 3.1. The now familiar pattern of social inequality was again repeated here. The mean Social Index scores of step-families (9.2), supported one-parent families (9.4), and lone one-parent families (9.5) and children living with foster parents or grandparents (9.1) indicate that on average these groups were worse off in socioeconomic terms than families with both natural parents (8.1). The Scheffe test (Nie *et al.*, 1975, p. 426) which is a very conservative or strict test for comparisons between group means showed that the observed differences in mean Social Index score between the types of families which had experienced disruption were non-significant. But the difference between intact and disrupted families was statistically significant ($p < .010$). Finally, adoptive families (Social Index mean = 7.4) were marginally better off ($p < .05$) than families with both natural parents present. The difference in mean score between intact and lone parent families was quite substantial and amounted to .7 standard deviations of Social Index score.

Explanations for the socioeconomic inequalities between these different types of family are of two kinds. Firstly, women of low socioeconomic status may be more prone to having children before marriage or experience marital breakdown, and in the absence of opportunity for upward mobility remain at a similar social level to their

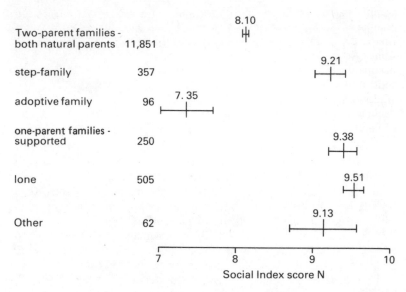

One-way analysis of variance $F_{i3115, 5} = 94.2$; $p < .001$

Figure 3.1　Mean Social Index score for each type of family showing 95 percent confidence intervals

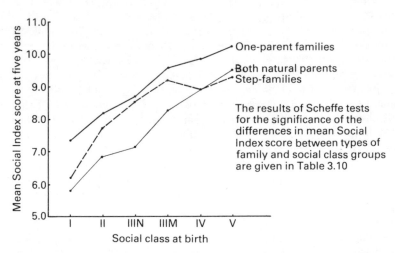

Figure 3.2　Mean Social Index score (modified) by type of family at five years and social class at birth

50

parents. There is some evidence from the CHES study that daughters of manual workers were somewhat more likely to be unmarried when their first child was born than were daughters of men in non-manual occupations. Also families headed by fathers in semi-skilled and unskilled occupations were slightly more likely than other occupational groups to split up between the child's birth and fifth birthday (Burnell and Wadsworth, 1981, Tables 7.2 and 7.3). Alternatively, however, a decline in socioeconomic circumstances may be a direct consequence of family disruption. It is this possibility that will be investigated here.

There is some evidence, then, to suggest that poor socioeconomic circumstances can increase the probability of subsequent family disruption. However, the differences observed were not large and could not account for the substantial social inequalities found between different types of family in the five-year study. What evidence do we have, therefore, for the alternative explanation, that family breakdown itself results in socioeconomic decline? This was investigated by comparing social class at birth with Social Index scores at five for three types of family (Figure 3.2).

Before discussing the results of this analysis, some methodological explanation is necessary. Firstly, a social class classification was not available for all families in the birth survey. About two-thirds of the unsupported mothers (single, widowed, divorced or separated) did not record an occupation for a male head of household. As insufficient social items were available from the birth study to compile a Social Index score as an alternative to social class, the social class of the maternal grandfather at the time the mother left school was used for unsupported mothers for whom occupational social class was not available in the birth study. Whilst this procedure admits some degree of error due to any social mobility of the mothers concerned, we doubt that this would seriously affect the results of the analysis.

Secondly, a modified version of the Social Index score was used for the purpose of this analysis. The modification was simply the exclusion of the five-year social class classification from the items comprising the Index. This was necessary in this particular analysis because we had no social class classification for one-parent families in the five-year study, which constitutes a separate group for analysis in Figure 3.1, and the analysis also entails a breakdown by birth social class categories.

If we consider all the families assigned to social class V at the child's birth for example, we know that a sizeable proportion of these families would still be in social classes IV or V five years later. These categories would then add a weight of one or two to the Social Index score. However, five-year social class data were only available for two-parent families and so to add the weights for these but not for one-parent families would introduce a serious bias. The same argument applied to the other social classes which contributed to the Social Index score, i.e. social classes I and IV. The simple solution, therefore, was to exclude the weights for five-year social class from the Social Index score so that all types of family in this analysis were treated in the same way.

Children who at the age of five were with neither natural parent, e.g. adopted and fostered children, were excluded from the analysis as the data for a large proportion of these were not matched with the birth study. Supported and lone one-parent families were combined because of the small numbers of children occurring in some of the categories and also because there was no significant difference in the mean Social Index scores of these families (see Figure 3.1). Thus three types of family appear in Figure 3.2; families with both natural parents, step-families and one-parent families.

As expected, the mean Social Index score increased in relation to the birth social class scale from the lowest point at social class I to the highest at social class V. But one-parent families had higher mean scores than families with both natural parents for every category of birth social class (the results of Scheffe tests for the differences between means are given in Table 3.10). In other words, for each social class at the time of the child's birth, children in one-parent families five years later were on average more socially disadvantaged, according to the Social Index, than were children in families which remained together.

The size of the difference in mean Social Index score between one-parent and intact families varied slightly according to the mother's original social class from an equivalent of .6 standard deviations of Social Index score (birth social class IV) to more than one standard deviation (both social classes I and III non-manual). Another way of conceptualising the degree of downward social mobility associated with one-parent families is to observe in Figure 3.2 that the mean Social Index score of children in one-parent families at age five was about the same as that of children with both natural parents at age five who started life two social classes lower. For example, families in social class II when their child was born and who were one-parent families when the child was five had a mean Social Index score which was about the same as intact families who originated in social class III (manual).

The pattern for step-families was less clear-cut than that for one-parent families. Although families who were in social classes II or III when the child was born appeared to be downwardly mobile if a natural parent was replaced by a substitute parent, this was not the case for step-families originating in social classes I, IV and V.

This analysis strongly suggests that the poor social and housing circumstances of the average one-parent family compared with intact families are attributable more to their downward social mobility after becoming a one-parent family than their tendency to have lower social class origins. One-parent families are most often headed by women who command lower incomes than men in the labour market. Their family circumstances also mean that with a preschool child it is more difficult to work full-time and part-time employment results in lower income and fewer benefits. The break-up of a marriage often results in the sale of the family home and a move to other less satisfactory accommodation. State benefits for lone parents are far from adequate to meet all the family's needs (Ferri, 1976, Chapter 7).

All these factors contribute to the decline in social circumstances of one-parent families that we have described. If the divorce rate continues to increase as it has done throughout the 1970s, more and more children will be subject to family disruption. The problems associated with family breakdown are, as we have shown, not necessarily resolved by the introduction of a substitute parent to create a step-family. The set-back created by family disruption appears to have a lasting effect on the socio-economic circumstances of the family.

Summary

One in ten of the children in the Study were not living with both natural parents by the time they reached their fifth birthday. These children lived in what we have termed 'disrupted' families. Half of these were in one-parent families and half were in step-families, had been adopted, or were living with grandparents or foster parents. In this study we have distinguished between one-parent families who shared accommodation with other adults who were a potential source of support and lone parents who lived in households with no other adults. Only about a third of the disrupted families had been in this situation since the child's birth. For the other two-thirds the parental change had taken place during the study child's first five years of life. Single parenthood was still a predominantly female phenomenon, with only a handful of families being headed by a lone father.

Disruption was somewhat more likely to occur in families of children with young and less well-educated mothers and mothers of low social class origin. There was also a slightly increased likelihood of disruption in families where the child's father was of low social class.

Whilst the parents' poorer social origins may have been partly responsible for the marked disparity in housing, amenities, domestic equipment and facilities of disrupted families compared with intact families, we suggest that for the most part it was the loss of a parent which precipitated a decline in the standards of living of these families. Whilst step-families and supported one-parent families were in consistently worse social circumstances than intact families, it was the lone

one-parent family which was most likely to be the most seriously deprived.

Chapter 4

Division of labour in the home

Domestic work and child-care have traditionally been the responsibility of women. Women who are wives and mothers typically spend long hours doing work that is physically and mentally demanding yet carries few tangible rewards. Because domestic work is largely carried out within the home the extent of exploitation through the sexual division of labour is not readily apparent. There is also no organisation that looks after the interests of housewives and mothers in the way that trade unions operate on behalf of other workers who are in paid employment.

Notwithstanding the potential vulnerability of housewives many women do not find housework onerous and see child-care as a challenge which is rewarding in itself. At the same time, other women would like to have the opportunity to obtain employment, pursue a career or develop other interests outside the home. Such ambitions need the co-operation of other members of the household, in particular the wife's husband, to share the domestic and child-care duties. Young and Willmott (1975) have suggested that in Western societies families are becoming more 'symmetrical' with husbands and fathers playing a greater part in the home than hitherto. However, they found little evidence of the breaking down of the traditional segregation of roles within the family:

> . . . , it was in virtually all (families) not expected that men should do more than *help* their wives at the work of child-rearing and housekeeping. The primary responsibilities for home and work were still firmly with one sex or the other, . . . (ibid., p. 96)

This appears to be the view of most commentators on role sharing in the family and many argue that the marriage relationship is still fundamentally exploitative of wives, (Oakley, 1974; Rowbotham, 1973).

Even in professional families, which were thought by Young and Willmott to set the standard for the rest of society in future generations (ibid., pp. 20-7), there remains a basic commitment to the traditional division of labour between married partners:

> There are some couples who have reallocated responsibilities in a more fundamental way — either by defining them as their joint responsibilities or on the basis of a new division of labour between husband and wife; but this is still rare even among the dual-career families in this study. (Rapoport, 1971, p. 304)

Modern technology, however, is modifying the nature of domestic responsibility through the introduction of labour-saving equipment, for example automatic washing machines and dishwashers, new fabrics that do not require ironing, food preservers and processors such as the deep freeze and microwave oven and convenience foods. In addition to these aids to home-management the dual-career family also makes use of paid help for both child-care and housework, so that the wife's responsibility becomes more a question of *organisation* of all these resources rather than actually carrying out the tasks herself.

At the other end of the social scale wives and mothers are often unable to introduce any planned organisation into their domestic or child-care responsibilities because of lack of resources. A study of families in depressed areas of a midlands city reveals that many mothers do housework and shopping on a day-to-day basis, which hardly allows any respite for them either to give extra attention to the children when they ask for it, or to take a rest themselves (Wilson and Herbert, 1978, pp. 90-92). In these families the fathers were much less likely to share in child-care activities than were fathers in the average family, even though their wives were in greater need of practical help (ibid., pp. 120-1).

A major reason why a father does not take a hand in looking after his children may be his preoccupation with his own employment, rather than a lack of concern for the day-to-day needs of his family. In families with young children there is an increased likelihood that the father will be absent from the home in the evenings or at weekends due to shift working or the need to work overtime either to increase family income or to improve career prospects (National Board for Prices and Incomes, 1970). After careful analysis of the transcripts of interviews with nearly 700 Nottingham mothers with a seven-year-old child, the Newsons (1978) suggest that the father's work not only serves to sustain the traditional differentiation of family roles but is also physically exhausting so that when they return home they are too tired to take an active interest in their children; in contrast non-manual workers tend to bring their work home with them and therefore appear too busy to become involved with their children (ibid., p. 301). Thus for one reason or the other mothers continue to fill the main nurturant role whilst the father helps out from time to time or engages more in leisure or 'educative' activities (Backett, 1982; Newson, 1970, p. 485; Wilson and Herbert, 1978, pp. 116-19).

The studies briefly reviewed above suggested that the 'symmetrical family' was expected to be so rare that it did not warrant special investigation in the CHES (1975) study. Thus, in line with these studies, our enquiries were limited to the help given by the father in a selection of specific domestic and child-care tasks, on the implicit assumption that the mother carried the main responsibility in the management of the home and child. In the rest of this chapter we describe the extent to which mothers in the study received help from their husbands or others in these activities, and then investigate the social and family factors that appear to affect the likelihood that mothers received help in the home.

Indicators of domestic and child care tasks

We enquired whether in the previous week the mother received help from the father or other persons (which could include members of the household, friends, neighbours, relatives and paid help) in any of the following ways; (a) doing housework and shopping, (b) looking after the child for part of the day while mother shops, attends appointments, does housework, etc., (c) taking the child to school/nursery/playgroup, etc., (d) putting the child to bed, and (e) babysitting in the evening. Whilst these five activities in no way encompasses the whole spectrum of housework and parent-child interaction, they do draw from a broad range of typical activities in which the father or others may be expected to play a part. In the discussion which follows it is vital to recognise that there would be considerable variation in the extent to which mothers received help in these ways. For example, helping to put the child to bed may only mean reading a story after the mother has completed the undressing and washing rituals preparatory to settling the child down for the night. Similarly, a mother who reported that she had been helped with housework or shopping may have had help daily or on only one occasion during the previous week. A second methodological consideration is that the majority of the survey interviews were conducted with the mother herself and therefore the response to the questions concerning the help she received is perhaps better understood in terms of her perception of being helped rather than an objective indication of help actually received. However, these factors in no way diminish the significance of the analysis presented in this chapter; they are mentioned simply to ensure that our results are seen in the correct perspective.

Type of family

One-parent mothers are clearly unlikely to be able to depend on the study child's father for help with domestic and child-rearing tasks. Such families, therefore, may depend on the good-will of other members of their family, friends and neighbours to help out from time to time. This expectation is borne out by the results presented in Figure 4.1 which show that very small proportions of one-parent mothers received any of the five types of help from the study child's father compared with mothers in two-parent families. This was compensated for to some extent by higher proportions of one-parent mothers obtaining the help of family, friends, etc., and this was particularly so in supported one-parent families (for definition see Chapter 18) where there were other adults in the household who were potential sources of help. For lone mothers, help from friends, relatives and others, who by definition were not members of the household, could not compensate entirely for the loss of help from fathers or other household members available to mothers in two-parent and unsupported one-parent families.

The contrast between lone mothers and mothers in two-parent families was greatest in those activities in which fathers in the latter were most likely to take part; these were housework and shopping and putting the child to bed (Figure 4.1(a) and (d)). The proportion of mothers who received no help with housework and shopping was 38 percent in two-parent families compared with 70 percent of lone mothers. Similarly 41 percent of mothers in two-parent families had no help putting the child to bed compared with 72 percent of lone mothers. The same kinds of trend can be seen in Figure 4.1 for the other types of help but the differences were not so large as for the two we have mentioned.

Because of these obvious differences in the availability of sources of help in one-parent compared with two-parent families the remaining analyses in this chapter will be based on the subsample of children in two-parent families. These include families with both natural parents, step-families and adoptive families (see Chapter 18 for definitions). Analyses will be in terms of socioeconomic differences using the Social Index, family composition (numbers of children older and younger than the study child) and mother's employment. These variables were selected for analysis in this chapter in the expectation that these were the kinds of factor most likely to influence the probability that

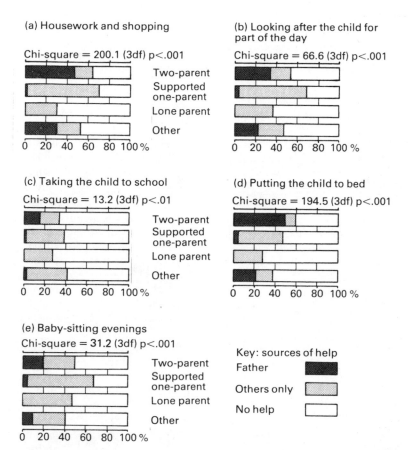

Figure 4.1 Help for mother by type of family

Notes
1 Help received from father *and* others (i.e. family, friends, neighbours and paid help) is included only in percentages for fathers.
2 Test for difference between types of family: help from father or others v. no help.

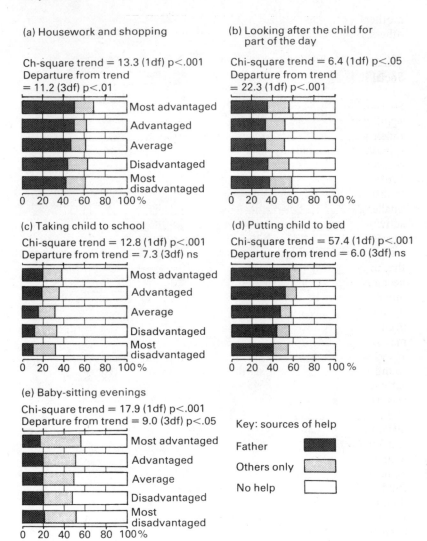

Figure 4.2 Help for mother by Social Index group

Notes
1 Help received from father *and* others (i.e. family, friends, neighbours and paid help) is included only in percentages for fathers.
2 Test for difference between types of family: help from father or others v. no help.

mothers obtained the help of fathers, friends, relatives and others.

Social Index group

Social class differences in family attitudes were expected to have a significant effect on the extent to which fathers in different Social Index groups helped their wives. Previous studies have contrasted the typically traditional ideology of working class families with the more egalitarian attitudes towards family roles of middle class parents (Kohn, 1969; Newson, 1978; Young and Willmott, 1975). Adherence to the traditional view of sexual division of labour in the family could result in smaller proportions of fathers taking part in domestic and child-care activities. This same traditionalism in working class families, however, suggests closer links with the extended family network and a more integrated and supportive neighbourhood community compared with the more self-sufficient and independent nuclear family which has become the middle class model (Willmott and Young, 1960). Furthermore the more acute difficulties and lack of domestic resources faced by socially disadvantaged mothers would mean that they are in greater need of help from family and friends. Finally, the father's employment may or may not provide the opportunity for him to help out at home. Working evenings, weekends, overnight and on shifts have all been found to influence the likelihood that a father is involved in child-care activities and these working patterns tend to be differentiated by social class (Osborn and Morris, 1982).

Figure 4.2 shows the variation in the proportion of mothers in different Social Index groups who received help with the five domestic and child-care activities. Half the socially advantaged fathers helped with housework and shopping compared with 42 percent of the most disadvantaged fathers. Only a third of the fathers looked after their child for part of the day so that the mother could get on with other things without the worry of having to cope with an active five-year-old at the same time. There was little social variation in this proportion. Even fewer fathers had taken their child to school in the previous week although this was more common in the most advantaged families (19.4 percent) than in the most disadvantaged families (11.8 percent). This suggests greater flexibility in the working hours of socially advantaged fathers. Moreover, we have shown elsewhere (Osborn and Morris, 1982) that 25 percent of fathers who worked nights or shifts took their children to school, which demonstrates how certain work patterns can increase the opportunity for a father to help out.

It is perhaps surprising that there was little variation between Social

Index groups in the proportions of mothers who were helped by friends, relations and neighbours with housework and shopping (14.9 percent), looking after the child whilst the mother did other things (19.1 percent) and taking the child to school (17.3 percent). There was little evidence here of a supportive working class community and extended family network from which help was forthcoming.

Figure 4.2(d) shows that fathers helping to put their child to bed were more frequently found in advantaged families than in disadvantaged families. But the trend was in the opposite direction regarding the proportion of others who helped in this way – this occurred more frequently in socially disadvantaged homes. This kind of help was unlikely to come from people outside the household and the results suggest that other members of the household, for example adult relatives and older siblings, were important sources of help for some mothers. As there was a marked tendency for socially disadvantaged families to be larger than disadvantaged families (Table 1.1) this could underlie the differences appearing in Figure 4.2(d) and is explored further later in this chapter.

Baby-sitting in the evenings occurred in half the families in this study (Figure 4.2(e)). This might have allowed mothers or both parents to go out and enjoy themselves for a few hours or in some cases to enable the mother to go out to work. There is some evidence to suggest that socially disadvantaged mothers were more likely to work unsocial hours (Chapter 12) and this might account for the 21.8 percent of fathers in the most disadvantaged families who looked after their children in the evenings compared with 17.2 percent of fathers in the most advantaged Social Index group. In contrast to this pattern, baby-sitting in the evenings by others, i.e. friends, relatives, etc., was more frequent at the advantaged end of the scale which can probably be attributed to the employment of paid sitters by the more well-off parents in the study.

In general, the pattern of results in Figure 4.2 has shown that socially disadvantaged mothers were somewhat less likely than their better-off counterparts to obtain help in the five specific ways we have described. The differences were small, however, and suggest that other factors may have been of greater significance than social inequality *per se*. There was little evidence in the results of a more supportive community or extended family network in the disadvantaged as compared with the advantaged groups.

Family composition

The number and age distribution of children in the family could have important implications with regard to the involvement of the father or

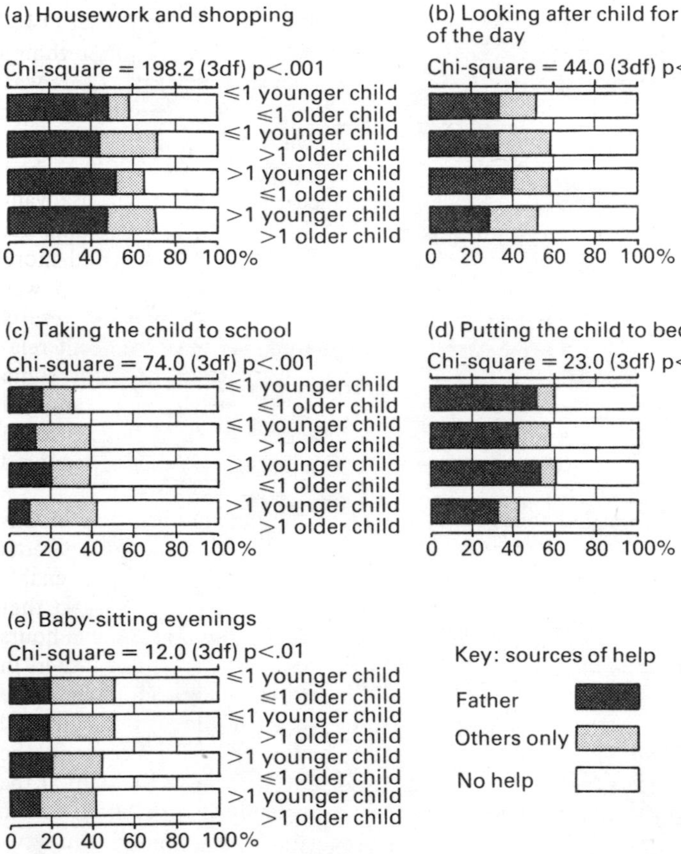

(a) Housework and shopping

Chi-square = 198.2 (3df) p<.001

≤1 younger child
≤1 older child
≤1 younger child
>1 older child
>1 younger child
≤1 older child
>1 younger child
>1 older child

0 20 40 60 80 100%

(b) Looking after child for part of the day

Chi-square = 44.0 (3df) p<.001

0 20 40 60 80 100%

(c) Taking the child to school

Chi-square = 74.0 (3df) p<.001

≤1 younger child
≤1 older child
≤1 younger child
>1 older child
>1 younger child
≤1 older child
>1 younger child
>1 older child

0 20 40 60 80 100%

(d) Putting the child to bed

Chi-square = 23.0 (3df) p<.001

0 20 40 60 80 100%

(e) Baby-sitting evenings

Chi-square = 12.0 (3df) p<.01

≤1 younger child
≤1 older child
≤1 younger child
>1 older child
>1 younger child
≤1 older child
>1 younger child
>1 older child

0 20 40 60 80 100%

Key: sources of help

Father

Others only

No help

Figure 4.3 Help for mother by number of children younger or older than study child (two-parent families only)

Notes
1 Help received from father *and* others (i.e. family, friends, neighbours and paid help) is included only in percentages for fathers.
2 Test for difference between types of family: help from father or others v. no help.

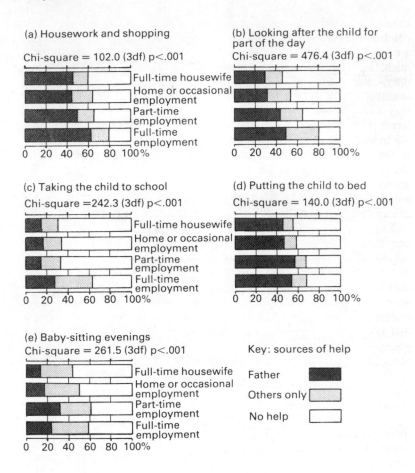

(a) Housework and shopping

Chi-square = 102.0 (3df) p<.001

Full-time housewife
Home or occasional employment
Part-time employment
Full-time employment

0 20 40 60 80 100%

(b) Looking after the child for part of the day

Chi-square = 476.4 (3df) p<.001

0 20 40 60 80 100%

(c) Taking the child to school

Chi-square =242.3 (3df) p<.001

Full-time housewife
Home or occasional employment
Part-time employment
Full-time employment

0 20 40 60 80 100%

(d) Putting the child to bed

Chi-square = 140.0 (3df) p<.001

0 20 40 60 80 100%

(e) Baby-sitting evenings

Chi-square = 261.5 (3df) p<.001

Full-time housewife
Home or occasional employment
Part-time employment
Full-time employment

0 20 40 60 80 100%

Key: sources of help

Father

Others only

No help

Figure 4.4 Help for mother by mother's employment

Notes
1 Help received from father *and* others (i.e. family, friends, neighbours and paid help) is included only in percentage for fathers.
2 Test for difference between types of family: help from father or others v. no help.

others in domestic and child-care activities. When there are only a few children the mother may feel that she can cope without help. If there are many young children the probability that the father would help might increase because of the additional work involved. If there are many older children, however, they may be seen as a more readily available source of help for the mother than the father, who in any case may need to work longer hours to meet the economic needs of his larger than average family. These possibilities are investigated in Figure 4.3 in which families are divided up according to the number of children in the household who were younger or older than the study child. As the majority of study children were just aged five at the time of the survey, children younger than the study child were in the preschool group, or babies and children other than the study child were aged over five and by definition under eighteen years.

Examination of Figure 4.3 suggests that in families with more than one child older than the study child smaller proportions of fathers helped with any of the tasks or activities described, and the proportion of 'others' involved increased markedly. This relationship held independent of the number of children younger than the study child. Fathers were most likely to help in families where there were several young children but few older children. These results confirm our expectation that fathers help where the need is greatest, i.e. in families with several younger children, but the father's involvement is likely to be reduced if others, for example older siblings, are on hand to help.

Mother's employment

As housework and child-care are widely regarded as fundamentally women's responsibilities, the possibility of a mother obtaining employment outside the home depends largely on the extent to which others can share these responsibilities. Figure 4.4 shows that mothers employed outside the home were far more likely to have had help than were full-time housewives. The contrast was greatest where the mother was in full-time employment. Also the extra help was more likely to come from the father than from other family members, friends or neighbours.

The proportion of fathers who helped with housework and shopping increased from 45.5 percent if the mother was not employed to 62.3 percent where the mother had a full-time job outside the home. 48.3 percent of children of mothers in full-time employment were looked after by their father whilst the mother did other things (which might include when the mother went out to work) compared with only 29.2 percent of children of full-time housewives. As many as 27.4 percent of fathers had taken their children to school during the previous week when the mother was employed full-time compared with 15.2 percent if the mother did not have a paid job.

Full-time maternal employment was associated with increased likelihood of certain kinds of help being available from other members of the family, friends, neighbours and paid helpers. Such people looked after 31.8 percent of the children of full-time employed mothers for part of the day (this would include paid child minders) and took 34.7 percent to school compared with 16.7 percent and 15.5 percent respectively of children whose mothers were not employed. Employment outside the home was associated with slightly increased proportions of mothers receiving help from family, friends, etc., in the other three ways described in Figure 4.4, but the contrasts were not so great as for the two described above.

These results suggest that fathers were the most likely source of general help for mothers who obtained employment outside the home, whereas others, such as family, friends, neighbours and paid helpers, were of assistance in specific ways. For many of these mothers it is likely that the availability of these various sources of help was a prerequisite for being able to seek employment outside the home. A corollary to this is that other mothers who may have wished to go out to work were unable to do so because of the lack of support either from within the family or from the wider community.

Summary

The sexual division of labour in the home means that child-care, housework, shopping and other domestic work are chiefly the responsibility of women who may receive, to a greater or lesser degree, the help of family members, friends or neighbours in such tasks. The extent to which mothers in the CHES sample received help with five specific types of activities from the study child's father was investigated. These types of activity were (a) housework and shopping; (b) looking after the child for part of the day whilst the mother did other things; (c) taking the child to school; (d) putting the child to bed; and (e) babysitting evenings.

About half the fathers helped with housework and shopping and putting the child to bed, but fewer than this had helped in any of the other ways. One-parent mothers were more likely to obtain help from other family members, friends and neighbours but this did not make up for the loss of help available from fathers in two-parent families. Lone mothers living in households with no other adults were especially vulnerable in this respect.

Analysis of differences in the proportions of mothers who received these types of help suggested that fathers were more likely to become involved in domestic and child-care activities in families where extra help was needed; for example, where there were many young children or where the mother had a job outside the home. It appeared also that mothers in households where there were older children were able to obtain help from them.

The general impression obtained from the evidence provided by these five examples of the types of help mothers might receive is that this was more forthcoming in households where the mother needed extra help and where the opportunity presented itself in the form of others in the household who were capable of helping.

Chapter 5

Social and family influences on child behaviour and ability and maternal depression

The early years of life are crucial for a child's subsequent cognitive and emotional development. Whatever the child's genetic endowment, the pattern of family life and the social condition of the home can accelerate or retard developmental progress so that by the age of five, some children are more prepared than others for formal education in the school system. Previous cohort studies have emphasised the profound impact of the home background on children's ability and school attainment (Davie *et al.*, 1972; Douglas, 1964). We have shown that important improvements have occurred in the social and housing conditions of children over the past twenty-five years (Chapter 2), yet despite this progress substantial socio-economic inequalities persist. Such inequalities may have important implications for the intellectual progress of children in Britain.

In this chapter we seek to discover which family and social factors were most strongly associated with differences in children's abilities and behaviour at the threshold of their school careers. In previous sections we have shown the tendency for many family characteristics to cluster together so that, for example, large family size tends to be associated with older mothers and with low socioeconomic position. Thus, if we wish to examine the relationship between family size and a child's ability or behaviour, it becomes necessary to take account of the separate 'effects' of mother's age and socioeconomic position in order to avoid spurious associations. However, it is never possible to isolate completely the 'effects' of a specific variable because social indices are inevitably crude and give only an approximate indication of what we are trying to measure.

An even greater problem for empirical research is that associations between measures of behaviour or ability and factors such as family size or socioeconomic position do not necessarily imply causal relationships. That is to say, family size *per se* might not directly influence a child's ability, but there may be some intermediary factors which are associated in a casual way with both size of family and a child's ability. The kinds of intermediary factor we are thinking of are, for example, the child-rearing methods adopted by parents with large families which may differ in important ways from those of parents of an only child. There may also be logistic reasons why family size is associated with differences in children's ability. For example, a mother with several children to care for has relatively less time to devote to her five-year-old compared with mothers with only one or two children. Resources may need to be spread more thinly in large families, resulting in poorer diet, fewer trips out to places of interest and a general reduction in quality of life in many unthought-of ways which, taken collectively, could have an adverse effect on the rate of cognitive development of children in such families.

Such considerations apply not only to family size but also to all the other family characteristics we discuss below (and in other parts of this report) in relation to our measures of the children's behaviour and ability. The point we are making is that although our statistical methods can separate out the associations between specific social factors and measures of children's ability and behaviour, the explanations for such associations remain implicit and sometimes open to alternative interpretations. However, these cautionary words are only addressed to the assumption of causality between these variables; the associations we describe actually existed for this sample even though we can only speculate about the real life processes which produce these associations. Awareness of such associations, however, is itself of value in directing attention to families where there may be greater need for intervention and the concentration of resources. The important point to grasp, however, is that a campaign to reduce family size, even if successful, would not necessarily produce a general increase in the educational potential of children, whereas it is possible that the promotion of community facilities to provide additional support for families which need it may well have a beneficial effect. The value of our study is that it can direct attention towards the types of families which are most in need of such resources and support.

It is in this spirit that we present the results of analyses of family and social factors related to outcomes obtained when these children were five years old. These measures are maternal depression score, child's antisocial behaviour score, neurotic behaviour score, Human Figure Drawing (HFD), Copying Designs score, and English Picture Vocabulary Test (EPVT). The tests and assessments and our approach to multivariate analysis are described further in Chapters 19 and 20.

The child's behaviour and maternal depression

The close relationship which normally exists between a mother and child in the early years means that the emotional state of either has a profound influence on the other. Home and family circumstances which may be stressful for the mother may also give rise to deviant behaviour in her child either through their direct impact or indirectly by how they affect the mother's responses to her child's needs. At the same time any behavioural problems the child develops constitute a further difficulty for the mother, which thereby aggravates the risk of her becoming depressed.

Thus the home and family circumstances, the mother's emotional state, and the child's behaviour work as an integrated system which can be mutually supportive or else spiral into worsening behavioural deviance on the part of the child and maternal depression. Given this complex interaction it was not surprising to find a correlation as high as .36 between our measures of behaviour and maternal depression (Table 19.8). Indeed, such a link between maternal depression and child behaviour has been reported from other studies of preschool age children (e.g. Richman, 1976).

We believe that deviant behaviour in children and maternal depression were likely to arise for similar reasons. In the most general non-clinical terms depression can be interpreted as a reaction to perceiving one's position in life as being intolerable or unacceptable and yet at the same time inescapable. Depression of this origin is not a sudden occurrence but rather builds up over time as efforts to make something of life seem to be constantly frustrated by things beyond the individual's control. It is very likely that similar frustrations are felt by children who may then give vent to their feelings in bouts of aggressive behaviour. For adults, however, such outward expression of their feelings is not generally permitted and the suppression of fears and insecurities can lead instead to depression.

Many of the preconditions for behavioural deviance in children and depression in mothers are to be found within the home and family context. Brown and Harris (1978) use the term 'vulnerability factors' to describe social and family conditions which increase the risk of clinical depression in women who are faced with acute problems. In the present study we looked at several factors which might constitute vulnerability factors in this sense. These results are presented in Figures 5.1, 5.2 and 5.3 which show the relative sizes of the associations between selected social and family factors and our scales of maternal depression and child behaviour. It is important to note that in these analyses the effects of any variable have been adjusted for the effects of all the other variables. Thus the separate effects of the individual

Analysis of variance: the effects of all independent variables are adjusted for the others

Sample size: 11,977

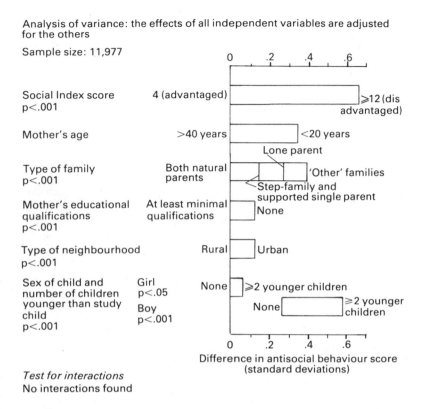

Figure 5.1   Analysis of social and family factors and antisocial behaviour

Analysis of variance: the effects of all independent variables are adjusted for the others

Sample size: 12,992

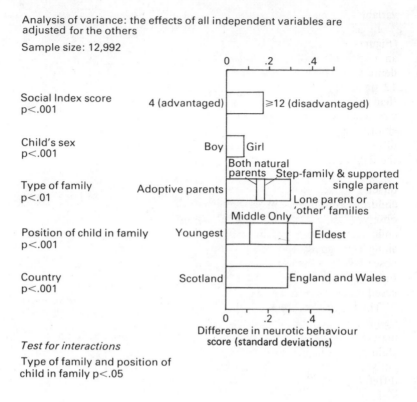

Figure 5.2 Analysis of social and family factors and neurotic behaviour

variables can be added together as explained in Chapter 20.

In all three analyses of child behaviour and maternal depression (Figures 5.1, 5.2 and 5.3) social inequality, i.e. Social Index score, was an important factor but its effect was greatest in terms of maternal depression where socially disadvantaged mothers (Social Index score of 12 or more) had a mean depression score which was .66 SDs higher than advantaged mothers (Social Index score of 4). Social inequality was associated with larger differences in antisocial behaviour in the children (.66 SDs difference) than in neurotic behaviour (.17 SDs difference). Clearly inequalities in the material and social resources of the family have a profound influence on the degree of stress experienced by the mother and which is reflected in her depression score. Inadequacies in the material environment may also create difficulties for children, but this is likely to be only a partial explanation for the observed differences attributed to the Social Index. We suggest that child rearing methods and other cultural factors which are organised along class or socioeconomic lines are the main contributors to the observed difference in behaviour scores associated with the Social Index. (These possibilities are to be the subject of future publications based on attitudinal data obtained in the five-year study.)

The type of family in which the children lived was also found to be a significant factor in antisocial and neurotic behaviour in children and maternal depression. Of particular importance was the finding that children of lone parents were more likely to be neurotic or behave in an antisocial manner than were children with both natural parents. The differences in mean scores were .27 SDs in antisocial behaviour score and .16 SDs in neurotic behaviour score. Lone parents were also most at risk of being depressed. This group had a mean depression score .32 SDs higher than mothers in families where both natural parents were present. Children living with neither natural parent, i.e. those who lived with grandparents or foster parents, were also more likely to be neurotic or antisocial, in fact their mean antisocial score was .12 SDs higher than that of children of lone parents. Mothers and children in step-families or supported one-parent families also had somewhat higher depression and antisocial behaviour scores than those in families with both natural parents but not so high as for families with a lone parent. Mothers and children in adoptive families did not differ significantly from families which included both natural parents.

These results are interesting in view of opposing opinions concerning the reason for behaviour problems in children of lone parents. This issue is discussed more fully elsewhere (Burnell and Wadsworth, 1981) and the two main arguments run as follows. One view is that children need to be brought up in a two-parent family so that they can benefit from the full-time love and care of one parent whilst the other parent's responsibility is to provide the family's economic needs (Pringle, 1980(a)). This could be termed the 'traditional' model of child-care. The alternative argument stresses the need that many women express to have interests outside the family as well as within it. This argument also holds that young children benefit more from a diversity of social experiences than from a single mother-child relationship (Hughes *et al.*, 1980, Chapters 1 and 2). This we shall call the 'radical' model as it rests on the premise that a woman cannot function effectively as a mother if she feels housebound and frustrated by the lack of opportunity to develop other aspects of her personality and other interests.

Proponents of the radical model suggest that when deviant behaviour occurs in children of one-parent families, this can be explained by their relatively poor socioeconomic circumstances. Indeed this study has shown marked downward social mobility in the single-parent families (Chapter 3), and our other findings indicate that socially disadvantaged children were more likely to show signs of behavioural deviance than their more favoured peers in well-off families. However, the difference in mean antisocial behaviour score between children with both natural parents and lone parents was only reduced from .42 SDs to .27 SDs after adjustment for the other social and family factors in the analysis. Adjustment for other factors made no difference at all to the mean neurotic behaviour score of children of lone parents relative to children with both natural parents. The difference was .16 SDs both before and after statistical adjustment. Thus differences in social or material well-being were only a partial explanation of the increased level of antisocial behaviour in children with one parent and accounted for none of the difference in neuroticism.

Advocates of the traditional model of parenting would claim that this supports their case that more adequate financial and social support could alleviate some but not all of the ill-effects and disadvantages associated with one-parent families but full-time care provided by one parent in a two-parent situation is the only kind to ensure optimal emotional, social and intellectual care and stimulation (Pringle, 1980(b), Chapter 3). However, this viewpoint was not vindicated by our results for children in step-families or those in supported single-parent families in the antisocial analysis; their mean antisocial behaviour score was also significantly higher (after adjustment) than that of children with both natural parents (a difference of .14 SDs) though not as high as the mean score of children with lone parents. If lone-parentness *per se* had been the crucial factor, then children in step-families or supported one-parent families would have been expected to be no different from children with both natural parents.

Thus it appears that family disruption, for example, the antecedent events leading to the breakdown of the family or the death of a parent, was associated with increased maternal depression and antisocial behaviour in the child but neurotic behaviour was associated mainly with lone-parent families.

There is clearly no adequate single explanation for the increased levels of depression in lone mothers and behavioural deviance in their children. The majority of such families have a history of social, emotional and economic deprivation which engenders more stress and worry than is experienced by the average two-parent family. It follows that families who have experienced such disruption to their lives are more vulnerable to behavioural deviance in their children and psychiatric disorders in the parents. It is evident from our results that improving the material well-being of one-parent families may do much to reduce stress even though this in itself may not provide a complete solution.

Other factors associated with differences in behavioural deviance and maternal depression included the family composition in terms of the number of children in the household, the mother's age and education, the type of neighbourhood or locality where the family lived and the child's sex. These factors did not affect all three measures of behaviour and depression in the same way, however, and each analysis will be discussed separately.

Antisocial behaviour was found to be increased in children of young mothers, mothers without educational qualifications and in children living in an urban, as against a rural, environment. The importance of maternal age was confirmed by the fact that children of very young mothers, under twenty years, had a mean antisocial behaviour score which was .34 SDs higher than that of children whose mothers were over forty years old. This was about the same as the difference attributed to social inequality and may reflect different tolerance levels in mothers of different ages to the types of behaviour listed in the questionnaire. This is unlikely to be a complete explanation, however, as there was no maternal age effect associated with children's neurotic behaviour. Perhaps older women with more experience were better able to control any tendency for aggression or disobedience in their children.

Another interesting result to emerge from our analysis of antisocial behaviour was the effect of the number of children in the household younger than the study child. Preliminary analysis indicated an interaction between the child's sex and the number of younger children with respect to antisocial behaviour. Investigation of this interaction revealed that the observed difference in antisocial score associated with the number of younger children was almost entirely limited to the boys in the sample. These effects we have tried to illustrate in Figure 5.1 by showing the differences in score attributable to numbers of younger children for boys and girls separately. The presence of younger siblings made very little difference to the antisocial behaviour score of the girls, but boys in families where there were two or more younger children had a mean antisocial behaviour score which was .32 SDs higher than boys with no younger siblings and .52 SDs higher than girls with two or more younger children.

These results suggest not only that boys were more likely than girls to display antisocial behaviour, but the presence of younger children in the home appeared to increase the likelihood of antisocial behaviour still more. It could be that the kind of aggressive, assertive and active behaviour that comprise the antisocial scale are more likely to be expected in boys than in girls. This does not explain the differences associated with the presence of younger children however. Perhaps girls, even at the young age of five years, become more involved with the younger children and babies than do boys. The latter, however, may feel that they are in competition with the younger ones for the parent's attention and respond accordingly in ways that in terms of our scale are defined as antisocial behaviour.

The associations with neurotic behaviour were quite different from that for antisocial behaviour. For example, mother's age and neighbourhood of residence were not significant factors in neuroticism. Girls were more likely to be neurotic than boys although the difference was small (.08 SDs). Curiously, Scottish children had a lower mean neurotic behaviour score than English or Welsh children (.29 SDs difference).

As in the antisocial analysis the number of children in the household had important implications for neuroticism, although a different pattern emerged. Figure 5.2 shows that eldest children amongst these five-year-olds (i.e. those with younger siblings but no older children) had the highest mean neurotic behaviour score, followed by only children (i.e. with no siblings) and middle children (i.e. with both elder and younger siblings) and children who were the youngest in the family had the lowest mean score. The differences between these four groups were all highly significant statistically ($p < .001$). The fact that first-born children were the most neurotic suggests this may be attributable to differences in parenting between first and subsequent born children. The parenting of the first child is often carried out with less confidence than with subsequent children. But the arrival of subsequent children increased the risk of neuroticism in first born children perhaps as a result of sibling rivalry.

The model is not strictly an additive one as an interaction was found between type of family and the age position of the study child. Further investigation of this interaction revealed that this mainly affected adopted children and children living with grandparents or foster parents but added little to the conclusions derived from the main effects model.

The mothers most at risk of depression were those with high ($\geqslant 12$)

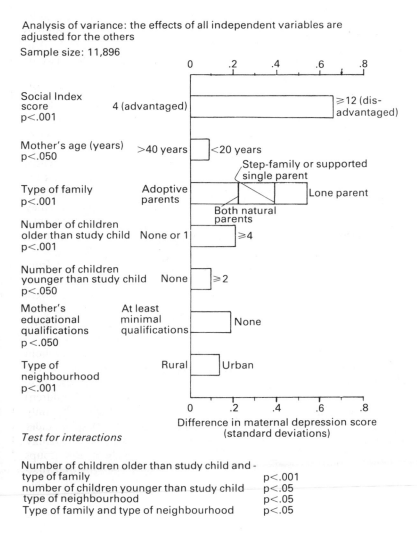

Analysis of variance: the effects of all independent variables are adjusted for the others

Sample size: 11,896

Test for interactions

Number of children older than study child and -
type of family   p<.001
number of children younger than study child p<.05
type of neighbourhood   p<.05
Type of family and type of neighbourhood   p<.05

Figure 5.3   Analysis of social and family factors and maternal depression

Analysis of variance: the effects of all independent variables are adjusted for the others

Sample size: 12,220

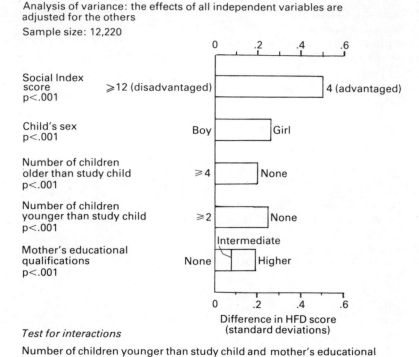

Test for interactions

Number of children younger than study child and mother's educational qualifications p<.05

Figure 5.4 Analysis of social and family factors and Human Figure Drawing

Social Index scores (i.e. severely disadvantaged) and those who were lone mothers as described above. In addition, however, Figure 5.3 indicates that young mothers (under twenty years old) and those without educational qualifications had increased risk of depression as were those living in urban rather than rural neighbourhoods.

Family size was a further contributory factor such that in families where the study child was the only child or if there was only one other older child, mothers were least at risk of depression. Increasing numbers of older or younger children, however, were associated with greater risk of depression.

The interaction between type of family and number of children older than the study child mainly concerned step-families and supported single-parent families. The higher mean maternal depression score associated with lone mothers compared with mothers in families with two natural parents was maintained irrespective of the number of older children. Where there had been a merging of families, however, as in step-families and in many supported single-parent families, the presence of two or more children older than the study child was associated with a larger increase in mean maternal depression score compared with mothers and children in families with both natural parents. This implies a compounding of the stresses arising out of a changing family situation when older children were also involved.

Further investigation of the other interactions in the analysis of maternal depression did not reveal any systematic trends and were of relatively low statistical significance.

Cognitive abilities and vocabulary

Formal education in Britain begins after a child reaches his or her fifth birthday. At this time children are expected to have acquired all the social and cognitive skills necessary for fitting in with and learning from the school environment. In only five years between the child's birth and this event parents provide all that is necessary to prepare their children for their introduction into one of society's major institutions. Unlike formal education, which uses special techniques and professionally trained teachers to achieve specific educational objectives (such as literacy, numeracy and knowledge of the wider world) the informal education provided by parents depends mainly on traditions − often implicit and intuitive − that are handed down from generation to generation. Parents do not deliberately set out to teach their children conceptual skills, yet by the example they set and through other every-day experiences, children gradually come to understand certain general principles concerning the world about them. All the activities which make up family life, such as mealtimes, bathtimes, bedtimes and play contribute vitally to the developing child's conceptual awareness so that he or she builds up pictures of the material and social worlds which constantly evolve and change shape with every new experience. Thus to the extent that the everyday life of children varies from family to family, so their conceptual and cognitive development may progress at different rates and follow different paths.

We recognise that we could not possibly grasp the full richness and range of cognitive abilities of these children when they were five years old. The tests we have used, however, serve to show how a child's conceptual and linguistic abilities may be profoundly influenced by family circumstances at the crucial time of entry into full-time formal education.

Human Figure Drawing test

The Human Figure Drawing (HFD) test, for example, is considered to provide an indication of a child's general conceptual maturity (see Chapter 19). It has also been found to correlate with tests of intellectual ability and its validity as a developmental test is corroborated by the fact that older children obtain higher scores on the test than do younger children. Thus, broadly speaking, children in the study with higher scores on this test were likely to be at a more advanced stage of cognitive development than children with lower scores. Figure 5.4 shows the differences in mean HFD score associated with a number of factors after adjustment for the effects of the other factors in the analysis of variance. Children with the highest scores were girls from socially advantaged families in which there were no siblings and the mother had higher educational qualifications (i.e. teacher's qualification, degree or higher professional qualification). Low HFD scores were found in socially disadvantaged boys from families with five or more children and whose mothers had no educational qualifications.

There is no ready explanation for the fairly substantial sex difference in HFD scores (.26 SDs). Harris (1963, pp. 126-130), who consistently found similar differences, was convinced that this was not an artifact of the scoring procedure. We are inclined to think that the girls simply enjoyed drawing more than the boys and perhaps had more practice.

The largest difference in HFD score was associated with socio-economic factors. Children from socially advantaged homes were half a standard deviation ahead of their less well-off peers. This is in line with other studies of child development and ability which consistently show large differences associated with social class and housing conditions, (e.g. Davie *et al.*, 1972). Much of this difference could be attributed to the material benefits accruing to the socially advantaged children in terms of superior diet, more space to play both indoors and out and other advantages stemming from a higher standard of living which are not available to socially disadvantaged children. Differences in child-rearing methods between socially advantaged and socially disadvantaged parents is another source of explanation for the observed variation in the cognitive ability of children. This possibility is suggested by a study of some 900 of this sample of children in the South West Region of England and South Wales at age 3½ years: the child-rearing attitudes of mothers from the lower socioeconomic strata were characterised as mainly authoritarian, whereas those of mothers from the higher social echelons were more democratic and child-centred (Osborn *et al.*, 1979). Whilst there is no guarantee that expressed attitudes are necessarily consistent with what mothers actually do, it is unlikely that mothers who have authoritarian views would in general behave in a child-centred manner towards their children, or vice-versa. Thus if child-centred parenting is more conducive to cognitive development in young children, this reported difference in child management could well provide at least part of the explanation for the observed socio-economic difference in conceptual maturity suggested by the HFD analysis.

The more children there are in a family, the more stretched are the family's resources and, in particular, the less time is available for any one child to have the undivided attention of an adult. How is this likely to affect a child's conceptual maturity? The HFD analysis showed family size to be a very important factor. Children with no younger siblings had a mean HFD score which was .25 SDs higher than those with two or more younger siblings. Similarly the mean score of children with four or more older siblings was .2 SDs lower than that of children with no older siblings. Thus children with no siblings were on average .45 SDs ahead in HFD score compared with children in families comprising seven or more children.

Preliminary analysis showed no urban/rural difference in HFD scores and the difference between children who lived in poor and well-to-do neighbourhoods disappeared after controlling for Social Index score. This was to be expected as these categories of the neighbourhood rating also contributed to the Social Index score. However, this makes the small difference (.19 SDs) attributable to mother's education all the more interesting as parents' education also contributed to the Social Index score (see Table 18.4). This finding suggests that mothers who had acquired at least minimal qualifications were likely to provide experiences which were more conducive to their child's general cognitive development than were mothers without formal qualifications.

Differences in mean HFD scores between children according to type of family were also reduced to statistical non-significance after adjustment for the other factors in Figure 5.4. It is worth mentioning, in addition, that it was not children in lone-parent families who had the lowest HFD mean score, but children in step-families. The elimination of differences in HFD scores after adjustment for social and other family factors adds weight to the argument that it was the circumstances within the different types of family rather than the parental situation *per se* that were influencing factors in any developmental problems attributed to lone parent and other 'non-normal' situations.

Copying Designs test

The ability to copy designs or geometric shapes is included as one element of assessment in many standard tests of intelligence. Design Copying shares with Human Figure Drawing the need for a child to have reached a certain level of conceptual development in order to be able to recognise the principles governing the different geometric forms. Some degree of overlap, therefore, was expected between the two tests used in this study. Indeed, a correlation of .4 was found between them (see Table 19.8). However, here the similarity ended, for whereas the Human Figure Drawing test was almost totally unstructured, the Copying Designs test demanded that the child copied given designs. Thus the test not only required the child to understand the principles of the designs given in the Test Booklet, but also to reproduce them. One difficulty with this test was that we do not know whether failure to copy a design was due to a lack of conceptual ability or to poor eye-hand coordination. However, we believe conceptual ability was probably the main factor as many children could copy one or two designs successfully which suggests that eye-hand coordination only became a problem for the children who failed to completely grasp the rationale of a particular design. The designs with which the children appeared to have most difficulty were the flag and the Maltese Cross. These produced some very curious results worthy of study in their own right but which would not be appropriate in the context of the present discussion.

Analysis of variance was again used to examine the relationships between social and family factors and Copying Designs score. The results obtained are presented in Figure 5.5 and were very similar to those for Human Figure Drawing except that larger differences were found in Copying Designs score attributable to the factors analysed. Children at extreme ends of the Social Index distribution had mean Copying Designs scores which were .86 standard deviations apart. Children whose mothers had teacher's certificates, degrees or post-

Analysis of variance: the effects of all independent variables are adjusted for the others

Sample size: 12,264

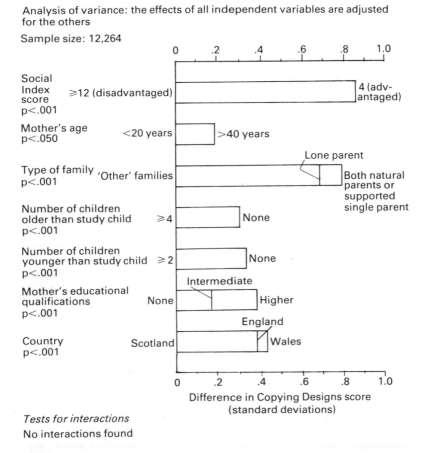

Tests for interactions
No interactions found

Figure 5.5 Analysis of social and family factors and Copying Designs score

Analysis of variance: the effects of all independent variables are adjusted for the others

Sample size: 11,498

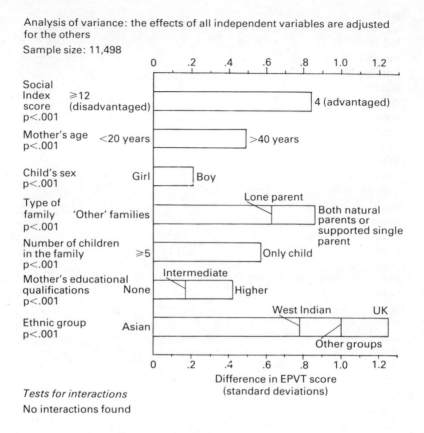

Tests for interactions
No interactions found

Figure 5.6 Analysis of social and family factors and English Picture Vocabulary test

graduate qualifications were .38 SDs ahead of children whose mothers had no formal qualifications. Children in families with no older children led those with four or more older siblings by .30 SDs, and children with no younger siblings scored on average .33 SDs higher than those in families with two or more younger children. By adding these two effects together, an only child would score about .6 SDs higher than children in families with six or more other children. In this analysis, unlike that for Human Figure Drawing, the parental situation was associated with a statistically significant ($p < .001$) difference in Copying Designs score. Children of lone parents were an average of .11 SDs behind children with both natural parents after adjustment for the other variables in the analysis. Prior to adjustment, the difference between children in these two types of family was .3 SDs so, again, it could be said that the social position of lone parents is likely to be a more damaging factor in the welfare of the child than the family situation itself. Children in 'other' family circumstances, i.e. living with grandparents or foster parents, however, performed least well in this test. This small group had a mean Copying Designs score which was .79 SDs lower than that of children with both natural parents.

Although there were no urban/rural differences in Copying Designs score after adjustment for the other variables in Figure 5.5, there were regional differences. Scottish children had a mean score which was .38 SDs lower than that for English children and .43 SDs lower than for Welsh children. As these differences were found after controlling for the effects of the other social and family factors there is no very easy explanation of why the Scottish Copying Designs scores were so much lower. This regional difference did not appear in the analyses related to Human Figure Drawing or EPVT. Perhaps more children in Scotland than in England or Wales have difficulty with abstract tasks. The National Child Development Study (NCDS) used a similar Copying Designs test in the seven-year follow-up of the 1958 birth cohort and also found that Scottish children were amongst those most likely to have poor scores (Davie *et al.*, 1972, pp. 107-8). These authors argued that the differences could be attributed to social class differences in the regions. This hypothesis was not tested in the NCDS, however, and we have found from the present study that the regional differences persist even after controlling for a number of socioeconomic and family factors. As the regional effect on Copying Designs score was large in comparison with other factors in the analyses it should not be ignored and suggests the need for further research.

English Picture Vocabulary test

Perhaps the skill of greatest importance at the beginning of formal education is language. This, more than anything else, determines how well a child can benefit from classroom experience. It was perhaps unfortunate that the survey methodology and the additional expense it would necessitate prohibited the use of any more probing tests of language than the English Picture Vocabulary test (EPVT) which was specifically a test of vocabulary. Further details of the test are given in Chapter 19.

The results of an analysis of social and family factors related to EPVT are given in Figure 5.6. Once more analysis of variance was used so that the independent effect of each factor could be estimated. There was one particularly important difference in this analysis compared with those already discussed, namely that large differences in EPVT score were associated with the children's ethnic background. The main effect concerned children from Asian families which in many instances were non-English speaking, and the 1.25 SDs difference in their scores compared with those of indigenous children suggests that for Asian children the language difference would be a serious disadvantage at school. Children from West Indian families had a mean EPVT score nearly half a standard deviation lower than that of indigenous UK children. Children from 'other' ethnic groups included those of mixed parentage, non-U.K. European children as well as children whose family origins were in other parts of the world. The mean EPVT score of children from 'other' ethnic groups was .25 SDs lower than that of UK children.

These differences in vocabulary score attributable to ethnic origin were a consequence of the extent to which English was not the exclusive or even primary language used by these families. They could not be attributed to poorer ability in non-indigenous children since little difference was found in Human Figure Drawing or Copying Designs scores according to ethnicity. Such differences in HFD and Copying Designs scores as were observed we considered too small to warrant reporting, and they may in any case have been due to language problems encountered during the administration of the tests. However, to the extent that English was not the exclusive language used by the family, children's vocabulary was adversely affected to their probable disadvantage upon school entry.

Poor vocabulary scores were also achieved by socially disadvantaged children whose EPVT scores were .84 SDs below those of children at the other extreme of the Social Index continuum. As with Human Figure Drawing and Copying Designs scores, the mother's education was an important determining factor in addition to the socioeconomic position of the family. Children of mothers with teaching or graduate qualifications had vocabulary scores which were .42 SDs above those of children whose mothers had no formal qualifications. Unlike the analyses of HFD and Copying Designs scores maternal age was an important factor in relation to the children's vocabulary. Half a standard deviation of EPVT score separated the children of young mothers (under twenty years) from children of the older mothers (over forty years) in this study.

The amount of parent-child contact perhaps underlies the now familiar finding that children with no siblings performed better in tests than did children in large families. The mean EPVT score of children in families with no other children was .57 SDs higher than children in families of five or more children. Also, children of lone parents had a mean EPVT score that was .23 SDs lower than children with both natural parents. The EPVT scores of children in supported single-parent families and step-families, however, were about the same as for children with both parents. Thus we suggest that any reduction in the opportunity for verbal contact between child and adult appears to reduce significantly the child's vocabulary and, by inference, linguistic ability. Children with the poorest vocabulary scores, however, were those living with grandparents or fosterparents. This group had a mean EPVT score which was .86 SDs lower than that of children with both natural parents.

The finding that the boys had a mean EPVT score which was .21 SDs higher than that of the girls was consistent with results described by the authors of the test who aver that this is a characteristic feature of orally administered vocabulary tests (Brimer and Dunn, 1962, pp. 30-3). However, the superiority of boys in this respect contrasts with the results for the HFD test (Figure 5.4) in which girls performed better on average than boys.

Summary

Throughout this chapter we have tried to show which family characteristics and environmental factors were most strongly associated with measures of child behaviour and ability and maternal depression. Some general themes have emerged. Social disadvantage, as measured by the Social Index, was consistently associated with increased risk of antisocial and neurotic behaviour, poorer general ability and reduced vocabulary, and a heightened risk of depression in mothers. With the exception of the poorer vocabulary of Asian children attributable to language differences, socioeconomic inequality was the most important single factor influencing all the outcomes in this study and illustrates very cogently how disadvantage is likely to be transmitted from generation to generation.

Family structure, i.e. numbers and ages of children relative to the study child, proved to be an important factor in analyses related to the child's general ability, vocabulary, behavioural deviance and maternal depression. It was found, however, that different family structures had different implications depending on the outcome under consideration. For example, children with no siblings were more likely to do well in tests of ability or vocabulary but were also more likely to be neurotic than were children who had siblings living at home.

Maternal education was associated with better test scores and reduced risk of antisocial behaviour and maternal depression. Other factors such as maternal age, child's sex, region and type of neighbourhood did not conform to any set pattern of relationships with the six outcomes we have examined.

A general conclusion of special significance concerns lone-parent families. On the basis of the evidence obtained from this study much of the adverse effect on behaviour and ability that is attributed to 'broken families' can be seen as a consequence of the poorer socioeconomic circumstances of these families compared with 'intact families'. However, these considerations did not account for the whole of the difference in test scores and behaviour of the children with a lone parent compared with two-parent children. Our interpretation of the results is that the loss of a parent reduced the opportunity for adult/child contact with detrimental consequences for the child's general ability and vocabulary. This interpretation was supported by the fact that in households with many children where the opportunity for adult/child interaction would have been similarly reduced, there was an associated decline in test scores. The EPVT analysis which showed no difference between supported single-parent families and two-parent families also supports this hypothesis in that where other adults were present, even though some family disruption had occurred, there was no loss of ability. The poor socioeconomic position typical of many lone-parent families would, however, serve to exacerbate the situation of family isolation and curtailed parent-child interaction.

The analyses of child behaviour and maternal depression differed from those of general ability and vocabulary in that increases in behavioural deviance and depression were associated to some degree with other families which had experienced disruption as well as to lone-parent families. This suggests that behavioural disturbance and maternal depression were less easily resolved by the advent of a substitute parent or other adult support.

Part Two

Preschool education and day care

Introduction

The factual history of nursery education and the development of the voluntary playgroup movement are well documented elsewhere (Blackstone, 1971, Chapters 2, 3 and 4; Van der Eyken, 1977, Chapters 6, 8 and 12; Tizard *et al.*, 1976, Chapters 3 and 4) and needs no further elaboration here. To place the present research in perspective, however, it is important to outline what we see as the main factors influencing the decline of day nurseries, the increase in provision of nursery education facilities and the expansion of voluntary playgroups to present-day levels.

Two broad theoretical perspectives or ideologies have transformed ideas about the needs of young children. The first of these perspectives was most clearly expressed in the work of John Bowlby (1951) as the maternal deprivation thesis. A central theme of the theory of maternal deprivation was the importance of maintaining a close mother-child relationship particularly in the early years of childhood. This need for young children to be at home with their mothers, however, had already been used by the Ministry of Health as a justification for closing war-time day nurseries even before Bowlby had provided the scientific basis for this belief (Ministry of Health and Ministry of Education, 1945) and resulted in a reduction in the female labour force in the 1950s. Closure of day nurseries and pressure on mothers not to go out to work but rather to fulfil their maternal role were legitimised by Bowlby's maternal deprivation thesis and also went some way to meeting the political objective of increasing the employment prospects of men returning to civilian life. Whatever the political motives for promoting the maternal deprivation thesis, however, the effect was an increased and widespread belief in the essential nature of the mother/child bond and the potentially damaging effect of long attendances at day nurseries due to the separation of child and mother. At that time, the emotional and developmental needs of the young child were vested in the family.

91

With passage of time, however, a partial redefinition of children's needs developed.

In the sphere of education considerable concern was expressed over the lack of educational mobility among children from different social backgrounds. The 1944 Education Act espoused the central idea of equality of opportunity, i.e. children were to be scientifically selected for grammar, secondary modern or technical education according to their level of ability as determined by the eleven plus examination. However, it frequently was observed that educational achievement and hence occupational opportunity was strongly related to home background. Perhaps the most influential research which related school performance to home background was based on the National Survey of Health and Development and published by James Douglas in *The Home and the School* (1964). This and similar research was rooted in and supported a burgeoning educational ideology which emphasised the powerful effect of the home environment on children's educational potential. A major theme in this area of thought was the profound qualitative difference in language skills between working class and middle class children (Bernstein, 1961), which meant that working class children were less able to cope with the middle class linguistic code of teachers. Developing out of this ideology was the concept of 'cultural deprivation' which had significant implications for children under five. The social and physical environment of children during the critical early years of development came to be seen as important determinants of their ability to benefit subsequently from the education system. The response to this, particularly in America, was the promotion of programmes of preschool education intended to 'compensate for cultural deprivation'. The American 'Headstart' programme is the best known example of this movement.

Whilst nursery education in Britain has never implemented the radically structured pedagogy of the American kindergarten (e.g. Bereiter and Engelman, 1966) the idea of increasing the educational potential of socially disadvantaged children has been the main force behind the expansion in nursery schools and nursery classes during the past twenty-five years. Thus the policy of positive discrimination expressed in a Department of Education and Science White Paper (1972) indicated official recognition that the philosophy of equality of opportunity embedded in the 1944 Education Act was insufficient to produce optimal standards of education for children from all levels of the social system.

In short, therefore, the level of Local Education Authority nursery school and class provision today can be seen as an official response to the needs of socially disadvantaged children. It is interesting that nearly a decade after publishing his theory of linguistic codes, which without doubt contributed to the philosophy of compensatory education, Bernstein claimed that he had been misinterpreted (1970(a)), that it is naive to expect that education programmes can compensate for the profound effects of social inequality and indeed to the extent that stratified cultures provide their own coping strategies within the class system it may be inappropriate to try to impose middle class culture on working class children. It is perhaps ironic that whilst Bernstein's earlier work contributed to an educational philosophy he opposes, his later views on this subject had less impact on official policy (Bernstein, 1970(b)). This is another graphic example of the way theoretical ideas are more likely to be taken up if they fit with the political and economic needs of the day.

The belief that some social environments are less than optimal for the developing child was an important shift from the essentially psychologistic idea of Bowlby that the emotional bond between mother and child was the single most important factor in the child's emotional and cognitive development. There was a recognition of the social and experiential needs of children as well as their personal/emotional needs. Nowhere was this more vividly expressed than in the work of Piaget. The stages of child development propounded in Piagetian theory depended on the child's contact with stimuli which evoked in the child by degrees the latent concepts essential for cognitive growth. Children starved of the appropriate stimulating environment were thus unable to progress at the same rate as others. This body of theory was widely publicised, not only in universities and colleges of education, but throughout the public consciousness and was largely responsible, we suggest, for the upsurge of middle-class demand during the 1960s for some kind of social and creative experience away from home for their preschool children which, in the absence of local authority provision, resulted in the appearance of playgroups.

Commentators on the emergence of playgroups seem to have accepted without question the fact that middle class mothers in the 1960s felt a need for their young children to be in contact with other children and adults. Whilst Belle Tutaev's historic letter to the *Guardian* Newspaper in 1960 (van der Eyken, 1977) may have sparked off the playgroup movement, the mood and perceived need for this was clearly already widely established. Increased geographical mobility, resulting in the establishment of the nuclear family as the norm, increased flat dwelling and heavily trafficked streets reduced the opportunity for children to play together and removed sources of support for the mother traditionally found in the wider family network. This changing pattern of family life also contributed to middle class demand for some kind of organised preschool experience for their children (Tizard *et al.*, 1976, pp. 76-8) but only insofar as mothers defined their children's needs as being unmet by the family situations in which they found themselves. Unlike the decline of day nurseries and the increase in LEA nursery education which derived from official policy, motivated partly by political and socioeconomic considerations, the playgroup movement, we suggest, represents a spontaneous response to a specific ideology concerning the needs of children and their mothers.

It is within this ideological and historical context that the next five chapters explore the preschool educational and day care experiences of children in the mid 1970s. The mixture of local authority, private and voluntary preschool provision in Britain, evolving as we have described in response to social and economic needs as well as to changing ideas of child development, has implications for who attends what types of preschool establishments and for what reasons. As this study is based entirely on a sample of children and their families, no information is given here about the preschool institutions themselves. Instead we focus on the factors likely to influence the type of organised preschool experience a child may have and we begin by considering the implications of differences in age at entry to infant school for the pattern of utilisation of different types of preschool experience by the children in our sample.

Chapter 6

Infant school entry

Statutory school entry age

In Britain, statutory school entry occurs at the beginning of the school term immediately following the child's fifth birthday. In other countries children begin their primary education at age six (e.g. United States of America, France, Belgium, West Germany) and in some as late as seven years (e.g. Denmark). However, many countries with a later school entry age compared with that of Britain have more comprehensive state provision of preschool services. In France, for example, 70 percent of children attend nurseries from age three years (Tizard *et al.*, 1976, pp. 112-21).

The time of year at which British children reach their fifth birthday has important implications for the length of time they spend in infant school. Children whose fifth birthday occurs in the Summer term or later are at a disadvantage compared with children born at other times of the year as they are not statutorily required to start school until the beginning of the school year (August/September) following their fifth birthday and thus spend six terms in infant school. Autumn-born children, however, must be admitted no later than the beginning of the Spring term following their fifth birthdays and therefore have eight terms in the infant school.

As there are no nationally agreed dates on which school terms begin and end these decisions are left to Local Education Authorities with the inevitable result that term dates vary from one LEA to the next. This creates large differences in statutory school entry age between children born at about the same time but who are resident in different authorities.

The fact that the fifth birthdays of the children in the CHES sample occurred during the week 5-11 April 1975 can be used to highlight the inequalities of educational opportunity resulting from the statutory method of deciding when a child should start formal education. In 1975 the start of the Summer term varied between Authorities by more than two weeks from 2 to 21 April, thus whilst in some Authorities CHES children were required to start school in the Summer term, for others living elsewhere the statutory school entry term was at least four months later in the Autumn.

In addition to these variations in the statutory age at which a child might expect to start school, many LEAs in Britain have, until the latter part of the 1970s, permitted early entry into infant schools either as a general LEA or national policy – as in Wales, where there has been a long tradition for children to start school at age four, or at the discretion of head teachers. Increased capitation, i.e. the financial allowance made to schools based on the number of pupils attending, has also been provided by LEAs for the education of under-fives admitted early to infant school classes.

A policy which has been widely adopted has been to admit children to infant school at the beginning of the school term in which they reached their fifth birthdays, i.e. as 'rising fives'. Rising five school entry, however, is more possible for Autumn born than Summer born children because the number of empty places in reception classes decreases as the school year progresses from term to term due to the intake of pupils in the Autumn and Spring terms. Thus fewer places are available for rising fives in the last (Summer) term who then have to wait until the following Autumn for an infant place. This further increases the difference between Autumn and Summer born children so that there can be up to a year difference in the length of time children spend in the infant school (Palmer, 1971).

The scope of head teachers to admit children before statutory age has declined since 1975 due to the reduction in central government expenditure on education during the latter part of the 1970s. Thus the timing of the CHES follow-up survey in 1975 which provided information on the pattern of school entry for this sample of children was most opportune.

Table 6.1 shows that more children started infant school at the beginning of the school year (Autumn 1974) when they were aged about four and a half years (42.1 percent) than in any other term. This suggests a strong inclination on the part of head teachers to have one intake at the beginning of the school year rather than in successive terms. Less than a quarter of our sample started school in the statutory Summer term (23.6 percent) and about the same number started in the Spring term (23.9 percent).

A small proportion of the sample (3.4 percent) were reported to have started at infant school before age four years and four months. At least some of these were children attending private schools and others, although reported by the mother as attending infant school, might have been attending nursery classes when they first started.

A further 7.1 percent did not expect to start school until the following school year when they would be over five years and four months of age. Thus for this sample of children born in the same week there was up to a year variation in the age at which they entered infant school.

Regional variation in age at infant school entry

We have suggested that variation in age at which children are admitted to infant school depends largely on policy differences at local authority level. Although it was not possible to analyse our data in terms of such small administrative units because of the small numbers of study children in each authority, regional analysis gives some indication of the collective policy of the local authorities within regions. Table 6.2 indicates substantial differences between regions in the proportion of children who started school before five. Children in Wales and the North and North West regions of England were more likely than children elsewhere to start school at the beginning of the school year prior to their fifth birthday or earlier (76.5 percent, 82.0 percent and 63.9 percent respectively). In Yorkshire and Humberside a higher proportion started in the rising five term (38.6 percent), compared with other regions. Nearly two thirds (64.7 percent) of the Scottish children did not start infant school until the beginning of the school year following their fifth birthday. This suggests that Scottish education authorities in 1975 did not admit children to infant school until the statutory age – the term following the child's fifth birthday.

The Scottish Education Act (1976), at the discretion of Scottish Education Authorities, allows children whose fifth birthday occurs before 1 February to enter infant school at the beginning of that school year. It is unlikely, however, that the pattern of school entry for children born at the same time of year as the CHES sample would be altered by this revision.

Most of the variation in age at infant school entry appearing in Table 6.2 was almost certainly due to policy differences between the regions and countries. To what extent, however, were educational policies affected by the social and family circumstances of the children?

Social circumstances and entry to infant school

Schools with different types of catchment areas might have operated different admissions policies. Figure 6.1 suggests small, though

97

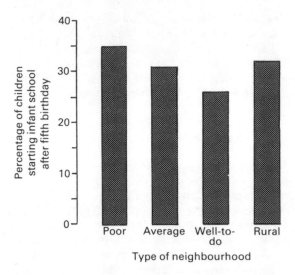

Figure 6.1   Age at infant school entry by type of neighbourhood

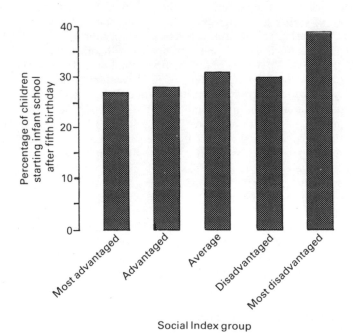

Figure 6.2   Age at infant school entry by Social Index group

significant, differences in school entry age between children who lived in different types of neighbourhood. Of children in well-to-do neighbourhoods, 26.1 percent started their infant education after their fifth birthday compared with 34.9 percent of those in poor neighbourhoods. Although this difference is not large, it does suggest that children living in poor neighbourhoods such as inner city areas are less likely to have the benefit of an early start to their formal education than children in more well-to-do or suburban areas. Children in rural areas, however, did not differ markedly from their counter-parts in the average urban neighbourhood in terms of school entry age.

Figure 6.2 looks at school entry age by Social Index groups. Here the difference between the most advantaged and the most disadvantaged groups was greater than that suggested by the neighbourhood analysis although it was still not very large. Little more than a quarter (26.9 percent) of the most advantaged children started infant school after their fifth birthday compared with 39.2 percent of the most disadvantaged children. Thus there was a tendency for a higher proportion of children from advantaged home backgrounds to start school early. Other factors such as parental situation, family size and mother's history of employment were associated with very small differences in infant school entry age and we conclude that the main source of variation was the difference in educational policy and demography between regions.

This analysis of infant school entry has not taken account of the provision of preschool educational or day care facilities and in the next chapter we examine the important relationship between uptake of preschool services and the age at which the child starts formal education.

Summary

In Britain, statutory school entry occurs at the beginning of the school term immediately following the child's fifth birthday. This results in some children spending up to a year longer in the infant school than others depending on the time of year of their date of birth. The children in the CHES sample were all born during one week in April 1970, but despite this there was still more than a year's difference in the ages at which they started at infant schools. This variation was attributed mainly to differences in policy at local authority level concerning early entry to infant schools which resulted in marked regional differences in age at school entry.

Chapter 7

Types of preschool provision

Classification of preschool experience

Studies concerned with provision and utilisation of preschool facilities usually express attendance rates in terms of the whole population of under fives or age bands considered to be appropriate for different types of provision. For example, nursery education might be deemed a facility appropriate for children aged three to four years but day nurseries usually can accommodate children of all ages up to four years. Whilst this method is useful for obtaining estimates of levels of provision of preschool services, other methods are needed to ascertain levels of utilisation of available preschool provision. One reason for this, as described in the previous chapter, is that children start infant school at different ages and this has implications for the age at which they might attend any preschool facility. This means that estimates of attendance rates in terms of a three to four years age group which have a proportion of children attending infant school miss the fact that many of these infant school children could have attended nurseries or playgroups prior to their entry into infant school. A consequence of this method of obtaining attendance rates is to underestimate the proportion of children ever to have experienced preschool education or day care provision although it is an adequate method for describing levels of provision (Osborn, 1981).

The difference between levels of provision and levels of utilisation can be illustrated by comparing the results of a 1974 O.P.C.S. survey of preschool services (Bone, 1977) with our own. The O.P.C.S. survey took a sample of 2,500 children aged between nought and four years with approximately equal numbers of children aged under one year, one year, two years, three years and four years but under five. Of the 533 children in the last age group, the four-year-olds, 35 percent were attending playgroup, 33 percent nursery/primary school, 6 percent day nursery or childminder and 28 percent were attending no form of day care (ibid., p. 10). Table 7.1 gives comparative figures for four age points between 3 years 10 months and 5 years obtained from the CHES survey. We found that the proportion of children attending playgroups declined from 45 percent to 5 percent over the period described due, of course, to the entry of these children into infant or, occasionally, nursery classes. The point is, however, that whilst the O.P.C.S. survey showed that the levels of provision of playgroups were sufficient to meet the needs of 35 percent of all four-year-olds, the CHES results indicate that a substantially higher proportion of children were attending playgroups at age 4 years 2 months (44.4 percent) but fewer at age 4 years 7 months (26.9 percent). The movement of children in and out of playgroups, and other types of facility, means that more children utilise preschool facilities than is apparent from figures describing levels of provision. This is illustrated further by considering the OPCS finding that 28 percent of four-year-olds were attending no form of educational or day care provision whereas the CHES study showed a rapid decline from 32 percent at age 3 years 10 months to under 5 percent at age five years. In fact, as we shall see below (Table 8.1) as many as 92.7 percent of the children in the CHES sample had some form of educational or day care experience prior to age five years even though the level of provision as estimated by the O.P.C.S. study was sufficient for only 72 percent of all four-year-olds.

The changing pattern of utilisation with age shown in Table 7.1 suggests that no one point in time could truly represent the level of uptake of preschool facilities of these five-year-olds. We decided, therefore, to take the placement just prior to infant school entry as their main preschool experience. This resulted in the distribution given in Table 7.2. This gives the child's most recent preschool placement as described by the mother. Over 80 percent of the children were attending infant school at age five (Table 7.1) and for these, any preschool experience they might have had prior to starting infant school appears in Table 7.2 as their main preschool placement. If a child had more than one type of preschool experience we have taken the most recent placement attended. Very few children attended two or more placements simultaneously, but where this occurred we have taken the one attended for the most sessions per week. Preschool placements which were attended for less than a term (or three months) were excluded from the classification.

This method, we suggest, provides the best possible estimate of the level of utilisation of different types of British preschool facilities experienced by children prior to age five. In the state sector we found that 8.1 percent of the study children went to nursery schools, 11 percent to nursery classes and 1.3 percent to LA day nurseries. Voluntary

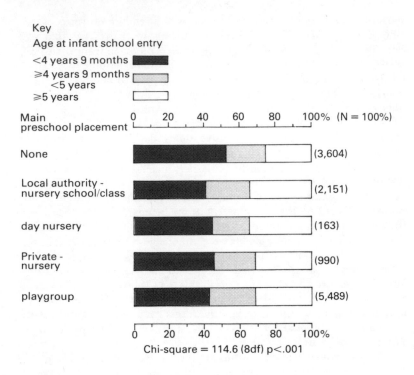

Figure 7.1   Age started infant school by main preschool placement

playgroups in the private sector accommodated more children than any other type of provision. As many as 43 percent of this sample went to playgroups. Also in the private sector, 5.6 percent went to independent nursery schools, 1.4 percent to other types of independent school and 1.1 percent to private day nurseries. To simplify analyses in the tables and analyses which follow, LEA nursery schools and classes will be combined as a single category and the different private facilities with the exception of playgroups will also be reduced to one group designated 'private nurseries'.

Infant school entry and the main preschool placement

It was possible that some of the main preschool placements the children attended may have been utilised in the early preschool years rather than just prior to infant school entry. It was found, however, that as many as 92 percent of the children stopped attending their main preschool placement no more than three months prior to infant school entry, and for 72 percent infant school followed on directly after the child's preschool experience. The only children at all likely to have stopped attending their main preschool placement more than a year before starting infant school were those who attended local authority day nurseries. Even so this applied to only 15 percent of children who went to LA day nurseries. It is also worth noting that for 92 percent of the whole sample the main preschool placement was the only preschool experience they had. Thus for most of the children in the study their main preschool placement was that attended just before starting infant school. What we now ask is whether children with no preschool experience started infant school at different ages from those who had attended a preschool placement.

Figure 7.1 suggests that children who had never attended a preschool placement were slightly more likely to start infant school early (52.9 percent) than were children who had done so (41.1 percent to 46.4 percent). It is not possible to say what caused this difference. Perhaps infant school head teachers were inclined to allow children with no preschool experience to start school early, or early infant school entry may have been more frequent in areas with fewer preschool facilities. It could also have been that some mothers preferred their children to start school early, where this was an option, rather than sending them to a nursery school or playgroup. Whatever the reason, however, entry to infant school before age five can clearly be seen as an alternative form of 'preschool' experience. We therefore decided to separate out the children who started infant school early without any other form of preschool experience into two groups; (a) rising fives, i.e. those who started infant school from age 4 years 9 months but before five, and (b) pre-rising fives which were children who started infant school before age 4 years 9 months. These two groups comprised 6.1 percent and 14.7 percent respectively of the total sample for whom preschool information was available (N = 12,945). Thus, for a fifth (20.8 percent) of our sample, early entry to infant school was the only preschool experience received. The significance of separating out these early infant groups will become apparent in subsequent chapters. At this point, however, to the extent that infant school can be accepted as an alternative form of education available to the under fives, the proportion of the total sample with no educational or day care experience prior to statutory school entry age was reduced to only 7.1 percent. It is important to note, however, that this figure applies only to Spring-born children. The proportion could be less for Autumn-born children and more for the Summer-born.

Validity of the main preschool placement classification

The distinctions between nursery school, nursery classes in infant schools, playgroups and day nurseries are not always very clear and we recognise that the mothers' names for the places their children attended may not always have conformed to our own definitions. The type of premises the child attended provided one means of checking the validity of our classification of preschool placements. Table 7.3 indicates that of the children who attended LEA schools and LA day nurseries, the large majority (over 90 percent) went to places described by their mothers as 'normal school or nursery premises'. In contrast, private nurseries and playgroups were more often to be found in community halls or private houses.

The figures for local authority provision and playgroups presented in Table 7.3 suggest that the mother's description of premises was generally consistent with the type of establishments they reported their children to have attended. Independent nurseries appear to be the least homogenous in terms of premises. This, we suggest, was due to the fact that under this common heading were private nursery schools, day nurseries and playgroups described as private nursery schools. The distinctions between these different types of private nurseries are often very hard to make and we have accepted that this group is likely to include quite diverse types of establishment.

Another means of checking the validity of the classification of main preschool placements is the pattern of attendance in different types of institution described in Table 7.4. This table shows that most children who went to local authority schools or nurseries attended five days per week either full-time or part-time. Over 95 percent of the children who attended infant school prior to age five went full-time for five days a week. These results conform with the normal pattern of attendance in the maintained sector. Few children who went to playgroups as defined by their mothers attended five days a week and the most common pattern of attendance was two or three mornings (61.9 percent). Again this is consistent with the norm for playgroups (Pre-school Playgroups Association, 1978). The majority of children who attended private nurseries went full-time or part-time five days a week (57.6 percent) which suggests a nursery school or day nursery, but a further quarter (26.4 percent) attended two or three mornings a week which was more consistent with the pattern for playgroups. This, together with the results describing the types of premises in which private nurseries function, suggests that the 'private nurseries' in our classification encompass many different types of educational or day care establishment. Playgroups, LEA schools and LA nurseries, however, in our classification, appear reasonably homogeneous in terms of the two criteria examined.

Finally, special preschool facilities for handicapped children comprised both LEA schools and voluntary playgroups, for example opportunity playgroups, as reported by the mothers. A third (34.1 percent) of the special preschool institutions attended by children in this study were located in premises other than schools, halls or private houses, many of these being hospital groups, and three quarters (74.5 percent) of the children attended full-time or for five mornings a week. As this category includes only 49 children who had no other form of preschool placement few reliable conclusions can be drawn about the children who attended special preschool facilities, particularly as these forms of provision were likely to be so varied. This category is nevertheless included in the tables presented in this and subsequent chapters.

Duration of attendance at the main preschool placement

Mothers were asked to include only those placements which their children had attended for at least one term or three months, this being considered the minimum time in which a child could be expected to derive any benefit from such attendance. The question of how long a child attended a preschool placement, however, was complicated by the variation in age at infant school entry described above. Early entry to infant school could either have resulted in a shorter preschool experience or it might have meant that children also started their preschool placements earlier. Figure 7.2 indicates a strong tendency for children who started their preschool placement early to have also started infant school

105

early. For example, 52.1 percent of children who started their preschool placement before age three years entered infant school before age 4 years 9 months compared with only 17.2 percent of the children whose preschool experience began after age 4 years 4 months. Conversely, 57.8 percent of the children who started a preschool placement after age 4 years 4 months entered infant school after age five whereas this occurred for only 23.7 percent of those who started their preschool experience before age three.

We found also that children were more likely to start early at some types of preschool placements than others. Thus, attendance at LEA nursery schools and classes began after age 3 years 4 months for nearly 80 percent of this sub-sample (Figure 7.3), whereas the majority of children who attended private nurseries or playgroups started before this age (55.6 percent and 59.6 percent respectively). Half (50.3 percent) the children who attended local authority day nurseries, however, started before age three years.

The results suggest two main patterns; children who went to playgroups or private nurseries tended to start attending these facilities early and also entered infant school early, whilst LEA nursery school/ class attenders began both their preschool experience and infant school late. Does this mean, therefore, that the duration of preschool attendance was much the same for children attending playgroups, private nurseries and LEA nursery schools and classes?

Table 7.5 suggests that the mean duration of attendance at private nurseries and playgroups was about five months longer than at LEA nursery schools and classes although there was quite considerable variation between children in the time they spent in their main preschool placements. The average time spent at LEA nursery schools and classes was just under a year (11.4 months, SD = 6.6) compared with over a year and four months at private nurseries and playgroups (16.7 months, SD = 8.0 and 16.4 months SD = 7.4 respectively).

Children attended local authority day nurseries for an average of twenty months but the considerable variability (SD = 13.1) meant that statistical comparison with other types of preschool placements was unreliable. Nevertheless it is clear that many children who attended local authority day nurseries did so for a longer period than did children who went to other types of placement.

Summary

One of the main advantages of the 1975 CHES follow-up is that it was carried out at the end of the preschool period for this sample of children when information could be obtained about the children's preschool

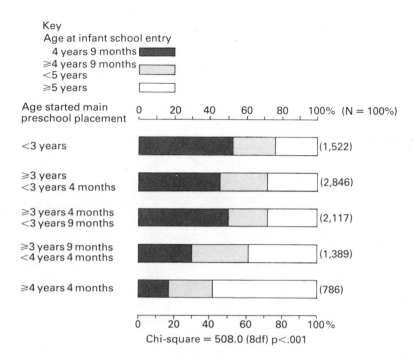

Key
Age at infant school entry
4 years 9 months
≥4 years 9 months
<5 years
≥5 years

Age started main preschool placement

<3 years (1,522)

≥3 years
<3 years 4 months (2,846)

≥3 years 4 months
<3 years 9 months (2,117)

≥3 years 9 months
<4 years 4 months (1,389)

≥4 years 4 months (786)

Chi-square = 508.0 (8df) p<.001

Figure 7.2 Age at infant school entry by age started main preschool placement

Preschool education and day care

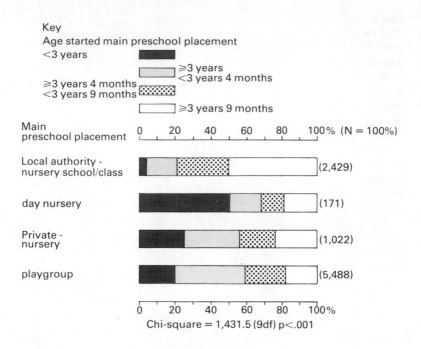

Figure 7.3 Age started main preschool placement by main preschool placement

educational and day care experience over the whole five-year period. This meant that we could document the children's preschool experience prior to infant school entry even though the age at starting infant school varied in this sample by as much as a year.

We found that more children attended playgroups than any other single type of provision. Playgroup attendance was usually for no more than two or three sessions a week, whereas LEA nursery school/class children typically attended five or ten sessions a week. Another difference concerned the ages at which children started and stopped attending different placements. This tended to occur at younger ages in playgroup children than in LEA nursery school/class children. Finally, children went to playgroups on average for about 16 months whereas those who went to LEA nursery schools/classes attended an average of only 11 months.

Having described the main characteristics of the various types of preschool placements attended by this sample of children as a whole, we now consider what factors influenced the patterns of utilisation of these facilities.

Chapter 8

Sources of variation in utilisation of preschool education and day care facilities

In Chapter 7 we established that half the five-year-olds in our sample had attended preschool institutions in the private sector and a fifth went to local authority preschool facilities. A further fifth, who had no designated preschool experience, started school as rising fives or earlier so that only 7 percent of the whole sample had had no form of educational or day care experience before reaching statutory school entry age at five years. In this chapter we describe how this system of mixed independent and local authority educational and day care provision is distributed between different social groups.

There are several factors which are likely to produce different patterns of utilisation between preschool institutions in the independent and local authority sectors, the most important of which is the fact that the former charge a fee for children to attend whereas LEA nursery schools and classes and many local authority day nursery places are free. The need for playgroups and private nurseries to make a charge will inevitably be a constraint on low income families who thus are more dependent on the local authority to provide preschool education and day care than families who can afford to pay fees. Other factors which are likely to influence the patterns of uptake of different types of provision are their admissions policy and the siting of institutions (Stevenson and Ellis, 1975). Heads of LEA schools, for example, may give priority to socially disadvantaged children or to children in one-parent families, whereas such a policy may not operate in independent institutions. Also preschool institutions tend to draw on the child population in their immediate locality, therefore those sited in inner urban areas are more likely to accommodate socially disadvantaged children than are institutions in suburban or rural areas.

In our analysis of the contrasting patterns of utilisation in the local authority and independent sectors we are ultimately concerned with those children who have no preschool educational or day care experience and the possible shortfall of places for children who are most in need of such provision. We examine first the national and regional variation in uptake of preschool provision in our sample.

Regional variation

We have already shown the marked regional variation in the age at which children entered infant school (Chapter 6). We shall now examine the regional differences that characterise the pattern of utilisation of preschool educational and day care provision by our sample of five-year-olds.

Table 8.1 shows substantial variation in utilisation of preschool services in the eight regions of England, in Wales and in Scotland. In England, Yorkshire and Humberside had the highest proportion of children attending Local Education Authority nursery schools and classes (25 percent) and the South West region the lowest (7.3 percent). Wales and Scotland, however, also had high proportions of children in LEA nursery schools and classes (26.6 percent and 24.9 percent respectively).

Although there was little regional variation in utilisation of private nurseries (the South East had the highest proportion with 12 percent), playgroup utilisation varied from 24 percent in Wales to 59 percent in the South West region and there was an inverse relationship between the proportion of children attending LEA nursery schools/classes and those attending playgroups.

There was marked variation also in early infant school entry by children with no designated preschool experience from 40.4 percent starting before age five in the North region of England to only one percent in Scotland. The North region had the highest incidence of children with no form of designated preschool experience (41.4 percent) but the very high proportion of children entering infant school early in this region meant that only one percent had no form of educational experience before age five. There was clearly widespread policy among LEAs in the North region to provide educational facilities for the under-fives in infant or nursery schools as this region also had a higher than average proportion of children who attended LEA nursery schools and classes (21 percent). The comparatively low proportion of children who attended playgroups in the North (29.3 percent) fits with the hypothesis that playgroups were less likely to appear where there were comparatively high levels of provision from the public sector. Wales was similar to the North of England in this respect in having a long tradition of early infant school entry. In Wales 63.5 percent of the children attended LEA nursery schools and classes or entered infant

111

school before age five and a relatively low proportion of children attended playgroups (24 percent).

Local authority day nurseries were the main preschool placement of only 1.4 percent of these children although more than twice this proportion attended day nurseries in the North West region (3 percent) which also had a high level of maternal employment (see Chapter 11). The smallest proportions of children to have attended LA day nurseries lived in Wales (0.5 percent) and East Anglia (0.4 percent) both of which are largely rural compared with other regions and therefore require less full-time day care provision than industrial and inner urban areas.

In terms of overall utilisation of preschool services, insofar as this reflects levels of provision, the North region and Wales were the worst off and the South East region was the most advantaged. However, since both Wales and the North had high proportions of children starting infant school early, it was children in Scotland (with its 1 percent early school entry) who were the most likely to have had no form of educational or day care experience before age five. This was true for more than a quarter (27.7 percent) of the Scottish children in this sample.

The proportions given in Table 8.1 are measures of utilisation and, as explained in Chapter 7 above, cannot be interpreted directly as an indication of the levels of provision in the different regions. However, insofar as utilisation is largely dependent upon provision, much of the observed difference in utilisation between regions must have been due to the variation in educational and day care policies of different local authorities within the regions and countries of our classification. These policies cover infant school entry, the maintenance and expansion of preschool educational provision or day nurseries and the support and encouragement of voluntary playgroups. Many Local Education Authorities in the North region, Yorkshire and Humberside and Wales appear to favour both nursery education and early entry to infant school whereas Scottish authorities provide more than average nursery school and class places but appear to have been opposed to early infant school entry. The Scottish Education Act (1976) is unlikely to affect the pattern of school entry for children born in the Spring or Summer (see Chapter 6). In the South of England the general policy has been to promote private nurseries and voluntary playgroups rather than expand LEA nursery schools and classes or allow early infant school entry.

In this discussion of the variation in utilisation of preschool services between regions, we are cognisant of the large differences between local authorities within regions. Such variations in provision and utilisation of preschool services at a local level are likely to be a response to the socioeconomic characteristics of communities and needs of individual groups. It is to these factors as possible sources of variation that we now turn.

Type of neighbourhood

Some of the observed regional variation in utilisation of services could be explained by whether a region was urban or rural in character. Higher levels of provision of local authority preschool services might be expected in areas of urban deprivation if official policy recommendations had been at all recognised (DES White Paper, 1972; Plowden, 1967), whereas the comparatively sparse preschool populations in rural areas perhaps make the establishment of nursery schools and classes more difficult.

Table 8.2 shows very large variations in utilisation according to the type of neighbourhood in which children lived. A third (33 percent) of children in poor neighbourhoods attended LEA nursery schools and classes compared with only 14.2 percent of children in well-to-do neighbourhoods and 8.7 percent in rural settings. We suggest that these differences are due to there being few opportunities for rural children to attend LEA nursery schools or classes, coupled with a disposition on the part of head teachers to use neighbourhood of residence as an index of educational need when deciding on priorities. There was a similar trend in LA day nursery attendance from 2.7 percent of children in poor neighbourhoods to only 0.4 percent of rural children. Private nurseries and playgroups were attended by far greater proportions of children in well-to-do than poor neighbourhoods. Nevertheless a fifth (20.8 percent) of children in poor neighbourhoods attended playgroups who otherwise, presumably, would have had no preschool experience. The important role of playgroups in the rural context is indicated by the fact that over half (55.3 percent) of children in rural neighbourhoods attended them. This was only possible because of the utilisation of community premises such as church and village halls by voluntary playgroup organisers notwithstanding the difficulties they experienced due to the necessity to put away equipment at the end of the day so that the halls could be used for other purposes.

A fifth (20.3 percent) of children in poor neighbourhoods had not attended preschool institutions but did start infant school early as pre-rising fives. This applied to fewer (7.4 percent) children in well-to-do neighbourhoods. However, we know from Figure 6.1 that a slightly larger proportion of children from well-to-do neighbourhoods started school early than did children from poor neighbourhoods. Thus many children in well-to-do neighbourhoods enjoyed the double benefit of attending a preschool institution and also starting school early, whereas for 27.3 percent of the children in poor neighbourhoods early school entry was the only educational experience they had before age five.

The policy in state schools and nurseries to take proportionately more children from poor neighbourhoods, counterbalanced to some extent the trend in private nurseries and playgroups to accommodate higher proportions of children from well-to-do neighbourhoods. Nevertheless 12.4 percent of children in poor neighbourhoods had received no preschool experience before five compared with only 3.2 percent of those in well-to-do neighbourhoods. If we discount early infant school entry as a form of preschool experience, the proportions of children from poor and well-to-do neighbourhoods who never attended a nursery or playgroup were 39.7 percent and 14.3 percent respectively. Thus although official emphasis has been on the educational needs of the urban disadvantaged and despite any policy of positive discrimination resulting from this which has contributed to the excess of children from poor neighbourhoods in maintained forms of provision, the net effect of the mixed system of local authority and private provision is that the urban poor are still the least likely to obtain a preschool place.

Socioeconomic status

The type of neighbourhood in which is a child lives is not necessarily indicative of his or her social situation at home. Indeed it has been argued that more children who are educationally at risk live outside designated poverty areas than within them (Barnes and Lucas, 1974) and we have found that fewer than half the most disadvantaged children in our study lived in poor neighbourhoods. It is important, therefore, to examine utilisation of preschool services in terms of the social circumstances of the individual children and their families. Before presenting our own findings, however, we shall review briefly those of two other national studies which have looked for social class differences in the utilisation of preschool educational and day-care services.

The General Household Survey (GHS) for 1975 found social class differences in the proportions of children under five years of age who were attending educational and day care facilities from 37 percent of children of professional fathers to 20 percent of children whose fathers were in unskilled manual jobs (OPCS *General Household Survey: 1975*, London, HMSO, Table 6.1). Most of this variation was accounted for by playgroup attendance which ranged from 26 percent of children of professional fathers to only 7 percent of unskilled manual workers' children. No systematic variation appeared in the proportions of children attending school placements.

The results of an 1974 OPCS survey of day care in England and Wales (Bone, 1977) were very similar to those of the GHS. Attendance at educational and day care establishments by children under five varied from 35 percent of children whose fathers were in social class I occupations to 24 percent of children with fathers in social classes IV manual

114

and V occupations (ibid., p. 11). Again most of the social class difference in attendance rates in the OPCS findings was explained by the difference in playgroup attendance from 24 percent of social class I children to 13 percent of social classes IV manual and V children. However, it was found that, 'Amongst children who actually used day provision . . . there was no difference between the social classes in the type of facility used' (ibid., p. 10).

An analysis in Section 10 of the OPCS report that used indices of children's needs for day provision (based on parental situation, adequacy of accommodation, mother's need to work, behaviour problems or handicap in the child and mother's mental health), found that higher than average proportions of children in need of day provision had attended nursery/primary school or day nursery, whereas the reverse pattern was found for playgroups (ibid., p. 56). It was suggested that these results were partly due to the preference amongst parents of children in the 'need groups' for the full-time attendance available in educational placements.

The social class differences amongst children who attended nursery/ primary schools in the OPCS study and the GHS were small and this is disappointing in view of official policy that maintained provision should give priority to children who are disadvantaged for social, family or other reasons. One reason for not finding social class differences in the children who attended nursery and primary schools was the combining of children who attended maintained or independent schools into one category. This was the method adopted in both the GHS and OPCS study and reflects the concern of these authors with levels of provision of educational facilities compared with playgroups or day nurseries rather than the question of utilisation (a short discussion of the distinction between provision and utilisation of preschool services introduces Chapter 7 of this book). Clearly the client group of private educational facilities is predominantly middle class families who are in a position to pay the necessary fees. LEA schools with places for under fives, however, are expected to give priority to children in special need of preschool education and such children are more likely to be from social classes IV and V. Thus by combining as one category the under-fives who attended independent and state schools the opposing social class trends of these two groups will tend to cancel each other out.

In Table 8.3 we present an analysis of the uptake of different types of preschool by children in different Social Index groups. Analysis by social class resulted in much the same conclusions as are presented below, but the increased sensitivity of the Social Index to social inequalities produced somewhat larger differences in proportions between the extreme categories than did social class.

The contrast between the state and independent sectors is

immediately evident in Table 8.3. Increasing levels of social disadvantage was associated with greater proportions of children who attended local authority schools and nurseries, and smaller proportions who attended private nurseries and playgroups. If we focus on the two main forms of preschool provision, for example, it can be seen that the proportion of children who attended LEA nursery schools and classes increased from 13.2 percent of the most advantaged to 29.6 percent of the most disadvantaged Social Index groups. In contrast, attendance at playgroups declined from 59 percent of the most advantaged to 19.4 percent of the most disadvantaged children. The opposing trends in uptake of local authority and private preschool facilities across Social Index groups did not, however, balance each other with the result that as many as 16.6 percent of the most disadvantaged children had no educational or day care experience before five, compared with only 2 percent of the most advantaged children.

Family situation

Parents who are bringing up their children single-handed have a greater need to obtain a place in a preschool nursery or playgroup, especially if it is necessary for the parent to go out to work. Although day nurseries are the only type of institution to offer day care of sufficient duration to enable a lone parent to work full-time, nursery schools and classes or playgroups also make possible part-time employment or at the very least can provide a respite from child care responsibilities so that the parent can shop or carry out other domestic tasks free from the child's demands. In addition to this day care function, nurseries and playgroups provide, among other things, the opportunity for children from one-parent families to come into contact with other adults. This is important for children whose adult contact might otherwise be limited to only one other person; i.e. the lone parent. Playgroups and nursery schools naturally promote contact between parents which reduces the social isolation experienced by many lone parents and provides a source of help if needed.

Awareness of the special needs of one-parent families on the part of those in charge of preschool facilities suggest that children from such families should be given priority when places are scarce. We examined our data to see whether greater proportions of children from one-parent families had indeed obtained preschool places. The only type of institution in which marked differences occurred in this direction was LA day nurseries.

Table 8.4 shows that of the children with supported single parents and lone parents 11.1 percent and 6.4 percent respectively went to LA day nurseries compared with less than one percent of children living with both natural parents. A relatively high proportion of children in step-families also went to day nurseries which could have been during a period of disruption before the family was reconstituted. LEA nursery schools and classes were attended by a somewhat higher proportion of children with lone parents than those in two-parent families but the difference was not very marked. Private nurseries and playgroups, however, in contrast took smaller proportions of children from one-parent and step-families compared with those living with two natural parents. Overall, about 10 percent of children who had experienced family disruption had had no form of preschool educational or day care experience compared with 7 percent of children who at five were still living with both natural parents.

There are two kinds of explanation for the reduced uptake of nursery school/class and playgroup places by one-parent families. The first is their need for all-day care which is necessary if the parent has to go out to work. This need is suggested by our figures in Table 8.4 showing the higher rates of uptake of LA day nursery places by one-parent families. Thus some of the children who had not attended preschool institutions may have been looked after by childminders instead.

Secondly, however, it is possible that some lone parents are so stressed by their circumstances that the effort required to find a pre-school place for their child and then to make the journey to and from the school or playgroup means that they find it easier to keep the child at home.

Family size

Like the parental situation, family size has important implications for a child's welfare and development. Socially disadvantaged families typically have many children (Chapter 1) and children in large families tend to do less well in tests of general ability (Chapter 5) and in subsequent school attainment (Davie *et al.*, 1972). Attendance by these children at a preschool institution, therefore, entails the double advantage of providing a respite for the mother by relieving her of the responsibility of at least one of her children for a few hours, as well as giving the child the opportunity to increase his or her capacity to benefit from subsequent infant education. The effectiveness of British preschool services in actually realising this potential is explored later in Chapter 10, but if educationally at risk groups fail to obtain preschool places then there is no possibility of any preparatory experience for these children.

The marked socioeconomic differences in how different types of preschool provision were utilised (Table 8.3) and the strong relationship between Social Index score and family size (Chapter 1) meant that the analysis of preschool attendance according to family size needed to take these social differences into account. Table 8.5 therefore, shows utilisation of preschool facilities by total number of children in the household, (a) for children with Social Index scores below the median (scores 4-8: Advantaged) and (b) with Social Index scores above the median (scores 9-16: Disadvantaged).

The pattern of preschool attendance related to family size was much the same for both Social Index groups. The proportion of children who went to LEA schools tended to increase with family size with the exception of the Disadvantaged group who attended LEA nursery schools/classes. It is probable that early infant school entry was more common amongst children whose elder siblings were already attending the same schools.

In the private sector the trend was reversed with declining proportions of children attending nurseries or playgroups with increasing family size. Although the cost of sending one or two children from a large family to a private nursery or playgroup would have been a constraint to many parents, the fact that the family size effect was present in the Advantaged, as well as Disadvantaged, group suggests that this was not the only consideration. The problem of transporting children to and from a playgroup for a three hour morning session may well be too much trouble for mothers with other children to cope with in addition to the one or two attending the playgroup; '. . . the most common complaint about the facility used related to availability – that is, that sessions were too infrequent, too brief, or that taking and collecting the child was difficult' (Bone, 1977, p. 17). This is particularly a problem for the mother who also has to take an older child to infant school which may be some distance from the playgroup. There is clearly a need for playgroups to be open longer with more flexible times of opening and closing although we recognise the difficulties this brings in terms of costs and availability of helpers. However, if voluntary playgroups are to be the mainstay of British preschool provision, as our findings suggest, then it is vital to find ways in which they can be helped to maintain and augment their service of meeting the needs of these most deserving groups of families.

Ethnic group

Children from West Indian or Asian homes are more likely than indigenous white children to live in poor urban neighbourhoods and be in relatively disadvantaged social situations (see Chapter 1). Thus, in view of our findings so far that socially disadvantaged children were more likely to attend local authority types of provision than private nurseries or playgroups, the pattern of results shown in Table 8.6 is as expected. However, the size of the variation in proportions of children from different cultural backgrounds who attended the different types of facility was surprising. Of European (UK) children, 18.5 percent attended LEA nursery schools and classes and 44.3 percent playgroups compared with 41.5 percent of West Indian and 30.9 percent of Asian children at LEA placements and 14.6 percent and 18.9 percent respectively at playgroups. The small frequencies in many of the cells in this table make many other comparisons somewhat unreliable. However, it is apparent that in families where one parent was of non-UK origin and the other was European (UK) the pattern of preschool utilisation was similar to that of children whose parents were both European (UK). It is possible that these families enjoyed a higher level of social integration with the general UK population, whereas in families where both parents were either West Indian or Asian the original culture was sustained. The results suggest that in regions of the country with relatively high proportions of ethnic minorities, e.g. the South East region and the West Midlands, Local Education Authorities are responding to the needs of the children and mothers from these groups in their provision of nursery schools and classes, but very few children of ethnic minorities are assimilated into playgroups. This is largely due, we suggest, to the tendency for playgroups to be located in well-to-do neighbourhoods and in rural areas, where there are few West Indian or Asian communities, whereas local authority provision is mainly found in inner urban settings where ethnic minorities are more concentrated.

Employed mothers

The part-time nature and long holiday periods of most forms of preschool provision (except for day nurseries) makes them generally unviable as places of care for children during their mothers' working hours, unless supplementary help is available from elsewhere. Indeed, fathers and other relatives were the main sources of care for the majority of children in the CHES sample whilst their mothers were at work (see Chapter 14). We were interested to see, however, how the preschool experience of children might have been affected by their mothers' employment situation in terms of opportunity for attending and type of facility utilised. For example, the opportunity for a child to attend a nursery school or playgroup may actually have been reduced if his or her mother had a substantial employment commitment. Previous

119

research suggests that children of employed mothers are more likely to be attending nursery/primary schools or day nurseries than are children whose mothers do not go out to work, whereas playgroup attendance is more frequent amongst children whose mothers do not work (Bone, 1978, p. 22).

Table 8.7 shows the main preschool placement of children in the CHES sample by the mother's employment situation when the children were aged five. As some of the mothers started their current jobs after their children had entered infant school the employed groups are divided into mothers who had been working for at least two years previously and those who had taken up work within the past two years. Thus the mothers who had been in their current employment for at least two years were at work during the period of maximum likelihood that their children would have been attending preschool facilities. The main differences shown in Table 8.7 concern the pattern of attendance at day nurseries and playgroups. Increasing work commitment by the mother (not employed or employed at home to part-time employment outside the home to full-time employment outside the home) was associated with increasing probability that her child would attend a local authority day nursery and decreasing probability of playgroup attendance. As expected, these trends were most pronounced if the mother had been employed for at least two years. For the children of these mothers, the proportion whose main preschool placement was LA day nursery increased from 1.1 percent of those whose mothers worked at home to 6.9 percent whose mothers worked full-time outside the home. The trend in playgroup attendance for these groups was reversed and went from 49.9 percent of children of home workers to only 28.6 percent of children of full-time workers outside the home. Similar trends to these were evident even when the mother had been employed for less than two years. Most of the children of mothers employed outside the home full-time would have been looked after by others during the mother's working hours in addition to their playgroup attendance. Our interpretation of these figures is that the opportunity for attendance at playgroup is reduced if the mother has a full-time job. An interesting point is that playgroup attendance was higher amongst children of mothers who worked at home than amongst those whose mothers had no regular employment. This could partly be explained by the fact that home employment was often undertaken by mothers in well-to-do or rural areas where higher than average proportions of children also attended playgroups.

Children whose mothers had worked for more than two years were more likely than other children to have attended private nurseries. This was probably attributable to the use of private day nurseries by employed mothers. Mothers' employment outside the home increased

120

the probability of their children's attendance at LEA nursery schools and classes hardly at all although home employment was associated with lower proportions of children in these placements. The highest proportion of children to have started infant school early were those whose mothers started full-time employment in the previous two years. It is likely that for many of these, entry into full-time infant school increased the opportunity for mothers to obtain full-time jobs, even though arrangements for 'after school' care would still need to be made.

Clearly the relationship between children's preschool educational and day care experience and mother's employment is very complex. In the main, however, it is only when the mother needs to work long hours that her being employed determines the type of preschool placement for her child. The majority of employed mothers worked only part-time and the preschool experience of their children was not markedly different from that of children of mothers with no regular job.

Summary

Regional differences in uptake of preschool facilities in Britain suggest that private nurseries and playgroups tend to be located in areas where Local Education Authority nursery schools/classes and local authority day nurseries are at relatively low levels. The independent sector is also more in evidence in well-to-do neighbourhoods and rural communities, whereas state provision tends to be concentrated in urban and inner city areas.

The siting of different types of facilities, the official policy of positive discrimination in local authority establishments and the need to charge fees in the private/voluntary sector, has inevitably resulted in socially disadvantaged children being over-represented in state schools and nurseries and under-represented in private nurseries and playgroups. This pattern applied to children from poor socioeconomic circumstances, one-parent families, large families and ethnic minorities. Because of the relative scarcity of places in state schools and nurseries disproportionately high numbers of children from all these groups had received no organised educational experience before the age of five.

The short periods of opening and long holidays of nursery schools and playgroups make them only partly compatible with the day care needs of children of working mothers, especially where mothers have a full-time job. There was a tendency, therefore, for higher proportions of children of working mothers to go to day nurseries whereas fewer than average went to playgroups where the periods of opening were the least conducive to meeting the needs of employed mothers. Maternal employment outside the home did not, however, lower the rates of children's attendance at LEA nursery schools/classes.

Chapter 9

Involvement of mothers in preschool institutions

A central feature of playgroup philosophy which distinguishes it from those of other forms of preschool educational provision is the role of parents in the educational activities and running of the group (van der Eyken, 1977, pp. 151-2). The expressed aim of the largest representative of the playgroup movement, the Preschool Playgroups Association (PPA), is '. . . to promote community situations in which parents can with growing enjoyment and confidence make the best uses of their own knowledge and resources in the development of their children and themselves.' (Published in every issue of *Contact*, the official journal of the PPA). The two main types of parental involvement are in the operation and management of the playgroup and in helping with the children during sessions.

A PPA survey of their membership found that 56 percent of playgroups in England and Wales were run by parent committees and in 81 percent parents helped in playgroup sessions (PPA, 1978, p. 15). It was estimated that the PPA survey covered 44 percent of all registered playgroups in England and Wales. As this sample was self-selected from the total membership of PPA, which comprises about two thirds of all registered playgroups, the findings may not be truly representative of all playgroups. Nevertheless, these figures and the fact that nearly all playgroups are initiated by parents demonstrates that parental involvement is a key feature of the playgroup movement.

In contrast, the contribution of parents is not an integral part of other forms of preschool educational and day care provision. In LEA nursery schools and classes management at both administrative and classroom levels is the responsibility of professional educators. This offers little scope for the participation of parents except at the consultative level through the parent-teacher association or as a parent representative on the school management committee.

However, staff in nursery schools and classes like to maintain close contact with the children's parents. In most schools parents are encouraged to come into the classrooms, especially when their children are just starting, to help ease the child's transition from home to school, but this involvement is less fundamental to the philosophy, existence and running of the nursery school than it is to the concept of play-groups. Indeed, parental involvement is often seen as an educative experience for the parent rather than of direct help to the nursery school (e.g. Department of Health and Social Security and Department of Education and Science, 1976, p. 14).

Lower levels of parental involvement are likely in day nurseries as they are attended almost entirely by children whose parents are in distressed family or social situations or who work full-time and cannot therefore be involved in the activities of the nursery.

Although the PPA survey suggested that in the large majority of playgroups parents help in one way or another, this does not mean that all parents of playgroup children are involved; in fact our own study shows that less than half (43.7 percent) of the mothers whose children went to playgroups said they took part or helped in some way at least once a term and only 24.3 percent helped at least once a month (Figure 9.1). In other types of educational and day care institutions, however, the level of maternal involvement was even lower. The proportion of mothers who helped at least once a term in private nurseries was 14.6 percent and in special institutions for handicapped children 15.2 percent. Both these groups were likely to include some institutions run on playgroup lines and this, therefore, would increase the likelihood of parental involvement to the observed levels. In LEA nursery schools and classes, 13 percent of the mothers helped at least once a term and 6.3 percent at least once a month. Levels of maternal involvement in infant schools and LA day nurseries were below 8 percent. Our results are very similar to those reported by Bone (1977, p. 18) who found that 46 percent of mothers whose children went to playgroups and 17 percent of those with children in nursery education 'sometimes spent time at the facility'.

These results clearly show that the likelihood that a mother is involved is to a considerable degree dependent on the type of institution her child attends. Involvement in infant schools and day nurseries was minimal and private nurseries and special facilities for handicapped children were likely to include institutions with diverse policies towards parental involvement. Children who attended any of these types of placement are therefore excluded from further analysis in this chapter and the following discussion of regional, social and family factors that influence maternal involvement in the child's preschool placement will be limited to those whose children had attended playgroups or LEA nursery schools and classes. Thus we shall compare playgroups, which

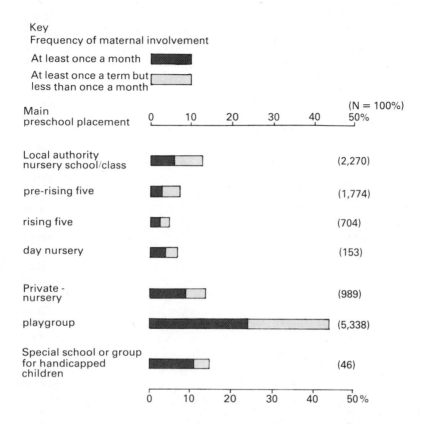

Figure 9.1 Maternal involvement by main preschool placement

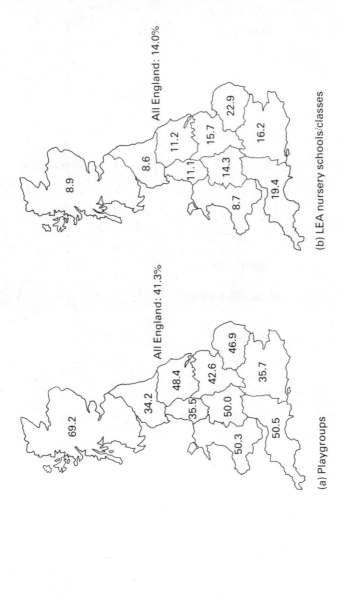

All England: 14.0%

8.9

8.6

11.2

11.1

15.7

14.3

22.9

8.7

16.2

19.4

(b) LEA nursery schools/classes

All England: 41.3%

69.2

34.2

48.4

35.5

42.6

50.0

46.9

50.3

35.7

50.5

(a) Playgroups

Figure 9.2 Maternal involvement in playgroups and LEA nursery schools/classes by region (percentage of mothers who helped at least once a term)

operate with a definite philosophy of embracing parental involvement, and LEA nursery schools and classes where the role of parents is less central.

Regional variation in maternal involvement

Figure 9.2 shows the regional variation in maternal involvement in play-groups and LEA nursery schools and classes. Comparisons of the two maps reveal similarities and differences in maternal involvement rates in the two types of preschool institution in different regions.

A higher proportion of Scottish mothers helped in playgroups (69.2 percent) than did English (41.3 percent) or Welsh (50.3 percent) mothers. There was, however, significant variation in involvement rates between the English regions. Regions with the lowest levels of mothers involved in playgroups were the North (34.2 percent), the North West (35.5 percent) and the South East (35.7 percent), whereas half the mothers of playgroup attenders in the West Midlands (50 percent) and the South West (50.5 percent) were involved in some way.

Maternal involvement in LEA nursery schools and classes showed a national variation quite different from that of playgroups, with some-what more English mothers involved (14 percent) than were their Welsh and Scottish counterparts (8.7 and 8.9 percent respectively). As with the playgroups there was variation between the English regions in the level of parental involvement in LEA nursery schools and classes and in at least some respects the findings were similar to those for playgroups. The North region again had the lowest level of maternal involvement (8.6 percent) with the North West (11.1 percent) and Yorkshire and Humberside (11.2 percent) coming close behind. As with play-groups, the highest level of maternal involvement in LEA nursery schools and classes was in the South West (19.4 percent).

There is no obvious explanation for these differences in level of maternal involvement between regions and countries. The rate of maternal employment, as a possible reason for non-participation, was not highest in the regions where involvement was at comparatively low levels (see Table 11.2). In some rural regions, e.g. the South West, and East Anglia, mothers were more likely than mothers in other regions to help in both playgroups and LEA schools but in other rural areas, e.g. Wales, maternal involvement was higher than average in playgroups but lower than average in LEA nursery schools and classes.

To explore further these urban-rural contrasts a comparison was made of rates of maternal involvement between mothers in different types of neighbourhood. This suggested that the locality of the home made little difference to the likelihood that mothers would help at all in LEA nursery schools or classes (Figure 9.3). Mothers in rural neighbourhoods, however, were somewhat more likely than those in urban neighbourhoods to participate in the child's playgroup; although of those who helped in playgroups, mothers from poor neighbourhoods were the ones who were most likely to help often (at least once a month).

Regional variations may also stem from differences in attitudes, policies and traditions of the mothers, playgroups and schools concerning the role of parents in preschool institutions. In addition, however, a mother's family circumstances and responsibilities may have a limiting or facilitating effect on the degree of involvement she has in her child's playgroup or nursery school. Some of these factors are examined below.

Social differences in maternal involvement

Social differences in the mother's perceived value of involvement for herself and her child and the opportunity for the mother to participate when there are other family and personal commitments are all factors influencing her decision to take part in the activities of the child's playgroup or nursery school. At the same time there may also be a tendency for preschool institutions to encourage the participation of mothers from some social groups and not others. This need not be a result of conscious discrimination on the part of nursery school teachers or playgroup organisers but is likely to be a consequence of the kinds of skill and ability required. There may also be a reluctance on the part of many working class mothers to become involved in what to them is an alien social or cultural setting in which they feel ill at ease and find it difficult to behave unselfconsciously.

Figure 9.4 compares the frequency of involvement of advantaged and socially disadvantaged mothers whose children attended playgroup or LEA nursery schools and classes. In both playgroups and LEA nursery schools and classes differences in socioeconomic circumstances were associated with only small differences in the proportions of mothers who were involved at all in the facility the child attended. The tendency was for slightly higher proportions of mothers from socially advantaged homes to be involved in their child's preschool placement than were socially disadvantaged mothers. In playgroups, however, this difference was entirely due to the higher proportion of advantaged mothers who helped only occasionally (less than once a month).

Playgroup philosophy particularly emphasises the value that involvement in playgroup activities may have for mothers who have difficult or stressful lives. Single-parent families and families with several preschool

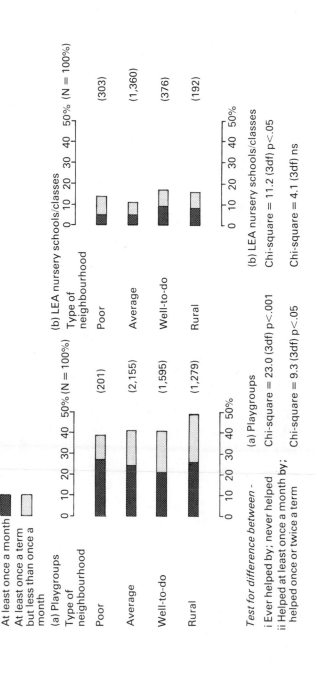

Figure 9.3 Frequency of maternal help in playgroups and LEA nursery schools/classes by type of neighbourhood

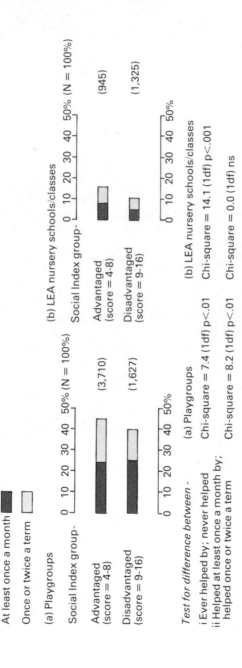

Figure 9.4 Frequency of maternal help in playgroups and LEA nursery schools/classes by Social Index group

children are examples of situations that are potentially stressful for mothers and, assuming that being involved in the child's playgroup does indeed provide a source of support for such mothers, higher proportions of these mothers might be expected to participate in playgroup activities. The same argument could apply also to mothers whose children attend LEA nursery schools and classes. However, although teachers often recognise the special needs of children in these family circumstances they do not necessarily perceive the mother's needs as part of their concern also. Thus whilst LEA schools' admissions policy may favour children from stressful home circumstances, the rate of involvement of mothers from these families might be no higher than that of other mothers. Indeed, mothers in stressful circumstances may feel reluctant to spare time to help the child's preschool placement or be unable to cope with other activities beyond the immediate demands of the family. This argument suggests that relatively fewer mothers in potentially stressful families may be involved in their children's preschool placements.

We found no significant difference between the proportion of mothers in single-parent and two-parent families who were ever involved in preschool activities. This applied to both playgroups and LEA nursery schools and classes. Whilst there is some measure of satisfaction in finding that single-parent mothers were no less likely than mothers from two-parent families to help in their child's preschool placement, we might have hoped that a higher than average proportion of them would have been involved. There was some indication that more lone mothers helped at playgroups (49.2 percent) than did supported single mothers (37.2 percent) but this difference did not achieve statistical significance.

Mothers who had two or more children younger than the study child were less likely than mothers with fewer younger children to help in the preschool activity their child attended (Figure 9.5). Having two or more younger children also resulted in mothers helping less frequently. This could be explained by the prevailing reticence in many playgroups and LEA schools to accommodate children under three, which thus precluded mothers with children of this age from being involved in school activities. One way of easing this problem would be to provide more mother and toddler clubs linked to nurseries or playgroups; this would then increase the opportunity for these mothers to become involved in their activities.

Reasons why mothers did not help

To ask why a mother did not help out at her child's preschool placement carries the implication that she ought to have helped, and the risk of the retort 'Why should I?' We have argued that playgroup philosophy has parental involvement at its core and many nursery schools and classes clearly welcome the help of the parents of the children who attend. Thus the question of why mothers were not involved is based on the assumption, not that they ought to have been, but that in some undefined way such involvement is a 'good thing'.

We have found, however, that more than half the mothers whose children attended playgroups had not helped at all and as many as 87 percent of mothers whose children went to LEA nursery schools and classes. Family situation, e.g. parental circumstances or family size, made little difference to the proportion of mothers involved in the child's preschool placement. We suggest, therefore, that the likelihood that a mother becomes involved depends largely on whether or not she believes that her help is needed or welcomed, the degree to which she feels she has sufficient time or the necessary skills to participate and also, perhaps, her own demands vis à vis her child's attendance at the preschool institution. In short, a mother's involvement in preschool activities probably depends on the value she places on such involvement and the benefits that she expects to ensue for her child and herself. For example, a mother who finds her child troublesome a lot of the time might see playgroup or nursery school primarily as a means of providing her with a few hours' respite from the child's demands and a place for her child to expend some of his/her energy. This mother is unlikely to offer to participate in the activities of the facility whilst others might enjoy the social interaction and activities of the nursery school or playgroup.

In the CHES study, mothers who had not participated in children's preschool placements were asked whether this was because their help was not required, because they were busy doing other things or because they preferred not to take part. Of these mothers 85.1 percent said they were not involved because their help was not required, 11.2 percent were busy doing other things and 3.7 percent preferred not to take part. These results, however, were structured in part by the fact that these categories were the only alternatives printed on the questionnaire. Nevertheless there were some small differences in response associated with the mother's social circumstances and the type of preschool facility her child attended. These are illustrated in Figure 9.6.

The mothers who were most likely to report that they were too busy or preferred not to take part were socially disadvantaged mothers whose children attended playgroups (21.6 percent). Conversely the group who were least likely to give these reasons for non-participation were socially advantaged mothers whose children attended LEA nursery schools/classes (8.2 percent). Figure 9.6 shows that there was a tendency for higher percentages of mothers whose children went to LEA schools

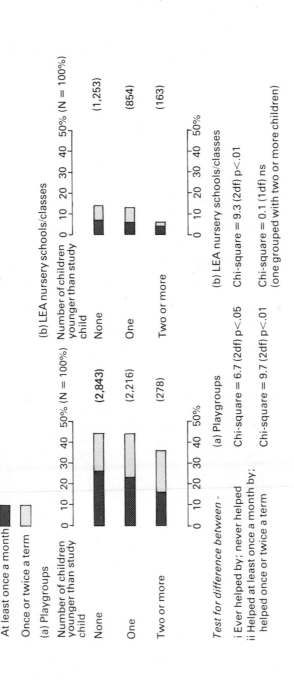

Figure 9.5 Frequency of maternal help in playgroups and LEA nursery schools/classes by number of children younger than study child

133

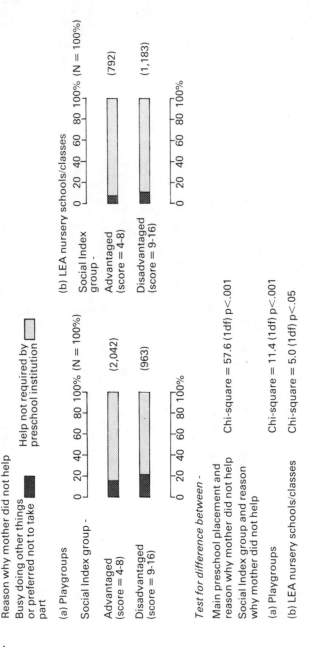

Key
Reason why mother did not help

Busy doing other things
or preferred not to take
part

Help not required by
preschool institution

(a) Playgroups

Social Index group -

0 20 40 60 80 100% (N = 100%)

Advantaged
(score = 4-8)   (2,042)

Disadvantaged
(score = 9-16)   (963)

0 20 40 60 80 100%

(b) LEA nursery schools/classes

Social Index
group -

0 20 40 60 80 100% (N = 100%)

Advantaged
(score = 4-8)   (792)

Disadvantaged
(score = 9-16)   (1,183)

0 20 40 60 80 100%

Test for difference between -

Main preschool placement and
reason why mother did not help   Chi-square = 57.6 (1df) p<.001

Social Index group and reason
why mother did not help

(a) Playgroups   Chi-square = 11.4 (1df) p<.001

(b) LEA nursery schools/classes   Chi-square = 5.0 (1df) p<.05

Figure 9.6   Reasons why mother did not help in playgroups and LEA nursery schools/classes by Social Index group

to report that their help was not needed compared with mothers of playgroup children. Also, in both playgroups and LEA schools, socially advantaged mothers were more likely than disadvantaged mothers to report that their help was not required.

Type of help given

Mothers who participated in the preschool facility their children attended were asked to describe the kinds of things they did. This was an open-ended question as we had no pre-conceived ideas about the range of responses possible and the mothers' replies were classified into five broad categories. The most common form of involvement was working actually with the children in the nursery or playgroup (84 percent) and this activity was more common in playgroups (86.6 percent) than in LEA nursery schools or classes (63.5 percent). The replies to this question did not lend themselves to being subdivided into smaller groups to give more detailed information about the kinds of thing mothers did. The next two categories of involvement, participation in management/advisory committees and giving general routine help, are similar to the first in that these three are concerned in some way with what actually goes on within the institution, whereas working parties and offering help at special occasions are supportive activities which, although important, do not have a direct bearing on what happens in the preschool institution. Figure 9.7 shows considerable differences between types of institutions in the kinds of maternal help which were undertaken. Of mothers who helped in playgroups 95.7 percent were involved in activities directly concerning the children, or management or day-to-day running of the playgroup whereas the corresponding figure for LEA nursery schools and classes was 70.5 percent. Help with working parties, fund raising, special occasions, etc., was more common in LEA nursery schools and classes (29.6 percent) than in playgroups (4.3 percent).

Notwithstanding these differences between the state and voluntary sectors, however, it is clear from our results that the majority of mothers who helped in the LEA schools their children attended were involved in classroom activities rather than the more peripheral tasks such as fund-raising and special occasions. We also found no differences between mothers from different social backgrounds (in terms of the Social Index) in the type of help in which they were involved. This was perhaps unexpected in view of the assumption that socially advantaged mothers, by virtue of their education and experience, may have had more skills to bring to the classroom than their socially disadvantaged peers.

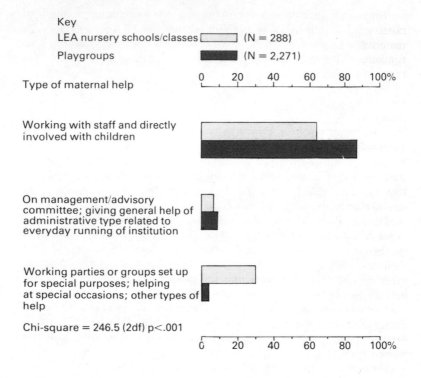

Key
LEA nursery schools/classes ▭ (N = 288)
Playgroups ▬ (N = 2,271)

Type of maternal help

Working with staff and directly
involved with children

On management/advisory
committee; giving general help of
administrative type related to
everyday running of institution

Working parties or groups set up
for special purposes; helping
at special occasions; other types of
help

Chi-square = 246.5 (2df) p<.001

Figure 9.7 Type of maternal help in playgroups and LEA nursery schools/classes

Thus although there were differences between playgroups and LEA nursery schools and classes in terms of the frequency and type of maternal involvement, these differences were not large in view of the fundamental differences in organisation and philosophy of these two types of facility.

Summary

Parental involvement is an integral feature of playgroup philosophy whereas in other types of preschool institutions, although parental participation is welcomed and encouraged, professionals at administrative and classroom levels determine policy and are responsible for the day-to-day running of the institution.

These differences were expected to give rise to differences between types of preschool institution in the rate and nature of involvement of mothers of children in the CHES sample who attended preschool facilities. Our results confirmed these expectations in that relatively more mothers of children who attended playgroups participated in their activities, were involved directly with the children and took part in management activities than did mothers of children who attended LEA nursery schools/classes or other types of preschool facility. Even so, fewer than half the mothers of children who attended playgroups had helped at all.

There were marked regional differences in maternal involvement in playgroups ranging from more than two thirds of Scottish mothers down to only a third of mothers in the North, North West and South East regions of England. This regional variation could not be attributed to the socioeconomic and urban/rural differences between regions as these factors were not strongly associated with differences in maternal involvement rates. Family factors such as parental situation and number of under-fives in the household also made little difference to the likelihood that a mother participated in her child's preschool facility. We suggest that the observed regional differences were likely to be attributable to broad policy differences in playgroups between geographical regions. Of the mothers who did not participate in their child's preschool facility more than four out of five averred that this was because their help was not required rather than because they were too busy or preferred not to take part.

In general, therefore, the main factors influencing the likelihood that a mother participated in her child's preschool facility were the type of institution the child attended and the region of the country in which the family lived. The mother's social and family circumstances were of far less significance.

Chapter 10

The association of preschool educational experience with behaviour and ability of the child and maternal depression

In previous chapters we have described the different types of preschool education and day care available to the children in our cohort, their patterns of attendance, the extent of parental involvement in the institutions and the variations in uptake of those services by families from different social backgrounds. We now address ourselves to the most compelling question of all – namely, what is the impact of the child's experience of preschool education or day care on his or her subsequent ability and behaviour? In posing this question we have to recognise that LEA nursery schools and classes, playgroups and day nurseries do not necessarily share the same objectives given that, as we have shown, they tend to accommodate children from different sections of the population who have different needs. Thus the value of such institutions does not depend solely on being able to demonstrate educational advantages that may come from having attended them (Hughes *et al.*, 1980). Nevertheless the curricula and activities of preschool institutions, particularly LEA schools and playgroups, have some significance for the cognitive development of children exposed to them. Activities which promote language development, materials that encourage reading and numerical ability, toys and equipment that facilitate fine and gross motor skills and stimulate creative activities all contribute to the child's intellectual development, while social skills and personal independence are elicited by contact with children of similar age in a group setting.

Furthermore, attendance at nursery school or playgroup may enhance the child's relationship with his or her mother, with their shared enjoyment of each other's company being greater after their short separation (Hughes *et al.*, 1980, p. 36). The fact that the time spent in a nursery or playgroup is an extension and enrichment of everyday life at home and essentially enjoyable to the child would suggest that these benefits ought to be reflected in tests of general ability and language, as well as in his or her behavioural adjustment.

Previous research

There has been no large-scale British research on the effects of preschool education on children's ability since Douglas and Ross (1965) looked at the educational progress of children who had attended nursery schools and classes in the early 1950s. Using a composite score based on tests of intelligence and educational performance, they found that these children had higher scores at eight years of age than did non-attenders. The difference had diminished by age eleven and by age fifteen the nursery school attenders were slightly behind. The findings of this study also suggested a small increase in the level of behavioural deviance in the children who attended nursery schools and classes. None of these differences were statistically significant, however, and in regard to the increased behavioural deviance the authors point out that this may be as easily attributed to the selection procedures for admission to nursery schools and classes as to the children's actual experience in them. At the time this research was carried out the powerful computing methods that are now used to statistically adjust for such intervening factors were not available. Even so, the results reported by Douglas and Ross suggest that the nursery schools and classes of the day probably had an influence on the general capabilities of the children who attended them.

The 1960s saw a tremendous surge of enthusiasm for preschool education as a means of intervention that would increase the educational potential of socially disadvantaged children. This movement was particularly strong in the United States where Headstart schemes were initiated as part of the national effort to reduce the effects of poverty. Britain's response to the same problem of social disadvantage was the setting up of Educational Priority Areas (Halsey, 1972). During this period, extensive, though largely unco-ordinated, research was undertaken in both countries to evaluate the effectiveness of Headstart and other intervention programmes.

As might be predicted, the findings of the various projects showed conflicting results which led to different conclusions being formulated on the effectiveness of preschool intervention in improving the later educational performance of children who had participated in the schemes. The conclusions of two substantial reviews of the research literature illustrate how different interpretations can be derived from essentially the same evidence. Barbara Tizard's (1974, p. 8) comment on the results of her review of preschool research was not encouraging. 'In so far, then, as the expansion of early schooling is seen as a way of avoiding later school failure or of closing the social class gap in achievement, we already know it to be doomed to failure.'

Smith and James (1977, pp. 310-11) reached a somewhat more optimistic conclusion. '. . . the evidence we have reviewed suggests that preschool intervention can make an impact, and with the right support this can be maintained for considerable periods.'

These differing conclusions stemmed mainly from the fact that there was great variation in the types of programmes studied, in the social circumstances of the children involved, the criteria by which the success of the intervention was judged and the expected duration of beneficial 'effects' after the intervention. Most British and American research was based on preschool programmes which were specially designed to achieve specific objectives, such as improving language skills. Children involved in the studies were from low income families, ethnic minorities, families living in poverty areas, or were disadvantaged in some other way. The differences between the various projects made comparison difficult and alternative interpretations or emphases easily led to the formulation of different general conclusions about the effectiveness of preschool education.

A major attempt to overcome these difficulties resulted in a report describing the pooled results of twelve American longitudinal studies which suggested that attendance at high quality Headstart programmes enabled more children from low income families to achieve the minimal requirements of their school system (Lazar and Darlington, 1978). The children who were enrolled in these schemes were less likely to be retained in the same grade or to be assigned to special education classes so that their progress through the school system was normal. Furthermore, they showed an increase in IQ scores which persisted for as much as three years after they had left the programme and, moreover, were independent of the child's sex, ethnic background, initial IQ, family structure and size and mother's educational level. Interestingly, Lazar and his colleagues found that the child's age when intervention started, duration of attendance (months) and frequency of attendance (hours per year) were unrelated to those outcomes. This finding, that the extent of child's contact with a preschool programme did not affect the outcomes described is surprising when contrasted with the results of a study of 40,000 French primary school children. These showed that children who had spent longer in a preschool education programme were less likely to repeat a year in the primary school because of failure to achieve the expected standard of education. This study was carried out in an area of France where the rate of school failure was above average (van der Eyken, 1982, pp. 45-6).

A point about which there is little argument is that preschool provision must be of good quality; there is, however, widely differing opinions on what constitutes good quality since that largely depends on the purpose and aims of different types of preschool provision. One type of facility may be geared to providing physical care in lieu of the parents and another may have a strong educational commitment. Even where the focus is explicitly educational, considerable diversity in pedagogy exists between the free play method practised in many British preschool institutions (Parry and Archer, 1974) and the progressive techniques such as those deriving from the approaches advocated by Bereiter and Engelman (1966). It is often assumed that 'Ordinary nursery education, with its emphasis on free play, does not in general produce (educational) gains, . . .' (Hughes *et al.*, 1980, p. 41).

The Oxford Preschool Research Group (Bruner, 1980) was also critical of certain practices in nursery schools/classes and playgroups. They concluded from their observations that the adults involved placed too much emphasis on management activity when they might have been profitably occupied in stimulating the children through play and use of structured materials. Notwithstanding this criticism, the observations made in the Oxfordshire preschool settings showed that the general standard of activity was by no means poor.

Despite this body of research of preschool educational provision and settings, very little attention has been given to the possible effects that existing nursery education has upon the behaviour and development of the children it serves. One exception was a study of 226 children aged three years who were attending various types of preschool educational and day care provision in a single London Borough (Stevenson and Ellis, 1975). However, this study found little difference in the children's behaviour or language skills which could be attributed to their preschool attendance. Most studies are concerned with the evaluation of specially designed programmes, without considering whether the typical run-of-the-mill nursery school or playgroup is already adequately meeting the needs of children by achieving appropriate educational ends. One reason why such research has not been undertaken is the appreciation of the *prima facie* benefits of existing forms of provision. Most play-groups and nursery schools and classes offer an enjoyable experience for the child, provide mothers with some respite from the demanding task of child care and also make it possible for them to take up a job if they wish it. With such obvious benefits, are further justifications for preschool provision necessary? These immediate assets of preschool education are clearly important and if they really do result in an improved quality of life for mothers and children, might this not be reflected in higher levels of ability in the children concerned, in the same way that they appear to be influenced by other life experiences?

Furthermore, when policy decisions are made on a cost benefit basis, it is important for policy makers to be assured that government funded provisions are being effective. A.H. Halsey (1980), for example, has argued strongly that expenditure on preschool services may result in saving funds that might otherwise have to be disbursed on expensive special educational provision for children at a later phase of their schooling. This point has been dramatically illustrated in an economic analysis of the long term financial advantages associated with the beneficial effects of an American Headstart programme (Weber *et al.*, 1978). This study demonstrated a substantial saving in public spending due to the reduced need for expensive special education programmes for school age children. For the individual children themselves there were higher anticipated lifetime earnings, which contributed to the gross national product. By contrast, school leavers who had needed to attend special schools found it more difficult to obtain employment than those who had remained within the normal educational system.

Summing up the significance of preschool education programmes in nurseries and playgroups we can make the following points. First, children exposed to preschool education can show short term and long term gains in educational attainment. Second, such favourable outcomes depend on the good quality of the experience children receive in the preschool facility. Third, the bulk of documented research has been focussed on evaluating specially devised preschool programmes. Fourth, there has been no recent large scale evaluation of preschool provision in Britain. Fifth, the advent of playgroups since the 1960s has added a whole new dimension to the question of the effects of early experience on children's ability and behavioural adjustment (Turner, 1977). The measures obtained from the CHES cohort at five years of age provide the means of evaluating the immediate effects attributable to the children's attendance at nursery schools and classes, playgroups, day nurseries and independent nurseries, and data from the ten-year follow-up of those children will in due course, provide information on the long term implications of this early experience.

Child behaviour

In Chapter 5 we described results of analyses which showed how the level of antisocial and neurotic behaviour of the children in our sample varied according to their family and social circumstances. Social inequality, parental situation, and family structure were three of the factors which exerted a powerful influence on neurotic and antisocial behaviour scores. These factors were also influential in determining the type of preschool placement the child attended (Chapter 8).

These complex inter-relationships have meant that we had to be specially careful to ensure that any observed differences in behaviour scores associated with preschool educational or day care experience could not be attributed to the different characteristics and home circumstances of the children who attended different types of institution. This was achieved by means of analysis of variance and using the

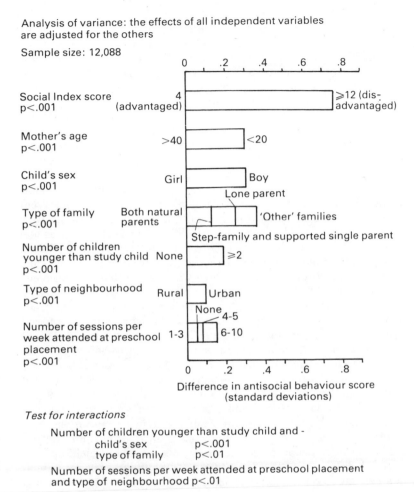

Figure 10.1 Analysis of preschool educational experience and anti-social behaviour

procedures described in Chapter 20.

Our analysis of the children's neurotic behaviour scores suggested that there was no association between this type of behaviour and the child's attendance at any form of preschool institution after statistical adjustment was made for the effects of a number of relevant social factors. Duration (number of months) and frequency (sessions per week) of attendance were also unrelated to neurotic behaviour score.

In contrast, differences in antisocial behaviour score were found between children according to the number of sessions per week they had attended preschool facilities although the type of facility they had attended was not a significant factor. The result of this analysis is shown in Figure 10.1 where it can be seen that, after statistical adjustment for the effects of all the other family and social variables, those children who spent more than five sessions a week in a preschool placement were more likely to display antisocial behaviour at home than children who attended 1-3 sessions (.16 SDs difference), non-attenders (.11 SDs difference) or half-time attenders (.08 SDs difference). This suggests that attendance for six or more sessions per week at any type of preschool institution was associated with a small, but not unimportant, increase in antisocial behaviour.

When we examined the interaction in this analysis of variance between frequency of attendance and type of neighbourhood we found that the higher mean antisocial score of children who attended more than five sessions a week occurred only in urban neighbourhoods. It is tempting to infer from this that the increased mean antisocial behaviour score associated with greater frequency of attendance could be attributed to the fact that certain preschool institutions in urban areas, i.e. local authority day nurseries and LEA nursery schools and classes, are likely to take a high proportion of children with behaviour problems on a full-time basis. However, our preliminary analyses did not confirm this as no behavioural differences were found between children who attended different types of institution. This supports our interpretation that the frequency of attendance, not the type of placement, was responsible for the differences in antisocial behaviour score.

Another possibility was that within institutions, children with behavioural problems were the ones most likely to have been selected for full-time attendance and thus could have contributed to these results. This explanation is unacceptable on two grounds. First, by statistically adjusting for the effects of all the other factors given in Figure 10.1 in the analysis of variance, such a selection effect should have been minimal. Second, the assessment of behaviour was made after the children's preschool experience and therefore can be more readily interpreted as a result of frequency of attendance rather than a determinant of it. A further point worth considering is that the typical nursery or playgroup curriculum places heavy emphasis on self-determination and freedom of choice which may encourage children to be more self-centred and less considerate of the wishes of others, which qualities may be deemed 'antisocial'. In this connection it is worth reiterating that no such difference was found in neurotic behaviour in terms of either type of institution or frequency of attendance.

Relatively few children attended more than five sessions a week — about 12 percent of all children who attended preschool institutions — and it may be assumed that only half those (6 percent) had increased antisocial scores of the order shown in Figure 10.1. Further support for the idea that preschool attendance is responsible for increased antisocial behaviour can be found in the mothers' responses to a question in the survey interview which asked if they had noticed any changes in the child which they attributed to preschool attendance. Only half the mothers thought there had been any change at all, 38 percent of all mothers described some kind of improvement in their child's behaviour, personality or skills which they attributed to his or her preschool attendance, and some kind of deterioration was mentioned by 4 percent. These were not necessarily the same children who were identified in the analysis of antisocial behaviour, but the point we are making is that some mothers spontaneously responded to an open-ended question by saying that their child's behaviour, personality or skills had deteriorated.

Maternal depression

For a mother, the opportunity to leave her child at a nursery or playgroup means that she has a few hours free from the demands of his or her care; this welcome respite enables her to visit friends, to do shopping or housework in peace, and opens up the possibility of obtaining a part-time job. Whatever a mother elects to do in these spells of freedom, she experiences some relief, if only short lived, from the stresses that are inherent in caring for a young child.

Figure 10.2 shows the results of an analysis of variance in which preschool attendance was found to have some effect on maternal depression after adjustment for the effects of other relevant family and social factors. Mothers whose children attended playgroups were slightly less likely to be at risk of depression scores than were mothers of children who did not attend any type of preschool institution. Risk of depression was also lower in mothers of children who went to LEA nursery schools/classes or private nurseries compared with mothers of non-attenders but the difference in mean depression scores between these groups failed to reach statistical significance. Mothers of children

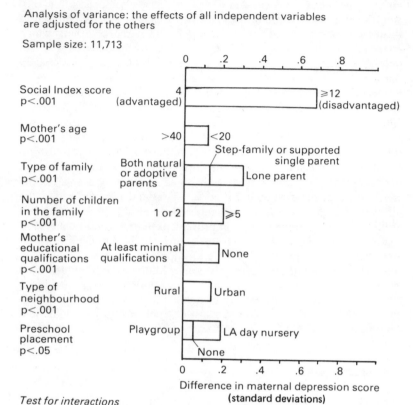

Analysis of variance: the effects of all independent variables are adjusted for the others

Sample size: 11,713

Test for interactions

Number of children in the family and type of family p<.01

Figure 10.2 Analysis of preschool educational experience and maternal depression

who attended local authority day nurseries were more at risk of depression than those of children who went to playgroups (.2 SDs difference in depression score). This does not support the hypothesis that respite from children's care reduces the risk of depression in the mother because if that were so the longer time that children were away from her care, i.e. as in full-time local authority day nurseries, the lower the level of depression expected. In point of fact the exact opposite result emerged from our analysis with the highest mean depression score being found amongst mothers of children in local authority day nurseries. Apart from this finding, there was no association found between maternal depression score and the frequency of their children's attendance at preschool institutions.

We suggest that the higher depression scores of mothers whose children attended local authority day nurseries can be attributed to the stressful circumstances in their lives which (a) necessitated their children's attendance at day nurseries and (b) engendered maternal depression. Indeed depression in the mother might have actually increased the likelihood that her child would obtain a place in a day nursery. The analysis of variance described in Figure 10.2 adjusts for many social and family factors which were associated with both type of preschool placement attended by the child and also maternal depression, but it is not possible to build into the analysis every contributory factor. We conclude, therefore, that the association between maternal depression score and children's preschool placement is attributable to differences in family background rather than a consequence of a child's attendance at one or other type of preschool facility.

Cognitive ability

The Human Figure Drawing test is conceived as a measure of intellectual maturity, but it depends also on a child's competence in drawing. Such a competence may be more readily acquired by children who attend preschool institutions where art work is one of the more common activities (Sylva *et al.*, 1980, pp. 173-84). Notwithstanding this emphasis on drawing and painting in preschool institutions and also the possibility that a child's attendance at a nursery or playgroup could be expected to enhance his/her cognitive progress, no relationship was found between the children's preschool experience and their subsequent HFD score. Age at entry to infant school was also not correlated with HFD score. These were the results from an analysis of variance which also included Social Index score, the child's sex, family size and mother's educational qualifications.

Copying designs is a more specific task than Human Figure Drawing,

Analysis of variance: the effects of all independent variables are adjusted for the others

Sample size: 12,097

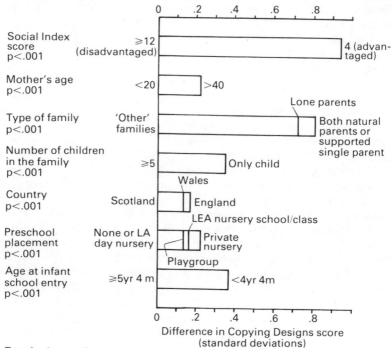

Test for interactions

Preschool placement and type of family p<.05
Age at infant school entry and country p<.001

Figure 10.3 Analysis of preschool educational experience and Copying Designs

depending on a child's ability to understand the patterns or structure of each design and to reconstruct it by drawing a copy. It is a more formalised skill that requires good eye-hand co-ordination and the ability to recognise patterns; both of which skills might be expected to develop through play with puzzles and matching and sorting exercises in preschool institutions.

The association between preschool experience and subsequent Copying Designs scores achieved by children in our sample, is investigated in Figure 10.3 where it is shown that attendance at all types of preschool facility, with the exception of local authority day nurseries, was associated with higher Copying Designs scores than were achieved by children with no preschool experience. The increase in mean score of children who attended preschool institutions was .13 SDs for play-groups, .16 SDs for LEA nursery schools/classes and .22 SDs for private nurseries. The difference in mean scores between the children who attended these three types of institutions, however, did not achieve statistical significance. These results were obtained after adjustment for a number of relevant social and family factors which are presented in Figure 10.3 where it is shown, in addition, that early entry to infant school was also associated with increased Copying Designs score.

This latter difference amounted to as much as .37 SDs between children who started school before 4 years and 4 months and those who did not start school until 5 years and 4 months or later. The relationship between Copying Designs score and age at infant school entry could not be attributed to national differences in the cognitive abilities measured by this test (Figure 5.5) coupled with the fact that many Scottish children started school on or after 5 years 4 months (Table 6.2) because country of residence was one of the factors for which statistical adjustment was made in this analysis (Figure 10.3). Investigation of the interaction between the child's age at infant school entry and his/her country of residence suggested that the former had less effect on Welsh children than on English or Scottish children. Thus the assumption of additivity of the model with respect to age at infant school entry was less reliable for Welsh children than for children in the other two countries. (See Chapter 20 for further explanation of interactions and additivity in analyses of variance.)

The size of the difference in Copying Designs score associated with preschool educational experience was not as large as that associated with socioeconomic inequality or type of family although it was comparable with other factors in the analysis such as mother's age, family size and country of residence. The importance of the preschool effect, however, should not be minimised as the contact with the nursery or playgroup environment is brief compared with the child's other life experiences at home and more dramatic effects should not, therefore, be anticipated.

Vocabulary

Stimulation of language skills is a cornerstone of preschool educational ideology and competence in linguistic expression and comprehension is such an essential precondition for successful learning at school that no professional concerned with the care and education of young children could be unaware of its importance. A child's attendance at a preschool institution, therefore, might be expected to increase his or her vocabulary skills, especially in institutions staffed by trained teachers as in LEA nursery schools/classes. Even without deliberate language stimulation by teachers and other staff or parents in preschool institutions, a child's contact with other adults and children beyond the immediate family circle may itself, through increased opportunity for verbal interaction, further his or her linguistic development.

The relationship between children's attendance at preschool institutions and their vocabulary as measured by the English Picture Vocabulary Test was examined by means of analysis of variance and the results are presented in Figure 10.4. It is immediately apparent from this diagram that the impact of early education on children's vocabulary was far less than that of other aspects of their lives such as their socioeconomic and family circumstances. Nevertheless, children who had attended any type of preschool facility had significantly higher mean EPVT scores than those without preschool experience.

Early entry into infant school was unexpectedly associated with *reduced* EPVT score. Thus children who started at infant school before age 4 years and 4 months were .11 SDs behind children who entered school on or after 5 years 4 months. This contrasts with the Copying Designs analysis in which scores of children who started school at an early age were higher than those who started later. There is no obvious explanation why starting school at an early age should be associated with improved general ability but reduced vocabulary skill and no further examinations of this finding were carried out at this stage.

Another unexpected result was that we found no relationship between the amount of preschool education experienced and our measures of children's ability and vocabulary. That is to say, when duration (in months) and frequency (in sessions per week) of attendance were entered into the analyses we have described, their relationships with the dependent variables were non-significant, and their presence in the analysis made no appreciable difference to the general pattern of results. Thus the higher scores in ability and vocabulary of children who attended LEA nursery schools/classes, playgroups and private nurseries compared with those who had no preschool experience were not significantly affected by the differences in duration and frequency of attendance between these types of institutions described

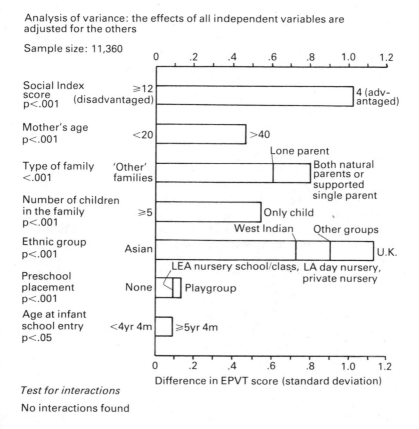

Analysis of variance: the effects of all independent variables are adjusted for the others

Sample size: 11,360

Test for interactions

No interactions found

Figure 10.4 Analysis of preschool educational experience and English Picture Vocabulary Test

in Chapter 7.

Further investigation may reveal methodological problems obscuring any effects associated with duration and frequency of attendance. Lazar and Darlington (1978) however, were also unable to demonstrate measurable effects attributable to the amount of time children spent in Headstart programmes (*op. cit.,* p. 177).

Summary

Previous research into the effects of preschool attendance on children's ability, attainment and behaviour has been inconclusive in that the results of one study are often contradicted by those of another. This is because most preschool educational research such as that carried out under the Educational Priority Area programme in Britain and Project Headstart in America, has been small scale and designed to evaluate the effectiveness of different innovatory curricula rather than the typical nursery or playgroup attended by most children. The tacit assumption appears to have been that the type of experience offered in the typical nursery school or class and playgroup cannot be expected to have any impact on children's cognitive development or behaviour.

Lazar and Darlington (1978) demonstrated substantial long-term benefits associated with children's attendance at Headstart programmes, and attendance at a good quality preschool placement was found to have lasting positive effects on children's later school careers. Their conclusions were reached after pooling the results of twelve different longitudinal studies, thereby averaging out, so to speak, the general impact of a variety of approaches to preschool intervention. This suggested that an analysis of British preschool institutions may yield similar results.

The object of the present CHES analysis of British preschool education was to see if attendance at a typical nursery school/class, playgroup or day nursery was associated with any appreciable change in children's behaviour or ability at age five. The main conclusions were as follows.

Children who attended LEA nursery schools or classes, playgroup or private nursery had higher Copying Designs and EPVT scores than those with no preschool experience. Differences in Human Figure Drawing scores between children with different preschool experiences, however, failed to achieve statistical significance. The size of the effect of preschool educational experience on Copying Designs score was comparable with the effects of other factors such as country of residence, age of mother and family size, but the effect on EPVT score was small compared with other factors. This suggests that preschool educational

152

experience has a greater influence on conceptual maturity or fine motor skills than on vocabulary.

Neither the frequency (sessions per week) nor duration (months) of a child's attendance at a preschool institution were associated with the level of his or her ability in terms of the three tests used. Frequency of attendance was, however, a significant factor in antisocial behaviour. Children who attended any type of preschool institution for more than five sessions a week were more likely to have higher antisocial behaviour scores than were non-attenders or children who attended no more than five sessions weekly. There was no difference between types of preschool institution in this respect and there was no measurable effect of frequency of attendance on neurotic behaviour.

Early entry into infant school was associated with a marked increase in children's Copying Designs scores but a small decrease in EPVT scores. Age at school entry, however, was not related to antisocial or neurotic behaviour in the child or to maternal depression.

The possibility was investigated that preschool attendance would provide a respite for the mother and hence reduce the risk of depression. Frequency of attendance was not found to be related to maternal depression but mothers of local authority day nursery attenders had higher depression scores than those whose children went to playgroups. A possible reason for this difference was the selection of children from stressful homes for day nursery attendance.

Part Three

Mothers in paid employment

Introduction

Nearly all women have a paid job at some time after completing their full-time education. In fact the employment rate of single women is very similar to that of single men, as we shall show in Chapter 11. Child bearing, however, effectively excludes women from the job market for as long as it takes for their youngest child to achieve independence. Thus the biological fact that it is women who bear children means that their work histories follow a fundamentally different pattern from those of men. Also, whereas the work histories of men follow a fairly well prescribed pattern, those of women are very diverse and depend on many interrelated and complex personal, family and socioeconomic factors (Elias and Main, 1982). For example, the choice between being employed or not may initially hinge upon the degree of gratification a mother anticipates that she can derive from a paid job as compared with that of devoting herself entirely to rearing her children and looking after the home. This apparently simple dichotomy is complicated, however, by the fact that the likelihood of obtaining satisfactory employment depends first on the range of job choices that it is possible for a mother with a given level of educational attainment and second, on local job availability. A third, crucial factor is the availability of alternative care for the dependent children of a mother who intends to go out to work. Mothers who wish or need to take up regular employment are often unable to do so because of the limited day care facilities available for young children. For some mothers the question of whether or not employment is a satisfying experience is of little consequence compared with the sheer economic need to supplement the family income by going out to work; lone mothers, for example, are especially vulnerable to this pressure to become employed.

These are just some of the ways in which a mother's response to the prospect of employment is structured by her personal needs, the demands of her family and the need to make adequate arrangements for

157

the care of her children so that the family rather than her job or career becomes her primary concern. In contrast to this, when a man becomes a father the loss of his wife's income means that there is increased pressure for him to remain in full-time employment and to consolidate his job or career prospects in order to ensure a regular future income to support the family. Male non-employment is usually due to lack of opportunity in the labour market, i.e. a constraint from outside the family, whereas female non-employment is mainly a result of the competing demands of family responsibility. The discontinuity of women in employment due to family formation also means that their future career prospects are not so good as those of men with similar initial training. Thus mothers who re-enter the labour market often take jobs of a lower status than their training merits (Elias and Main, 1982).

Changes in social attitudes towards the role of women which are reflected in new laws and regulations engendered by the Sex Discrimination Act of 1975 suggest that more mothers of young children would like to go out to work if adequate arrangements could be made for the care of their children (Equal Opportunities Commission, 1978; Hughes *et al.*, 1980). The proportion of such mothers had, indeed, been increasing up until 1975 and thereafter remained constant during a period when employment rates of men had been falling (OPCS *General Household Survey: 1980*, London: HMSO, Chapter 5). The employment of mothers will have affected the lives of the children in our sample in many ways, for example, reduction in mother-child contact, increase in the child's contact with other adults, increase in father's involvement with the child (see Chapter 4) and increase in standard of living because of additional income.

In the five chapters that follow we investigate some of the family and socioeconomic differences between mothers in our survey who were in paid employment and those who were not, the hours and type of work done by employed mothers, their attitudes towards employment, the day care arrangements made for the children and the differences between the behaviour and ability of children of employed and non-employed mothers. We also consider whether the risk of maternal depression is reduced in mothers who have jobs.

Chapter 11

Which mothers go out to work?

Employment trends

The 1960s saw a rapid growth in the numbers of employed mothers who had young children (Tizard *et al.*, 1976, p. 124). This trend continued until 1975 when as many as 28 percent of mothers of under fives were going out to work. Notwithstanding the worsening economic climate in the second half of the 1970s when male employment rates were falling, the proportion of mothers with young children who were employed remained relatively stable and reached 30 percent in 1980 (*General Household Survey: 1980*, London: HMSO, Tables 5.3 and 5.4). Not surprisingly in view of the shortage of day-care provision for under fives (Hughes *et al.*, 1980), this employment trend was mostly a result of increasing numbers of mothers obtaining part-time jobs (i.e. working no more than 30 hours per week). Full-time employment rates of mothers with under-fives remained between 5 and 7 percent throughout the 1970s.

Two preconditions were necessary to effect this trend: firstly, there must have been a previously unmet demand for employment from women with dependent children; and secondly, the job market must have become responsive to this demand for employment. We suggest that employers developed a preference for part-time female workers during this period of economic depression because they are low paid and less likely to be affiliated with a union than are full-time male employees (Elias and Main, 1982). Also the rapid growth of certain industries in recent years such as those involving the assembly of electronic components, has been highly conducive to the employment of relatively unskilled people, and many women returning to work part-time after a period out of the labour force associated with family formation are willing to accept jobs at a level of skill below that of their employment prior to starting a family (Elias and Main, 1982).

The relationship between family formation and employment rates of women and men is shown in Figure 11.1 where it can be seen that the pattern for women is quite different from that for men. In 1980, married men with or without dependent children had higher employment rates than single men. In contrast to this, although the proportion of single women who were employed was very similar to that of single men, the employment rate of married women with no dependent children was much lower than that of their male counterparts and many women worked part-time. Only 30 percent of the women with a child aged under five were in paid employment, with the large majority working part-time. As the age of the youngest child increased more mothers went out to work and greater proportions worked full-time; even so, the majority of employed mothers with dependent children worked part-time.

We can infer from these figures that the traditional domestic arrangements in which the mother looks after the home and children whilst the father earns the family income was still very much in evidence in 1980 (see also Chapter 4). This, together with the growth in part-time employment among mothers with dependent children, suggests that about one in three mothers with a child aged under five is undertaking two jobs; one, being responsible for the home and family, and two, doing paid work.

The demands of home and family responsibilities often result in a mother relinquishing her job so that over a given period of time more mothers will have been employed than appears from employment rates which are calculated at one point in time. From the broad perspective of the National Training Survey, women's work histories are characterised by periods of employment interspersed with periods of non-employment which are associated with child bearing and family formation (Elias and Main, 1982). Earlier studies, however, found that frequent moves in and out of work were common among mothers with young children (Douglas and Blomfield, 1958, p. 118; Yudkin and Holme, 1963, Chapter VI). The changeable pattern of women's employment prompted us in our own study to distinguish between mothers who were currently in regular employment, those who worked occasionally and those who had given up regular employment in the previous five years.

Table 11.1 compares the mother's employment situation at the time of the survey, when the children were aged five years, with their history of employment outside the home since the time of the children's birth. Although as many as 47.5 percent of all mothers had been regularly employed outside the home for at least some of the time during the previous five years, far fewer were currently employed in full-time (5.8 percent) or part-time (26.9 percent) jobs outside the home. A large part

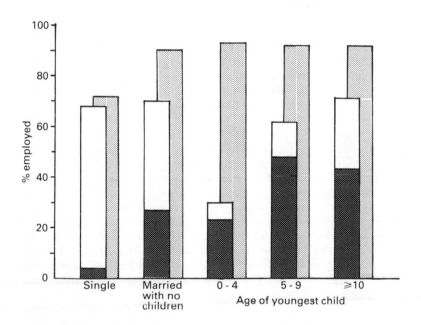

Figure 11.1 Employment of men and women by their marital status and age of youngest dependent child

Source: *General Household Survey*, Great Britain, 1980, Tables 5.5 to 5.9

of the difference was accounted for by the 12.5 percent of mothers who gave up jobs outside the home to become full-time housewives. A further 2.3 percent of the sample who had worked outside the home in the previous five years were currently employed regularly at home, did occasional work or were students or voluntary workers.

Although this table does not reveal all the variation in the pattern of mother's employment (such as changing jobs, increasing or decreasing the hours and days worked) over the five-year period since the child's birth, the relatively high proportion of mothers who had given up jobs and were no longer employed in any way (12.5 percent) is indicative of the way in which employment is, for many mothers, a very tentative situation. In the following analyses, therefore, the mothers who gave up jobs outside the home to become full-time housewives are separated from the 45.2 percent of all mothers who were full-time housewives for the whole of the child's preschool period. By doing this we are able to give some recognition to the changeable and unstable nature of mothers' employment whilst focussing for the most part on their current occupational situation at the time of the survey.

Most studies of women's employment concentrate only on women who are employed outside the home. In addition to those working outside the home on a regular basis, our study shows that 4.4 percent were regularly employed at home. The most frequently mentioned types of work in which these mothers were engaged were clerical work for their self-employed husband and helping with the family business such as a shop or farm. Very few of these mothers were out-workers, i.e. people who manufacture articles at home on a piece work basis. A further 4.4 percent worked occasionally, e.g. doing seasonal work such as fruit picking or other harvesting, providing tourist accommodation, doing temporary office work and acting as mail order firm agents. A small number of mothers (0.8 percent) were involved in unpaid activities, e.g. as students or voluntary workers, which they considered significant enough to mention during the survey interview. Thus nearly one in ten (9.6 percent) of these mothers, although not regularly employed outside the home, were engaged in activities in addition to those of housewife and mother. We consider it important to recognise the activities of these mothers as well as those of mothers who went out to work on a more regular basis.

Whilst the full richness and variation of a mother's employment experience were reduced by focussing only on her current employment, this method nevertheless produced a reliable and valid indication of the pattern of employment of these mothers at a critical point in time, when their children were at the threshold of their school careers.

Regional differences in the employment of mothers

Two important influences determine whether a mother obtains employment; local job opportunities in the area and her social and family circumstances. Job availability varies considerably from one part of the country to another, for example, the industrial north of England has traditionally employed a large permanent female work force, whereas in the more rural parts of the country female employment rates are low. These factors are reflected in the proportions of employed mothers in different regions shown in Table 11.2.

The North West region had the highest proportion of mothers who were regularly employed outside the home with 39 percent in full-time or part-time jobs, compared with predominantly rural East Anglia which had the lowest proportion (28.9 percent) of mothers going out to work. Other rural regions also had comparatively low employment rates; notably the South West region (31.8 percent) and Wales (30 percent). Scottish mothers were only slightly less likely than their English counterparts to go out to work (31.1 percent and 33.2 percent respectively). Differences between regions were also found in the number of hours mothers worked each week. In the West Midlands, for example, the overall proportion of mothers working outside the home (33 percent) was close to that for the whole of Great Britain, but 7 percent of mothers in that region worked full-time; this was twice the proportion found in East Anglia (3.5 percent) and second only to that of the North West region (7.7 percent).

Rural regions had higher than average proportions of mothers who worked regularly at home or undertook occasional or seasonal jobs. The 15.1 percent for East Anglia and 12.5 percent for the South West contrasts with the overall proportion for the whole of Great Britain of 8.8 percent. This was consistent with the high levels of agriculture and tourism in those regions which create seasonal and home employment such as harvesting and the provision of holiday accommodation.

At the time of the survey Scotland had the highest proportion (62.8 percent) of mothers with no form of employment or occupational commitment other than that of housewife and mother. Wales followed closely with 61.6 percent of non-employed mothers. The regions with the lowest proportions of full-time housewives were the North West and the South West regions with 54.1 percent and 54.7 percent respectively. This unexpected similarity between these two regions, following all the other observed differences, is partly explained by the 14.1 percent of mothers in the North West region who were full-time housewives at the time of the survey having given up a job in the previous five years. This occurred in only 10.7 percent of the mothers in the South West region.

These variations in patterns of mothers' employment are not large

163

but they are important in illustrating the way in which work opportunities are influenced by the geographical and economic characteristics of the different regions. However, there are limitations to regional analysis, in that variation *within* regions is at least as great as *between* regions. For example the mining and industrial areas in South Wales with their concentration of population contrasts sharply with the sparsely populated farming communities of mid-Wales and the centres of tourism in West and North Wales. The demographic and economic characteristics of these different parts of Wales will have important implications for the job opportunities of mothers and will undoubtedly result in variations in employment rates of mothers who live in these different areas.

Differences in social structures between regions may constitute a significant intervening factor for explaining different proportions of employed mothers in various parts of the country. The North West region, for example, not only provides women with the opportunities to work, but it also is characterised by high levels of social and economic disadvantage (see Figure 1.1) which itself may motivate mothers to take advantage of these opportunities. In addition, in areas such as the North West which have an accepted tradition of mothers going out to work, certain problems may be lightened for the individual mother. There is less likelihood of her feeling guilty or suffering from the disapprobation of her neighbours and as the position of her children is identical with that of many of their peers there is less chance that they will feel that they are missing something. Finally, local arrangements for the care of the children are likely to be an accepted part of the social scene in such neighbourhoods (Yudkin and Holme, 1963). These considerations suggest that the industrial composition of a region may be of less consequence than the existence of a tradition of female employment in determining the proportion of mothers who go out to work (Gales and Marks, 1974).

Type of neighbourhood

Our regional analysis suggested that mothers in predominantly rural regions had a distinctly different pattern of employment from those in other regions. This urban-rural contrast was explored further by using our neighbourhood classification (see Chapter 18) and the results are given in Figure 11.2.

This figure shows that relatively few mothers who were living in rural neighbourhoods worked outside the home on a regular basis, but they were more likely to be employed at home or occasionally than were mothers in urban neighbourhoods. Comparisons between the three

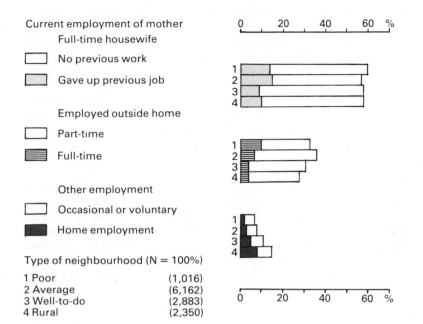

Figure 11.2 Current employment of mother by type of neighbourhood

types of urban neighbourhood reveal important differences in the proportion of mothers who worked outside the home. As many as 10.1 percent of mothers from poor neighbourhoods went out to work full-time compared with only 4.1 percent of mothers from well-to-do neighbourhoods. Part-time employment, however, was more common among mothers from average neighbourhoods. The group who were most likely to have been full-time housewives for the whole five-year period since the child's birth were those in well-to-do neighbourhoods.

These variations in employment rates according to type of neighbourhood of residence reflect differences in employment opportunity and also differences in mothers' demand for paid work. The urban conurbations have concentrations of industry, commerce and services which employ large numbers of women, and day care resources for young children are more readily available in the towns than in the country. Mothers living in poor urban neighbourhoods were more likely to seek a full-time job, because of the financial needs of their families, whereas those in well-to-do neighbourhoods were in less need of extra income and in such neighbourhoods employment opportunities are fewer. This contrast between the employment circumstances of socially disadvantaged and advantaged mothers is an important theme which will recur throughout this and subsequent chapters.

Household moves

Family mobility can exert a very disruptive influence on the mother's employment pattern. As well as having to find a new job in the area to which the family has moved, the mother with a child under school age faces the problem of making alternative day care arrangements. Moving away from an area usually entails leaving a network of family, friends and neighbours on whom the mother could depend for sources of information and help about day care, mutual cooperation in transporting children to and from school or nursery and help in times of emergency. In the new locality she will, in all likelihood, be unfamiliar with the network of support available and be unable, at first, to link up with the reciprocal child care arrangements operating between mothers who go out to work.

An American study of working wives (Long, 1978) found that any geographic move, other than a purely local one, was unfavourable to a married woman's continued participation in the labour force. Not only did a move, normally undertaken because of the husband's job, make it more likely that a wife would give up her job, but it also entailed lower earnings if she *was* able to continue working (Gallaway, 1969). Other research (e.g. Rapoport and Rapoport, 1971; Holmstrom, 1972; Wolfe,

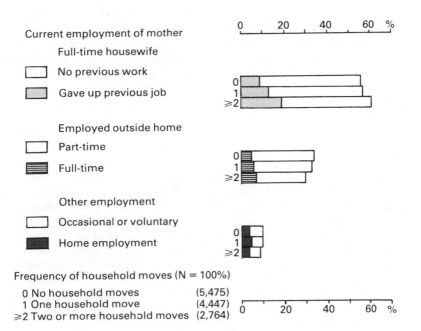

Current employment of mother

Full-time housewife
☐ No previous work
▨ Gave up previous job

Employed outside home
☐ Part-time
▤ Full-time

Other employment
☐ Occasional or voluntary
■ Home employment

Frequency of household moves (N = 100%)

0 No household moves	(5,475)
1 One household move	(4,447)
≥2 Two or more household moves	(2,764)

Figure 11.3 Current employment of mother by frequency of household moves

167

1971), supports Long's conclusion that the migration of husbands inter-feres substantially with the formulation of clear occupational goals among women. Indeed it might even be argued, although there is as yet no evidence to support this, that the likelihood of having to move for the purposes of the husband's career could influence a woman's initial choice of occupation. One reason for the continued concentration of more highly educated women in the traditional 'woman's' occupations – nursing, teaching, secretarial work (see Chapter 12) may be that these professions can be practised in many parts of the country and transfer between jobs is thus much easier (Stromberg and Harkness, 1978).

Figure 11.3 shows the effects of household moves upon the employ-ment of mothers in our sample. The proportions of mothers who had given up their jobs away from home to be full-time housewives were as many as 18.6 percent of those who had moved at least twice compared with only 8.7 percent of those who had never moved. Smaller propor-tions of mothers went out to work part-time if they had moved two or more times (22.9 percent) compared with those who had never moved (28.9 percent). Unexpectedly, however, the proportion of mothers who went out to work full-time was higher for the mothers who moved at least twice (7.1 percent) than for those who had not moved (5.1 percent). Although this difference is small, the trend associated with full-time employment is opposite to those related to part-time work and giving up jobs described above. It was possible that the observed trend may have derived from the different social composition of the more mobile social groups compared with those who were not mobile. In an analysis in which the relationship between full-time employment and family moves was examined whilst controlling for Social Index group, the trend described in Figure 11.3 remained, though it was slightly reduced.

Apart from the results for full-time employment, Figure 11.3 shows a reduced probability of employment in mothers who had experienced household moves which was mainly attributable to the tendency for such mothers to have given up their jobs. As more than a third (35.1 percent) of all the mothers in our sample had moved once, and more than a fifth (21.8 percent) more than once during the previous five years, family mobility is a not insignificant factor in determining whether or not a mother goes out to work. Care should be taken, however, in making causal inferences, as factors precipitating a family move, for example the birth of younger siblings resulting in the need for larger accommodation, may also be the primary reason for a mother to give up her job.

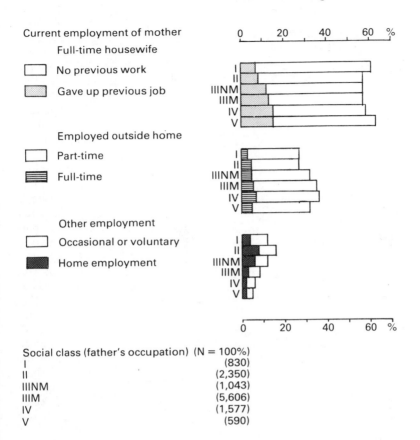

Figure 11.4 Current employment of mother by social class (father's occupation)

Mothers in paid employment

Current employment of mother
Full-time housewife

☐ No previous work

▨ Gave up previous job

Employed outside home

☐ Part-time

☰ Full-time

Other employment

☐ Occasional or voluntary

■ Home employment

Social Index group	(N = 100%)
1 Most advantaged	(1,228)
2 Advantaged	(3,473)
3 Average	(4,721)
4 Disadvantaged	(1,963)
5 Most disadvantaged	(1,435)

Figure 11.5   Current employment of mother by Social Index group

Socioeconomic status

Past research has paid little attention to the socioeconomic circumstances of mothers who go out to work. What evidence there is suggests that those mothers who obtain employment when their children are of preschool age tend either to be women whose families are in economically deprived circumstances, or women with a strong commitment to work for its own sake (Gowler and Legge, 1982). Yudkin and Holme (1963) found that the highest proportion of mothers in paid employment were those in social class III (using the husband's occupation as the index of class position) but Hunt (1968) showed slightly higher employment rates among women with preschool age children if their husbands were in manual jobs compared with those who were married to non-manual workers. Somewhat different results were found in an unpublished study of a small, socially mixed area of London which suggested that mothers with professional or managerial class husbands had higher employment rates (51 percent) than those with husbands in manual employment (43 percent) (Tizard *et al.*, 1976, p. 131).

The use of male occupations as an index of the social position of their wives has been subject to some criticism (Equal Opportunities Commission, 1982; Kingsley and McEwan, 1978; Osborn and Morris, 1979; Rodmell and Smart, 1982) and the Social Index has been devised for our study as an alternative to social class based on the father's occupation (see Chapter 18). However, for the purpose of comparison with earlier studies we shall first describe the results of an analysis of mothers' employment by social class using the father's occupation, and follow this with our analysis by Social Index group.

Figure 11.4 shows clear social class trends in which wives of manual workers were more likely to have a job outside the home than were mothers whose husbands were in non-manual occupations. Women whose husbands did semiskilled manual work had the highest employment rates and were also the ones who were most likely to have given up a job in the previous five years. Thus 51.2 percent of these mothers had been in employment at some time since the birth of their child compared with only 35 percent of wives of men in social class I or II occupations.

The analysis by Social Index gave a similar pattern of results to that obtained in the social class analysis. The proportions of mothers working outside the home when the children were aged five years showed small differences which ranged from 29.7 percent of the most advantaged group to 35.1 percent of the average group (Figure 11.5). Full-time working, however, increased with increasing social disadvantage from 3.7 percent of the most advantaged to 7.2 percent of the most disadvantaged — nearly double the proportion. Increasing disadvantage

171

Mothers in paid employment

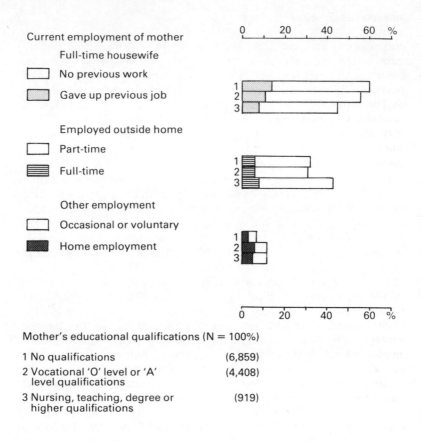

Current employment of mother

Full-time housewife

☐ No previous work

▨ Gave up previous job

Employed outside home

☐ Part-time

▤ Full-time

Other employment

☐ Occasional or voluntary

▰ Home employment

Mother's educational qualifications (N = 100%)

1 No qualifications (6,859)
2 Vocational 'O' level or 'A' (4,408)
  level qualifications
3 Nursing, teaching, degree or (919)
  higher qualifications

Figure 11.6 Current employment of mother by mother's educational qualifications

also corresponded with increasing proportions of mothers who had been in full-time or part-time jobs in the past five years but were currently full-time housewives. This trend went from 7.2 percent of the most advantaged to 17.3 percent of the most disadvantaged mothers. Disadvantaged mothers were also less likely to work at home or only occasionally than were mothers in the socially advantaged groups.

The most disadvantaged mothers probably worked full-time from necessity rather than from choice (see Chapter 13) but some of them may also have had to give up work because of their social circumstances. Arrangements for the care of their children may well have proved unsatisfactory, because they had less income at their disposal to pay for reliable day-care. They were also more likely to have been in unskilled employment (see Chapter 12) where job security was at a minimum.

Mother's education

One of the arguments for increasing the opportunity for women to return to employment is the potential wastage of educational and occupational skills acquired by women — often at public expense (Equal Opportunities Commission, 1978, p. 20). There are two types of wastage, (a) the non-employment of qualified women, and (b) the employment of women below their level of competence in terms of education and training.

Of all the mothers in our sample 7.4 percent had a degree or higher qualification, a Certificate of Education (teaching) or nursing qualifications equivalent to State Registered Nurse. A further 21.5 percent had GCE 'O' or 'A' level qualifications or the equivalent, 14.4 percent had vocational training such as shorthand and typing or hairdressing, and one percent had other qualifications which we were unable to classify. As many as 55.7 percent of the mothers had no qualifications or vocational training.

The proportion of mothers who were not currently employed varied from 60.3 percent of mothers with no qualifications down to 45.3 percent of mothers with professional qualifications. The results in Figure 11.6 show that a higher proportion of professionally qualified mothers were employed at least part-time outside the home (43.1 percent) than were mothers with qualifications at or below GCE 'A' level (31.3 percent) or without qualifications (32.3 percent). In terms of wastage of educational resources, however, close to half of the most highly trained and qualified mothers were unemployed at the time of their child's fifth birthday even though substantially more of these mothers were working than were mothers with lower levels of education.

The reasons for the non-employment of highly trained and qualified mothers might have been lack of opportunity for employment, poor provision of day care facilities for their children, or it may simply have been that the mothers preferred not to seek employment. Whatever the reasons, however, the non-usage of acquired skills represents a loss to the economy even though education is clearly of personal benefit to the mothers themselves and to their families. To the extent that the latter point is considered an important aspect of educational attainment, it is perhaps disturbing that over half of the mothers in this sample had acquired no formal qualifications or training.

To examine the second potential source of under-utilisation of qualified mothers we compared the mother's own occupational status (OPCS social class classification) with her educational qualifications. This revealed a strong association between the education and occupational status of those mothers who were in regular employment at the time of the survey. The great majority of nurses (84.5 percent), teachers (84.8 percent) and mothers with at least degree level qualifications (77.8 percent) were in social class I or II occupations and were thus likely to be engaged in the type of work for which they were trained. Mothers with GCE 'A' level or 'O' level qualifications or vocational training were mostly in non-manual occupations (71.1 percent, 60.8 percent and 56.8 percent respectively) and particularly social class III NM (48.4 percent, 47.6 percent and 40.8 percent respectively). Unqualified mothers tended to be in manual occupations (70.6 percent). These results suggest that in very general terms the occupational status of the majority of employed mothers was generally commensurate with their educational attainments.

However, other research suggests that within these broad occupational classifications, mothers were more likely to have poorer pay and fewer opportunities for promotion compared with women without children. Hunt (1968) reported that 8 percent of employed women without responsibility for children felt that they did not have the opportunity to use past training or qualifications in their present jobs compared with 19 percent of women with dependent children. Moss (Fonda and Moss, 1976, p. 12) concluded from his review of research on employed mothers that: 'there is some evidence that married and non-married working mothers are doing jobs at present which are at a lower level than their usual jobs,' and that mothers of preschool children in particular are: 'most restricted in job choice, most likely to work part-time, and gain the least financially from employment.' (p. 14)

Moss suggests that:

the disproportionate share of family responsibilities that women with children assume, together with the absence of adequate child

174

care facilities, often limits the type of work they can undertake; they must, for instance, work near home or seek part-time work which fits in with school hours or husbands' availability. (ibid., p. 12).

Although our results indicate that most qualified mothers in our sample were employed at the occupational levels appropriate to their training, other research suggests that they may, nevertheless, have been engaged in the least rewarding types of job within these levels and also have limited opportunity for promotion (Oakley, 1976, Chapter 4; Stromberg and Harkness, 1978).

Ethnic group

Culture and historical tradition are important influences on whether or not mothers seek and obtain paid employment and these factors certainly bring about some of the social and regional variation in employment rates described above. Such factors are likely to be of even greater significance, however, when considering the proportions of mothers of different ethnic groups who go out to work. For example, West Indian mothers who have 'been brought up with the idea that women worked wherever employment was available' (Hood *et al.*, 1970, p. 44), and who in the West Indies have traditionally been able to leave their children in the care of grandmothers or other relatives can be expected to continue this tradition in Britain. Half of Hood's sample of 101 West Indian mothers of one-year-olds living in Paddington were working, most of them in full-time unskilled work. Another study of mothers of three-year-olds in Brixton found that 64 percent of West Indian mothers were employed compared with 37 percent of English mothers (Pollack, 1972).

In line with these studies we also found high proportions of West Indian mothers in paid employment (Figure 11.7). In our sample, of the 176 mothers (1.4 percent) who were of West Indian origin as many as 56.8 percent were employed outside the home and the majority worked full-time (31.8 percent). A further 18.2 percent of West Indian mothers who were currently full-time housewives had been in paid employment in the previous five years. These figures combined show that three-quarters of the West Indian mothers had either a full-time or part-time job outside the home at some time during their child's preschool years compared with 45.2 percent of European UK mothers.

The 266 (2.1 percent) Asian mothers in our sample presented an entirely different picture, with only a quarter (25.5 percent) working outside the home at the time of the survey, although the majority of these — 15 percent of the entire Asian group — were employed full-

175

Mothers in paid employment

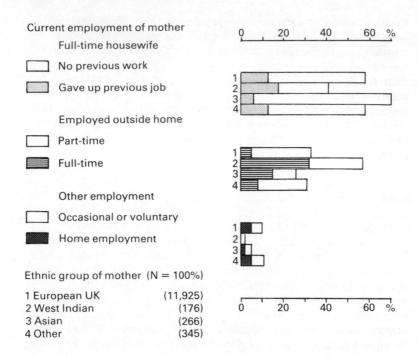

Current employment of mother

Full-time housewife

☐ No previous work

▨ Gave up previous job

Employed outside home

☐ Part-time

▤ Full-time

Other employment

☐ Occasional or voluntary

■ Home employment

Ethnic group of mother (N = 100%)

1 European UK (11,925)
2 West Indian (176)
3 Asian (266)
4 Other (345)

Figure 11.7 Current employment of mother by ethnic group of mother

time. A further 6.4 percent of the Asian mothers had given up a job and were currently full-time housewives. In total, only 31.9 percent of these mothers had been employed full-time or part-time outside the home at some time during their child's preschool years – a far lower proportion than for the European UK and West Indian groups. This does not conform with the trend predicted by Tizard *et al.* (1976, p. 135) who suggested that the employment rates of Asian mothers were becoming similar to those of West Indian mothers. It is possible, however, that there were cultural variations in the interpretation of the questions in our survey concerning employment. For example, Asian mothers working in a family business may have regarded this as a taken-for-granted part of their lives rather than 'employment', whereas European women would certainly regard this as employment.

One-parent families

Many of the problems faced by one-parent families stem from the fact that all the family responsibilities that are normally shared between two parents are shouldered by only one. Mothers in two-parent families can often depend on their husbands for child care or for helping out in other ways and therefore make it possible for them to go out to work. In supported single-parent families other adult members of the household may be able to provide similar assistance for the working mother, but such help would not be available to lone mothers (see Chapter 18 for definitions of family types). These differences in family circumstances will affect both the need and the opportunity for a mother to go out to work.

Figure 11.8 gives the proportions of employed mothers in different types of family. For the purposes of this analysis step-families and adoptive families are combined with families with both natural parents as all these were two-parent families. The mother figures in the 'other' types of family were all grandmothers or foster mothers and it is not surprising that as many as 83.1 percent were not in paid employment at the time of the survey.

The proportion of mothers who were working outside the home was, as expected, greatest in the supported one-parent families, 46 percent, compared with 31.7 percent of lone mothers and 33.7 percent of mothers in two-parent families. The main difference between these groups was in the proportion who went out to work full-time; the highest full-time employment rate was 23.4 percent in supported one-parent families, followed by 11.5 percent of lone mothers and 5.3 percent of mothers in two-parent families. These figures are remarkably similar to results from the 1977 *General Household Survey* (Table 4.6)

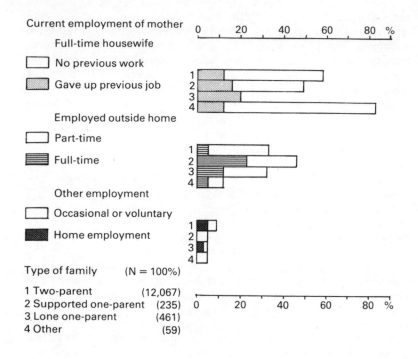

Figure 11.8 Current employment of mother by type of family

for mothers with a youngest dependent child aged 0-4 years which reported that 14 percent of the mothers who were unmarried (single, widowed, divorced or separated) and 5 percent of those who were married worked full-time. Comparable figures in the 1980 *General Household Survey* (Table 5.7) were 16 percent and 6 percent respectively which suggests that there has been little change over time.

Although the overall proportion of mothers who were going out to work at the time of the survey was about the same in all three main types of family, a higher proportion of lone mothers (20 percent) and supported one-parent mothers (25.8 percent) had given up jobs in the previous five years compared with mothers from two-parent families (11.6 percent). Thus the circumstances of being the sole parent in a single-parent family could have been a compelling reason for these mothers to both seek and relinquish their work. The proportion of mothers employed at home or occasionally, however, was lower in the one-parent families (5 percent) than in two-parent families (9.2 percent).

In general, it cannot be said that single-parent status inevitably results in a mother going out to work even though in the majority of cases family disruption leads to financial hardship and a deterioration in the family's standard of living (see Chapter 3). Nevertheless, greater proportions of mothers in one-parent families had been out to work in their children's preschool years compared with mothers from two-parent families, and relatively more of the former worked full-time. Our expectation of higher employment rates among supported one-parent mothers was also borne out by our results.

Family size

The financial needs of families with several children are greater than those of families with only one or two to clothe and feed. Thus the pressure on a mother to go out to work might be greater if she has a large family. At the same time, however, her presence in the home is needed that much more because of the extra domestic work created by a large family. In addition, it is more difficult for the mother to make arrangements for the care of several children during her working hours than if there are only one or two children. In large families then, the mother's need for increased income may be off-set by her increased domestic responsibility and the problem of finding alternative care for several children whilst she is absent at work. Alternatively, a large family may be a sign of a mother's home-centredness and reflect a preference for staying at home in the traditional role of wife and mother.

179

Figure 11.9 shows that increasing family size was associated with decreasing likelihood that a mother had been out to work at any time during the five years preceding the survey. Over half (55.2 percent) of the mothers with five or more children had not had a job outside the home since the study child was born, compared with less than a third (32.7 percent) of mothers with only one child. In families where the study child was the only child 13.3 percent of the mothers went out to work full-time and 32.4 percent part-time; in families with five or more children, however, 5.6 percent of the mothers worked full-time and 20.1 percent part-time. Home or occasional employment did not vary markedly with family size. The comparative ease of making day-care arrangements for only one child rather than for several children, and the possibility that some of these mothers deliberately restricted their family size in order to be able to continue employment are likely explanations for the higher employment rates of mothers with one child.

A further important reason for the higher proportion of the mothers with one dependent child who were in employment was the fact that the study child was aged five and many had already started school. The age of the mother's youngest child is a strong determinant of whether or not she goes out to work. Results from the 1977 *General Household Survey* (*Social Trends*, 1979, London: HMSO, p. 59) showed that the proportion of mothers working full-time increased from 6 percent of mothers whose youngest child was aged 0 to 2 years to 29 percent of mothers with a 10 to 15 year old youngest child. The trend for part-time workers was 14 percent to 40 percent for mothers whose youngest children were in these two age groups. This reflects mothers' views about the ages at which their children can be left unsupervised and the increasing availability of alternative care as children grow older; i.e. preschool educational provision after age three and full-time schooling from age five.

To examine this effect in our own data we compared the employment rates of mothers with no children younger than the study child with those who had one or two or more younger children; the results are presented in Figure 11.10. This shows the relationship between increasing numbers of children under the age of five and the mother's employment. As many as 82.5 percent of mothers with two or more preschool age children in addition to the study child were full-time housewives at the time of the survey compared with 46.4 percent of mothers with no children younger than the study child. More mothers with younger children had given up jobs, almost certainly because of the birth of the subsequent children. The presence of additional preschool children reduced the opportunity for mothers to work part-time or full-time outside the home and smaller proportions of these

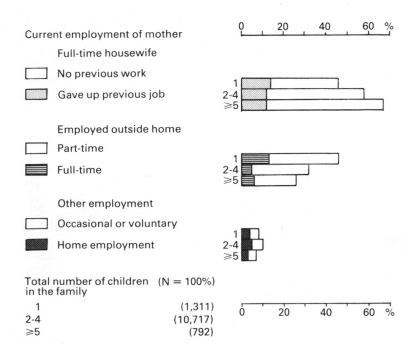

Figure 11.9 Current employment of mother by total number of children in the family

Mothers in paid employment

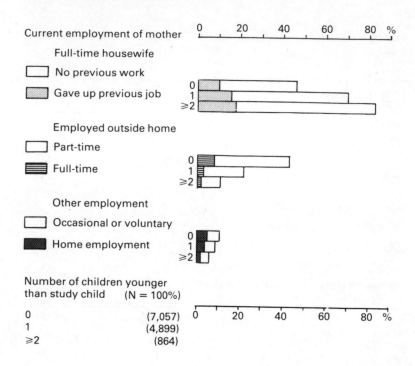

Figure 11.10 Current employment of mother by number of children younger than study child

182

mothers could even work at home or occasionally. Of all the social and family factors we have considered as possible influences on the likelihood that a mother goes out to work, the presence in the household of one or more children under the age of five is the one which most reduces the chances that a mother obtains any form of paid employment.

It is very likely that more mothers with children under five would like to have the opportunity to go out to work and this points to the need for an expansion of resources and other services which can provide day care facilities for under fives (Hughes *et al.*, 1980).

Mother's age

Young mothers are more likely to be the ones who adopt contemporary attitudes towards the role of women in society, and therefore be more avid for employment than older mothers. Young families are also at an early stage of the life cycle when they are trying to establish a home, and it is at this time that the financial need for a second income is greatest. At the same time, however, these mothers have younger children who are more demanding and for whom day care arrangements are difficult to make. There are, therefore, many conflicting pressures on women of different ages which can influence their decision to go out to work, but the age of the children in the family is likely to be the most important factor.

We found that 73 percent of mothers aged under 25 at the time of the survey had one or more children who were younger than the study child compared with only 11.3 percent of mothers aged 45 or over. Also, we know that in families where there were one or more children younger than the study child, mothers were considerably less likely to go out to work (Figure 11.11); this will be a major factor, therefore, influencing the relationship between a mother's age and her employment. Because of this it is important that in our analyses of mothers' employment related to their age we control for the presence of younger children in the family.

If we consider first the mothers with no children younger than the study child (Figure 11.11(a)) employment outside the home declined from 47.7 percent of mothers who were under 25 to 30.6 percent of those aged 45 and over. A high proportion of young mothers (15 percent) worked full-time compared with only 5.9 percent of mothers aged 45 and over. More than half (54.9 percent) of the latter group had never been employed during the previous five years compared with only a quarter (24.5 percent) of mothers who were under 25 years of age. The under twenty-fives were also more likely to have had a job which they had given up. For these mothers, in families where there were no

183

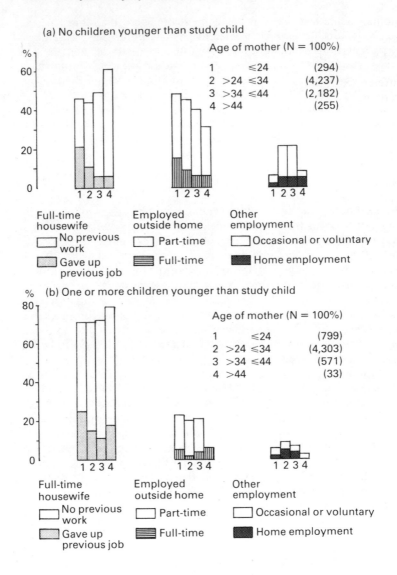

Figure 11.11 Current employment of mother by age of mother and number of children younger than the study child

children younger than the five-year-old study child, increasing age was associated with reduced likelihood of being in paid employment.

Figure 11.11(b) describes the employment situation of mothers with at least one child younger than the study child. There was no significant difference between age groups in the proportion of these mothers who were going out to work part-time, but slightly higher proportions of younger and older mothers (5 percent of mothers under 25 and 6.1 percent of mothers 45 and over) worked full-time compared with mothers aged 25-44. Young mothers were also more likely to have had jobs which they had given up at some time since their child's birth.

Our results suggest that mother's age was a significant factor in whether or not she obtained employment only after her youngest child attained school entry age. Young mothers were then more likely to obtain employment than were older mothers and this applied particularly to full-time employment. Conversely, older mothers were more likely than younger ones to have been full-time housewives for the whole five-year period since their child's birth. Young mothers may have been more motivated to seek paid employment because of the greater need for a second income in young families who were still struggling to establish themselves both in the area of housing, domestic furnishings and equipment, and in the area of the husband's job, compared with older families who were more likely to be settled and to be consolidating their social position. It may also have been the case that younger mothers were more influenced by the contemporary climate of opinion concerning women's role in society which urges greater freedom of choice for women as individuals, so that they did not necessarily see their maternal role as being incompatible with other work roles.

Summary

Throughout the 1960s and 1970s there had been a steady growth in the proportion of mothers in paid employment and, by 1980, 30 percent of mothers whose youngest child was aged under five years were going out to work. This trend is the more surprising when compared with the rising level of male unemployment during the same period. In our own sample, 32.7 percent of the mothers were employed outside the home at the time of the 1975 survey when the study children were aged five years. A further 12.5 percent had been out to work at some time since their child's birth but had given up their job and were currently full-time housewives.

The probability of whether or not a mother went out to work depended on many factors which included, 1. the mother's own wishes, 2. the financial needs of the family, 3. the demands on the mother

185

within the home, 4. the availability of day care provision, and 5. the availability of work in the locality of the mother's home. The effect on the mothers' employment rate of some of these factors can be found from the differences in the family and social circumstances of the employed and non-employed mothers in our sample.

Regional analysis showed the highest employment rates occurred in those regions where there was an established tradition of female employment; and mothers living in rural areas were the ones who were least likely to go out to work. The social and family circumstances of the mother also affected the likelihood that she would go out to work; higher employment rates were found for mothers with professional qualifications and for other mothers who were living in poor socio-economic circumstances. West Indian mothers had very high employment rates but Asian mothers were less likely to go out to work than mothers with British ancestry. Large family size resulted in fewer mothers going out to work, particularly where there were children under the age of five. After controlling for whether or not there were children in the family who were under five, increasing age of mother was associated with lower employment rates.

Only 5.8 percent of our sample of mothers worked full-time but this proportion increased if the mother was in a one-parent family or the family was socially disadvantaged. Events which increased the likelihood that a mother gave up her job were childbirth and geographical mobility.

Of all the factors examined in this chapter, the one which exerted the greatest influence on the probability that a mother did not go out to work was the presence in the family of at least one child under the age of five. Part of the reason for this is that some women limit their family size in order to be able to go out to work whilst others who wish to have more children are prepared to give up their jobs. This is not a complete explanation, however, as we know that many of the mothers who do not go out to work when their children are under five take up employment once their children reach school age. This suggests that some women with preschool age children would like to go out to work, even if only part-time, if adequate day care provision was available. The arrangements made by the employed mothers for the care of their children whilst they were absent at work are described in Chapter 14 where it would be seen that there was a heavy dependence on the family and friends rather than on formal day care facilities. These facts point to the poor levels of day care provision in Britain which means that many mothers who would like to be able to go out to work are prevented from doing so.

In the next chapter we focus on those mothers in our study who did have jobs and describe the type of work they did and how their working week was organised.

Chapter 12

Patterns of employment

We have described so far the family and social characteristics of employed mothers compared with mothers who were not in regular paid employment. In this chapter we focus on the days worked and the kind of work done by those mothers who were in regular full-time or part-time employment at home or outside the home at the time of the survey. Finally, we compare the circumstances of mothers who had worked for several years with those who had been employed for a relatively short time.

Occupational status

All the evidence concerning women's work suggests that although the proportion of women in professional and semi-professional jobs is increasing, women still hold the larger share of the least skilled and least responsible jobs in the labour market and that at all levels they tend to be concentrated in the 'traditional women's' and 'nurturing' occupations, e.g. teaching, nursing, catering, the food and clothing industries, retail sales work and clerical work (Oakley, 1974). Although women comprised little more than a third of the total labour force in 1971, more than half of all employees in unskilled manual or junior clerical jobs were women (Tizard *et al.*, 1976). Thus women employees tend to be concentrated in the lower levels of the non-manual and manual employment hierarchies.

Figure 12.1 shows that higher proportions of married women than married men were in low status occupations compared with single men and women. In particular, a higher proportion of single women than men were in social class II occupations and hardly any were in social class V. For married women, however, fewer were in social class II and more were in social class V occupations than were married men.

Key   single   married
Men   N = 367,401   1,132,396

Women   N = 247,381   539,681

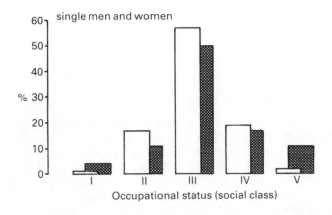

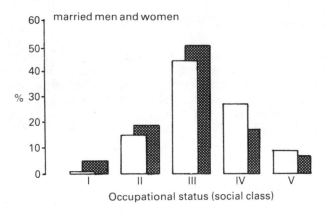

Figure 12.1   Occupational status (social class) by marital status and sex

Source: *Census*, 1971, Economic Activity Tables, Part IV (10% sample) Table 29.
Great Britain

These data demonstrate the differences in the occupational structures of men and women according to their marital status. How do these differences affect the occupational status of wives compared with their husbands? Oakley (1974, p. 10) used data from the 1971 Census to show that 94 percent of wives whose husbands were in social class I occupations would, on the basis of their own occupations, be categorised as of a lower social class. This was partly due to the low probability that both husband and wife would have been in social class I jobs. If we look at the statistics the other way round, however, we find that only 66 percent of husbands whose wives were in social class I occupations were themselves in lower status jobs. At the other end of the social scale, of the married men in social class V jobs, 77 percent had wives in higher status occupations, and of the married women in social class V jobs, 85 percent had husbands in higher status occupations. Thus at either end of the social class hierarchy, differences in occupational status favoured the men so that more wives had jobs of lower social status than their husbands than *vice versa*.

We hypothesised that women with children would suffer an exacerbation of all the employment disadvantages of women generally, since they assume a disproportionate share of family responsibilities, are frequently limited in their job choice and most often work part-time (see Chapter 11). A comparison of the occupation of the mothers' and fathers' occupation in the CHES sample (Table 12.1) shows that only 28.1 percent of the mothers had occupations in the same social class category as their husbands (i.e. those on the diagonal of the table). Part of the discrepancy is accounted for by the tendency for non-manual social class III occupations (clerical work, typing, etc.) to be done by women, and manual social class III occupations (skilled manual work) to be done by men. Table 12.1 shows that there were as many as 13.6 percent of the families in the CHES sample in which both parents were employed where the father was in a social class IIIM job and the mother was in a social class IIINM occupation. If social classes IIINM and IIIM are treated as having the same occupational status in this table, then the occupational status of 42.4 percent of these mothers was the same as their husbands'.

Thus well over half the employed mothers were in occupations of different occupational status from that of their husbands and most were of lower status. Whilst 44 percent were in lower status jobs than that of their husbands, only 13.6 percent were in higher status occupations if social class IIINM is treated as equal to social class IIIM in Table 12.1. The tendency for employed women to be in lower status occupations than their husbands which we described above is even more pronounced in this sample of mothers with young children. This contrast is shown in Figure 12.2 in which the occupational status of wives is compared with that of their husbands for three groups of couples: (a) those who were newly married for whom the occupational status of bride and groom prior to marriage was obtained, (b) married couples with employed wives, (c) parents with a child aged five in our own sample. This figure shows increasing proportions of wives who were employed in occupations of lower status than that of their husband from 27.1 percent at the time of marriage to an average 35.5 percent for all employed married women with or without children and 44.3 percent of mothers with a five-year-old child. A corresponding decrease is shown in the proportion of wives in occupations of higher status than that of their husbands across the three groups although this was not so marked as for wives whose status was lower than that of their husbands. The proportion of newly married women in higher status occupations than their husbands (21.6 percent) was not very different from the proportion in occupations of lower status than their husbands (27.1 percent); the corresponding proportions for the mothers in the CHES sample, however, was 13.3 percent and 44.3 percent.

Three reasons are suggested for this disparity in occupational status between husbands and wives with young children. Firstly, most wives give up employment on the birth of their first child and do not return until the last of perhaps several children is at school. During these years of concentrated motherhood, occupational skills acquired before marriage deteriorate, the mother feels out of touch with new developments in her trade or profession and there is often a loss of self-confidence. These factors may persuade mothers to limit their aspirations and prejudice employers against taking on women who have been unemployed for several years (Elias and Main, 1982).

We were able to examine the relationship between occupational mobility and childbirth by comparing the current occupation of the mother with her occupation before the birth of her child. For this purpose analysis was limited to those mothers for whom the study child was the first-born and who were in paid employment both before pregnancy and at the time of the five-year follow-up survey (N = 1,371). In this way we could compare the occupation of a woman when she had no children with her occupation five years after the birth of her first child. We found that half (50.8 percent) of the mothers were in occupations of the same status before and after pregnancy and 17.3 percent were in higher status occupations than they were prior to the birth of their child. Nearly a third (31.9 percent) of this group of mothers, however, were in jobs of lower status than the ones they were in previously. If so many mothers were prepared to accept jobs of lower status after only five years, a more prolonged absence from the workforce would be expected to result in even more mothers accepting jobs of lower status than they once had.

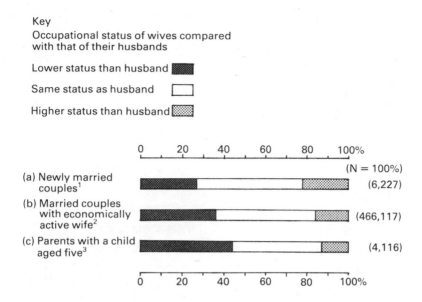

Key
Occupational status of wives compared
with that of their husbands

Lower status than husband

Same status as husband

Higher status than husband

Figure 12.2 Occupational status of wives (social class) compared with
that of their husbands[4]

Notes
1 Leete et al., 1977, p. 4. Figures reworked from Table 5.
2 *Census*, 1971, 10 percent sample, England and Wales. Economic Activity
   tables, Part IV, Table 52.
3 CHES sample – England and Wales only for optimal comparison with the
   Census data. The proportions obtained for the whole of Great Britain, however, were very similar and differed by less than 1 percent from those given.
4 OPCS (1971) social class classification of occupations was reduced to three
   categories:
   social class I and II
         IIINM and IIIM
         IV and V.

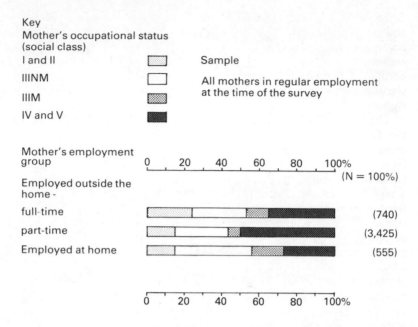

Key
Mother's occupational status
(social class)
I and II   Sample
IIINM   All mothers in regular employment
IIIM   at the time of the survey
IV and V

Mother's employment
group

Employed outside the
home -

full-time   (740)
part-time   (3,425)
Employed at home   (555)

Figure 12.3 Mother's occupational status (social class) by mother's employment group

Secondly, the difference in occupational status between husbands and wives with children is partly due to the fact that the husband continues to further his career during the period when his wife is engaged in child rearing. On her return to work, therefore, the mother's occupational status is the same, or possibly lower, than it was before starting a family whereas her husband may well have progressed to higher occupational positions.

The third reason for status inequality between husbands and wives is the fact that many mothers but few fathers take part-time jobs and these are more often of lower status than full-time occupations (Hurstfield, 1978, p. 20). The contrast between full-time and part-time employment in terms of occupational status is shown in Figure 12.3 where it can be seen that half the mothers employed part-time outside the home were doing semi-skilled or unskilled manual work (occupational classes IV and V) compared with little more than a third (34.8 percent) of those employed full-time. Conversely, the proportions of mothers in occupational classes I and II were 24.2 percent of full-time employees compared with 15 percent of those who worked part-time. Mothers who were employed at home tended to be concentrated in occupational classes IIINM (14.1 percent) and one of the more frequently mentioned jobs undertaken by these women was doing clerical work for her self-employed husband.

In Chapter 11 we showed how mothers from socially disadvantaged homes were likely to work longer hours than those who were socially advantaged (Figure 11.4). The fact that full-time employment was also associated with higher occupational status than part-time work makes the interrelationship of these three factors — social circumstances, hours of work and occupational class — worthy of further examination. This has been done in Figure 12.4 by comparing the mean Social Index scores of mothers in jobs of different occupational status for three employment groups — full-time or part-time employment outside the home and home employment.

Two clear effects can be seen to be associated with increasing mean Social Index score, i.e. increasing social disadvantage. Firstly, for all three employment groups, the upward sloping lines indicate that increasing Social Index score was associated with decreasing occupational status. Thus mothers from the poorest home and social environments were the ones most likely to be employed in semi-skilled or unskilled manual jobs. The second effect was that full-time employment outside the home was associated with higher mean Social Index scores than was part-time work for all occupational classes, and part-time employment was associated with higher mean Social Index scores than home work for all occupational classes except I and II. Thus socially advantaged mothers (with low Social Index scores) tended to work part-time in occupational status I and II jobs, whereas mothers from relatively poor homes were the ones who were most likely to work full-time outside the home in semi-skilled or unskilled manual jobs (classes IV and V). For socially advantaged mothers, therefore, the world of work was possibly a poor escape from a depressing home environment although many welcomed the social contact with others (see Chapter 13).

Mothers who worked at home in occupational class I and II jobs did not fit in with the general pattern shown in Figure 12.4 in that their mean Social Index score was considerably higher than that of mothers who were employed part-time outside the home in jobs with the same occupational class. This result was almost certainly due to mothers whose husbands were self-employed describing their occupations as 'company director' or 'company secretary' because of business and tax benefits deriving from this. Many of these women would in fact have been engaged in routine clerical or secretarial work for the family business and a more appropriate occupational class might have been IIINM. Indeed, the mean Social Index score of these mothers was much closer to that of other home workers doing class IIINM jobs.

On the whole, however, regular work at home was associated with lower mean Social Index scores, i.e. was carried out by relatively advantaged mothers. One reason for this could be that higher proportions of socially advantaged mothers had skills which enabled them to work at home. A second possibility is that the income resulting from home employment may have been so low that socially disadvantaged mothers who worked mainly for reasons of financial need were more likely to seek better paid employment outside the home.

Days worked

One method by which working mothers overcome the problem of day-care for their young children is to work what might be termed 'unsocial hours', i.e. to work at times when their husbands or other adult members of the household are at home, in the evenings, early mornings, or at weekends. In a 1965 survey of women's employment (Hunt, 1968), 6.5 percent of employed mothers worked evenings, early mornings or overnight. By comparison among employed mothers without children, only 1.5 percent worked during these hours, emphasising again that the pattern of employment among mothers reflects the need to rely on other members of the family for child care. The OPCS *Protective Legislation Survey* (Marsh, 1979) estimated that 11 percent of mothers with children under five in areas of high female employment worked weekends. Women with children of school age or less also work variable

Sample: All mothers in regular employment at the time of the survey

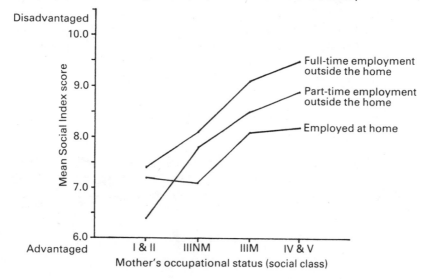

Figure 12.4 Mean Social Index score by mother's occupational status for three employment groups

Mothers in paid employment

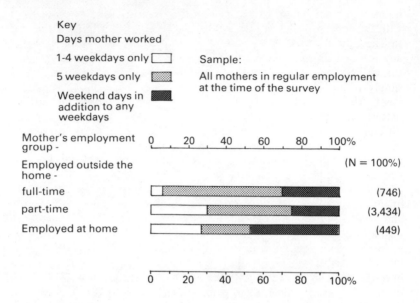

Figure 12.5   Days mother worked by mother's employment group

196

hours of no set pattern in order to fit in their hours of employment with the demands of their family responsibilities (Hunt *et al.*, 1973).

The great variation in the pattern of working amongst mothers defies any form of simple classification. For our present purposes, therefore, the CHES data on mothers' patterns of employment will be described simply in terms of the days worked during their last week of employment. This method overcomes the problem of describing the work pattern of mothers, who, although regularly employed, worked at different times from one week to the next. The majority (80.4 percent) of employed mothers, however, confirmed that the pattern of employment described was the same every week. Regularity of employment was similar for full-time and part-time work except that a higher than average proportion of full-time workers (8.5 percent) worked shifts. As might be expected, home workers had the most varied work pattern and over half (55.5 percent) of these mothers reported that they had no regular routine.

Mothers employed at weekends were considered to be working unsocial hours insofar as Saturdays and Sundays are times when families have the most opportunity to be together. Weekend employment may be more significant in this respect than evening work which the mothers were able to do after the children had gone to bed.

Table 12.2 shows that most employed mothers worked weekdays only (71.7 percent) and that many (45.7 percent of all employed mothers) worked a five day week. Only 3.2 percent of all employed mothers worked just at weekends but as many as 25.1 percent worked Saturday or Sunday in addition to during the week making a total of 28.3 percent working weekends. Figure 12.5 suggests that full-time workers were more likely to work a five day week (64 percent) than at weekends (29.6 percent) in order to bring their working hours to over thirty. Part-time workers were employed at weekends only slightly less frequently than the full-timers (25.4 percent). Home-workers, however, were much more likely to work weekends (47.4 percent).

In the absence of information about the extent to which other economically active groups are employed at weekends, it is hard to say whether the proportion of these mothers employed Saturdays and Sundays is high or low. However, almost one in three of these employed mothers, which is about one in ten of all mothers in the sample, were employed at home or outside the home for part of the weekend and the majority of these also worked at least some days during the week.

It was hypothesised that socially disadvantaged mothers would be more likely to work unsocial hours than advantaged mothers because greater need to work and less opportunity for making regular arrangements for the care of their preschool children was a pattern expected to be more common in the former group. An analysis of days worked by

Social Index score tended to support this hypothesis as with increasing social disadvantage greater proportions of mothers were employed at weekends. The difference was fairly small, however, with the trend going from 22.2 percent of the most advantaged to 31 percent of the most disadvantaged mothers working weekends. The most common pattern of working amongst the most disadvantaged mothers was a five day week from Monday to Friday (51.2 percent) and comparatively few worked 1 to 4 weekdays (17.8 percent). In contrast, as many as 42 percent of the most advantaged mothers worked 1 to 4 weekdays.

The type of work the mother did could have been an influencing factor in producing these differences in patterns of employment according to the mother's social circumstances if disadvantaged mothers were doing jobs which were more amenable to weekend employment. Therefore we compared the days worked by mothers from different Social Index groups for those in (a) non-manual and (b) manual occupations; these results are presented in Figure 12.6.

Firstly, over 40 percent of the most advantaged mothers worked 1 to 4 weekdays compared with under 20 percent of the most disadvantaged mothers. Thus socially advantaged mothers who were regularly employed were likely to work less than five days a week and not at weekends. This held for advantaged mothers in both manual and non-manual occupations.

Secondly, for manual workers there was a very marked difference between the advantaged and disadvantaged mothers in the proportion who were working a five day week from Monday to Friday. Up to 57 percent of the disadvantaged mothers in manual occupations worked five weekdays compared with only 28.4 percent of the most advantaged mothers. This social difference did not occur, however, in the mothers employed in non-manual occupations. We suggest that the reason for these differences is that socially disadvantaged mothers were prepared to work five days a week doing what would frequently have been onerous semi-skilled and unskilled manual work, whereas few advantaged mothers would have been so prepared. Non-manual occupations, however, were possibly less physically arduous and more acceptable work for women to do, thus no social differences appeared in the proportion of mothers working Monday to Friday in these types of job.

Finally, social differences in the proportions of mothers who worked weekends were found only where mothers were in non-manual occupations; there was no social difference in the proportion of mothers in manual jobs who worked at weekends. 21.7 percent of the most advantaged mothers in non-manual jobs worked weekends compared with 42.5 percent of the disadvantaged mothers. Why did more disadvantaged mothers in non-manual occupations work weekends compared with advantaged mothers? We suggest that this was because the type of

Key

Social Index group
1 Most advantaged
2 Advantaged
3 Average
4 Disadvantaged
5 Most disadvantaged

Sample:

All mothers in regular employment
at the time of the survey

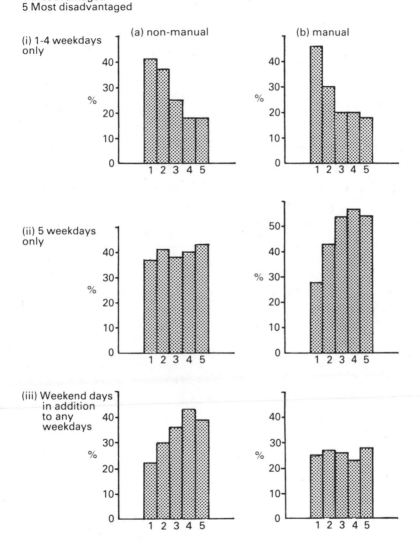

Figure 12.6 Days mother worked by mother's occupational status and
Social Index group

Mothers in paid employment

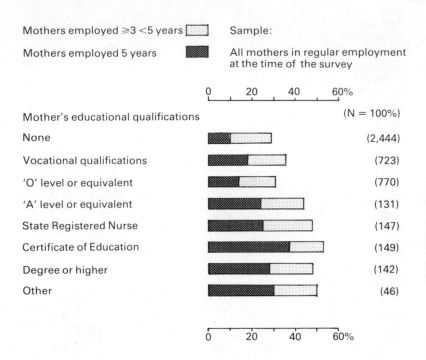

Figure 12.7 Number of years employed by highest educational quali-fication of mother

non-manual work that was being done by disadvantaged mothers was amenable to weekend working, e.g. Saturday shop assistants, whereas the type of work being done by socially advantaged mothers was less so, e.g. office work.

These are, of course *post hoc* explanations for observed social differences in the pattern of days employed and thus require more investigation. Our original hypothesis, however, has been partially supported — more socially disadvantaged mothers worked weekends than did advantaged mothers although this applied only to non-manual occupations. The general picture gained from these analyses is that socially disadvantaged mothers worked a full five-day week or at weekends whereas advantaged mothers were less inclined to work weekends and were more likely to work less than five weekdays. It is clear from these results, also, that the type of job a mother had was likely to be an important factor in her work pattern. It is possible, also, that many women seek out jobs that enable them to work hours that fit in with their family responsibilities.

Whilst there is no evidence from the CHES data on the effects on family life of either the father or the mother working unsocial hours on a regular basis, it is obvious that this reduces the opportunity for all members of the family to enjoy leisure periods together and this is a deprivation of normal family life. It is a particular cause for concern that this pattern of working occurs most frequently among families who are already disadvantaged.

Number of years employed

Very few mothers return to work as quickly as two years after the birth of their baby (Elias and Main, 1982, Figure 2.3), and only 11.5 percent of all the mothers in the CHES sample had been out to work for three or more years in the five-year period since their child was born. However, this represents as many as one in three (32.9 percent) of all mothers who were in regular paid employment at the time of the survey, and a number of factors contributed to the likelihood that a mother had been employed for most of her child's first five years. The mother's education and training was one such factor.

Figure 12.7 shows that working mothers with educational qualifications at GCE 'A' level and above were more likely to have worked for three years or more than were mothers with lower level qualifications. This applied especially to teachers of whom more than half (53 percent) had worked for at least three years and 36.9 percent for the whole five years since their child's birth. Comparable figures for working mothers without qualifications were 28.7 percent and 9.7 percent respectively. Thus mothers with higher educational or professional qualifications were not only the ones who were most likely to obtain employment (see Chapter 11) but those who were employed tended to have been working for more years than mothers without qualifications or with only minimal qualifications. These results suggest that professional qualifications provide the means of access to occupations of sufficient flexibility to enable many mothers with very young children to accommodate the demands of both employment and family responsibilities. A mother's education, however, may also be indicative of different attitudes towards family life and her employment. For example, a qualified teacher may feel a greater personal need to continue teaching, notwithstanding the domestic difficulties, than does a mother for whom employment is not seen as a career or profession. Indeed, teachers, nurses, social workers and other qualified professionals need to maintain continuous employment in order to retain or further their professional status.

Another factor which may strongly influence a mother's attitude towards employment is her ethnic origin. We have shown in Chapter 11 that West Indian mothers were far more likely to be employed than were European (UK) mothers, and that Asian mothers were the least likely to have a job. Figure 12.8 shows that West Indian mothers were not only more likely to be employed, the majority (59.4 percent) of those who were working had done so for more than half the child's preschool period and one in five (19.8 percent) for the whole five years. This compares with 30.5 percent of employed Asian mothers and 32.1 percent of European (UK) mothers who had worked for at least three years.

The birth of subsequent children was expected to affect the number of years a mother had worked during the preschool period of the study child, and Figure 12.9 shows that a higher proportion of mothers with no children younger than the study child had worked for at least three years (34.9 percent) compared with mothers with two or more children younger than the study child (24.8 percent). This difference, however, was small compared with the substantial effect the presence of younger siblings had on the probability that the mother had a job at all (Chapter 11); indeed the proportion of working mothers who were employed for the whole of the child's preschool period was unaffected by the number of younger siblings.

A second type of family change that was expected to have implications for the duration of the mother's employment was family mobility. We have already shown that moving house increased the probability that mothers gave up their jobs (Chapter 11), and Figure 12.10 suggests that there was also a tendency for the duration of employment of mothers who had moved house to be shorter than that of mothers who

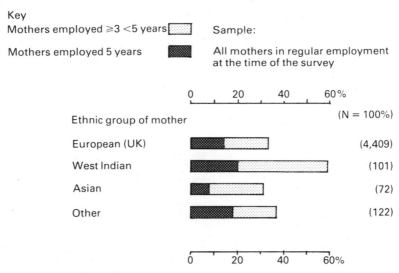

Figure 12.8   Number of years employed by ethnic group of mother

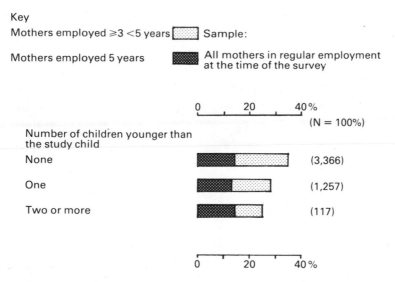

Figure 12.9   Number of years employed by number of children younger than study child

Mothers in paid employment

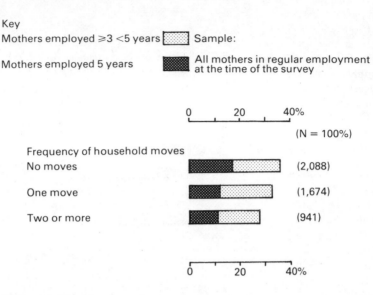

Key
Mothers employed ≥3 <5 years ▨ Sample:

Mothers employed 5 years ■ All mothers in regular employment at the time of the survey

Figure 12.10 Number of years employed by frequency of household moves

had never moved.

From these figures we can see that changes in family circumstances such as the birth of subsequent siblings and household moves made little difference to the number of years these mothers had worked compared with the mother's educational qualifications or ethnicity. We suggest that a mother's attitude towards employment is the key factor influencing the number of years she worked.

For West Indian women the custom is that they return to work as soon as possible after having their children (Pollack, 1972); the West Indian culture, therefore, in contrast to that of the indigenous British population, serves to endorse rather than discourage the employment of mothers. This positive attitude towards employment would result in the high employment rate of West Indian mothers described in Chapter 11 and also the tendency for many of these mothers to have been working for the greater part of the five years since their child's birth.

The attitudes of the West Indian mothers were prescribed by their culture, but the attitudes of working mothers with higher qualifications were likely to have derived from their commitment to a profession or career (Holmstrom, 1972; Rapoport and Rapoport, 1971). Such a commitment would have provided an incentive encouraging the mother's prompt return to work after having the baby in order to minimise any discontinuity which might have impeded her career prospects. The mother's attitudes towards their work are explored further in the next chapter where we describe how the reasons why they work varied according to their social and family circumstances.

Summary

Fewer women than men are in high status occupations. This difference is larger for married women and larger still for women with children. Married women who are employed are likely to be in lower status jobs than their husbands and, again, this difference is increased in families with dependent children. In our own study, one in three of the mothers who were employed at the time of the survey were in jobs of lower status than the one they were in prior to having their baby, and as many as 44 percent were in occupations of lower status than their husbands. Nearly half (45 percent) of these employed mothers with five-year-old children were doing routine semi-skilled or unskilled manual work compared with only 18 percent of all the fathers in the study.

Socially disadvantaged employed mothers were more likely than socially advantaged mothers to be in full-time, low status occupations and to work at weekends. The pattern of employment of these mothers depended on the relationships between their domestic responsibilities, their perceived needs and aspirations, job opportunities and the availability of day-care for their children. We suggest that the acceptance of low status work was the result of a compromise between the mother's desire to obtain employment, for whatever reason, and her acceptance of the major responsibility for the day-to-day care of the children which led also to a demand for part-time employment at times when other family members were available to look after the children.

One in three of all mothers who were employed at the time of the survey had worked for three years or more during the five years since the child's birth. Mothers of West Indian origin and those with higher level qualifications were the ones who were most likely to have worked this many years. Mothers with other children who were younger than the study child and those who had moved house were slightly less likely to have worked for three years or more. These factors were of less significance, however, than the mother's ethnic origin or education.

The fact that so many of the mothers in our study were prepared to accept low status jobs and work unsocial hours suggests that their desire or need to go out to work was very great. In the next chapter, therefore, we discuss the mother's own views on why they were in paid employment.

Chapter 13

Mothers' attitudes towards employment

In the previous two chapters we have shown that social conditions and family circumstances are important factors influencing the likelihood that a mother goes out to work. The mother's own needs and aspirations, however, may also be persuasive elements in her decision to seek employment. In this chapter, therefore, we compare the employed and non-employed mothers in terms of their attitudes towards certain maternal roles, and investigate whether their expressed reasons for working varied according to the social and family circumstances of the employed mothers.

Attitudes towards maternal roles

There is a considerable body of research and comment on the demands of motherhood, the way in which marriage is generally exploitative of wives and how the lives of mothers might be improved, for example by the provision of more day care for young children (Hughes *et al.*, 1980; Oakley, 1981; Pringle, 1980(b)). Apart from anecdotal evidence, however, we have been unable to find any attempt to ascertain what mothers themselves think about some of these issues which are discussed so often by experts. We have attempted to fill this gap by inviting the mothers in our study to express their opinions about a number of relevant issues which include maternal employment and the position of women in society. This has been done by means of an attitude scale comprising forty-three items (see Appendix, Maternal Self-completion Questionnaire). Using the results from the items in the scale concerned with sex equality, the quality of life of women and maternal employment, we have compared the responses of employed mothers with those of non-employed mothers to see whether the opinions of these two groups differed. These results are presented in Tables 13.1 and 13.2.

We hypothesised that mothers who went out to work would be more radical in their views on sex equality than mothers who were not employed, whilst the latter might be expected to have a more traditional attitude towards the roles of men and women. This proved not to be the case, however, as the pattern of responses to the first four items in Table 13.1 was much the same for both housewives and employees. About 80 percent of the mothers thought that 'women should have the same work opportunities as men', and more than 85 percent disagreed with the view that 'girls should accept marriage and motherhood and not start a career'. These results suggest a much stronger commitment to sex equality in employment in Britain than was found in the United States in 1973. A survey carried out in Washington found that 44 percent of women were not in favour of more women being employed although this proportion reduced to 28 percent in women younger than 35 (Hoffman and Nye, 1974, p. 12).

The small statistically significant differences between the employed and non-employed mothers in our sample indicate slightly larger proportions of the former favouring sex equality, but the differences are very small. More than three quarters of the mothers believed that 'girls are as capable as boys of learning to be engineers' — traditionally a man's occupation — although as many as 13 percent were undecided about this. There was no difference at all between the employed and non-employed mothers in their views on the potential engineering capability of girls. Neither did they differ in their views concerning the position of the husband as the head of the household. It is surprising that in 1975 when in most families the mothers were responsible for the day-to-day running of the home, more than half of the mothers in our sample held the view that their 'husband ought to have the main say-so in family matters'.

Over 80 percent of the mothers thought that 'women need something more from life than they can get by just looking after the home and children', and about the same proportion felt that 'mothers need a break from their children from time to time during the day'. These views were held somewhat more strongly by the employed mothers for whom going out to work might have increased their independence and self-esteem and provided social contact which they felt was lacking in their role as housewife and mother.

The largest differences between employed and non-employed mothers were in their attitudes towards whether or not mothers ought to go out to work. All the items in Table 13.2 show that there was greater opposition to the idea of mothers going out to work amongst the non-employed mothers than in the employed group. Indeed, it would be surprising if such a difference in attitude had not resulted from the responses to these items. What is of greater importance, however, is that, despite the large differences between employed and non-employed mothers, there were sizeable proportions of employed mothers who, according to their responses to these items, believed that mothers of young children ought not to go out to work. More than half (51.2 percent) agreed that 'a mother's proper place is at home with her children', 19.8 percent agreed that 'a mother who leaves her children with someone else in order to go out to work is not fit to be a mother unless she needs the money for food and clothes', 12.3 percent disagreed with the view that 'there is nothing wrong with a mother going out to work if her children can be properly cared for by someone else', 23.5 percent thought that 'a wife must sacrifice her right to go out to work once she has children' and 20 percent were opposed to the opening of more State run day nurseries. It is worrying that this substantial minority of mothers were going out to work when they believed they ought to be at home with their children. These were mainly mothers who were in semi-skilled or unskilled manual employment where the level of job satisfaction is likely to be low and thus engender a negative attitude towards their work. Such a contradiction between a mother's beliefs about her maternal role and her actual employment status, however, is likely to engender stress which is not only detrimental to the mother's health but is likely to have adverse consequences for the emotional and behavioural adjustment of her children.

The other type of contradiction shown in Table 13.2 concerns the non-employed mothers who expressed the belief that mothers should be able to go out to work. It is possible that many of these mothers experienced frustration because of not having a paid job. Nearly two thirds (61.1 percent) of the non-employed mothers thought that the State should provide more day nurseries so that mothers could go out to work. Two thirds believed that 'there is nothing wrong with a mother going out to work if her children can be properly cared for by someone else', over half (51.8 percent) did not agree that 'a wife must sacrifice her right to go out to work once she has children'. Thus the opinion of the majority of full-time housewives was that mothers with young children should be able to go out to work if they want to. At the same time, however, three quarters of these mothers (74.5 percent) agreed that 'a mother's proper place is at home with her children'. This illustrates the dilemma faced by many mothers who would like to be able to go out to work but are unable to find adequate alternative care for their children. Further evidence of this was found in a survey which was carried out on our sample of children who at age three years were living in the South West region of England and South Wales. Of the 707 mothers in the survey who were not employed at that time 73 percent said that the main reason why they did not go out to work was the need to look after their children, and only 13 percent said it was because they did not wish to go out to work. Many mothers would be satisfied with a part-time job which they could fit into the hours during which their children attended nursery school or playgroup, but there is insufficient flexibility in the labour market to accommodate this pattern of employment.

To take the analysis of these attitudinal data a stage further we carried out a principal components analysis on the five items in Table 13.2 in which the first component explained 48.8 percent of the total variance in the five items. This confirmed their homogeneity as a set of items having a common underlying dimension representing attitudes towards maternal employment. The component scores, which were produced by the same procedures as is described in Chapter 19 for the behaviour scales, conformed to a standard normal distribution (mean of zero, standard deviation of one) in which respondents with high scores favoured the employment of mothers whilst those with low scores were relatively opposed.

This scale was used as the dependent variable in the analysis of variance presented in Figure 13.1. Here, the effect of the mother's current employment status on her attitudes towards maternal employment is compared with her socioeconomic circumstances (Social Index score), age and educational qualifications. It is immediately apparent from this diagram that the mother's current employment had a far greater independent effect on her attitude towards maternal employment than the other variables in the analysis; with the largest difference in opinion occurring between full-time housewives and mothers employed full-time outside the home (.95 SDs).

This difference in attitude towards maternal employment between employed and non-employed mothers reflects the general pattern of results in Table 13.2. The more favourable attitude towards maternal employment in the employed group of mothers is partly due to the fact that mothers who were strongly committed to this view were more likely to be the ones who would seek employment, and also mothers would attempt to minimise dissonance between their actual employment status and their responses to the attitude items (Festinger, 1957).

A favourable attitude towards maternal employment was also more likely to be found in younger mothers, socially disadvantaged mothers and mothers with professional qualifications (i.e. nursing, teaching, degree level or higher qualifications). The difference attributed to the mother's age reflects a greater commitment to traditional beliefs in older mothers, whilst young mothers are more willing to adopt modern ideas. The comparison between socioeconomic position (Social Index score) and mother's education is interesting in that both professionally qualified mothers, who were the least likely ones to be socially disadvantaged, and those who were socially disadvantaged expressed

Analysis of variance: the effects of all independent variables are adjusted for the others

Sample size: 12,052

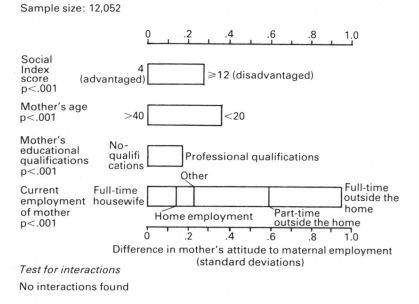

Test for interactions

No interactions found

Figure 13.1 Analysis of mother's attitude towards maternal employment

favourable attitudes towards maternal employment. We suggest, how-ever, that the reasons for their shared beliefs were likely to be quite different in that the socially disadvantaged mother would favour employment as a means of reducing financial hardship, whereas the professionally qualified mother is anxious to pursue her career at least partly for reasons of personal satisfaction.

Reasons why mothers go to work

Certain ideological assumptions are involved in asking mothers 'Why do you work?', a question whose equivalent in a study of men's work attitudes is 'Why aren't you working?' (Oakley, 1974). The question carries the implication that it is the mother who should assume the major responsibility for child-care and domestic arrangements rather than that these roles might be shared between the parents, and that paid work for mothers, if it is considered at all, is only a secondary consideration. Nevertheless we justify the use of the question on several grounds; one is that it reflects views about the role of mothers which, as we have demonstrated above, are still widely held in Britain – quite frequently by working mothers themselves – secondly it enables com-parisons to be made with earlier studies which have also asked this question, and thirdly the reasons which prompt a mother to work out-side the home have an important direct effect on the family situation because:

> If she goes unwillingly to work for reasons of sheer economic
> necessity, the result, in terms of her own and her children's reactions
> will be very different from the results when she works to escape
> from the loneliness of the restricted life she leads with a small
> family in a block of flats. (Yudkin and Holme, 1963, p. 43)

The implications for the family are likely to be different again if a mother has an interest in and involvement with the work she is doing.

The responses to the question of why a mother works are inevitably highly subjective as many mothers may take a job for, say, social reasons but then come to depend on the extra income and eventually define the income as 'essential'. Responses may also be influenced by the degree to which working mothers who might assume societal disapproval, experience a sense of guilt. Thus mothers could believe that working from necessity appears more acceptable than working for social or career reasons which may seem to spring from selfish motives. Whatever the deep-rooted motivations and social mores which prompt particular responses to the question of why mothers work, the differences in response provide some insights into the varied perceptions of mothers in different social, educational and family circumstances.

In 1963, Yudkin and Holme found that financial reasons were by far the most important single factor influencing mothers to take paid employment. However, only 13.4 percent of their sample of mothers gave absolute financial necessity as the main reason for working. A far higher proportion, 70.2 percent, were working to improve the standard of living of their family and 16.4 percent worked to escape boredom at home or because they enjoyed the companionship at work, for professional or vocational interest or for other non-financial reasons.

More recently, Banfield (1978) has shown that maternal employment rates fall as the level of family income from the father's employment and other sources increases. However, the age of the mother's youngest child was shown to be a more important factor in whether or not the mother went out to work than was family income. Other research suggests that financial considerations are still the basic reason why mothers go out to work, although other aspects of the job situation such as companionship and social stimulation, enjoyment of the work itself and dissatisfaction and boredom with life at home are reported as being very important contributory factors in the mother's motivation to seek employment (Tizard *et al.*, 1976; Mayall and Petrie, 1977; Moss *et al.*, 1973). As many as 21 out of 27 mothers in the Mayall and Petrie study said that they would still go out to work if more money were available from another source. This suggests that, despite the low status of many women's jobs, most employed mothers find more satisfaction in working than in staying at home all day and that some see work as an escape from 'isolated, unsatisfactory and stressful' lives (Tizard *et al.*, 1976, p. 151).

Ann Oakley's (1974) finding that 70 percent of women from both her middle class and working class samples of mothers were dissatisfied with their position as housewives adds support to this, although more working class than middle class women in her sample saw housework as an appropriate role for women, even though they disliked doing it.

These studies have shown that a mother's reasons for working are complex and that her responses depend a lot on the wording of the question asked. In general the results of previous enquiries suggest that money is a fundamental reason for working but that other motivations such as enjoyment of the work, social contact and escape from housework are also important contributory factors.

As in these previous studies many mothers in our sample gave more than one reason why they were employed and these are reported in Table 13.3. In this table financial reasons are contrasted with social or career reasons for being in paid employment. 'Social reasons' included working for the company of others at work, making friends and relief of boredom — where the social contact at work rather than the work itself was important. 'Career reasons' was coded if the mother indicated that she enjoyed the job itself or if she saw her job as a career. Financial reasons were mentioned by 78 percent of the regularly employed mothers. This is only slightly fewer than the 83.6 percent of employed mothers in Yudkin and Holme's study (1963) who worked from absolute financial necessity or to improve their standard of living.

A total of 60.8 percent of the employed mothers in our sample mentioned social, career, family business or other reasons for working. Thus there was a considerable overlap in the financial and social/career reasons why the mothers worked so that as many as 38.8 percent of the employed mothers gave both types of reason for working, 39.2 percent gave only financial reasons and 22 percent gave only social/career reasons. These figures demonstrate the prominence given by these mothers to the financial aspects of their employment, whilst the social and career aspects were for the majority of mothers likely to be a secondary but none the less important consideration.

We have attempted to distinguish between mothers who worked from financial necessity (contribution to housekeeping, rent, purchase of clothes, etc.) and those who worked for financial advantage (savings, household appliances, luxuries, car, to gain independence). We recognise, however, that the distinctions between 'necessity' and 'extras' are arbitrary and are sure to be influenced by a mother's experience and expectations. What is defined as a taken for granted necessity by one household, e.g. holidays, a car and decent clothes, may be thought of as luxuries by families who find it difficult to make ends meet. Nevertheless, the results do provide an insight into the mother's perceptions of her reasons for working.

We found that 22.5 percent of working mothers reported that they worked because of financial necessity with no other reason given. A further 20.1 percent mentioned other reasons as well as financial necessity. Mothers who were not working from financial necessity, however, were likely to mention a combination of reasons which suggested that they enjoyed their work experience and also welcomed the extra income which resulted from it.

To overcome the problem of trying to resolve the complexities resulting from all the different combinations of reasons for working given by these mothers as presented in Table 13.3, we asked the mothers to specify what they believed to be the *main* reason why they were in paid employment. This is reported in Table 13.4 which shows an increased emphasis on the financial aspect of employment. Thus, for example, although in Table 13.3 a total of 27.6 percent of employed mothers mentioned their career as one of their reasons for working, Table 13.4 shows that only 10.6 percent of all employed mothers said that this was the main reason. Similarly the 39.9 percent of employed mothers who mentioned social factors as one of their reasons for working was reduced to 20.5 percent who saw this as the main reason. Conversely, 36.2 percent of the mothers gave financial necessity as the main reason for working compared with 42.6 percent who mentioned this reason at all, which was a much smaller reduction than in the previous two examples.

These figures confirm the general conclusions of earlier studies that mothers work mainly for the income that employment brings but that many of them enjoy the company and work they do in addition to the financial benefits. In this they are probably no different from most other employed people, whether men or women. However, mothers constitute a special case in that they are still seen as the central figure in the family responsible for child care and socialisation. This is despite a limited increase in recent years in the father's share of the domestic and child-care responsibilities at home (see Chapter 4 and Osborn and Morris, 1982).

The majority of women who are not mothers have jobs (see Chapter 11), thus it could be said that it is 'normal' in Western industrialised societies for women to be employed. This merely emphasises the anomalies inherent in the situation of mothers who face a conflict between realising their expectations as women and fulfilling their socially defined maternal responsibilities. Thus a mother's reasons for working provides a useful insight into how she rationalises her decision to obtain a job and make other arrangements for the care of her child in the face of still strong social pressures to focus all her energies on her maternal role.

Social variation in reasons given for working

We hypothesised that socially disadvantaged mothers, mothers in low status occupations and those working long hours at unsocial times would be the ones who were most likely to define their main reason for working in terms of financial need. Mothers with professional qualifications in high status occupations, however, were expected to be more likely to mention their career or interest in the job as reasons for working. These hypotheses embody the idea that a mother's perceptions of why she works may be as much a reflection of the degree of intrinsic satisfaction she experiences from her job as an account of her original motive for seeking employment.

Previous research suggests that mothers' reasons for working vary with their socioeconomic position and their education. A study of two samples of mothers — one in Kirkby, a predominantly working class

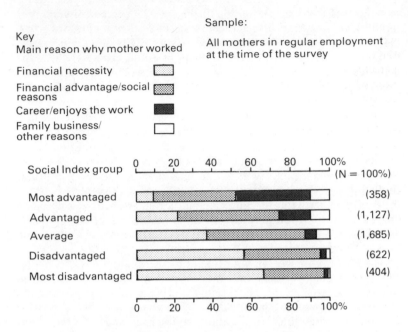

Key
Main reason why mother worked

Financial necessity

Financial advantage/social reasons

Career/enjoys the work

Family business/ other reasons

Sample:

All mothers in regular employment at the time of the survey

Social Index group

Most advantaged (358)
Advantaged (1,127)
Average (1,685)
Disadvantaged (622)
Most disadvantaged (404)

Figure 13.2 Main reason why mother worked by Social Index group

216

area near Liverpool, and the other in a socially mixed area in London — found that of those mothers who said that they would like to return to work immediately, 68 percent in Kirkby mentioned money as one of the reasons for this as opposed to 33 percent in London. However, 46 percent and 47 percent respectively in the two areas referred to the need for social contact and a break from home as a motive for returning to work. This suggests that the latter reasons occur equally in all social groups, whilst financial reasons are mentioned more frequently by working class women (Moss *et al.*, 1973). In the Government Social Survey of women's employment (Hunt, 1968), 68 percent of manual workers' wives, as against 52 percent of non-manual workers' wives, gave financial reasons for returning to work. Only 3.1 percent of married women in households with children gave 'interest in specific field of work or to use qualifications' as reasons for resuming work. However, amongst those who finished their education at 19 or over, the proportion giving these reasons rose to 21 percent. As we shall show below, this would be an under-estimate of the current significance of vocational or professional motives for mothers working, as in the mid-1960s, when Hunt carried out her survey, the rapid growth of further education for women had not yet had its full impact on women in their twenties and thirties (Tizard *et al.*, 1976, p. 150).

The socioeconomic circumstances of the families in our study had a marked effect on the reasons mothers gave for being employed. Figure 13.2 shows a steep trend from 8.9 percent of the most advantaged to 65.6 percent of the most disadvantaged mothers who said they worked for reasons of financial necessity. A reverse trend was found in the proportion of mothers who gave career or enjoyment of the work as the main reason why they worked. This went from 38 percent of the most advantaged mothers to only two percent of the most disadvantaged mothers. Advantaged mothers were also more likely than disadvantaged mothers to work for social reasons.

Thus there was a strong correspondence between the Social Index, an objective indicator of the mother's social situation which suggested the degree to which additional family income might be needed, and her perceived main reason for working. These results again suggest a qualitative difference in the work experience of socially disadvantaged mothers compared with socially advantaged mothers which we noted in Chapter 12. For many of the former, employment and its benefits were seen in purely extrinsic terms, i.e. the additional family income needed for the purchase of essential things like food, clothes and payment of rent. Mothers not in socially disadvantaged circumstances, however, who did not work from sheer necessity, were perhaps more inclined to see their employment as an end in itself and as an enjoyable activity or part of their career.

Other mothers of whom high proportions said they worked from economic necessity (see Table 13.5) were those living in poor neighbourhoods (60.1 percent), lone mothers (83.4 percent), supported single-parent mothers (73.2 percent), Asian mothers (66.2 percent) and West Indian mothers (81.1 percent) compared with 36.2 percent of all mothers. Mothers who were most likely to work because they enjoyed the work or saw their job as a career were those with professional qualifications such as SRN (33.9 percent), teacher's certificate (45.3 percent) and mothers with degrees or higher qualifications (59.8 percent) compared with an average of 10.6 percent of all mothers.

These results offer consistent evidence that the employed mothers in potentially stressful or disadvantaged social situations often described their main reason for working as being that of financial necessity. Mothers in average or better than average social circumstances tended to give reasons in terms of financial advantage or social factors. Finally, it was mothers who were professionally qualified who asserted that the pursuit of a career was their main reason for working.

Type of employment and reason for working

Although social and family factors are important influences on a mother's motivation to obtain paid employment, the actual job the mother does is also likely to influence the mother's attitude towards her employment. Mothers engaged for many hours a week in routine and arduous manual work are more likely to do this from necessity than from choice. Mothers employed for only a few hours a week doing work they find interesting are, perhaps, more inclined to say they do this for social or career reasons. Figures 13.3 and 13.4 give some indication that this is so although it should be noted that the type of work a mother did was strongly associated with her social situation (Chapters 11 and 12) which as we have seen (Figure 13.2) also related to her reasons for working.

Figure 13.3 shows that the majority of mothers employed full-time outside the home said the main reason they worked was financial necessity (56.3 percent) compared with only a third (33.9 percent) of part-time workers and a quarter (24.3 percent) of home workers. Thus mothers with a strong work commitment, i.e. the full-time workers, were more inclined to define their employment as economically essential than were the mothers in the other employment groups. Higher proportions of mothers working part-time gave financial advantage, social factors or career as reasons for working compared with full-time workers and home workers. A large proportion of home workers (31.6 percent) gave their family business as the main reason for working

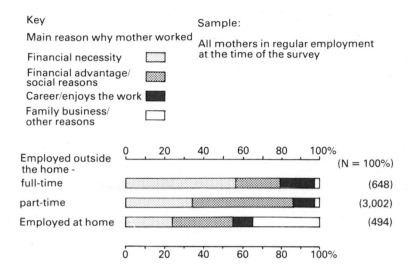

Figure 13.3 Main reason why mother worked by mother's employment group

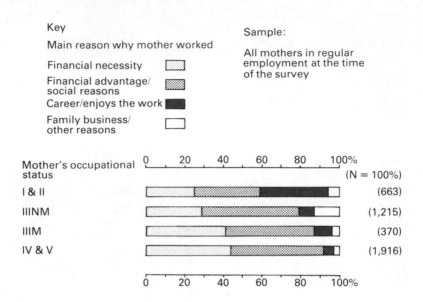

Figure 13.4 Main reason why mother worked by mother's occupational status

compared with less than 2 percent of full-time and part-time workers outside the home. These results suggest that mothers who work more than thirty hours a week do so because they feel the need to do so financially whereas part-time workers see their employment as a more enjoyable experience or as having financial advantages.

It was hypothesised that financial necessity would be the main reason for working given by mothers doing low status manual work. Figure 13.4 indicates that higher than average proportions of mothers in manual employment worked from financial necessity and the overall trend went from 25.3 percent of mothers in social class I and II occupations to 43.5 percent of those in social class IV and V occupations. Similarly, 19 percent of social class I and II mothers gave financial advantage as their main reason for working compared with 28.2 percent of mothers who were doing semi-skilled and unskilled manual work.

Most of the mothers in professional and managerial occupations (social classes I and II) had degrees or were qualified teachers or nurses. Therefore the 34.7 percent of these mothers who worked for career reasons or because they enjoyed the work roughly corresponds with the proportions of mothers with these qualifications (Table 13.5). In comparison only 4.2 percent of mothers in social class IV and V occupations gave these as the main reason for working.

Thus we have found that both home situation and the status level of the mother's occupation were associated with their expressed reasons for being employed. In Figure 13.5, therefore, we show the mothers' main reasons for working in terms of both home and occupational situations together. In this diagram can be seen the same hierarchy of 'main reasons why the mother worked' for each occupational status level. Thus no matter what kind of job the mother had, from professional/managerial occupations to semi-skilled/unskilled manual work, the mothers who reported that they were working because of financial necessity were those who were the most socially disadvantaged (i.e. had the highest mean Social Index score) of their occupational group. However, because of the positive association between the mother's socioeconomic circumstances and her occupational status, which is represented in this diagram by the upward slope of the lines, the mothers in social class I and II occupations who were working for reasons of financial necessity had the same mean Social Index score as the mothers in social class IV and V occupations who reported that the main reason why they worked was because they enjoyed their job. Thus although in objective terms the socioeconomic circumstances (Social Index score) of these two groups of mothers were very similar, their expressed reasons for working were quite different. It is even more surprising that some mothers in professional or managerial jobs should assert that they are doing it principally for the money, whilst others

221

Sample:
All mothers in regular employment at the time of the survey, N = 3,885
Mean Social Index score for sample = 8.3

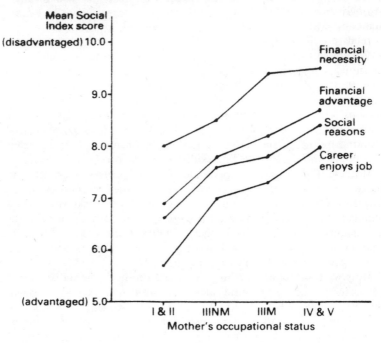

Figure 13.5 Mean Social Index score by mother's occupational status and main reason why mother worked

who are among those engaged in semi-skilled or unskilled manual work report that they work mainly because they enjoy their job.

We suggest that a mother's attitude to the reasons why she works is strongly influenced by her awareness of her own socioeconomic circumstances relative to others in similar types of occupation. If the mother is relatively deprived she will think of her work as an economic necessity. Conversely, mothers who are socially advantaged relative to others in similar occupations with whom they come in contact will not feel that the money is so important and will instead explain their reasons for going out to work in terms of their enjoyment of the job or social reasons.

In brief, the results of our analysis of the reasons mothers gave for working are:

1 Mothers who described their reason for working in terms of financial necessity were socially and economically worse off than others in similar occupations to themselves. The point here is that mothers compare their own social situation with that of their colleagues and workmates rather than the wider society in defining their social and economic needs.

2 Mothers in non-manual occupations who gave financial advantage or social reasons for working came essentially from the same social group, but non-manual workers who gave career or enjoyment of the work as their reason for working comprised a distinct group which was more socially advantaged than other non-manual workers.

3 Mothers in manual occupations, especially semi-skilled and unskilled manual workers, who gave social reasons or career/job enjoyment reasons for working were from similar social circumstances, and we suggest that for many of these mothers 'enjoyment of the job' mainly consisted in enjoyment of the social contact with workmates rather than the work process itself. There was a tendency, however, for manual workers giving financial advantage as their reason for working to be less well-off socially than the mothers who worked for social reasons, although in this respect the statistical significance was achieved only for mothers in social class IV and V occupations.

Summary

A comparison of employed and non-employed mothers in terms of their attitudes towards sex equality and quality of life for women showed little difference of opinion between mothers in the two groups.

223

The majority of the mothers agreed that women should have the same work opportunities as men and not simply opt for marriage and starting a family. However, more than half this sample of mothers believed that the father should have the final word on family matters. Slightly larger proportions of employed mothers than non-employed mothers thought that mothers need more from life than just looking after the home and children but the overwhelming majority of *both* groups concurred with this view.

Notwithstanding the similarity between employed and non-employed mothers with regard to their attitudes, the former group responded far more favourably to the idea of maternal employment than did the latter group. Although full-time housewives were less likely than employees to favour maternal employment, at least half of the former agreed that mothers should be able to go out to work if they wanted to. A more worrying finding, however, was that of the employed mothers at least one in five felt that mothers of young children ought not to go out to work, and half believed that a mother's place is at home with her children. Such a conflict between the necessity for a mother to go out to work and her belief that she ought really to be at home looking after her children can impose stresses likely to have serious consequences for the mother's health and hence for her child's welfare also. The mothers who were most likely to have a favourable attitude towards maternal employment were those employed outside the home, young mothers, mothers with professional qualifications and those in poor socio-economic circumstances.

About one in three employed mothers said that the main reason why they went out to work was because of financial necessity and one in ten for career reasons or because they enjoyed the work. The proportion who worked because of financial necessity was much higher in one-parent families and in socially disadvantaged families. Middle class mothers, i.e. those who were professionally qualified or employed in occupational status I or II jobs, were far more likely to report that they worked for career reasons or because they liked their jobs. However, we found that a mother's perceptions of her reasons why she went out to work were strongly influenced by her awareness of her own socio-economic position compared with others in similar occupations. Thus professional mothers whose socioeconomic circumstances were less afluent than others in similar occupations were likely to report that they worked from financial necessity, but mothers doing semi-skilled and unskilled manual work who were less disadvantaged than most others in this kind of job were likely to say that they worked because they enjoyed the job.

Chapter 14

Day care of children of employed mothers

The extent of preschool day care provision

The only officially recognised services for looking after the preschool age children of employed mothers are day nurseries and registered childminders. Day nurseries run by the local authority are expensive compared with other forms of day care provision and places are occupied mainly by children in special need because of family difficulties or handicap (Leigh, 1980, pp. 157-8), although attempts are made to keep a balanced community of children if possible (Garland and White, 1980, pp. 16-18). Independent day nurseries receive no state subsidy, although local authorities sometimes pay for children to attend a private nursery if they are in special need of day care and there is no alternative provision available. In general, however, a mother who sends her child to an independent day nursery must pay the full economic cost of the place which proves too expensive for the majority of working mothers.

Childminders offer the cheaper solution to the problem of day care for children of working mothers both from the point of view of the mothers and the local authorities whose only responsibility is to see that the childminder's home meets minimal standards of health and safety at the time of their registration. Studies of childminding are unanimous in their observation of the poor quality of care provided by many childminders (Bryant *et al.*, 1980; Jackson, 1979; Mayall and Petrie, 1977). These studies also point out, however, the very poor working conditions of childminders who work long hours in their own home with low pay and high expenses. A survey carried out in 1978 in an Inner London Borough revealed that two thirds of the childminders studied were earning no more than twenty pence an hour (Leigh, 1980, p. 156). It is not surprising therefore that the service provided was less than adequate.

In 1976, the total provision for full-time care in local authority and independent day nurseries and by childminders in Great Britain was sufficient to accommodate only 3.4 percent of the population of children aged 0-4 years, although there was considerable variation between local authorities in the level of provision (Central Policy Review Staff, 1978, Annex 5). This proportion had increased only slightly by 1980 when there were full-time places for barely 4 percent of the age group even though there had been an 8 percent reduction in the total population of under-fives from 3.6 million in 1976 to 3.3 million in 1980. There was, however, a noticeable shift in the type of provision available away from day nurseries and towards childminders. The small increase of about 1,700 (5.6 percent increase) full-time places in local authority day nurseries between 1976 and 1980 was more than offset by the loss of more than 4,000 places (15.1 percent decrease) in private nurseries which suggests their non-viability during this period of economic stringency. The number of children going to childminders, however, rose by 14.2 percent from 65,300 to 74,500 (Department of Health and Social Security, 1982; Welsh Office, 1980; Scottish Education Department, 1982). In addition to those with registered childminders, numbers of children, possibly as many as 100,000, are being looked after by non-registered minders where the quality of care is likely to be even less satisfactory than that provided by registered minders (Jackson, 1979, pp. 13-14). Thus the growth in day care provision, small though it is, is occurring most in the very area in which there is the greatest concern for the quality of care offered; a concern which has been expressed by many of the mothers who use childminders as well as by researchers (Bone, 1977, p. 15; Leigh, 1980, p. 157).

This trend can undoubtedly be attributed to the worsening economic climate in the latter half of the 1970s which limited expansion of local authority day nurseries and made private nurseries a less profitable proposition. The rise in childminding can be seen as a response to the increased demand for their services because of the decline in day nursery provision; also more women might have seen childminding itself as a ready means of increasing family income. In addition, official policy was to seek ways of providing low cost preschool day care services, to spread existing provision between a greater number of under fives by encouraging part-time rather than full-time use of services, and by discouraging the use of day care places by children under the age of two or three years (Department of Health and Social Security and Department of Education and Science, 1976, p. 1). All these measures discriminated against the mothers of young children who wished or needed to go out to work and increased their dependence on childminders, friends and relatives.

Although full-time places in day nurseries and with registered child-minders are sufficient for only 4 percent of the population of children aged 0-4, other types of preschool provision with primarily educational objectives, such as nursery schools, nursery classes in infant schools and playgroups, can offer a partial solution to the problem of day care for children of employed mothers. Indeed, evidence suggests that mothers generally prefer their children to attend a placement with an educational content rather than a day nursery or childminder where care rather than education is the primary function (Bone, 1977, Table 3.5). However, nursery schools/classes and playgroups, although providing a valuable educational and social experience for the child, cannot meet the full day care requirements of a mother who goes out to work, particularly if she works full-time (David, 1978). The short school day and long holidays mean that additional arrangements must be made for the care of the child outside school hours, especially if the mother works full-time. Also nursery schools/classes and playgroups rarely take children younger than three years old and so day nurseries and child-minders are the only officially recognised means of day care for children under three years old. The division of responsibility for the care and education of under fives between social services and education departments respectively exacerbates an already complex situation and the development of a more coordinated approach to the provision of services for the under fives is long overdue (Bradley, 1982; Department of Health and Social Security and Department of Education and Science, 1978; Study Commission on the Family, 1983, p. 28). Much of the problem could be resolved if it could be recognised that the social and educational needs of young children and the desire of the mothers of these children to enter the labour market are not in conflict and that appropriate day care provision could satisfy both exigencies (David, 1982; van der Eyken, 1978; Hughes *et al.*, 1980). Several innovatory schemes have been tried with varying degrees of success (Bibby and Thomas, 1980; Ferri *et al.*, 1981; Moss, 1978); what is now needed is official action to expand existing provision and develop the ideas that have already been proved successful in experimental schemes.

Data from our own study can contribute to this debate by giving an account of the arrangements made for the care of their children by mothers who were in paid employment, and by describing how certain family circumstances affected these arrangements. A major factor for children at age five is their entry into full-time education.

How entry into full-time school affects children's day care needs

We have seen that the proportion of mothers who were employed increased with the age of their children from 30 percent of mothers with a youngest child aged 0-4 years to more than 60 percent of mothers with a youngest child aged 5-9 years (Figure 11.1). This was due partly, if not mainly, to the fact that the children had entered full-time school and the problem of day care was thus partially resolved. We also know, however, that even in the preschool period the proportion of employed mothers increases with the age of the youngest child. Bone (1977, Table 4.2) found that maternal full-time and part-time employment increased from 12 percent of mothers with a youngest child aged under one year to 36 percent of mothers with a youngest child aged three or four. To what extent, then, did children's entry into full-time preschool education or day-care situations contribute to this trend?

Table 14.1 shows the relationship between a mother taking a full-time or part-time job outside the home and the age at which her child entered a full-time educational or day-care placement. By full-time placement is meant attendance at nursery school/class, playgroup, day nursery or infant school morning and afternoon from Monday to Friday. No account has been taken of the duration of sessions or whether the child stayed to lunch. This table is limited to mothers with no other children younger than the study child as, clearly, any effect of the study child's entry to full-time education or day care on a mother's opportunity to seek employment would be considerably reduced in families where there were other younger children at home. Also, in this table and throughout this chapter mothers who worked at home or occasionally are excluded from the employed group as the question of day-care is concerned mainly with the children of mothers employed outside the home. Table 14.1 shows a tendency for mothers to obtain a job when their children entered a full-time placement. The highest proportion of mothers who started their current job before the child's third birthday occurred where the study child also started a full-time placement before age three (45.4 percent compared with an average 18.6 percent). A similar, though not so marked, correspondence between age of child at entry to a full-time placement and mother starting employment occurred in the fourth and fifth years of these children. The importance of the child's age at entry to a full-time placement can also be seen in the increasing proportion of non-employed mothers from 41.1 percent of those whose children were attending before age three to 63.2 percent of those whose children started full-time school after their fifth birthday. Notwithstanding the comparatively short hours and long holidays of most full-time educational placements, our results suggest that the youngest child's entry to a full-time placement

228

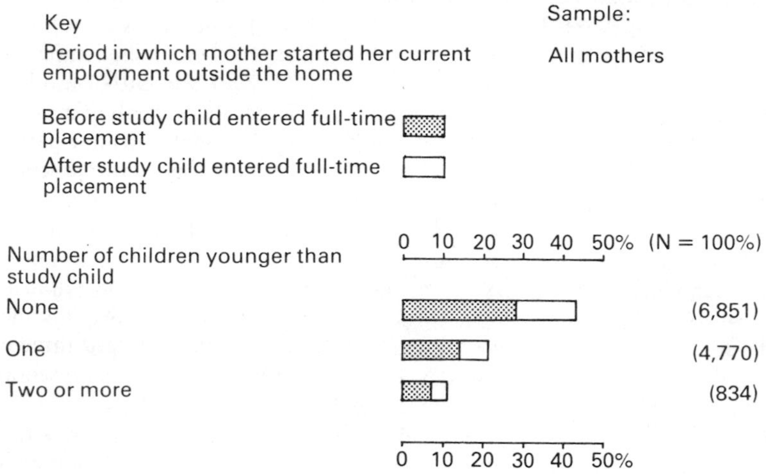
Key
Period in which mother started her current employment outside the home
Before study child entered full-time placement
After study child entered full-time placement
Sample:
All mothers
Number of children younger than study child
0 10 20 30 40 50% (N = 100%)
None
(6,851)
One
(4,770)
Two or more
(834)
0 10 20 30 40 50%

Figure 14.1 Mother's employment and child's entry to a full-time educational or day care placement by number of children younger than study child in the preschool years increases the probability that the mother obtains employment. Nevertheless, in Figure 14.1 we find that a higher proportion of mothers started their current employment *before* their children entered a full-time placement than after. Of mothers with no other children younger than the study child 27.9 percent started their current job before the child's entry into a full-time placement and 15 percent after. The same pattern, but with reduced proportions, was found for mothers with other children younger than the study child.

From this we conclude that a child's entry to full-time education is not a major influence on a mother's decision to go out to work although in some instances it may be a contributory factor. The increase in maternal employment rate associated with increasing age of the youngest child is more likely to be due to growing independence in the children as they get older so that mothers become more willing to leave them in the care of others and in the case of children in the 5-9 year range, to let them look after themselves until the parents return home from work. However, the after-school care of young children who attend full-time school presents different problems for employed mothers than those faced by mothers whose children have not yet started school (Simpson, 1978).

At the time of our survey three quarters of the children of employed mothers were attending nursery schools, infant schools or playgroups full-time, i.e. ten sessions a week, and this provides the opportunity to look at (a) the day care arrangements for children *not* attending a full time educational placement and (b) the after-school care for children who *were* attending full-time school. Details of these are given in Table 14.2. The term 'after-school care' here refers to arrangements made for the care of children outside normal school hours which includes before and after school during the week and at weekends. Our discussion of the after-school care of children who were attending full-time school will follow our account of the day care arrangements made for children who were not yet going to school full time.

Day care of children not in full-time school

Half of the children not attending a full-time educational placement were looked after by their father whilst their mother was at work. This does not necessarily imply that these fathers were unemployed themselves. It is more probable that the mother worked at times when the father was home from work, for example evenings or weekends (Chapter 12). Some mothers and fathers may also have worked alternate shifts and there is some evidence that mothers with children under five living in areas with high rates of female employment are more likely than other employed women to work shifts (Marsh, 1979). We hypothesised, therefore, that more shift-working fathers would have looked after their children whilst the mother worked than fathers not on shifts, but our results refute this hypothesis; shift-working fathers in this sample were no more likely to look after their children during the mother's working hours than were other fathers. Other research has shown that wives of shift-workers are less likely to be employed than other wives despite the tendency for shift-workers to have heavier family financial commitments than comparable day-workers (National Board for Prices and Incomes, 1970). Thus our conclusion is that where children are looked after by their fathers, mothers are very likely to be working unsocial hours.

After fathers, Table 14.2(a) indicates that adult relatives, e.g. grandparents, aunts, etc., were the most commonly mentioned source of care (18.4 percent). Some children (4.4 percent) were looked after by their mother at work and a further 1.7 percent by their older siblings. Thus altogether three-quarters (75.4 percent) of the children not in a full-time educational placement were in the care of their own parents or other family members during the time their mothers were at work. Part-time attendance at an educational placement such as nursery school or class or playgroup was the main place of care for 13.7 percent of these children and only 3.4 percent were attending day nurseries (this included both full- and part-time day nursery attendance). Paid childminders looked after 3.1 percent and friends or neighbours 4.4 percent of these children whilst their mothers were out at work. It must be emphasised that we have recorded only the main place of care of these children and some of them experienced more than one of the types of day care mentioned.

The arrangements made by employed mothers for the care of their preschool age children have changed considerably since the 1950s when only 13 percent of the fathers were reported to be looking after their children aged 0-4 years (Yudkin and Holme, 1963, p. 53) compared with 35 percent of 3-4 year olds in 1965 (Hunt, 1968, p. 94) and 51 percent in 1975 in our own study. This large increase in paternal involvement in child care can be attributed to changes in sex roles within the family, the reduction in availability of other family members due to increased geographical mobility, and the closure of day nurseries. The proportion of preschool age children looked after by relatives during their mother's working hours has halved since Yudkin and Holme's (1963) survey from 40 percent to 20 percent in the CHES sample; the proportion cared for in day nurseries has declined from 17 percent in 1948 (Douglas and Blomfield, 1958, p. 123) to 6 percent in 1965 (Hunt, 1968, p. 94) and only 3 percent in our own sample; and childminders, friends and neighbours who in the 1950s looked after

17 percent of children of working mothers (Yudkin and Holme, 1963, p. 53), were responsible for only 12 percent in 1965 (Hunt, 1968, p. 94) and 8 percent in 1975 as shown by our own survey.

Day care of children in full-time school

Earlier surveys have commented on the absence of any formal arrangement for looking after the school age children of employed mothers outside of school hours and during school holidays (Equal Opportunities Commission, 1978; Hunt, 1968, p. 97; Yudkin and Holme, 1963, pp. 57-65). Local authorities are empowered to provide 'out-of-school-hours' services for school age children and in 1975 at least three quarters were running such schemes. Many of these schemes, however, had major limitations that considerably reduced their value to working parents (Simpson, 1978). The extent of these provisions, moreover, was completely inadequate to meet the needs of even a small proportion of the school age children of employed mothers. A contemporary estimate suggested that about 15 percent of the 5—10-year-olds with working mothers were left alone after school and approximately 20 percent during the school holidays (Simpson, 1978, p. 5). In the late 1950s Yudkin and Holme (1963) found that 18 percent of 5—11-year-olds were managing alone after school and 22 percent during the holidays. Thus there is little evidence of any significant change in the proportion of this age group with employed mothers who are left unsupervised outside of school hours.

The pattern of after-school care of the children in our sample who were attending full-time educational placements given in Table 14.2(b) was strikingly similar to that of 14.2(a) in that the ranking of after-school caretakers was virtually the same as for the children who were not full-time attenders. Fathers were the most frequently mentioned caretaker outside school hours (33.3 percent), adult relatives came next (11.2 percent) and mothers at work and older siblings followed, each with 2.7 percent of these children. Only 2.2 percent of children were cared for by friends or neighbours and 1.6 percent by paid childminders outside school hours. Comparison with earlier studies (Hunt, 1968; Yudkin and Holme, 1963) showed similar historical trends to those we described for preschool age children. The after-school day care involvement of fathers has increased from 12 percent in the late 1950s to 20 percent in 1965 and 33 percent in 1975. Dependence on other relatives for after school care had declined during this period from 21 percent to 16 percent by 1965 and 14 percent in 1975.

As many as 46.3 percent of mothers in our sample whose children attended a full-time educational placement said that school was the only place of care whilst they worked. It is very likely that many of the mothers citing only school as the place of care may have not mentioned all after-school caretakers and simply given school as the *main* place of care. For example, 61.3 percent of the mothers who mentioned no after-school care had help from the father or others in 'looking after the child for part of the day whilst the mother went shopping, attended appointments, did housework, etc.' Over a third (37.7 percent) of these mothers also had help in taking their children to school. As these proportions were not markedly different from those of mothers who did mention other forms of care outside school hours we conclude that many of the former mothers failed to mention all types of help they may have received when describing who looked after their children during their working hours. We may assume, however, that the mothers who mentioned no day care other than school felt that any other help they received was small compared with that of school attendance. In Table 14.2(b), as in 14.2(a), after-school care was more often provided by the child's own parents or relatives (49.9 percent) than by childminders, friends or neighbours (3.8 percent) and both tables demonstrate the importance of the father in looking after the children whilst the mother was at work.

For the purposes of subsequent analysis some of the categories in Table 14.2 have been grouped together. Adult relatives and older siblings were combined, and childminders have been grouped with friends and neighbours. This was done mainly to reduce the problem of small numbers in these categories but also because 'friends and neighbours' in some cases may have been euphemisms for 'childminders' if respondents anticipated a negative attitude to the use of childminders on the part of the interviewer.

Social and family differences in preschool day care

Mothers of preschool age children who wish to go out to work need to seek a compromise between (a) the type and hours of employment they undertake, and (b) the availability of adequate day care facilities. Frequently, too, the range of job opportunities for wives is limited because the area in which they live is determined by the location of their husband's job and there may be no local employment suited to the wives' skills and abilities. Thus the relationship between the pattern of employment and arrangements for the day care of children depends on a resolution of several factors which include the mother's skills and abilities, job opportunity, and availability of day care facilities. It is important to recognise the inter-relatedness of these processes which underlie the results described below.

Table 14.3 describes the day care of children who were not attending a full-time educational placement for the five Social Index groups. The main social differences in the pattern of day care concerned the use of day nurseries and part-time nursery schools/classes or playgroups. The proportion of children attending day nurseries increased from 1.2 percent of the most advantaged to 5.8 percent of the most disadvantaged Social Index groups, which probably reflects admissions policies giving priority to socially 'at risk' children. Conversely, the proportion cared for in part-time educational placements decreased from 22.9 percent of the most advantaged to 6.6 percent of the most disadvantaged groups. There is also a suggestion that socially disadvantaged mothers were more likely to obtain the help of relatives to look after their children than were the socially advantaged mothers. The proportion of children who were looked after by their fathers during the mother's working hours was about the same in all Social Index groups.

The absence of the father resulted in greater dependence on other sources of day care in families headed by a single-parent mother who went out to work (Table 14.4). Whilst 17.2 percent of children in two-parent families were looked after by relatives, the proportion was as high as 42.1 percent of lone mothers and 58 percent of supported single-parent mothers. Of the latter, many were living with their own parents who were thus able to look after the child whilst the mother was at work. In contrast, more children of lone mothers were looked after by friends, neighbours or childminders (18.4 percent). Day nurseries were more likely to be attended by children from single-parent families (supported 12 percent, lone 18.4 percent) than by those in two-parent families (2.4 percent). This can be seen as a result of the policy in day nurseries to give priority to children from potentially stressful family circumstances. The presence of younger children in the household increased the probability that the father would be the main caretaker whilst the mother was at work such that 68.8 percent of fathers were cited as the main caretaker where there was at least one child younger than the study child compared with 41.8 percent in families where the study child was the youngest.

We have said that the mother's employment routine is likely to be associated with different patterns of day care; Table 14.5 illustrates some of these differences. Full-time employment was associated with greater proportions of children being looked after by relatives, (34.8 percent), friends, neighbours, or childminders (12.4 percent) and day nurseries (8.7 percent) compared with part-time employment. More than half (55.7 percent) of the children of mothers employed part-time were looked after by their fathers compared with only 28.6 percent of children whose mothers worked full-time. These results suggest that although fathers were the most frequently mentioned caretakers of children who had not yet started full-time school, this applied mainly to mothers employed part-time and that others, especially relatives, were needed to look after children of full-time workers. The importance of fathers as the main caretakers also increased to 68.9 percent when mothers worked at the weekend compared with about 35 percent where the mother worked weekdays only.

The pattern of after-school care was found to vary quite considerably according to the social and family circumstances of the mother. Children who were least likely to require day care outside school hours were those of mothers with teaching or degree level qualifications of whom 81.3 percent and 72.8 percent respectively mentioned no after-school care. A further 5.6 percent of teachers' children accompanied their mothers to work and in some cases may have attended the schools at which their mothers taught. This reflects the advantage for teachers in working school hours and holidays corresponding with those of their children.

A third of the children of the mothers employed outside the home were looked after outside school hours by their fathers. This occurred more frequently, however, if there were also other children in the family who were younger than the study child (52.8 percent). This is to be expected in view of the fact that for children who were not attending a full-time educational placement the main source of day care was the father (Table 14.2(a)) and thus the presence in the family of other children not yet attending school increased the likelihood that school children were also looked after by the father.

Higher proportions of fathers helped with the after-school care of children whose mothers were qualified nurses (48.8 percent) which was due perhaps to the greater opportunity for nurses to work at times when their husbands were at home, e.g. evenings, overnight or weekends, compared with mothers in other occupations. Mothers in the most disadvantaged Social Index group were also more likely to depend on the child's father for after-school care (40.4 percent) which again may have been associated with the longer or unsocial hours worked by many of these mothers (Chapter 12). The mothers in the most advantaged Social Index group, in comparison, tended to work shorter hours and not at the weekend, hence a higher than average proportion of their children (69.1 percent) were at school during the hours the mothers were employed with no other care mentioned. The most advantaged Social Index group also included a relatively high proportion of teachers and mothers with degrees who, as we have already seen, were more likely to have working hours which coincided with normal school hours.

Relatives, including grandparents, aunts or older siblings, were responsible for the care of 13.9 percent of the children of working mothers outside school hours and were an important source of help for single-parent mothers. This particularly applied to supported single-parent mothers of whom 41.2 percent depended on relatives for the after-school care of their children compared with 23.2 percent of lone mothers and indicates an advantage for single parents who shared a household with relatives. Higher than average proportions of single-parent mothers mentioned friends, neighbours and childminders as sources of after-school care (9.2 percent of supported mothers and 8.4 percent of lone mothers) although most lone mothers mentioned no day care other than school (64.2 percent).

The fact that nearly two-thirds of the children of lone mothers received no other day-care outside school hours is surprising in view of the expectation that this group of mothers would need to work full-time. It suggests that for these mothers the non-availability of informal sources of help from the child's father or other relatives, and the almost total lack of local authority provision for after-school care means that they can work only during the periods that their children are at school. This limits their hours of work and job opportunity with increased likelihood of low income and dependence on social security. The loss of self-esteem for the mother and the consequences of poverty for her children need hardly be spelt out. Whilst local authority provision of adequate day-care for children of unsupported parents clearly cannot compensate for all the difficulties of single-parenthood, it could alleviate one of the more central problems facing these parents.

Asian mothers mainly depended on relatives for after-school care (34.9 percent) and the fathers played a minimal role (11.6 percent). West Indian mothers, however, were more inclined to obtain day care help from friends, neighbours or childminders (9 percent) or, unlike the Asian mothers, involved the father in looking after their children outside school hours (39.7 percent). Differences in sex roles, family structure and community integration within West Indian, Asian and European cultural groups are probably the best sources of explanation for these observed differences in after-school care (Pollack, 1972).

The hours a mother works and the type of day care she arranges for her children are mutually dependent. Thus for a mother who wishes to work full-time some forms of day care are more suitable than others. Conversely a mother may be more inclined to seek full-time employment if a ready source of all day care is available. Table 14.6 suggests that relatives, friends, neighbours or childminders were used more by full-time workers than by part-time workers, whereas the father was more likely to look after the child outside school hours if the mother worked part-time than if she worked full-time.

It was surprising that as many as 41.2 percent of mothers who worked more than 30 hours per week were able to fit their working hours and travelling time between home, school and place of work, within the average school day. It is possible, however, that these mothers were helped out by friends or relatives for a short time before or after school yet did not regard this as a form of care. Some of these mothers, however, must have omitted to mention some after-school care because we found that 27.4 percent of mothers who worked at least some of the time outside the home at week-ends mentioned only school as the main place of care. It is highly probable that these children were looked after by other family members whilst the mother was at work as half of the children whose mothers worked at least some of the time at week-ends were in the care of their fathers. It is very likely that many mothers decided to work partly at weekends, when the father was at home, as a means of reducing the problem of finding other sources of day care.

National variation in day care arrangements

A key factor in the pattern of day care in different regions is the variation in the age at which children start school (see Chapter 6). In Scotland comparatively few children had entered full-time school by age five and only 11.8 percent of the children of Scottish mothers employed outside the home were attending a full-time educational placement compared with 81.4 percent in England and 85.2 percent in Wales. Despite this considerable disparity in the proportion of Scottish children who had entered school by age five compared with those in the rest of Great Britain, the proportion of Scottish mothers who were employed was not markedly different from the proportion employed in England and Wales (see Table 11.2). Because of this, different patterns of day care were expected in Scotland compared with England and Wales. We found that the patterns of day care of children who were not in a full-time educational placement at the time of the survey were very similar in Wales and England with the exception of part-time preschool placements which were the main place of care for 21.2 percent of Welsh children compared with 15 percent of English children and only 9.6 percent of Scottish children. Scottish mothers were more likely to leave their children with relatives, friends, neighbours or childminders (37.5 percent) than were English or Welsh mothers (23.5 percent and 18.2 percent respectively). In Scotland 43.6 percent of the children were mainly looked after by the father whilst the mother went out to work, compared with as many as 60.6 percent of Welsh children and 53.9 percent of English children.

The pattern of after-school care in Scotland was also different from that in England and Wales although it should be noted that only 42 children with working mothers were in a full-time educational placement.

237

Two thirds of Scottish children had no after-school care compared with 41 percent and 46 percent in Wales and England respectively. Scottish mothers who did use other day care arrangements in addition to school were more likely to mention friends, neighbours or childminders (7.7 percent) than were Welsh and English mothers (2.4 percent and 3.8 percent respectively). About half the Welsh and English children (56.8 percent and 49.9 percent respectively) were looked after by their fathers, mother at work or relatives outside school hours compared with only a quarter (25.6 percent) of Scottish children. Thus in Scotland, whether or not the child had started full-time school, fathers were less likely to occupy a child care role than were fathers in England and Wales. Scottish mothers, both before and after their children had entered full-time school, were also more likely to rely on the help of friends, neighbours or childminders than were the English and Welsh mothers. These findings suggest differences in the pattern of family and community life in Scotland compared with other parts of Great Britain which have implications for wives and children and merit further research.

Summary

Our description of the arrangements made by mothers in this study for the care of their children whilst they went out to work shows a diversity which results from the chronic lack of sufficient organised provision for meeting the day care needs of such children. We have found that the mother's cultural and social background, her education and training and her family situation all have different implications for the method of day care used. This is likely to be modified after the child enters a full-time educational placement and is clearly also dependent on the types of job opportunity available.

The mother who wishes to go out to work must make the best arrangements she can for the care of her children and may decide to work evenings or weekends, if such work is available, so that the father can look after the children. Comparisons with earlier studies over a period of 25 years show that fathers have become of much greater significance in the child care role than hitherto, whereas dependence on relatives, friends and childminders has considerably lessened. In recent years, however, there appears to be a significant increase in childminding. Fathers were more prominent in families with more than one child under five years old for whom the problem of day care was increased in proportion to the number of preschool age children. Some mothers were more prepared than others to work unsocial hours. Nursing, for example, is one of very few occupations employing large numbers of women on a shiftwork basis and more qualified nurses in this study were able to leave their children with their husbands than were mothers in other occupations. Socially disadvantaged mothers were also more prepared to work full-time or unsocial hours but for reasons of economic need rather than being qualified for a particular type of job. These mothers were more likely than socially advantaged mothers to obtain the help of the father or other relatives in looking after their children. Socially advantaged mothers tended to work hours which fitted with their children's school attendance, even if the child only attended a part-time nursery or playgroup, or obtained the help of friends, neighbours or childminders. We know that socially advantaged mothers tend to work part-time (Chapter 12), thus there is less pressure on them to make additional arrangements for the care of their children outside school or nursery hours.

The fact that most employed mothers depend entirely on informal day care arrangements points to the need for a major review of current policy on this important issue. Increasing proportions of mothers of preschool age children are desiring and obtaining paid employment; this fact is recognised in other countries where more adequate day care facilities are being provided (Organisation for Economic Cooperation and Development, 1979). Expansion of nursery provision in Britain would not only meet the day care needs of children whose mothers go out to work, it would also provide the opportunity of giving these children a valuable educational experience. This service would be particularly important for families where poor socioeconomic circumstances necessitate the mother's employment and also hinder the child's developmental and educational progress.

Chapter 15

The association of mother's employment with behaviour and ability of the child and maternal depression

A mother's decision on whether to go out to work or to devote all her time to domestic and child care activities has profound implications for the family. However, the nature and extent of these implications are hard to predict as the circumstances of employed mothers are so complex. Going out to work means that a mother must find alternative care for the children and also arrange for housework and shopping to be done. If her work is well paid it may be possible for a mother to find good all day care in a nursery or with a registered childminder, to pay someone to come and do housework, to buy labour saving domestic equipment such as an automatic washing machine, tumble drier, dishwasher, etc., and to make use of convenience foods (Strober and Weinberg, 1980). By contrast mothers in less favourable circumstances whose employment is necessary to supplement or provide the basic income cannot dispense their earnings in these ways and have instead to cope with housework, shopping, cooking and seeing to the needs of the children in whatever time is available outside of their working hours. It follows, therefore, that unless such mothers receive some help from their husbands, relatives or friends they will inevitably have less time to spend with their children than mothers who are not employed. Although there has been a significant increase in maternal employment over the past twenty years this has not led to any significant changes in the traditional division of labour between the sexes in the home, and while mothers in employment are more likely to receive help from their husbands with their domestic duties, than mothers who are full-time housewives (see Chapter 4) they still have the primary responsibility for organising these activities (Beckman and Houser, 1979; Watt, 1980).

The question of what impact maternal employment has upon the children involved is the subject of considerable controversy. One view holds that there is a basic conflict between the needs of mothers, for whom working may be a positive benefit, and the needs of their children who may suffer from the diminished attention from which this may result (Bruner, 1980; Pringle, 1980(a)). Although the latter has some vigorous proponents, it is being subjected to growing criticism (David, 1982; Hughes *et al.*, 1980) and it has been suggested that if this potential conflict between a mother's perception of her maternal responsibility and her desire to obtain employment is not satisfactorily resolved it may have undesirable consequences for her own emotional state and on her children (Farel, 1980). This conflict is clearly evident in our analysis of mothers' attitudes in Chapter 13 where we found that they had a strong commitment to their maternal role whilst at the same time agreeing that mothers should be able to go out to work. These divergent opinions illustrate how commitment to the traditional child-centred role of mothers is being challenged by the idea that they should have the right to go out to work if they wish. Many mothers reconcile these differing demands by working only part-time, but even a part-time job makes inroads on the time available for the demands of home making and child care.

In the face of such controversial assertions it is vital that we examine the evidence to see whether the employment of mothers has any adverse effect on their young children. Some studies have concluded that there is no firm evidence that maternal employment has a detrimental effect on children's ability or social adjustment (Hughes *et al.*, 1980; Rutter, 1976). Other research, however, suggests that mothers working full-time may have significant implications for their children. Results from the National Child Development Study suggested that children aged seven whose mothers were working outside the home had poorer social adjustment at school than children of mothers who were not employed. Maternal employment in the preschool period, however, had no measurable effect on the children's social adjustment at seven years (Davie *et al.*, 1972, p. 46). Children whose mothers worked full-time in the preschool period had poorer reading and arithmetic scores at age seven than children of mothers who had not been employed or who had part-time jobs (ibid., pp. 44-5). These associations between maternal employment and children's behaviour and attainment were found after adjustment for socioeconomic differences in home background. Similar results were obtained in a study of ten-year-old children which compared the social adjustment and ability of children whose mothers had full-time jobs with children of non-employed mothers (Gold and Andres, 1978). These studies emphasise the impact of full-time maternal employment on children's development and behaviour. By contrast there is no evidence that part-time employment of mothers has any effect on their children, either adverse or beneficial.

This earlier research paid very little attention to the type of work on which the mothers were employed and its possible impact on both their health and ability to fulfil their maternal role. These points in fact deserve greater consideration as they probably exert quite a significant influence; for example, the mother who is in a job that is physically demanding may be exhausted at the end of her day's work and less able to meet her child's normal demands for attention. Conversely, a stimulating occupation may augment a mother's self-esteem and enrich the relationship between her child and herself. Yet again another mother may have to select a certain type of work to fit in with her domestic commitments (Shimmin *et al.*, 1981). Thus any effects on child or mother ascribed to type of employment may in fact be due to the stresses involved in organising their lives so as to accommodate both paid job and domestic work.

To pursue this point about type of employment further, it is safe to assume that in general more physically demanding work is in the manual sector, while jobs that are stimulating and have an intrinsic interest tend to be non-manual in character. Broadly speaking the professions and vocations, administrative and secretarial posts are both less tiring and more rewarding than routine factory work, domestic service or similar manual employment. Another facet of employment which should be considered is its duration; part-time is more satisfying than full-time employment, especially when it applies to the manual sector (Moss and Plewis, 1977). In view of the importance of both duration and type of work done by mothers that this earlier research points to, the classification of mother's employment used in the present study was based on full-time (more than 30 hours per week) or part-time (up to 30 hours per week) in manual or non-manual employment.

In addition we identified mothers who were employed at home and those who had had a job outside the home at some time in the previous five years, which they had given up in order to become full-time housewives. We then compared mothers in the different employment situations we have described with mothers who had been full-time housewives for the whole period since their children's birth. Those mothers who were only in occasional employment were excluded from the analysis as insufficient was known about the hours and type of work involved.

The associations between mothers' employment status and experience and the different levels of ability and behaviour shown by their children were investigated using analysis of variance. By this means statistical adjustment was made for the effects of social and family differences between employment categories which might otherwise have been responsible for any association found between mothers' employment and children's ability and behaviour (Chapter 20 gives further details of our methods of analysis).

Using this approach our findings on the relationship between

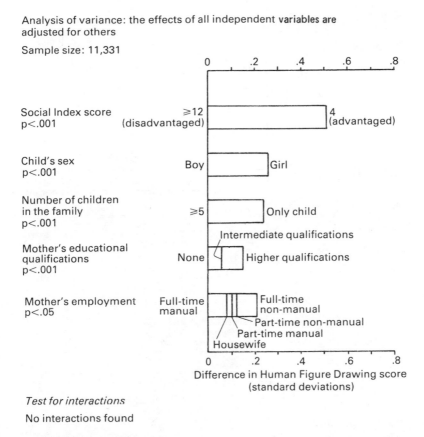

Analysis of variance: the effects of all independent variables are adjusted for others

Sample size: 11,331

Figure 15.1 Analysis of mother's employment and Human Figure Drawing

Analysis of variance: the effects of all independent **variables are adjusted** for others

Sample size: 11,385

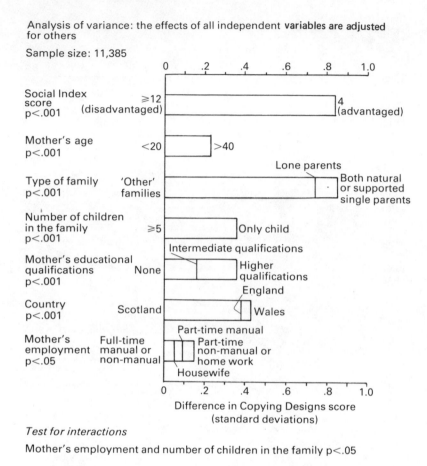

Difference in Copying Designs score (standard deviations)

Test for interactions

Mother's employment and number of children in the family p<.05

Figure 15.2 Analysis of mother's employment and Copying Designs

maternal employment and the development and behaviour of the children yielded interesting insights.

Cognitive ability and vocabulary

Cognitive ability was measured by the Human Figure Drawing Test (Figure 15.1) and the Copying Designs Test (Figure 15.2). (See Chapter 19 for details of tests and assessments.) There was no evidence on the basis of these tests that a mother's employment outside the home necessarily had an adverse effect on her child's level of general ability. Although children with mothers in full-time manual employment had lower mean scores than children of women who were full-time house-wives, the difference was non-significant after adjustment for other social and family factors in the analysis. There was some indication that children whose mothers had a part-time non-manual job scored higher on these tests than those whose mothers did not work. (.05 SDs differ-ence $p < .05$ and .10 SDs difference $p < .01$ respectively.) However, these differences in score associated with maternal employment were very small, especially compared with those attributed to socioeconomic inequality and family factors, and were not sufficient in themselves to offer any other conclusion than that maternal employment had no demonstrable ill-effect on children's general ability as measured by these particular tests.

Vocabulary was measured by the English Picture Vocabulary Test, and the results using this test differed from those just reported on cognitive ability in that the highest mean EPVT score was achieved by children whose mothers were full-time housewives and the lowest by children of mothers in full-time manual employment, the difference between these two groups being .16 SDs ($p < .001$). The next lowest score was that of children with mothers in part-time manual jobs which differed from that of children of full-time housewives by .10 SDs ($p < .001$). Children whose mothers were in non-manual employment, worked at home, or had given up their job had very similar mean EPVT scores and were grouped together in Figure 15.3 as 'other employment situation'. This group also had a mean EPVT score which was slightly lower than that of children of full-time housewives (.05 SDs difference, $p < .05$).

This pattern of results suggests that physically demanding employ-ment and long hours of work were associated with poorer vocabulary skills in the children of these mothers. Although the overall difference in mean score attributable to mother's employment was small com-pared with other factors in Figure 15.3 it was more conclusive, in a statistical sense, than were the results for Human Figure Drawing and

Copying Designs. Our interpretation of these findings is that mothers in full-time manual employment were likely to have less time to be with their children as well as being physically exhausted by their work so that scope for verbal interaction between them was likely to be reduced. Verbal interchange is obviously essential for increasing a child's vocabulary, and although verbal interaction is also recognised as an important factor in the development of cognitive abilities it is probably of greatest significance in the case of language development. In other words, general intellectual development depends on a far wider range of experiences than verbal interaction alone, but vocabulary depends entirely on a child's access to spoken language. Thus, if the mother's employment cuts down the opportunity for verbal interaction with her child, this will have greater consequence for the latter's language or vocabulary skill than for his or her general cognitive progress.

Child behaviour

If a child reacts in some way to his mother's working outside the home, this reaction is likely to be revealed in his or her pattern of behaviour. We have already seen in Chapter 5 how family composition and structure, as expressed in the parental situation and number and ages of other children in the household, profoundly influence a child's likelihood of exhibiting antisocial or neurotic behaviour. In fact, family circumstances were associated with larger differences in neurotic behaviour than were socioeconomic factors. From this we may infer that when a mother's employment situation affects the organisation of her child's home life, this factor could be deemed responsible for differences in the child's behavioural adjustment. Differences in antisocial and neurotic behaviour were indeed found in relation to mother's employment and these are shown in the results of analyses of variance presented in Figure 15.4 and Figure 15.5.

Children of mothers in full-time manual employment had a higher mean antisocial behaviour score than children whose mothers had never been out to work in the previous five years (.24 SDs difference, $p <$ .001). Full-time non-manual employment was also associated with an increased level of antisocial behaviour compared with children whose mothers had not been employed (.11 SDs difference, $p < .05$). Children of mothers who worked only part-time (manual or non-manual), however, had only a slightly higher mean antisocial score (.07 SDs difference, $p < .001$) than children of non-employed mothers.

These results support the hypothesis that children of mothers working full-time in physically demanding jobs are likely to experience some disruption in their home background which can produce increased risk

246

Analysis of variance: the effects of all independent variables are adjusted for the others

Sample size: 10,771

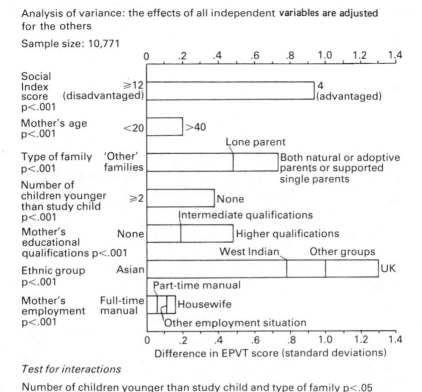

Test for interactions

Number of children younger than study child and type of family p<.05

Figure 15.3 Analysis of mother's employment and English Picture Vocabulary Test

Analysis of variance: the effects of all independent variables are adjusted for the others

Sample size: 11,218

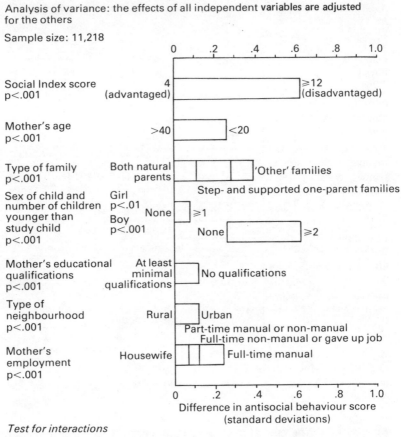

Test for interactions

Sex of child with number of children younger than study child and type of family
p<.05

Mother's educational qualifications and type of neighbourhood p<.05

Figure 15.4   Analysis of mother's employment and antisocial behaviour

of antisocial behaviour. However, children whose mothers had pre-viously worked outside the home and then given it up also had a higher mean antisocial score compared with those whose mothers had never worked at all. This finding challenges the hypothesis that the child's behavioural deviance is simply a result of the mother's absence from home.

The fact that a similar association was found in regard to neuroti-cism (Figure 15.5) suggests that this was not a chance finding. The children with high neuroticism scores were those whose mothers had given up a job outside the home in the previous five years, whereas, the mean neuroticism score of children whose mothers had jobs, whether manual or non-manual, full-time or part-time, was very little different from those children whose mothers had never been employed outside the home.

As we showed in Chapter 13 there are a variety of reasons why a mother wants to be in active employment but if she feels that her primary responsibility is the care of her child this obvious conflict of interest may engender a sense of guilt and even be responsible for her giving up her job. From the opposite standpoint this decision to stop working, either for the reason just suggested or others such as the arrival of subsequent children, may generate a feeling of frustration and even resentment towards the children which could undermine her rela-tionship with them and perhaps lead to reactive behaviour disorders on their part (Farel, 1980).

These are merely speculations but they serve to indicate the kind of family dynamics that operate within a given set of cultural mores that may produce the kinds of effects that we have found in our analyses of antisocial and neurotic behaviour associated with the mother's employ-ment status.

Considerations of this kind lead us to our next point, namely an analysis of how the mother's employment may influence her risk of depression.

Maternal depression

Studies of the association between maternal employment and depres-sion do not agree in their findings and outcome. Brown and Harris (1978), in their study of working class women in Camberwell, found that vulnerability to depression was reduced in women who were employed outside the home. By contrast Moss and Plewis (1977) and Richman (1978) who carried out research on samples of mothers of preschool age children living in other parts of inner London did not find that the proportion of those who were depressed was related to whether they had a job or not.

The explanation for many apparently contradictory findings may lie in the methodological and conceptual differences between the different studies. For example, Brown and Harris showed that employment reduced the risk of depression specifically in mothers who were predisposed or vulnerable to this condition for other reasons. The other investigations, however, explored the question of whether employment reduced the risk of depression in all mothers, not just those who were especially vulnerable. These different findings pose the question of whether employment can have a beneficial effect on the mental health of mothers in general or whether the postulated benefits are confined to specific groups who are particularly at risk of depression.

We began our investigation of this question by looking at the relationship between the classification of mothers' employment and our scale of maternal depression (see Chapter 19) using the same method as for the analysis of children's ability and behaviour described above. After making statistical adjustment for a number of factors we knew were associated with both maternal depression and the likelihood of the mother obtaining work, we found a marked relationship between the circumstances of the mothers' employment and their susceptibility or otherwise to depression (Figure 15.6). This analysis suggests that mothers in certain categories of our employment classification were associated with reduced risk of depression and others with increased risk. Mothers who had non-manual jobs had a lower mean depression score than mothers who had never had a job outside the home (.07 SDs difference, $p < .01$). Part-time manual employment was also associated with slightly lower depression scores but the difference was not statistically significant. Full-time manual employment was associated with increased risk of depression compared with housewives but, again, this difference did not achieve statistical significance. However, the most depressed group were those who had been employed outside the home in the previous five years but had given up their jobs. These mothers had a mean depression score which was .15 SDs higher than full-time housewives ($p < .001$) and .22 SDs higher than mothers in non-manual jobs ($p < .001$). This difference in the depression score related to the mother's employment situation was smaller than the differences associated with social inequality and family composition but greater than the differences associated with mothers' educational level, family size and type of neighbourhood in which the family lived. This clearly indicates that employment can be a significant factor contributing to or mitigating maternal depression.

In speculating on why relinquishing a job should be closely associated with susceptibility to depression, we suggest that the mothers in this situation missed the financial and social benefits that they had derived

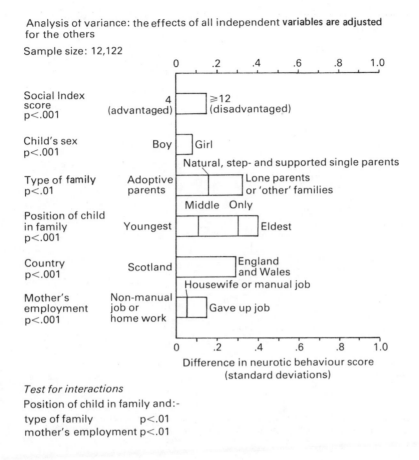

Analysis of variance: the effects of all independent variables are adjusted for the others

Sample size: 12,122

Figure 15.5 Analysis of mother's employment and neurotic behaviour

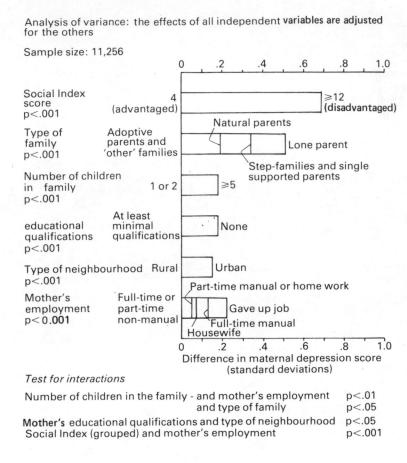

Analysis of variance: the effects of all independent variables are adjusted for the others

Sample size: 11,256

Figure 15.6 Analysis of mother's employment and maternal depression

from their work and that their depressive symptoms were a reaction to this deprivation. A second plausible explanation is that the circumstances which necessitated the mother's giving up her job may themselves have been responsible for her being depressed. Whatever the explanation, our findings point to the fact that women who give up their jobs to become full-time housewives and mothers are at increased risk of depression.

Brown and Harris found that employment may be more beneficial in reducing the risk of depression for certain vulnerable groups of women than for others. On the basis of this premise we would expect such an effect to show up in our analysis as an interaction between mother's employment situation and one or more of the other factors in the analysis. Interactions were indeed found between the mother's employment and the number of children in the family (p < .01) as well as between employment and grouped Social Index score (p < .001 – for a description of the statistical methods adopted please see Chapter 20). Although we did not find that the interaction of this variable with family size showed a consistent or simple pattern of any theoretical interest, the interaction with the Social Index did have interesting implications which merit further discussion.

Unlike Moss and Plewis (1977) who reported no social class difference in the proportion of mothers they studied with 'mental distress', we found that socioeconomic inequality was the factor which was associated with the greatest differences in maternal depression. Socially disadvantaged mothers were most at risk of depression and, following Brown and Harris, were hypothesised as being the group most likely to derive a psychiatric benefit from being employed. This hypothesis was explored following the statistical procedures described in Chapter 20 concerning interactions in analyses of variance. The results presented in Table 15.1 compare the expected mean depression scores obtained from the main effects analyses of variance (summarised in Figure 15.6), with the observed mean depression scores for each employment category within three Social Index groups. Interest centres on those categories where there were large differences between expected and observed mean scores as these were the ones where the effect of employment situation on depression score deviated from that predicted from the main effects (i.e. additive) model in Figure 15.6.

Socially disadvantaged mothers who were in any of the types of employment described earlier had lower mean depression scores than did the full-time housewives in this social group; even those disadvantaged mothers who had full-time manual jobs had lower scores than expected, while those unfortunate ones who had previously been in employment but had given it up were at even higher risk of depression. These results support Brown and Harris' hypothesis that employment

can reduce the risk of depression in women with a particular vulnerability to this condition; in our case the vulnerable mothers were those
defined as being socially disadvantaged.

The implications of employment related to depression were quite
different for socially advantaged mothers from those for disadvantaged
mothers. The mean depression scores of advantaged mothers in non-
manual jobs differed little from that of housewives, whereas manual
employment, especially if full-time, was associated with greater risk of
maternal depression. Advantaged mothers who gave up their jobs were
slightly more depressed than mothers from similar backgrounds who
had never been employed, but the increase was considerably less than
that shown by disadvantaged mothers who had given up jobs.

These results go one stage further than the formulation put forward
by Brown and Harris and suggest that socially advantaged women, who
are at risk of becoming depressed, may increase that likelihood if they
take up physically demanding employment, particularly if it is on a
full-time basis. However we should exercise caution against too readily
accepting a causal explanation for these effects and be prepared to consider other reasons. It may be that mothers rated as socially advantaged
according to the Social Index who were yet in manual employment
(which is a contradictory finding) belong to socially aspiring families
who are struggling to maintain a standard of living beyond their normal
income. The stress generated by this economic pressure may be responsible for the higher levels of depression found in these mothers. This
explanation cannot be applied to socially disadvantaged mothers,
however, and our results suggest that for these women employment
outside the home can reduce the risk of depression.

Summary

There is little evidence of any erosion of the traditional gender based
division of labour between parents within the home. Mothers who wish
to go out to work can do so only if they can also fit in their domestic
responsibilities outside of their working hours or else obtain help from
elsewhere. The basic conflict between the traditional view of the
mother as the parent with primary responsibility for child care and her
own desire to have a paid job outside of the home may generate stress
in the family. Such stress may lead to psychiatric problems for the
mother and accompanying behavioural deviance in the child.

Previous research has not shown that mothers' employment has
serious detrimental effects on child behaviour or ability, unless they
were employed full-time. These studies have not, however, considered
the possible implications of the type of work the mother did, and this is

likely to be a key factor in providing her with satisfaction in her job. In the present study a comparison was made of children of non-employed mothers and those of mothers who worked full-time or part-time in manual or non-manual jobs, revealing significant though small differences in tests of general cognitive ability. The scores on vocabulary tests showed larger differences, with children of mothers in full-time manual employment having lower than average scores. These differences persisted after statistical adjustment for other social and family factors.

Full-time maternal employment was associated with an increased risk of antisocial behaviour in the child, especially when the mother had a manual job. However, children of mothers who had given up a job outside the home in the previous five years were also more likely to be antisocial or neurotic. These behavioural effects that were associated with different patterns of maternal employment were probably a consequence of the mother's own response to her employment status. Maternal depression was found to be reduced in socially disadvantaged mothers who were employed, and mothers in this social group who had given up a job were more depressed than housewives who had not had a job in the previous five years. This effect was not found in socially advantaged mothers who, on the contrary, were more depressed if employed in manual occupations.

Part Four

Research methods

Chapter 16

The survey

Why a week of births?

The present study takes as its sample all the children in England, Wales and Scotland who were born during the week 5-11 April 1970. In this it follows the blueprint devised in 1945 by a Joint Committee of the Population Investigation Committee (PIC) and the Royal College of Obstetricians and Gynaecologists for the purposes of obtaining specific information on the use made of the maternity services and on the cost of having children (Douglas and Blomfield, 1948). Taking a population of children born during one week was considered an adequate means of obtaining the required information, reduced administrative problems and, hence, kept costs to a minimum. The week 3-9 March 1946 was simply the earliest time that it was possible for the PIC survey to take place. The Joint Committee could not have known at that time that their decision would set a precedent for at least two further national studies of childbirth which also took one week of Spring births; the first in 1958 (Butler and Bonham, 1963) and the second in 1970 (Chamberlain et al., 1975). Neither could they have foreseen that the original 1946 cohort would subsequently be followed up throughout childhood and into adulthood in a series of studies known as the National Survey of Health and Development (Atkins et al., 1980) as are the 1958 and 1970 cohorts also.

In all these studies the choice of one week of births was a practical solution to the problem of carrying out national perinatal and obstetric surveys of newborn children and their mothers. Seasonal variation in perinatal mortality and morbidity rates, however, could mean that prevalence estimates might not be correct for children born at other times of the year. Furthermore, the established practice of following up these children in successive surveys entails further methodological difficulties (Douglas, 1976). Respiratory infections in early infancy, for

259

example, are likely to be fewer among those born in the Spring than in the Autumn, and so are accidental burns which are particularly likely to occur when a child is learning to walk at a time of year when fires are in use. The season of the year is also important in relation to age at infant school entry since Summer born children may have up to a year more primary education than those born in the Autumn (Palmer, 1971).

These methodological objections in following up children born during one week must be set against the administrative convenience of tracing children born in a given week compared with, for example, sampling births spread throughout the year. Also if one of the purposes of the study is to follow up small but important risk groups such as children who experienced perinatal complications, or who were born with congenital malformations, or who were illegitimate at birth, then the whole of the original one week birth cohort would be needed in order to have sufficient numbers of these groups (e.g. Davie *et al.*, 1972, Chapters 8, 14 and 16; Chamberlain and Davey, 1975 and 1976). Sometimes it is not until a later stage of the longitudinal study that defects or problems become apparent. It is important in these cases to be then able to refer back to earlier data to seek possible causes of subsequently emerging problems.

It should be recognised also that the possibility of seasonal variations, such as those suggested above, mainly affect prevalence estimates. Analyses concerned with associations between factors, for example, between social class and preschool experience, are unlikely to be affected by seasonal differences in rates of uptake of different types of preschool provision. Similarly, longitudinal analysis concerned with change or growth over periods of time may be satisfactorily based on data obtained from one week of births (Goldstein, 1968, pp. 98-9). Sometimes the fact that all the children were born in one week can be used to make a point that would not be easy to demonstrate using other sampling methods. For example, although all these children were the same age there was still a year's variation in age at school entry and considerable regional variation which possibly reflects policy differences between the regions (see Chapter 6). In short, seasonal considerations are unlikely to seriously affect the majority of analyses based on a one week birth cohort.

Tracing the children

The children in England and Wales were traced through the cooperation of the registration division of the Registrar General's Office (RGO), the National Health Service Central Register (NHSCR) and Family

Practitioner Committees (FPCs). The RGO produced a computer listing of every child whose date of birth was registered as occurring during the week 5-11 April 1970. Using the details provided by the RGO the NHSCR was then able to identify the Area Health Authority (AHA) in which each child was last registered with a NHS general practitioner. The NHSCR could also say if a child had gone abroad, was registered with a Service Medical Officer, i.e. if the father was a member of HM Forces, or had died, in which case a copy of the death certificate was supplied. Using the NHS number provided by the NHSCR, Family Practitioner Committees could pinpoint the home address of children who had not emigrated or died. This information was passed to the community nursing service of the AHA in which the FPC was located, and the local health visitors personally approached the families in question, inviting them to participate in the study. This procedure ensured that information confidential to the health authorities such as the home address of the study child was not disclosed to the research team unless the parents had agreed to take part.

A similar procedure was adopted in Scotland, but because the administrative structure was slightly different, the Scottish NHSCR was provided with the names of the children who had taken part in the British Births (1970) study. They added the child's NHS number and located the Health Board in which the child was last registered with a NHS general practitioner. Administrators of Primary Care in each Health Board used this information to identify each child's home address which was communicated to the health visitors who then invited the parents' participation.

The whereabouts of children of servicemen who were registered with a Service Medical Officer were determined with the help of the Service Children's Education Authority. This group included 64 children of service families who were interviewed by nurses of the Soldiers, Sailors and Airmen Families Association (SSAFA) in West Germany, Malta, Gibraltar and Singapore. These children were included in the survey because they were members of the British Births cohort and although they were overseas in 1975 were likely to return to Britain and be included in future follow-ups of the cohort.

These methods of tracing depended entirely on the availability of information obtained at the time of the children's birth. Thus children who were born outside Great Britain but were resident here in 1975 could not be traced in this way. Health visitors located some of these children by scanning child health records for children born during the study week, but immigrant children were inevitably under-represented in the sample. The NHSCR could provide no information about children who were adopted for reasons of confidentiality. Some adopted children were located from child health records, but information obtained on these children at age five could not be linked with that obtained at birth because of the lack of necessary information concerning their origins.

The cohort size in 1975 was estimated to be 16,284 children (Table 16.1). Of these, 13,135 (80.7 percent) were successfully traced and interviewed on or shortly after their fifth birthdays in April 1975 (Table 16.2). This was considered to be a reasonable response rate considering the difficulty of tracing children in the preschool period. Nevertheless, in order to obtain information on as many of the cohort children as possible, a second follow-up was mounted in 1977. Tracing was this time carried out with the cooperation of Education Authorities throughout Great Britain and independent schools with children in this age group. Class teachers were able to identify children in the 1970 birth cohort by scanning their registers for all children born during the study week. This resulted in information being obtained on a further 1,917 (11.8 percent) of the cohort using a short questionnaire specially designed for this purpose. It was not possible at this stage to administer the full range of questionnaires and tests used in the five-year survey. The main purpose of the seven-year survey was to check for certain sources of bias in the data obtained in the 1975 survey (see Chapter 17).

Table 16.2 shows that only 3.9 percent of the parents declined to take part in either five- or seven-year surveys and 1.2 percent were traced but not interviewed for other or unknown reasons. As a result of the tracing exercises at five and seven years only 2.5 percent remained unidentified and information was obtained on 92.5 percent of the total cohort.

Data collection

Four research documents (reproduced in the Appendix) were used in the five-year survey. These were:

1 Home Interview Questionnaire
2 Maternal Self-completion Questionnaire
3 Developmental History Schedule
4 Test Booklet

These documents were designed to obtain different types of information.

1 The Home Interview Questionnaire (HIQ) was administered by health visitors who carried out the interviews in the children's own

homes. Usually the interviewee was the mother (92.3 percent). Relatively few fathers were present at interviews (7 percent). Fewer than one percent of the interviews were carried out with persons other than the child's parents. Many questions in the HIQ had precoded response categories where a finite number of responses could be anticipated. Other questions were of the open-ended type which required responses to be written down. This approach was used where the potential range of responses was unknown in advance. Replies to open-ended questions were coded according to schema devised by scrutinising a thousand randomly selected questionnaires.

2 The Maternal Self-completion Questionnaire (MSQ) was designed for completion by the mother herself. This was done mainly to reduce the effect of interviewer bias in completing the attitudinal data. However, this also served to reduce the duration of the home interview. More than half the mothers (56.4 percent) completed the MSQ out of the presence of the health visitor and a further 28.1 percent completed it unaided during the health visitor's visit. The health visitor's help was needed by only 15.5 percent of the mothers, some of whom had difficulty in reading or required an interpreter. The MSQ contained questions concerning the child's behaviour at home and maternal depression. These were based on the Rutter A Scale of behavioural deviance and the Malaise Inventory (Rutter *et al.*, 1970). There were also forty-three attitudinal items designed to elicit attitudes towards child rearing, maternal employment, television viewing and hospital visiting.

3 The Developmental History Schedule (DHS) was designed to obtain information from child health records. Details of developmental screening throughout the preschool period were obtained by reference to child health clinic and health visitor records where these were available. As these records contained prospective observations, details such as early surveillance by the child health service did not depend solely on the mother's memory. Child health records were also used to corroborate details in the HIQ obtained from the mother of handicap or developmental problems. Results from the DHS, however, are not included in this report but are to be published separately.

4 The Test Booklet (TB) was administered by the health visitor during her visit to the child at home. Several tests were completed and those included in this report are described in detail in Chapter 19.

To achieve a reasonable degree of consistency in the manner in which interviews and tests were carried out nationally, a comprehensive set of explanatory notes was prepared for the health visitor interviewers. In addition, briefing meetings were held at regional centres throughout Britain. Criticism of the deployment of health visitors as survey interviewers (Newson, 1970, p. 19) is totally misplaced in studies of this type (Douglas, 1976, pp. 11-13). Nearly half the families in this study were known to the health visitor interviewers through previous professional contact. Health visitors are seen by the mothers as medical workers with a legitimate interest in all aspects of the children's health, development, social and family circumstances. Health visitors also had access to child health records which provided an important additional source of information on the early health surveillance of these children as well as the means of tracing additional children born in the study week.

The main period of data collection took place over six months in 1975, during which time information was obtained on 95 percent of the traced sample (Figure 16.1). Thus, inferences can be made about children aged between five and five and a half years. The same statistical considerations apply to this sample as to that of the National Child Development Study. (Davie *et al.*, 1972, p. 216 and Pringle *et al.*, 1966, p. 10, concisely summarise these considerations.)

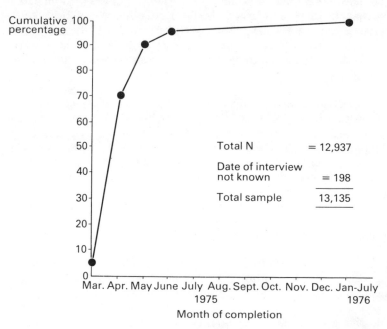

Figure 16.1　Month of completion of Home Interview Questionnaire

Chapter 17

Non-response

Almost all empirical research faces the risk of non-response. Non-response presents a problem because usually it is impossible to know how the absence of certain information may affect the results of the research (Cox *et al.*, 1977). Thus it is important firstly to ensure that non-response is kept to a minimum and, secondly, where it cannot be avoided, to attempt to ascertain how the results of a study might be affected.

There are basically two types of non-response which we shall term specific and gross non-response.

Specific non-response

Specific non-response occurs where respondents cooperate in the study but fail to complete every part of it and results in some questions having a proportion of 'not stated' responses. This may be due to respondents accidentally missing out a question or section of a questionnaire or to their deliberately not answering a question because they object to its content or do not understand it. Some questions are more prone to specific non-response than others because of the manner in which they are presented on the page of the questionnaire or are arranged in such a way that respondents fail to notice them. Piloting questionnaires reduces these problems but can never eliminate them.

Some forms of response cannot make a useful contribution to analysis and are consequently treated as specific non-response. For example, where a numerical answer is required respondents sometimes put 'often' or 'rarely' or 'many' or similar non-numerical responses which are unusable. A valid response to some questions is 'not known' which means that the respondent understands the question but is unable to provide an answer. Although this accurately portrays the situation at the time of the interview, such a response can contribute nothing to most analyses and therefore is treated as a specific non-response.

Some questions in the present study were affected more by specific non-response than others. For example, information about the parental situation was obtained on every child, but information about the father's experience of any unemployment was not available for over 30 percent of the children. Specific non-response for unemployment was so high that it was decided to exclude this variable from the report. The majority of variables, however, had a specific non-response rate of under 5 percent.

Multivariate analysis involving several independent variables was most affected by non-response because only cases with complete data could be included. This results in between 1 and 18 percent of the children being omitted from the analysis depending on the particular subset of variables involved. The social and family characteristics of children excluded in this way from selected multivariate analyses were compared with children with complete data and no important differences were found.

In cross-tabular analysis the distribution of specific non-responders on one variable could be examined with respect to the variable with which it was cross-tabulated. This showed whether the specific non-responders on one variable differed significantly from the rest of the sample with respect to the second variable. No once and for all check for possible bias due to specific non-response in a particular variable could be done as bias could appear in some tables but not in others. However, examination of many tables used in this study revealed no bias of any significance resulting from specific non-response which would substantially alter the conclusions reported.

Gross non-response

In almost every empirical enquiry there is a proportion of individuals who form part of the sample being studied for whom no information is obtained at all. This we term gross non-response. The two main causes of gross non-response in the CHES (1975) survey were failure to trace children born in the study week and unwillingness on the part of some families to cooperate in the study. The total gross non-response rate in the 1975 survey was only a fifth (19.3 percent) of the estimated sample size (see Table 16.2), despite the difficulty of tracing the children before they had all entered infant school. It was decided, however, to trace and obtain limited information about the children who were missed in the 1975 study in order to check whether these differed in any important respects from those who were successfully traced and interviewed. This additional survey took place just two years later, when the children were seven.

There was little regional variation in trace rates (Table 17.1). Children in the South East region of England were somewhat under-represented in the 1975 survey (27.4 percent compared with 32.7 percent in 1977) and there were fewer Scottish children in 1975 (8.9 percent compared with 11.9 percent in 1977). These differences may be attributed to the relatively high mobility rates in the South East region, and the different method of tracing used in Scotland in 1975 (Chapter 16). Movement between regions since the children's fifth birthdays were likely to be minimal since less than a third of the 1977 sample (31.9 percent) had moved at all since their fifth birthday and many of these moves would have been *within* regions, thus the regional distribution in 1977 provides a reasonable comparison with that of 1975.

The social class distributions in the two surveys were also very similar (Table 17.2). There was a suggestion that it was children of non-manual workers who were slightly under-represented in the 1975 sample but the observed differences were too small to introduce any serious bias into the results based on the 1975 data.

Whilst broad parameters such as region and social class show little evidence of bias in the 1975 sample, factors more directly related to the problems of tracing and interviewing cohort members, such as geographical mobility and family disruption, proved to be more important considerations. A selection of such factors are presented in Table 17.3.

Lower proportions of children in the 1977 survey were living with their natural parents. Of the children in the 1975 sample, 98.1 percent were with their natural mothers compared with 91.9 percent of the 1977 sample children. Children still with their natural fathers were 90.9 percent and 78.2 percent in 1975 and 1977 respectively. This suggests that children in families which experienced some form of parental disruption were more difficult to trace for interviewing and thus were slightly under-represented in the 1975 survey. It was anticipated that the children for whom there was a sizeable loss from the 1975 survey were adopted children. Only 0.7 percent of the children in the 1975 study were with adoptive mothers compared with 4.5 percent in 1977. The figures were 1.2 percent and 6.1 percent respectively for adoptive fathers. It is possible that some children may have lost one or other of their natural parents *since* the 1975 survey took place. However, this happened for only 15 percent of children with substitute mothers and 12 percent of children with substitute fathers in the 1977 sample.

Children of ethnic minorities were more difficult to trace, especially if they had come into Britain since the time of their birth. Interviewing difficulties, especially where there were language differences, further

267

increased the risk of bias in the study. The 1975 survey found 92.3 percent of the children were with parents who were both of UK origin, i.e. not members of an ethnic minority, but in 1977 this figure was down to 84 percent. Only 26 children (1.4 percent) in the 1977 survey were not born in the UK and arrived after their fifth birthday, thereby precluding the possibility of taking part in the 1975 survey. Thus immigration since 1975 makes little difference to our conclusion that non-UK children were slightly under-represented in the 1975 survey.

Families which are geographically mobile are expected to be difficult to trace. Results in Table 17.3 suggest that this factor could have been a major reason why some families were not traced in time for the 1975 survey. Only 26.4 percent of children in the 1977 survey had never moved before their fifth birthday compared with 43.1 percent in the 1975 survey. To the extent that mobility is often associated with family disruption this could be a significant source of bias in some analyses. Even with this sizeable difference between the children in the two surveys, however, the relatively large size of the sample interviewed in 1975 compared with the 1977 sample means that any bias resulting from the loss of children in mobile families will be trivial for analyses involving the whole 1975 survey sample. Analysis carried out on a subsample of highly mobile children (i.e. those who moved more than twice in five years), however, would be very prone to error because over a fifth (22.9 percent) of this group were untraced for the 1975 survey.

Another group of children we thought might have been difficult to locate in the preschool period were those who had been taken into care or lived in residential institutions. Table 17.3 indicates a significant difference ($p < .001$) between the 1975 and 1977 surveys in the proportion of children ever in these situations during the preschool period, (2.5 percent in 1975 and 4.1 percent in 1977 surveys). Part of this difference may have been due to the relatively high specific non-response rate in the 1975 survey (20.1 percent). Also the small proportions of children taken into care in a residential home means that general bias in the 1975 sample as a result of not tracing some of these children was minimal.

Finally, we examined the possibility that the housing conditions of children in the 1977 sample differed from those of children in the 1975 sample. Comparisons were made in terms of overcrowding (persons per room ratio), and availability of four basic household amenities (kitchen, bathroom, indoor lavatory and hot water supply). The observed differences were so small that statistical significance was achieved for only two of the five housing indicators — crowding and availability of a kitchen (Table 17.3). These items suggested that the 1975 sample had a slight excess of children in poor housing conditions. The differences, however, were not sufficient to create a bias in the 1975 sample.

Implications of non-response

In general specific non-response has not been found an important source of bias although we have avoided the use of variables with relatively large specific non-response rates. We have found gross non-response to be associated with the factors we expected as a result of our method of tracing, e.g. adopted children, immigrant children and geographically mobile children. In other respects, e.g. the regional distribution, children in care, social class and housing factors, the children traced and interviewed in 1975 did not differ markedly from the whole sample as suggested by the results of the follow-up of previously untraced children in 1977. It is important to recognise, however, that there may be important differences between the traced and untraced parts of the sample about which we have no information, and, indeed, the 1977 survey was itself subject to some degree of non-response. It is possible, also, that the group of respondents who refused to take part in the study in 1975 may have contained, for example, higher proportions of deviant families or children with behavioural problems (Cox *et al.*, 1977). However, the refusals in 1975 constituted only 4.7 percent of the total estimated sample, whereas the main loss was due to the 14.6 percent untraced in 1975. (These figures do not appear in Table 16.2 as 137 families that had refused to participate in 1975 agreed to take part in the 1977 survey which reduced the overall refusal rate to 3.9 percent as given in Table 16.2.) Cox *et al.*, concluded that where refusal rates were kept below 10 percent '. . . the distortion of total population rates which results from missing data is trivial' (p. 136). Thus on this evidence bias resulting from a 4.7 percent refusal rate in the CHES (1975) survey is likely to be negligible. Analysis of non-response in the National Child Development Study (Davie *et al.*, 1972, p. 220) suggested that the behavioural adjustment of children whose parents refused or were untraced was no different from other children but their reading ability was slightly poorer than those whose parents were in the study. Although direct comparisons between the NCDS (1965) and CHES (1975) surveys are limited by the fact that the children were of different ages (7 years and 5 years) and the methods of tracing were different, the NCDS results do indicate that bias resulting from gross non-response was minimal in terms of behavioural deviance and school attainment of the children.

Our examination of specific and gross non-response based on our own data and the findings of other studies leads us to conclude that bias resulting from non-response in the 1975 survey was likely to be small. Certain subgroups, however, were more vulnerable to omission from the 1975 survey and these were children who had experienced family disruption or were geographically mobile and children in ethnic minorities.

Chapter 18

Variables which require definition

The majority of variables used in this report are self-explanatory and require no further definition. However, variables that have been specially devised for this study or are based on specific classifications do need explanation and the derivation of such variables is described below.

Region

Regional analysis is important insofar as it highlights geographical differences in social structure, industry and services. There are, of course, important variations within regions but this fact need not detract from the significance of the marked regional differences described in this report. We have used the standard regional classification as defined for the 1971 census for optimal comparability of our data with those of other national surveys. Great Britain is subdivided into Wales, Scotland and eight regions in England. A comparison of the CHES sample with families with children of all ages in the 1971 census revealed only small differences between the regional distribution of the two samples. For some analyses in this report the English regions were grouped together to provide a contrast between the three countries of Great Britain. This was only done where no major differences appeared between the English regions.

Social class

The occupations of both father and mother were coded using the Office of Population Censuses and Surveys' Social Class classification (OPCS, 1970). We have adopted this classification for purposes of comparison with other studies and also when interest focussed specifically on occupational status (for example Chapters 2 and 12). Beyond this limited usage occupational social class has not been employed as a general indicator of social inequality. Instead we have devised a composite Social Index for this purpose which is described later in this chapter. The father's occupation, however, is a contributory factor in this Index.

In order to acquire a working knowledge of the classification of occupations and its application, four members of the CHES coding staff spent two days at the OPCS headquarters. During the course of the study the OPCS also checked randomly selected occupational data. The agreement rate between the experienced OPCS staff and our own coders exceeded 98 percent for the coding of occupations.

Comparison of the CHES sample with 1971 census families suggest a somewhat greater concentration of families in social class IIIM and fewer in social classes IV and V compared with families with children of all ages. The lower proportions of CHES families in social classes IV and V cannot be attributed to biases due to tracing difficulties as the seven-year follow-up of children not traced at five years revealed very small social class differences between the five- and seven-year samples (Table 17.2).

Age of parents

This variable gives the age of the people recorded as parents at the time of the five-year follow-up survey. This included substitute parents who were members of the household. The parents' age was that as at the time of the study child's fifth birthday.

Family size

The number of people in the household included all who were resident at the same address and who were catered for by the same person or benefiting from a common housekeeping. This included people who were unrelated to the study child as well as those who were related by birth or by legal processes (e.g. adoption and marriage). The number of children in the household who were older than the study child is not synonymous with parity as all older children are included, not just the study child's natural siblings. Also this takes no account of earlier pregnancies of the mother which parity requires. Similarly, the number of children younger than the study child includes unrelated children as well as siblings. This approach was adopted for this report in which the emphasis is on social and economic considerations rather than biological issues.

Type of family

The classification of family structure and composition devised for this study reflects the fact that the focus of our research is the child. For the child, the most important family dimensions are his or her relationships with the people acting as parents. Thus it is this relationship, as defined by the parents themselves, which forms the basis for the family classification. The relationship between the parents themselves — whether or not they are legally married — is of almost no direct consequence for the child, although the quality of the marital relationship or informal partnership, and its degree of stability, may have crucial implications for the child. For the purposes of this classification parents who lived permanently away from their child's home were not regarded as parents. These principles follow closely those adopted by the Finer Committee on One-Parent Families (1974) and the National Child Development Study (Lambert and Streather, 1980, p. 55). However, our six-category classification has some important innovations over those used by the Finer Committee and the NCDS.

Table 18.1 shows the resultant CHES classification which is described in more detail below. The first three groups constitute different types of two-parent families.

1 Both natural parents. Ninety percent of children were living with both their natural parents at the age of five. Whilst it is possible that some of these children may have experienced some kind of disruption in their family life, such as living away from home for a period or a temporary separation of the parents, the fact that the original family unit was intact five years after the child's birth indicated that it was still functioning with a measure of stability. In contrast to this majority the remaining 10 percent of children had lost either one or both original parents and were living in a variety of family circumstances.

2 Step-families. We have designated as step-families those in which the child lived with one natural parent and a substitute parent. This family grouping formed 2.7 percent of the sample. Although the children in this situation may have had an unsettled period in their earlier family life, by the age of five they were in an apparently stable family unit. Included in this step-family category are children whose substitute parent was the cohabitee rather than spouse of the natural parent. These numbered 93 and in 79 cases the cohabitees were father substitutes. Our rationale for including cohabitees was that the parents defined this relationship themselves and in all probability it differed from the average family structure only by the absence of a legal marriage. Furthermore we suspect that a similar situation prevailed in a number

of the families where children were described as living with both natural parents. It would therefore be a distortion of the real picture to cate-gorise families with a natural parent and cohabitee as one-parent families. Also under the step-family heading were 60 children who had been adopted by one of their natural parents — usually the putative father. Children adopted by both parents, however, were classified separately.

3 Adoptive families. This category consists of families in which the child has been adopted by both parents; they comprise less than one percent (N = 96) of the children in the sample, but this figure must be regarded as an underestimate because the strict confidentiality sur-rounding adoption procedures made it much more difficult to trace adopted children in the preschool period (see Chapter 17). Data from the seven-year follow-up study, which was not subject to the tracing constraints of the 1975 survey, suggest a more accurate estimate of the proportion of children aged five who had been adopted by both parents to be 1.2 percent. A further sixty children had been adopted by one of the parents, all but one of whom were adoptive fathers, usually legalis-ing their relationship to a child of their wife's former union. These sixty children were included not in the adoptive group, but with children living in what we have described above as step-families.

4 Supported one-parent families. Although 5.7 percent of CHES children at age five had only one natural parent, 1.9 percent were in a household which included at least one other adult living there on a permanent basis. These additional adults were grandparents or others who may or may not have been related to the child and did not neces-sarily fulfil a parental role. The term 'supported one-parent family' is meant to suggest that the other adult members of the household were at least available to help the single parent in various ways, such as looking after the child whilst he or she was at work. Economic support may also have been forthcoming through the provision of a home or in financial emergencies.

5 Lone one-parent families. In contrast to the previous group were 3.8 percent of children who lived in households in which the natural parent was the only resident adult. These lone one-parent families were more isolated emotionally and socially with the single parent carrying the full burden of maintaining a separate home. Except for a purely descriptive account by Leete (1979, Table 6) there is no record to our knowledge that this distinction between supported and lone one-parent families has ever been explored in any other research study. This is an important point to be considered, particularly when taken in conjunction with the

finding that the proportion of five-year-olds in one-parent families in this study (5.7 percent) is considerably higher than the figure of under 3 percent found by the NCDS among seven-year-olds in 1965 (Ferri, 1976, Table A5.3). This difference reflects the increased prevalence of one-parent families over the decade (National Council for One Parent Families, 1980).

6 Other families. 62 children (0.5 percent) were not living with either natural parent at the time of the survey. Of these 34 were living with grandparents, 26 with foster parents and two with other relatives.

A further 14 children were living in residential institutions at the time of the survey. As the home circumstances of these children differed so markedly from those of children in the typical family unit they have been excluded from the classification.

Ethnic group

Our interest in the ethnic group of the study child and his or her parents lay in the cultural differences in family life that were likely to have implications for the child's health, development and education in the context of British society. Preliminary examination of the data on ethnicity revealed that many children whose natural parents were both given as, say, West Indian, were nevertheless recorded as European (UK), based on the child's nationality rather than his or her ethnic origin. To counter this we have devised a special variable based on the ethnic group of both present parents (see Table 18.2). According to this classification 92.3 percent of the children in the sample were with parents of British descent. The ethnic minorities which were of most interest to this report were the West Indian (1.3 percent) and Asian (2.0 percent) families. These groups were likely to be under-represented, however, because of tracing difficulties (see Chapter 17). Where interest centred on one or other parent rather than the child, that parent's ethnic group was used; for example, when looking for ethnic differences in maternal employment rates (Chapter 12), the mother's own ethnic origin was applicable.

Type of neighbourhood

The type of neighbourhood in which a family lives has been found to have many social and psychiatric implications affecting quality of life in general (Osborn and Carpenter, 1980). In this study we hypothesised that a child's neighbourhood of residence could have an important influence on both health and well-being as well as on utilisation of health and education services.

A simple classification of neighbourhoods was achieved by asking the health visitors to say which of four brief descriptions best characterised the district in which the study child lived (see question H.2 in the Home Interview Questionnaire in the Appendix). The classification contains three urban categories (labelled Poor, Average and Well-to-do). In addition, a fourth 'rural' category was provided mainly to overcome the difficulty of rating a small community where well-to-do and poorer families live fairly close together. Where the health visitor felt she was unable to assign a neighbourhood to one of these four categories, she was asked to describe the neighbourhood in her own words. This occurred in 11.2 percent of the sample and these were assigned to the four basic categories by coding staff on the basis of given criteria.

One difficulty associated with subjective ratings is the risk of low inter-rater reliability; to check this a study was designed and carried out in the county of Avon (Osborn and Carpenter, 1980). Two independent ratings were obtained on each of the 322 neighbourhoods selected at random from a street gazeteer of Avon. The Kendall's Tau B rank correlation between the two sets of results was .70 (p < .001) which is a satisfactory level of agreement for a rating of this type. One of the principal sources of disagreement between ratings concerned the Well-to-do and Rural categories, with some health visitors clearly rating relatively well-off families living in the country as 'Well-to-do' and others recording this as a 'Rural' situation. This neighbourhood classification would be improved by rating the 'urban-rural' dimension separately from the 'quality of neighbourhood' dimension; but in a study where questionnaire space was at a premium this was not feasible.

The distribution obtained using the neighbourhood rating is shown in Table 18.3, where it is also compared with the classification of father's occupation. The majority of children lived in an Average (49.7 percent) or Well-to-do (23.2 percent) neighbourhood, while less than one in five (18.9 percent) lived in a rural environment. A sizeable minority (8.2 percent) lived in Poor neighbourhoods, usually located in inner city areas. Whilst there was a strong association between the type of neighbourhood in which a child lived and the family's social class position, different types of neighbourhood contained families from all social classes. A third (34.1 percent) of families in Poor neighbourhoods were in the lowest social class groups (IV and V) and more than a third (37.7 percent) of all families in Well-to-do neighbourhoods were in manual social classes, rather than the professional or managerial social classes as might be expected. Rural neighbourhoods had an excess of social class I and II families but the proportions of the other social class groups in Rural areas were not much different from average.

The important point is that the neighbourhood rating identified some-what different 'advantaged' and 'disadvantaged' groups from those identified using the social class classification of father's occupation and has provided an alternative social classification which in certain contexts, e.g. utilisation of preschool education services, may be of greater explanatory value because of the geographical basis for the provision of services and the development of different communities.

Social Index

Occupational status has been a traditionally accepted index of social inequality and is strongly predictive of many social and economic differences (Central Statistical Office, 1975, pp. 13-32; Reid, 1981). The convention adopted in studies of child development has been to use the father's occupation as an index of the family's social class position. Osborn and Morris (1979) have argued that using occupational status in this way in child studies creates difficulties and to overcome them have developed a Social Index to provide an alternative indicator of social inequality. The rationale and significance of the Social Index is described in Chapter 1. In the present chapter we describe the system of scoring the items comprising the Index and the possible effects of non-response.

The Index is comprised of eight variables hypothesised as being indices of a common socioeconomic dimension. These variables and the weighted scores of their categories are given in Table 18.4. A total Social Index score is obtained by summing the weighted scores of the variables and adding ten to give a positive total score. For example, a child whose father was in a Social Class I job (score -1), whose mother had a teaching qualification (score -2), who lived in a Rural neighbourhood (score 0), in a house (score 0) where there were five rooms for a family of three (score 0), which the parents were buying (score -1), but lacked a bathroom (score 1) and had no car (score 0) would have a total Social Index score of 7 ($10 - 3$). The minimum possible score was 4 ($10 - 6$) and the maximum 18 ($10 + 8$) although the actual range achieved was 4 to 16 as indicated by Table 18.5 which gives the resultant distribution of Social Index scores.

As the system of scoring has both positive and negative weights a zero weighting for items where information was missing caused little bias to the resultant total score. Clearly only cases with the most complete information could have achieved scores which approached the extremes of the distribution and cases with information missing on several items had scores which tend towards the mean where any bias due to non-response had least effect. This can be seen in Table 18.6

where 74.3 percent of families with information missing on two or more Social Index items had scores between 8 and 10 compared with 51.4 percent of families whose scores were within this range and had complete information. Thus the system of scoring ensures that the groups on which most research interest centres, i.e. the extreme scorers, were the very ones for whom the most complete information was available. In fact less than one percent of the sample had missing information on more than one item. The Social Index was particularly useful in analyses involving families where there was no father figure and hence no social class classification. The possibility of any bias resulting from this has been investigated and found to be negligible (Osborn and Morris, 1979). The correlation between the standard Social Index score and a score based on a modified Social Index which excluded the weights for the classification of father's occupations was .96 (Pearson's r, N = 12,267). This correlation was calculated for the subsample of families for whom an occupational classification was available. The high correlation was partly due to the fact that only the scores of children whose fathers were in occupational classes I, IV or V were affected by the omission of this variable from the Social Index and this applied to only 25 percent of the sample. This example illustrates how absence of information on one item in the Social Index affects the ranking produced only minimally and that the limitations of individual items were compensated for by the others.

One of the advantages of the Social Index compared with the social class classification is that mean scores can be used when appropriate thereby simplifying certain kinds of analysis (e.g. Figure 3.1 in Chapter 3). As a covariate in analysis of variance, the Social Index provides a more adequate method of controlling for socioeconomic differences than social class based only on father's occupation; in particular it means that fatherless children can be retained in the analysis. For tabular analyses the Social Index scores have been grouped into five categories. How this grouping was decided is described in Chapter 1, but one objective was to have approximately 10 percent of the sample in each extreme category thus providing substantially more cases in the most advantaged and disadvantaged categories than were in the social class distribution. Table 18.7, which compares Social Index and social class classifications, shows that the Social Index groups had 9.6 percent most advantaged compared with 6.9 percent in social class I and 11.3 percent most disadvantaged compared with only 4.9 percent in social class V. This is useful in tabular analysis where, even with a large sample such as we have, the numbers in some cells can be reduced to a level where statistical inference becomes unreliable if categories of variables contain too few cases.

In addition, Table 18.7 shows that whilst there was a strong association between occupational status and Social Index scores, there was also considerable deviation with most of the occupational classes being spread over four or five Social Index groups. Perhaps the most important feature of this table concerns the 854 children with no social class classification, most of whom were fatherless. Of these, 56.8 percent were in the disadvantaged or most disadvantaged Social Index groups compared with 24.5 percent of the children with a social class classification. This indicates a significant source of bias in the social class classification attributable to the group for whom no occupational information was available which has a negligible effect on the Social Index score for these cases.

Chapter 19

Measures of ability, behaviour and maternal depression

Tests and assessments of the children's ability and behaviour were needed in this study to provide a means of comparing the significance of different types of social and emotional experience for the development and welfare of young children. The relative importance of different forms of inequality, e.g. being in a one-parent family or living in poor socioeconomic circumstances could be determined by comparing their effects on the child's ability and behaviour. The most serious deprivations would be expected to have the most marked effect on these measures. Without such criteria it would be impossible to gauge the significance of different events and conditions in a child's life. It was not our intention, however, to use the measures for diagnostic purposes in the way an educational psychologist might assess a child's need for special education. The objective was to make comparisons between groups of children in terms of ability and behaviour rather than probe the underlying cognitive processes (Evans and Sparrow, 1975). Thus relatively simple tests touching on different aspects of a five-year-old child's abilities were required.

The choice of tests was limited by the fact that there are few standardised tests for five-year-olds that could reasonably be carried out in the children's own homes. Psychological assessment is not among the many skills acquired during health visitor training and, as the survey was being carried out by more than six thousand health visitors, on the spot assessment of children's test performance would have been subject to considerable variation between health visitors. Thus tests were selected which could be performed by young children at home, required no assessment of the child's competence by the tester and which could be scored at the survey headquarters by trained coders. The tests selected included the Human Figure Drawing Test, Copying Designs Test and the English Picture Vocabulary Test. These tests are described below followed by our scales of behavioural adjustment and maternal depression.

Human Figure Drawing Test

The Human Figure Drawing Test used in the present study is a modified version of the Draw-a-Man Test originally devised by Florence Goodenough (1926) and later developed by Dale Harris (1963). The Harris-Goodenough test has been subjected to extensive evaluation as a measure of IQ and correlations with conventional IQ tests (Binet, Wechsler, etc.) averaging between .4 and .5 have been reported (Scott, 1981). Harris himself suggested that the test is more indicative of 'conceptual maturity' than IQ (*op. cit.*, p. 5). This shift in emphasis gets away from the notion of unitary intelligence, and permits consideration of children's concepts of the human figure as an index or sample of their concepts generally.

The drawings produced by the CHES children at age five were relatively simple and did not warrant the implementation of the full Harris-Goodenough scale of 73 items. The CHES scoring scheme was based on thirty developmental items suggested by Elizabeth Koppitz (1968) but used the Harris point system of scoring. This scoring scheme is summarised in Table 19.1. One point was scored for each item represented in the drawing giving a maximum possible score of thirty. In fact the actual range achieved was 1 to 23 as shown in Table 19.2.

Copying Designs Test

Previous studies (Davie *et al.*, 1972; Rutter *et al.*, 1970) have tested children's ability to copy designs as a means of assessing their visual-motor coordination. Children in our sample were asked to make two copies of each of the eight designs shown in the Test Booklet reproduced in the Appendix. The following principles were followed when scoring the drawings.

1 The drawing must have the right general shape and look like what it is supposed to be.
2 It should be approximately symmetrical.
3 Angles should not be rounded.
4 The drawing should not be rotated, e.g. the point of the triangle should be uppermost.
5 Angles must be approximately opposite each other (except for the triangle).
6 Slight bowing or irregularity of lines is allowed.

7 As long as the other criteria are met, neatness is not important.

8 Lines should meet approximately but as long as other criteria are met small gaps at junctions are acceptable.

9 Slight crossing and overlapping of lines is permitted.

Not all children completed two drawings of each design, therefore a score of one was given if at least one good copy was made of a given design. The total score was the sum of the scores obtained on each design, thus giving a range of 0 to 8. Zero score was obtained when a child attempted to copy at least one design but all attempts were judged to be poor copies. The distribution obtained is given in Table 19.3.

English Picture Vocabulary Test

The English Picture Vocabulary Test (EPVT) is an adaptation by Brimer and Dunn (1962) of the American Peabody Picture Vocabulary Test. It consists of a series of 56 sets of four different pictures with a particular word associated with each set of four pictures. The child is asked to point out the one picture which corresponds to the given word, and the test proceeds with words of increasing difficulty until he or she makes five mistakes in a run of eight consecutive items. The final item achieved is designated the ceiling item. The EPVT raw score is the total number of correct items occurring before the ceiling item. The resulting distribution of raw EPVT scores was unacceptably skewed and so the scores were transformed using the proportions under the standard normal distribution to give a mean of zero and standard deviation of one.

Scoring the tests

Five coders were trained to score the tests using the first thousand Test Booklets for this purpose. Inter-scorer reliability (i.e. between scorers) was checked on 273 randomly selected Test Booklets and was found to be .94 for Human Figure Drawing which compares favourably with other studies reported by Scott (1981, p. 489), .7 for Copying Designs and .96 for EPVT. Intrascorer reliability (i.e. for a person scoring the same test on separate occasions) was .9 or more for all three tests. Having established that the tests were being scored reliably, coding proceeded on the whole set of Test Booklets. The first thousand were recoded again at the end to eliminate the possibility of errors being attributed to scoring during the training period. Although five coders

281

were trained, the bulk of the Test Booklets (94.6 percent) were scored by only three coders, the other two having left after completing only 707 Test Booklets.

The scoring of two of the tests, i.e. Human Figure Drawing and Copying Designs, necessitated some degree of subjective judgement in that coders had to decide whether the drawings performed by these five-year-olds conformed with the standards specified in the scoring instructions. This was not always easy and the reliability checks carried out before scoring of the whole sample commenced could not indicate whether a coder was consistently more lenient or harsh in scoring than the other coders. This could only be observed at the end when the coding was completed.

A comparison of the mean test scores for each of the three tests as scored by the five individual coders suggested that the test which was most vulnerable to systematic variation in scoring was Human Figure Drawing. The mean Human Figure Drawing score in Test Booklets scored by one coder was 10.2 (standard deviation 3.0) compared with a mean of 10.6 (standard deviation 3.2) in those scored by one of the other coders. This difference was statistically significant ($p < .001$) but was equivalent to only .14 standard deviations of Human Figure Drawing score. The difference between coders' scoring of the Copying Design Test was very small (maximum difference between means was .05 standard deviations, $p < .05$). The mean EPVT scores showed no such difference between the coders which clearly reflected the fact that subjective judgement was not required in scoring this test.

These differences in test score that are attributable to the individual coders who scored the original tests are interesting in that they demonstrate how the subjective element in scoring tests can marginally increase or decrease a child's score. This is not a serious problem when scores are being used for research purposes, as in the present study in which Test Booklets were randomly assigned to coders. Moreover, analysis inevitably focuses on group averages, therefore it is unlikely that any bias would ensue, even though coder variation has introduced additional unexplained variance into our analyses. However, it is important to bear in mind that when tests requiring individual judgement on the part of a tester are used for diagnostic purposes, then there is the risk that deviations from test norms are partly a function of tester differences and that due allowance should be made for this.

Child behaviour scales

To provide scales of antisocial and neurotic behaviour we used items from a psychiatric screening instrument devised for the Isle of Wight study of children aged nine to twelve years (Rutter *et al.*, 1970, pp. 412-21). Items which were most likely to be indicative of (a) antisocial behaviour and (b) neurotic behaviour were identified by means of principal components analysis. A total of twenty-seven items were analysed and of these eleven loaded highly (i.e. component loading greater than .46 after rotation) on a dimension we have interpreted as being indicative of antisocial behaviour. Five antisocial items as defined by Rutter *et al.* (1970) appeared in this dimension. These were items describing children as disobedient, destructive, lying, bullying and stealing ('takes things belonging to others'). The second dimension in the analysis contained nine high loading items (i.e. component loading greater than .32 after rotation) which were indicative of neurotic behaviour. These two dimensions explained 23 percent of the total sample variance. Further behavioural dimensions were not explored as the analysis planned for this report required only a broad assessment of behavioural adjustment for the purposes of evaluation of the children's social and emotional experiences as described earlier in this chapter. This resulted in items which did not load highly on either dimension being excluded from further analysis; these were night-time wetting, day-time wetting and soiling, 'not much liked by other children', 'has twitches, mannerisms or tics of the face or body', 'frequently sucks thumb or finger', and 'frequently bites nails or fingers'. The wetting and soiling items tended to go together in the factor analysis as a separate dimension and are to be discussed more fully in other reports of this study.

The two subsets of items identified by the above procedure were next subjected to separate principal components analyses. The results of these are given in Tables 19.4 and 19.5 together with the frequency distribution of each item. The reason for analysing the two sets of items separately was to obtain scores on the antisocial and neurotic scales which would permit some degree of correlation. Factor scores extracted from the original two-factor solution would have been orthoganal, i.e. have a correlation of zero, and this we suggest, would have imposed an artificial constraint.

Table 19.4 shows that the component loadings for the eleven items of the antisocial behaviour subscale varied from a maximum of .67 ('is often disobedient') to a minimum of .49 ('sometimes takes things belonging to others'), thereby confirming that all the items contributed substantially to the implied underlying dimension. Also the first principal component explained 33 percent of the total variance in the eleven items comprising the analysis. Rutter *et al.* (1970) found that items suggesting hyperactive behaviour were associated with psychiatric disorders of all types. In our analysis these items, i.e. 'very restless', 'cannot settle' and 'squirmy or fidgety', were mainly associated with the antisocial dimension.

The items in the neurotic behaviour scale had loadings from a maximum of .66 ('often worried') to a minimum of .34 ('has sleeping difficulty') and the first principal component explained 22.9 percent of the total variance in these nine items (Table 19.5). The four highest loading items provided the best definition for this scale – children who were worried, miserable or tearful, fearful or afraid, and fussy. Three of the neuroticism items as defined by Rutter *et al.* (1970) which describe children as worried, fearful and having sleeping difficulty are included in this scale.

The total score on either of these scales is given by:

$$\sum_i \frac{x_i - s_i}{sd_i} \cdot F$$

Where s_i is the individual's item raw score
x_i is the item mean
sd_i is the item standard deviation
F is the factor score coefficient given in Tables 19.4 and 19.5
and i ranges over the N items in the scale

This information derived from these results for this national sample of five-years-olds will enable other researchers using the same scale items to compute antisocial and neurotic behaviour scores for smaller or local samples. The advantage of this is that (a) the factor score coefficient (F) weights the items in accordance with the strength of their relationships with the underlying dimension; (b) the resulting scores conform to a standard normal distribution which is more amenable to statistical treatment than scores based on the raw scores only; and (c) the results of other studies would be directly comparable with those obtained from the CHES national sample. This means that scores obtained in studies of specific groups, e.g. children in areas of poor housing, can be compared directly with this national random sample of five-year-olds.

Maternal depression

The 24-item Malaise Inventory also originates from the Isle of Wight study (Rutter *et al.*, 1970, pp. 339-43) and was extracted from the Cornell Medical Index Health Questionnaire (Brodman *et al.*, 1952). The scale had been found to discriminate reasonably well between women with and without psychiatric disorder, as determined by independent interview (Richman, 1978; Rutter *et al.*, 1976, p. 323) and had an acceptable level of test-retest reliability (r = .91, N = 35, Rutter *et al.*, 1970, p. 340).

Mothers in the CHES study were asked to indicate all the items from the list of 24 (Table 19.6) which they thought applied to themselves. Positive responses to items were scored one and negative responses zero. The total score using this point system of scoring was simply the sum of the raw scores for the 24 items, thus giving a theoretical range of 0 to 24. This method of scoring assumed that all items contributed equally to the hypothesised underlying dimension. The assumption of item equality was tested using principal components analysis which showed that some items loaded more strongly on the scale than others. The loadings obtained and the associated component score coefficients for each item are also given in Table 19.6.

The high loading items (those with loadings greater than .40) were mainly concerned with depression, nervousness and being worried. The low loading items focussed more on physical symptoms such as rheumatism, indigestion, backache and upset stomach and contributed little to the component scores obtained. Mothers who felt depressed, miserable, nervous or worried scored high on this scale and low scorers were those who did not express these feelings. Average scores would have been associated with some degree of depression, nervousness and worry. The component scores obtained with this analysis conformed to a standard normal distribution (mean of zero, standard deviation of one). The simple point method of scoring produced a downwardly sloping, i.e. one-tailed, distribution and 48.9 percent of the mothers in the sample scored less than four whilst 51.1 percent scored between four and twenty-three. This could not be transformed to approximate a normal distribution and thus imposed limitations on the way in which the scale could be used, rendering it particularly unsuitable for use as a dependent variable in multivariate analysis. So the normally distributed scores obtained using principal components analysis had the additional advantage of being more amenable to statistical treatment. However, the correlation of component scores with the point system of scoring was .99 (N = 12,834). Thus the principal component method of scoring differed little from the point method in the ranking of the mothers on the scale whilst providing a more usable distribution of scores. The highest loading items also support interpretation of the scale as a measure of maternal depression or anxiety.

Child's age at testing

Cognitive, conceptual and linguistic skills are developmental in nature and increase with age, therefore tests of these abilities should be responsive to differences in children's ages. In the present study two thirds of the children were tested within a period of one month following their fifth birthdays (Table 19.7) which reduced the scope for variability in test scores due to the age factor. Nevertheless, small but statistically significant (p < .001) age differences in test scores were found and are reported in Table 19.7. For all three tests children who were tested at a late stage in the fieldwork, i.e. after age 5 years 6 months, had significantly higher scores than children tested just before their fifth birthdays. These results confirm the developmental character of the cognitive tests, but as expected the measures of behaviour and maternal depression did not vary with age at testing.

Relationship between tests and assessments

The indices of children's abilities and behaviour described above were each intended to measure different aspects of the child's cognitive and social development. However, some degree of overlap between them was inevitable since they all depend in similar ways on social and genetic factors.

The HFD and Copying Designs Tests both involved drawing and although the former was intended to measure conceptual development and the latter visual-motor coordination it is a fair assumption that ability to draw and a given level of cognitive development were basic prerequisites for performance in both tests. This was reflected in the relatively high correlation of .40 obtained between these two tests, (Table 19.8). Vocabulary is also dependent on conceptual and other cognitive abilities and so the correlation of .25 between EPVT and HFD and .34 between EPVT and Copying Designs was not surprising.

The negative correlations between antisocial behaviour score and the three ability tests shown in Table 19.8 (−.12 to −.19) suggest that the more antisocial, aggressive, disobedient, etc., children were somewhat less likely to do well in the tests, or *vice versa*. These relationships remained even after controlling for Social Index score and sex. There was little or no correlation, however, between neurotic behaviour and the three tests of ability. The positive correlation of .31 between antisocial and neurotic behaviour scores was surprising, suggesting as it does that children who are disobedient destroy things and fight are also likely to be worried, miserable or distressed, fearful or afraid and fussy in line with the high loading items of the two dimensions. The positive correlations between maternal depression and the two behaviour scores (.36 with antisocial score, .34 with neuroticism score) suggested that the association between the behaviour scores might have been due to maternal depression. This, indeed, was partly borne out in that a partial correlation between antisocial and neurotic behaviour scores was reduced to .21 (p < .001, N = 12,955) after controlling for depression score.

The relatively high correlations between the antisocial and neurotic behaviour and maternal depression can be explained in two ways. The first explanation is methodological and attributes the correlations to what has been termed the 'grumble' factor (Rutter *et al.*, 1970, pp. 161-2). Both Malaise Inventory and behaviour scale were completed by the same mothers, so those who were disposed to see symptoms in themselves could also be expected to report symptoms in their children. In other words mothers who grumble about their own worries, aches and pains may extend this attitude to their children's behaviour.

The second type of explanation for the association between deviant child behaviour and maternal depression relates to the emotional relationship between child and parent. Mothers of children whose typical behaviour was antisocial had a greater likelihood of being depressed themselves. Or equally, children whose mothers were chronically depressed might be more disposed to deviant behaviour. Thus the mutual interaction between a depressed mother and her antisocial or neurotic child is likely to result in a worsening of conditions in both mother and child.

Which of these two types of explanation is most likely to be correct? The results of the Isle of Wight studies suggest that the 'grumble' and 'real' factors both contribute to the association between child behaviour and maternal depression, but the authors conclude that: 'While the grumble factor may have played some part in mothers' response to the Malaise Inventory, it seems that reality factors were more important' (Rutter *et al.*, 1970, p. 161).

Whatever is the relative contributions of the 'grumble factor' and 'reality factors' in creating the associations between behaviour and maternal depression scores, there was no way in which the 'grumble factor' could be eliminated by statistical manipulation of the data. For this reason, our interpretation of the results of analysis involving behaviour and depression scales must be in terms of the mother's perception of her own symptoms and her child's behaviour and not an independent objective diagnosis.

Chapter 20

Methods of analysis

All analysis was carried out using the Statistical Package for the Social Sciences (Nie *et al.*, 1975). The options within this package allow considerable scope for variation in analytic procedures and our decisions concerning methods of analysis are described below.

Tabular analysis

Most of the descriptive analyses for this report made use of two-way or three-way contingency tables. The tables did not always include the whole sample of 13,135 children, however, as information was sometimes not available for small proportions of children for various reasons.

Firstly, as occurs in most surveys, some questions were simply left unanswered without explanation. Interviewers may have overlooked them by mistake or left them out deliberately and occasionally respondents declined to answer questions for reasons of their own. Secondly, the respondent might not know the answer to a question, as, for example, when a mother is ignorant of her husband's educational qualifications or is unable to remember the information required. Thirdly, certain circumstances rendered some questions inapplicable. In families where there was no father figure, for example, there would be no information about the father's occupation, education, age, etc.

Children in respect of whom information on a particular question was not stated, not known or not applicable were excluded from tables, and other analyses utilising that question. Thus the percentages and statistics were calculated on the basis of the sample of children for whom data were available for a particular table. A discussion of possible bias due to non-response is presented in Chapter 17.

288

Analysis of variance

Analysis of variance has been used when we needed to examine the separate effects of several interrelated factors on our measures of child ability and behaviour or maternal depression which are described in Chapter 19. This method allows us to observe the size and strength of the association between each independent variable and the outcome measures after adjustment for the effects of all the other variables in the analysis.

The basic model in all analyses was a main effects one, i.e. it was assumed that the effects of the different independent variables were additive. In some analyses, however, certain factors were found to 'interact'. That is, the effects on a dependent variable of two factors in combination were significantly larger or smaller than the sum of their independent effects obtained in the main effects analysis. For example, in Chapter 5 (Figure 5.1) we describe the results of an analysis of social and family factors related to the child's antisocial behaviour score. From the main effects analysis the difference in score attributed to the child's sex was .31 SDs and for the number of children younger than the study child it was .20 SDs. Thus the assumption of additivity would lead to the conclusion that the total difference attributable to these two variables would be .31 + .20 = .51 SDs. However, the significant interaction ($p < .01$) between sex and number of children under five years prompted further investigation. This was done by compiling an 'interaction variable' which consisted of every combination of the categories of the two interacting factors. The interaction variable was then introduced into the analysis of variance in place of the two interacting factors so that the adjusted means were obtained for all the combinations of the interacting factors whilst controlling for the effects of the other variables in the analysis. In this way it was possible to see where the interactions were occurring. In the above example this showed that the difference in mean antisocial score associated with having two or more younger siblings was .32 SDs for boys but only .06 SDs for girls instead of the average .20 SDs obtained from the main effects model. The overall difference in score for sex and number of younger children in combination was .58 SDs rather than .51 SDs obtained from the main effects model. All significant interactions are reported but are only discussed in the text where they were thought to be of theoretical importance. It should also be noted that an interaction between two independent variables with respect to a given dependent variable can disappear if other independent variables in the analysis are changed. For example, the interaction between type of family and type of neighbourhood reported in Figure 5.3 did not occur in the analysis described in Figure 10.2. Generally, only highly significant interactions (p < .001) withstand variations in the design of the analysis.

Certain independent variables, i.e. those that were at least ordinal scales such as Social Index and mother's age were introduced into the analysis of variance as 'covariates'. Unlike categorised variables such as sex and type of family, covariates cannot interact with other independent variables. Sometimes, however, theoretical considerations lead us to believe that a variable which is normally analysed as a covariate might interact with another independent variable with respect to a certain outcome. This happened in the analysis described in Figure 15.6 where an interaction was hypothesised between Social Index score (a covariate in the main effects model) and maternal employment with respect to depression. To test this hypothesis it was necessary to classify the covariate (Social Index score) into groups and introduce it into the analysis as a factor. This was done by using the same Social Index groups as for tabular analysis throughout the report (see Chapter 18). This procedure confirmed the existence of the hypothesised interaction which is reported in Table 15.1.

Classifying a scale or continuous variable in this way necessarily involves a somewhat arbitrary grouping which could conceivably influence the likelihood of finding interactions. This was not, however, thought to be a serious source of error compared with simply ignoring the possibility of interactions.

A second problem concerning covariates in analysis of variance was that their relationship with a dependent variable was expressed as a partial regression coefficient which was not immediately comparable with the adjusted mean scores of categories in variables that were classified into discrete groups such as sex and type of family. Thus a method was needed to express the partial regression coefficient for covariates as an overall difference in dependent variable score so that the effects of covariates in analysis of variance could be compared with the categorised variables. This was achieved by multiplying the partial regression coefficient by four times the standard deviation of the covariate. This provided an estimate of the difference in score over four standard deviations of the covariate, or to express this another way, between the lowest and the highest scorers over 95 percent of the sample.

The distributions of Copying Designs and HFD Tests were not standardised so the differences in raw scores were divided by the square root of the residual mean square from the AOV to give scores which could be expressed in terms of standard deviations. This provided a means of comparison with the standardised dependent variables, i.e. EPVT, behaviour and maternal depression scores. Thus it was possible to see in what ways different family and social experiences had the greatest effects. For example, Social Index had a regression coefficient of .19 related to Human Figure Drawing and .22 related to Copying Designs. But as the scores of the two tests were not comparable these coefficients gave no indication of whether the Social Index produced greater relative differences in HFD or Copying Designs. In accordance with the procedure described above the coefficients were transformed into differences in standard scores over four standard deviations of the Social Index score (SD = 2.0). (The figures presented here are from the analyses of variance performed for Chapter 5.)

Thus for HFD, (Residual mean square = 9.370)
$$\frac{.19 \times 4 \times 2.0}{\sqrt{9.370}} = .50 \text{ SDs}$$

And for Copying Designs (Residual mean square = 3.482)
$$\frac{.22 \times 2 \times 2.0}{\sqrt{3.482}} = .94 \text{ SDs}$$

Thus difference over four standard deviations of Social Index score corresponded to .5 standard deviations of HFD and .94 standard deviations of Copying Designs score. From this we concluded that the ability to copy designs was more affected by socioeconomic differences than were the general conceptual abilities indicated by the Human Figure Drawing Test. It should also be mentioned, however, that such differences between tests were also partly due to the test characteristics themselves such as their sensitivity and specificity; but as these were unknown, further refinement of the analyses was not possible.

Selection of variables for analysis

One of the problems besetting the present study was to decide which of the hundreds of variables in the data set were likely to be most important in analyses related to the measures of children's ability and behaviour and maternal depression. This was largely determined by theoretical considerations but, even so, it was anticipated that some variables would prove to be more important in their predictive power than others.

For the most part our analyses of variance were designed to enable us to examine the effects on an outcome of a particular factor, say maternal employment, whilst controlling for the effects of 'intervening' variables. An intervening variable is one which is related to both the factor of special interest (maternal employment) and also the dependent variable. Failure to control for such intervening variables may result in effects being spuriously attributed to factors like maternal employment. Our objective, therefore, was to select a subset of variables which, by virtue of their relatively strong relationship with the dependent variables, were likely to be important intervening variables in the analyses we planned.

On the basis of other research which suggested their importance in terms of children's ability and behaviour, fourteen variables were selected from the total data set as potential independent variables. One-way analysis of variance was used to test the simple relationship of these variables with each of the six outcomes used in this study (Table 20.1). Most independent variables were associated with all the outcomes at a high level of statistical significance (p < .001) with the exception of neurotic behaviour score which was strongly related to only half of the fourteen variables. We decided to select items which explained at least one percent of the variance in a dependent measure as potential intervening variables. Table 20.1 shows the percentage of variance explained by the fourteen independent variables for each of the six outcome measures. We recognise that a variable with large differences in mean scores between categories might only explain a small proportion of total variance if the categories contain only a small number of cases. For example, type of family explains more than one percent of the variance in only one outcome measure (EPVT), although analysis of variance (e.g. in Chapter 5) shows large differences in mean outcome scores between children in different types of family. However, the amount of variance explained is a more important consideration when selecting intervening variables as it is this which is most likely to influence the relationship between other independent variables and a particular outcome.

The percentages of explained variance given in Table 20.1 are based on the simple association of each independent variable with the outcome without controlling for the effects of any other variable. Thus considerable overlap in explained variance would be expected, for example, between father's education, mother's education, type of neighbourhood and social class. Nevertheless, the analysis serves to show that certain independent variables were more important in terms of some outcomes than others. For example, ethnic group of parents explained 3.8 percent of EPVT variance, but less than one percent of the variance of other outcomes, even though some of the categories of this variable contained relatively few cases.

Independent variables which explained less than one percent of the variance of a particular outcome measure were generally not included as intervening or explanatory variables in the analyses of variance presented in this report. The exception to this occurred where a variable had particular theoretical relevance as, for example, the type of family in analyses that were specifically concerned with family differences. Also, social class and father's education have not been used since these were subsumed by the Social Index. Mother's education and type of neighbourhood in which the family lived have been included as intervening variables in some analyses because they were found to explain additional variance over and above that of the Social Index. In particular, the type of neighbourhood variable provides a contrast between urban and rural areas which was a different dimension from that of the Social Index which was specifically designed to indicate socioeconomic inequality.

This method of selecting factors as potential intervening variables resulted in different combinations of variables appearing in analyses that related to different outcomes. For example, analysis of Human Figure Drawing included the total number of children in the family; Copying Designs and EPVT the number of children older and younger than the study child, antisocial behaviour, number of children younger than the study child and neurotic behaviour, the study child's age position within the family. Again, however, theoretical considerations were sometimes allowed to over-ride the one percent variance explained rule. For example, our analyses of social and family factors related to maternal depression used the number of older and number of younger children instead of total children, as Table 20.1 suggests. This was because we thought the ages of children in the family was of theoretical importance in analysis related to maternal depression.

Coda

by Brian Jackson

All these children were born within the same seven days. Yet how curiously life's chances are now being dealt out to them. At first the cards seem to fall at random — the place where you are born, a father losing a job or a mother finding one, a check-up at the hospital, a new playgroup opening or a younger sister born, a slight shift in government policy, an accident, a budget day change in tax allowances, the inexplicable break-up of your parents' marriage. But looking through this meticulously detailed evidence, we can see that, in the social laboratory, patterns begin to emerge. Some children will break the mould, and perhaps we have not yet attended enough to that remarkable number who defy all expectation. Nevertheless, though social science cannot predict what might happen to the individual child, it can record, analyse and make a fair forecast about larger groups of boys and girls.

That is implicit in the data here. Standing back from these children who are now, in research terms, five years old — but whom we may meet again when they are ten or twenty — one theme stands out. That is inequality. Some have more chances to be equal than others. The cards are being shuffled all through the first five years. It is not a question of whether an equal chance to be equal is either desirable or attainable. That is a judgement everyone will make for themselves and on a different plane. What we see here is the flow and collision of forces through which some children have more opportunity than their parents and others have less — but we also glimpse at least an outline of how disadvantage can be transmitted from one generation to the next. Unequal opportunity may at first seem a clear concept, but in the untidy movement of life it is very much more complex. Sometimes it is a matter of luck, serendipity, happenchance. Sometimes it is deliberate, avoidable, artificial. At other moments it can be oversight, accidental, an unforeseen result of a quite different decision. New

294

initiatives or creative drives for one child may put another at unexpected disadvantage. These tables are studded with that evidence.

The analysis here only draws on a fraction of the data collected. It is not about the crucial medical and social health dimensions (handicap, lead poisoning, diabetes, rickets, vulnerability to disease); nor about the delights of a young child's life today, nor about such traumas as child battering or the terrifying facts of accidents that could be avoided. That comes in other publications. But even looking only at this part of the child's situation — preschool care and education, mothers and outside work, starting school — we can see how the intertwined weave might affect any child in this complex tapestry. Let me suggest examples which take us from the general to the particular.

Alison remains an only child at five. Clare finds that she now has a younger sister. The evidence is that the first or only child has more opportunity to listen to, and to talk with, an adult. That may mean a developing vocabulary and a stronger grasp of concepts. Alison has that. She may flourish. On the other hand such total attention may have unexpected effects which show up on other scorelines. Meanwhile Clare suddenly has to share all the attention with a younger child. That may slow up her conceptual progress, but it may or may not enhance her ability to form and accept relationships. The whole subject of birth order — and the spacing between children — remains, I think, under-researched and not well enough understood by parents. Yet at whatever level of advantage or disadvantage, it remains a powerful factor.

Jacqueline's parents remain happily married. But Jamie was gently but suddenly told that his mother and father were splitting up. Mother and father, like day and night, were simply fixed rhythms in his universe. But now, by the age of five, he joins one in every ten children. For many, as we saw in Chapter 5, that can mean not only a reduction in their standard of living, but also in their quality and awareness of living. Survival pressures may mean that the remaining parent just cannot give him the same span of attention that might be possible in a two-parent household.

Geoffrey was born in Yorkshire. Denis was born in Middlesex. Because Britain allows great local autonomy, and because that is linked with the presence or lack of local wealth and responsiveness, then at once they face different provision. Any consideration of the tables shows how considerable the difference can be for the child. We are a small island. But this card in the life-shuffle may depend upon your growing up in the country, the suburb, the inner city street; or whether you are born a hundred miles north or a hundred miles south. We remain two nations, if not more.

Katharine went to a playgroup for two or three sessions a week.

Lindy went to a nursery school every day, nine till three. The play-group was there because there was little official provision, but every encouragement was offered to voluntary groups. Some parents sent their child to the playgroup and became involved. Just as many did not join in. Nevertheless in Katharine's area, like most, such informal provision dominated. Meanwhile Lindy found herself in a nursery packed with children, many of whose parents had serious problems and so, like her, had qualified for a place. We saw here evidence of the likely and different results on their development.

Nick's mother went out to work part-time. Mutazah's mother stayed at home. The different balances of advantage and disadvantage tilt again. Nick's mother may have made her decision, like one in three, on what she saw as financial grounds. The family needed the cash. Or like one in ten such women she may have thought of the enjoyment of work, of its social buzz, or of a career advancing. Both mothers face a dilemma, and its tensions can be radiated to the child. Possibly Nick's mother has twinges of guilt; for one in five who were employed felt they should be back at home, and half fundamentally agreed that the mother's place was with the child. But there is also the counter-tension: Mutazah's mother may want to work — but opportunity eludes her or culture denies her. The vibrations touch the child.

Esther entered her infant class when she was four years and four months old. Tania joined her first class when she was five years and four months old. Both were born on the same day. The difference in educational result can be considerable. Inside school the teachers may group, allocate, informally select, and maybe later stream. Esther has an accidental year's advantage. The consequences can be perfectly clear in later results.

These are immediate examples of how children find themselves placed. There are of course genetic differences, physical and psychic variations which are outside the present scan. And above all, in an unequal society, there is the great and persistent difference in social and economic background and in the cultures and expectations that emerge from it. The simple concept which I pose — equal opportunities to be equal — comes, like the child, under multifarious pressures. Never-theless as we step away from this research I doubt if the concept loses any literal, statistical or moral legitimacy. Evidence strives to be neutral, but demands assessment. And assessment here could begin by looking at the data upside-down.

To what degree does it suggest that these children enjoy more oppor-tunity and escape more disadvantage than previous generations? For example, only a modest proportion of the poorest children attended a playgroup. Yet only one generation back it would not have needed a computer to count them. They were as rare as the ospreys on Loch

Garten. Turn back the clock to the beginning of the century, and the very notion of being concerned whether every small child entered school at four years, four months or five years, four months would have been laughed at as fancy moonshine. With a child's medical history over that period — typhoid, scarlet fever, malnutrition, measles, tuberculosis, diphtheria — the record is even more dramatic. If we view the data like this, we see what has been done, what can be done, what might be done.

The children grow, circumstances change, aspirations alter. Even the very questions we ask, begin to shift. And perhaps looking back on these data, and our privilege in being able to monitor the child like this, we could ask several fresh questions.

Some about the fiscal patterns in society which support or do not support the child. Some about a universal and adaptable preschool policy. Some about a more flexible relationship, both for men and for women, between the dual worlds of home and work. And perhaps most of all about the status, servicing and meaning of parenthood.

This enquiry, however preliminary and limited, is a modest raid on the frontier of our social ignorance. It began on Sunday, 5 April 1970. This is one dispatch back. Simply to file the reports is to propose investment in future children.

Appendices

Appendices

Appendix 1 Tables

TABLE 1.1 Different family characteristics by Social Index group

Family characteristic	Social Index group					All %
	Most advantaged %	Advantaged %	Average %	Dis-advantaged %	Most dis-advantaged %	
(a) Mother aged under 25 years[1]	1.1	4.4	9.4	14.3	14.7	8.6
(b) Father aged under 25 years[1]	0.3	1.1	3.2	5.5	4.9	2.8
(c) Number of children in family -						
Only child	7.3	10.7	11.1	10.7	7.8	10.2
2-3 children	84.5	81.6	73.6	63.7	56.1	73.3
4 or more children	8.2	7.7	15.3	25.6	36.1	16.5
(d) Ethnic group of parents -						
European - UK	94.1	94.7	92.6	91.5	85.4	92.3
West Indian	0.1	0.4	1.1	2.0	4.7	1.3
Asian	0.7	0.9	1.8	2.8	5.1	2.0
Other	5.1	4.0	4.5	3.7	4.8	4.4
Total (N = 100%)[2]	1,255	3,542	4,835	2,010	1,479	13,121

Notes

1 Age at time of child's fifth birthday.

2 Percentages are based on totals which differ slightly from the numbers given due to small variations in the proportion of missing information on individual items.

TABLE 1.2 Housing conditions by Social Index group

Description of housing	Social Index group					
	Most advantaged %	Advantaged %	Average %	Dis-advantaged %	Most dis-advantaged %	All %
Lives in –						
(a) accommodation rented from local authority	0.1	2.5	36.7	69.1	67.0	32.3
(b) privately rented accommodation[1]	0.2	1.7	6.4	8.9	18.1	6.3
(c) accommodation above ground floor	0.4	1.6	6.5	12.6	18.1	6.8
(d) small accommodation[2] (≤ 3 rooms)	1.4	6.3	15.3	20.7	28.1	13.8
Total (N = 100%)[3]	1,255	3,542	4,835	2,010	1,479	13,121

Notes

1 Living in privately rented furnished accommodation contributes to the Social Index score.

2 Excludes kitchen, bathroom or any rooms used solely for business purpose.

3 Percentages are based on totals which differ slightly from the numbers given due to small variations in the proportion of missing information on individual items.

TABLE 1.3 Lack of household amenities by Social Index group

| Household amenities lacked or shared with another household | Social Index group | | | | | | All % |
	Most advantaged %	Advantaged %	Average %	Dis-advantaged %	Most dis-advantaged %	
(a) Kitchen	0.1	0.2	0.4	1.3	3.8	0.8
(b) Bathroom[1]	0.1	0.3	1.5	5.4	18.4	3.5
(c) Indoor lavatory	0.3	0.9	3.3	8.6	20.2	5.1
(d) Hot water supply	0.1	0.3	1.2	3.8	12.5	2.5
(e) Garden or yard	0.6	1.5	6.3	13.2	23.4	7.4
Total (N = 100%)[2]	1,255	3,542	4,835	2,010	1,479	13,121

Notes

1 This item contributes to the Social Index score.

2 Percentages are based on totals which differ slightly from the numbers given due to small variations in the proportion of missing information on individual items.

303

TABLE 1.4 Domestic equipment and facilities by Social Index group

Equipment and facilities available	Social Index group				Most dis-advantaged %	All %
	Most advantaged %	Advantaged %	Average %	Dis-advantaged %		
(a) Television –						
colour	58.7	62.5	53.9	40.0	30.2	51.9
black and white only	39.5	36.1	44.7	58.4	67.8	46.6
none	1.8	1.4	1.4	1.6	2.0	1.5
(b) Refrigerator	99.2	98.6	94.9	85.7	74.4	92.6
(c) Washing machine	97.3	95.3	90.6	84.0	74.7	89.7
(d) Car or van[1]	98.8	95.0	78.2	29.6	15.3	70.2
(e) Telephone	92.9	80.3	53.8	29.0	22.0	57.4
Total (N = 100%)[2]	1,255	3,542	4,835	2,010	1,479	13,121

Notes

1 This item contributes to the Social Index score.

2 Percentages are based on totals which differ slightly from the numbers given due to small variations in the proportion of missing information on individual items.

TABLE 1.5 Health visitor's assessments of home and relationship with neighbours by Social Index group

Health visitor assessment	Social Index group					
	Most advantaged %	Advantaged %	Average %	Dis- advantaged %	Most dis- advantaged %	All %
(a) Furniture and equipment -						
well equipped or luxurious	88.1	78.7	67.0	35.6	20.9	58.2
low or very low standard	0.2	0.3	2.2	8.6	19.0	4.4
(b) State of home -						
very tidy or over-tidy	42.4	40.3	30.6	23.6	16.8	31.7
untidy or chaotic	1.7	2.8	5.4	11.8	18.3	6.8
(c) Relationship with neighbours -						
family on good or very good terms with neighbours	76.6	71.4	59.3	49.8	41.4	60.8
family does not mix or are on bad terms with neighbours	2.0	2.3	4.9	8.8	14.3	5.6
Total (N = 100%)[1]	1,255	3,542	4,835	2,010	1,479	13,121

Note

1 Percentages are based on totals which differ slightly from the numbers given due to small variations in the proportion of missing information on individual items.

Appendix 1

TABLE 2.1 Changes in social class distribution between 1950 and
1975

Social class (Occupation of male head of household)	Children aged four NSHD (1950) %	House-holds[1] Census (1951) %	Children aged five CHES (1975) %	House-holds Census (1971) %
I	3.9	3.3	6.9	5.3
II	14.9	18.3	19.6	19.4
IIINM	11.4 } 49.5		8.7	11.5
IIIM	41.4		46.7	38.3
IV and V	28.4	28.7	18.1	25.5
Total (N = 100%)	10,616	123,372	12,267	1,394,794
No male head	2.6% (10,906)	-	5.0% (13,135)	20.2% (1,831,716)

Note

1 In 1951 census, social class was based on occupation of female
  head in household with no male head. This has the effect of
  slightly increasing the proportion of 1951 households in
  social classes IV and V and slightly reducing the proportion
  in social classes I and II.

TABLE 3.1 Marital status of mother (at time of child's birth) by type of family (at age five)

Type of family (at age five)		Marital status of mother (at time of child's birth)			
		Married	Single	Widowed, divorced or separated	All (N=100%)
Two-parent families -					
both natural parents	%	97.7	1.6	0.7	11,512
step-family	%	63.9	27.7	8.4	346
adoptive family	%	13.2	73.5	13.2	68
One-parent families -					
supported	%	61.1	29.9	9.0	244
lone	%	75.5	15.2	9.3	486
Other	%	50.0	38.3	11.7	60
All[1]	%	94.6	3.9	1.5	12,716
Untraced or unmatched in 1975	%	85.8	11.3	3.0	3,832
Total in birth survey[2]	%	92.5	5.6	1.9	16,561

Notes

1 13 children living in residential institutions in 1975 are omitted from this table.

2 All children born in England, Wales and Scotland.

TABLE 3.2 Child's age when present parental situation began by type of family

Sample: children not with both natural parents at age five

Type of family		Child's age when present parental situation began				
		< 3 mth	> 3 mth < 3 yr	≥ 3 yr	Not stated	All
Two-parent families –						
step-family	N	61	139	99	58	357
	%	17.1	38.9	27.7	16.2	100.0
adoptive family	N	56	24	1	15	96
	%	58.3	25.0	1.0	15.6	100.0
One-parent families –						
supported	N	71	61	65	53	250
	%	28.4	24.4	26.0	21.2	100.0
lone	N	70	138	199	98	505
	%	13.9	27.3	39.4	19.4	100.0
Other	N	23	20	17	2	62
	%	37.1	32.3	27.4	3.2	100.0
All	N	281	382	381	226	1,270
	%	22.1	30.1	30.0	17.8	100.0

TABLE 3.3 Reason for loss of parent by lost parent

Sample: children not with both natural parents at age five

Lost parent		Reason for loss of parent					
		Death	Divorce/ separation	Single mother at birth	Other reason	Not stated	All
Father	N	76	380	234	252	85	1,027
	%	7.4	37.0	22.8	24.5	8.3	100.0
Mother	N	12	20	–	47	6	85
	%	14.1	23.5	–	55.3	7.1	100.0
Both[1]	N	5	24	73	19	37	158
	%	3.2	15.2	46.2	12.0	23.4	100.0
All	N	93	424	307	318	128	1,270
	%	7.3	33.4	24.2	25.0	10.1	100.0

Notes

1 For children who lost both natural parents, data related to mother figure are given.

2 A further 182 children whose mothers were single at the time of birth were with both natural parents at age five.

TABLE 3.4 Reason for loss of parent by type of family
Sample: children not with both natural parents at five

Type of family		Reason for loss of parent					All
		Death	Divorce/ separation	Single mother at birth	Other reason	Not stated	
Two-parent families –							
step family	N	8	155	95	59	40	357
	%	2.2	43.4	26.6	16.5	11.2	100.0
adoptive family[1]	N	0	9	50	4	33	96
	%	0.0	9.4	52.1	4.2	34.4	100.0
One-parent families –							
supported	N	27	77	70	61	15	250
	%	10.8	30.8	28.0	24.4	6.0	100.0
lone	N	53	168	69	179	36	505
	%	10.5	33.3	13.7	35.4	7.1	100.0
Other[1]	N	5	15	23	15	4	62
	%	8.1	24.2	37.1	24.2	6.5	100.0
All	N	93	424	307	318	128	1,270
	%	7.3	33.4	24.2	25.0	10.1	100.0

Notes

1 For children who lost both natural parents, data related to mother figure are given.

2 A further 182 children whose mothers were single at the time of birth were with both natural parents at age five.

TABLE 3.5 Different family characteristics by type of family

Family characteristic	Two-parent families			One-parent families			All
	Both natural parents %	Step-family %	Adoptive family %	Supported %	Lone %	Other %	%
(a) Mother aged under 25 years[1]	7.5	27.1	1.1	27.5	13.7	0.0	8.6
(b) Father aged under 25 years[1]	2.4	18.7	0.0	3.5	0.0	4.3	2.8
(c) Mother without educational qualifications	54.8	67.7	45.3	64.8	64.9	78.2	55.7
(d) Father without educational qualifications	47.8	60.7	33.3	58.3	73.5	67.5	48.2
(e) Father in manual occupation	64.4	77.3	49.0	75.4	71.4	71.1	64.8
(f) Number of children in family –							
only child	9.0	14.8	21.9	36.8	17.8	17.7	10.2
2-3 children	74.9	63.3	70.9	45.6	61.2	48.4	73.3
4 or more children	16.1	21.8	7.3	17.6	21.0	33.9	16.5
(g) Ethnic group of parents –							
European – UK	92.4	93.5	96.9	88.2	90.2	91.8	92.3
West Indian	1.1	1.7	0.0	3.7	5.4	3.3	1.3
Asian	2.1	0.0	0.0	0.8	0.8	0.0	2.0
Other	4.3	4.8	3.1	7.3	3.6	4.9	4.4
Total (N=100%)[2] for (a) and (c)	11,851	357	96	244	470	62	13,080
for (b), (d) and (e)	11,851	357	96	92	35	48	12,479
for (f) and (g)	11,851	357	96	250	505	62	13,121

Notes 1 Age at time of child's fifth birthday.
2 Percentages are based on totals which differ slightly from the numbers given due to small variations in the proportion of missing information on individual items.

TABLE 3.6 Housing conditions by type of family

Description of housing	Two-parent families			One-parent families			All
	Both natural parents	Step-family	Adoptive family	Supported	Lone	Other	
	%	%	%	%	%	%	%
Lives in –							
(a) accommodation rented from local authority	30.2	51.1	11.5	53.8	59.8	59.7	32.3
(b) privately rented accommodation	5.6	11.8	1.0	13.0	14.3	4.8	6.2
(c) accommodation above ground floor	6.0	14.0	4.2	9.1	21.7	8.1	6.8
(d) small accommodation (< 3 rooms)	12.7	22.7	8.6	16.5	33.6	13.3	13.8
(e) overcrowded accommodation (> 1.5 persons per room)	3.4	5.7	0.0	7.5	2.8	6.7	3.5
Total (N = 100%)[1]	11,851	357	96	250	505	62	13,121

Note

1 Percentages are based on totals which differ slightly from the numbers given due to small variations in the proportion of missing information on individual items.

TABLE 3.7 Lack of household amenities by type of family

Household amenities lacked or shared with another household	Two-parent families			One-parent families			All
	Both natural parents	Step-family	Adoptive family	Supported	Lone	Other	
	%	%	%	%	%	%	%
(a) Kitchen	0.6	1.7	0.0	6.5	2.2	0.0	0.8
(b) Bathroom	3.1	6.5	1.1	10.2	8.3	1.6	3.6
(c) Indoor lavatory	3.4	7.2	1.1	10.1	7.9	8.6	3.8
(d) Hot water supply	2.1	4.6	2.1	11.5	5.9	1.6	2.5
(e) Garden or yard	6.3	16.3	4.2	15.8	23.4	4.9	7.4
Total (N = 100%)[1]	11,851	357	96	250	505	62	13,121

Note

1 Percentages are based on totals which differ slightly from the numbers given due to small variations in the proportion of missing information on individual items.

313

TABLE 3.8 Domestic equipment and facilities by type of family

| Equipment and facilities available | Two-parent families | | | One-parent families | | | All |
| | Both natural parents | Step-family | Adoptive family | Supported | Lone | Other | |
	%	%	%	%	%	%	%
Television –							
colour	53.4	38.5	62.5	42.6	28.6	48.4	51.9
black and white only	45.1	60.4	37.5	55.8	67.4	51.6	46.6
none	1.4	1.1	0.0	1.6	4.0	0.0	1.5
Refrigerator	93.5	85.4	97.9	82.7	80.3	83.9	92.6
Washing machine	90.9	81.7	90.6	76.3	73.0	83.9	89.7
Car or van	73.3	59.8	88.5	36.1	20.9	51.6	70.2
Telephone	58.9	38.2	82.3	42.2	36.8	61.3	57.4
Total (N = 100%) [1]	11,851	357	96	250	505	62	13,121

Note

1 Percentages are based on totals which differ slightly from the numbers given due to small variations in the proportion of missing information on individual items.

TABLE 3.9 Health visitor's assessments of home and relationship with neighbours by type of family

Health visitor assessment	Two-parent families		Adoptive family	One-parent families		Other	All
	Both natural parents	Step-family		Supported	Lone		
	%	%	%	%	%	%	%
(a) Furniture and equipment –							
well equipped or luxurious	60.5	35.8	73.7	40.7	29.5	42.6	58.2
low or very low standard	3.7	9.3	0.0	12.0	14.2	8.2	4.4
(b) State of home –							
very tidy or over-tidy	32.6	19.4	36.9	22.3	23.2	18.0	31.7
untidy or chaotic	6.0	13.7	8.5	14.1	16.4	19.7	6.8
(c) Relationship with neighbours –							
family on good or very good terms with neighbours	62.3	42.1	66.3	42.9	44.9	52.8	60.8
family does not mix or are on bad terms with neighbours	5.0	9.6	3.5	10.3	14.0	13.2	5.6
Total (N = 100%)[1]	11,851	357	96	250	505	62	13,121

Note

1 Percentages are based on totals which differ slightly from the numbers given due to small variations in the proportion of missing information on individual items.

TABLE 3.10 Scheffe tests for the significance of difference between means given in Figure 3.2

Types of family being compared	Social class at birth					
	I	II	IIIN	IIIM	IV	V
Both natural parents by:						
step-family	n.s.	$p < .001$	$p < .01$	$p < .001$	n.s.	n.s.
one-parent family	$p < .001$	$p < .001$	$p < .001$	$p < .001$	$p < .001$	$p < .001$
Step-family by:						
one-parent family	n.s.	n.s.	n.s.	$p < .050$	$p < .010$	$p < .001$

TABLE 6.1 Age at infant school entry

	N	%
< 4yr 4m	428	3.4
≥ 4yr 4m < 4yr 9m (Autumn term 1974)	5,275	42.1
≥ 4yr 9m < 5yr (Spring term 1975)	2,995	23.9
≥ 5yr < 5yr 4m (Summer term 1975)	2,956	23.6
≥ 5yr 4m (Autumn term 1975)	888	7.1
All	12,542	100.0
Attended special school for handicapped children	47	
Not known	546	
Total	13,135	

TABLE 6.2 Age at infant school entry by region and country

Region	Age at infant school entry				
	< 4yr 9m	≥ 4yr 9m < 5yr	≥ 5yr < 5yr 4m	≥ 5yr 4m	All N=100%
English regions					
North	82.0 %	15.4	2.3	0.3	778
Yorkshire and Humberside	48.1 %	38.6	12.9	0.5	1,203
North West	63.9 %	26.9	8.3	0.9	1,647
East Midlands	31.9 %	29.7	33.1	5.4	819
West Midlands	46.7 %	24.3	27.2	1.8	1,374
East Anglia	58.9 %	24.7	16.0	0.4	470
South East	34.9 %	26.2	37.6	1.3	3,425
South West	45.7 %	27.2	26.1	1.0	938
England	47.6 %	26.9	24.0	1.4	10,654
Wales	76.5 %	9.4	3.6	0.4	688
Scotland	1.1 %	2.5	31.8	64.7	1,138
Great Britain	45.5 %	23.8	23.6	7.1	12,480

Note

64 service families interviewed overseas are excluded from this table.

318

TABLE 7.1 Educational and day care attendance at four ages

Educational and day care attendance	Education and day care at age			
	3 years 10 months [1] %	4 years 2 months [1] %	4 years 7 months [1] %	5 years [2] %
None	31.8	27.1	15.4	4.5
Local authority –				
nursery school/class	12.6	15.4	13.3	5.1
infant class	0.9	2.5	36.4	81.5
day nursery	1.2	1.2	0.7	0.2
Private –				
nursery	8.4	9.0	6.9	3.3
playgroup	44.8	44.4	26.9	4.9
Special school or group for handicapped children	0.3	0.4	0.4	0.5
All (N = 100%)	10,360	10,331	11,738	12,742
Not known N =	2,775	2,504	1,397	393
Total N =	13,135	13,135	13,135	13,135

Notes

1 The ages were chosen to approximately correspond with the midpoints of school terms.

2 Child's placement at time of the survey.
Over 70% of the interviews were conducted in the month following the child's fifth birthday.

319

Appendix 1

TABLE 7.2 Main preschool placement

	N	%
No designated preschool experience	3,632	28.1
Local Education Authority -		
nursery school	1,049	8.1
nursery class	1,429	11.0
Local authority day nursery	174	1.3
Private -		
nursery school	724	5.6
nursery class	125	1.0
infant school	57	0.4
day nursery	136	1.1
playgroup	5,570	43.0
Special school or group for handicapped children	49	0.4
All	12,945	100.0
Not known	190	
Total	13,135	

TABLE 7.3 Main preschool placement by type of premises

Main preschool placement		Type of premises					All N=100%
		School or nursery premises	Community or church hall	Private house	Factory premises	Other	
Local authority -							
nursery school/class	%	95.7	2.9	0.1	0.0	1.2	2,374
pre-rising five	%	99.6	0.2	0.1	0.1	0.1	1,794
rising five	%	99.6	0.3	0.0	0.0	0.1	743
day nursery	%	93.9	3.0	1.2	0.6	1.2	165
Private -							
nursery	%	25.9	29.4	33.2	1.7	9.8	1,012
playgroup	%	4.3	76.2	8.5	0.1	10.9	5,451
Special school or group for handicapped children	%	43.9	19.5	2.4	0.0	34.1	41
All	%	47.2	39.2	6.9	0.3	6.4	11,580

TABLE 7.4 Main preschool placement by weekly periods of attendance

Sample: children who attended educational or day care institutions before age five

Main preschool placement		Weekly attendance							
		5 days per week			2-3 days		All	Not	
		Full-time	Mornings	Afternoons	Mornings	Other	N=100%	known	Total
Local authority -									
nursery school/class	%	32.6	36.7	24.6	1.6	4.5	2,305	173	2,478
pre-rising five	%	96.1	1.8	0.6	0.0	1.5	1,792	117	1,909
rising five	%	95.3	2.3	0.5	0.0	1.9	743	41	784
day nursery	%	73.7	9.9	7.9	1.3	7.2	152	22	174
Private -									
nursery	%	21.0	34.3	2.3	26.4	16.0	982	60	1,042
playgroup	%	0.7	12.4	0.9	61.9	24.1	5,340	230	5,570
Special school or group for handicapped children	%	68.1	6.4	0.0	4.2	21.3	47	2	49
All	%	31.4	16.9	5.9	31.7	14.2	11,361	645	12,006

TABLE 7.5 Mean duration of attendance at main preschool
placement

Sample: children who attended a preschool placement

Main preschool placement	Duration of attendance (months)		
	Mean	Standard deviation	N
Local authority -			
nursery school/class	11.4	6.6	2,401
day nursery	20.6	13.1	169
Private -			
nursery	16.7	8.0	1,010
playgroup	16.4	7.4	5,455
All	15.2	7.7	9,035

Test for difference between LEA nursery schools/classes and
private nursery or playgroup (Scheffe); $p < .001$.

TABLE 8.1 Main preschool placement by region and country

Region	None	Local authority				Private			All
		Nursery school/ class	Pre- rising five	Rising five	Day nursery	Nursery	Play- group	Special school/ group	N=100%
English regions	%	%							
North	1.0	21.0	36.1	4.3	1.4	6.5	29.3	0.4	795
Yorkshire and Humberside	3.8	25.0	17.0	12.1	0.9	5.7	35.0	0.6	1,265
North West	3.0	19.1	21.8	7.6	3.0	5.1	39.8	0.5	1,714
East Midlands	11.3	17.0	10.5	8.3	0.7	6.5	45.6	0.2	879
West Midlands	7.9	19.6	15.6	7.3	0.8	5.2	43.3	0.4	1,395
East Anglia	4.3	15.5	18.1	5.7	0.4	5.3	50.5	0.2	491
South East	6.7	17.5	7.1	4.6	1.4	12.0	50.3	0.4	3,556
South West	5.2	7.3	11.4	5.8	0.6	10.2	59.0	0.5	970
England	5.6	18.1	14.8	6.7	1.3	8.1	44.9	0.4	11,065
Wales	1.5	26.6	34.5	2.4	0.5	10.1	24.0	0.4	743
Scotland	27.7	24.9	0.3	0.7	2.0	6.0	38.6	0.0	1,073
Great Britain	7.2	19.2	14.7	5.9	1.4	8.0	43.2	0.4	12,881

TABLE 8.2 Main preschool placement by type of neighbourhood

Main preschool placement	Type of neighbourhood				
	Poor %	Average %	Well-to-do %	Rural %	All %
None	12.4	8.1	3.2	7.6	7.2
Local authority –					
nursery school/class	33.0	23.4	14.2	8.7	19.3
pre-rising five	20.3	17.9	7.4	13.0	14.7
rising five	7.0	7.2	3.7	5.6	6.1
day nursery	2.7	1.7	0.9	0.4	1.4
Private –					
nursery	3.5	5.3	14.6	9.0	8.1
playgroup	20.8	35.9	55.8	55.3	43.0
Special school or group for handicapped children	0.3	0.4	0.3	0.5	0.4
All N = 100%	1,009	6,230	2,938	2,368	12,545

TABLE 8.3 Main preschool placement by Social Index group

Main preschool placement	Social Index group					
	Most advantaged %	Advantaged %	Average %	Disadvantaged %	Most disadvantaged %	All %
None	2.0	3.0	7.7	10.2	16.6	7.2
Local authority -						
nursery school/class	13.2	13.4	19.7	24.3	29.6	19.2
pre-rising five	4.0	8.6	16.5	23.4	21.4	14.7
rising five	1.4	4.1	7.0	8.8	8.2	6.1
day nursery	0.8	0.9	1.2	2.2	2.2	1.3
Private -						
nursery	19.3	12.0	6.0	3.3	2.0	8.1
playgroup	59.0	57.8	41.7	27.0	19.4	43.0
Special school or group for handicapped children	0.2	0.3	0.3	0.8	0.6	0.4
All N = 100%	1,251	3,518	4,757	1,968	1,438	12,932

TABLE 8.4 Main preschool placement by type of family

Main preschool placement	Two-parent families			One-parent families			All
	Both natural parents	Step-family	Adoptive family	Supported	Lone	Other	
	%	%	%	%	%	%	%
None	7.0	10.4	2.1	9.5	10.2	9.7	7.2
Local authority -							
nursery school/class	18.8	19.3	10.4	21.4	26.3	25.8	19.2
pre-rising five	14.5	17.6	13.5	16.0	18.0	12.9	14.7
rising five	6.0	7.8	4.2	5.8	5.6	9.7	6.1
day nursery	0.8	5.8	0.0	11.1	6.4	3.2	1.3
Private -							
nursery	8.3	5.5	15.6	6.2	4.2	6.5	8.1
playgroup	44.2	32.6	54.2	29.6	28.3	30.6	43.0
Special school or group for handicapped children	0.3	1.2	0.0	0.4	1.0	1.6	0.4
All N = 100%	11,685	347	96	243	499	62	12,932

TABLE 8.5 Main preschool placement by number of children in household and Social Index

Main preschool placement	4-8 (Advantaged) Number of children				9-16 (Disadvantaged) Number of children			
	1-2 %	3-4 %	≥5 %	All %	1-2 %	3-4 %	≥5 %	All %
None	3.0	4.9	12.3	3.7	8.1	12.8	20.7	11.4
Local authority -								
nursery school/class	14.2	15.7	20.0	14.8	23.1	25.6	25.1	24.4
pre-rising five	8.3	12.3	16.1	9.6	17.4	22.9	28.5	20.9
rising five	3.7	5.3	9.0	4.3	6.8	9.4	9.5	8.2
day nursery	1.0	0.8	2.6	1.0	2.2	1.4	1.6	1.8
Private -								
nursery	12.6	10.2	7.7	11.8	5.0	2.5	1.4	3.6
playgroup	57.0	50.6	32.3	54.6	37.0	24.7	12.3	29.2
Special school or group for handicapped children	0.3	0.2	0.0	0.2	0.3	0.7	0.8	0.5
All N = 100%	4,798	2,091	155	7,044	2,832	2,415	641	5,888

TABLE 8.6 Main preschool placement by ethnic group of parents

Main preschool placement	Ethnic group of parents						
	European (UK) %	European (other) %	West Indian %	Asian %	UK + other %	Other ethnic group %	All %
None	7.1	6.7	8.2	16.5	5.5	6.9	7.2
Local authority –							
nursery school/class	18.5	19.7	41.5	30.9	18.3	23.6	19.1
pre-rising five	14.5	24.7	19.9	19.3	13.2	16.7	14.8
rising five	6.0	6.2	6.4	7.6	7.4	8.3	6.1
day nursery	1.2	1.7	4.7	1.2	1.6	8.3	1.3
Private –							
nursery	8.1	5.6	4.1	4.8	11.3	12.5	8.0
playgroup	44.3	35.4	14.6	18.9	42.1	23.6	43.1
Special school or group for handicapped children	0.4	0.0	0.6	0.8	0.6	0.0	0.4
All N = 100%	11,841	178	171	249	311	72	12,822

Appendix 1

TABLE 8.7 Main preschool placement by mother's current employment

Main preschool placement	Mother's current employment							All
	Not regularly employed	Employed under 2 years			Employed at least 2 years			
		At home	Outside the home Part-time	Outside the home Full-time	At home	Outside the home Part-time	Outside the home Full-time	
	%	%	%	%	%	%	%	%
None	8.3	4.1	4.6	11.6	4.6	5.6	7.9	7.3
Local authority –								
nursery school/class	18.2	11.6	21.2	21.0	14.4	21.9	22.2	19.1
pre-rising five	14.8	14.5	14.8	19.9	10.6	13.0	16.3	14.7
rising five	6.5	5.2	5.3	6.5	6.8	4.7	4.8	6.1
day nursery	0.9	0.6	1.3	3.6	1.1	1.5	6.9	1.3
Private –								
nursery	7.5	5.8	7.7	6.8	12.3	10.0	13.0	8.0
playgroup	43.3	58.1	44.8	30.4	49.9	43.2	28.6	43.1
Special school or group for handicapped children	0.4	0.0	0.3	0.0	0.3	0.2	0.3	0.4
All N = 100%	8,018	172	2,125	336	367	1,258	392	12,668

TABLE 11.1 Current employment of mother by history of employment outside the home since study child's birth

All percentages (given in brackets) are based on the grand total, N = 12,820

Current employment of mother	History of employment outside the home of mother since child's birth		
	Never employed	Employed	All
Full-time housewife	5,787 (45.1)	1,603 (12.5)	7,390 (57.6)
Regularly employed outside the home:			
full-time	-	746 (5.8)	746 (5.8)
part-time	-	3,452 (26.9)	3,452 (26.9)
Regularly employed at home	471 (3.7)	90 (0.7)	561 (4.4)
Employed occasionally	402 (3.1)	166 (1.3)	568 (4.4)
Other situations, e.g. voluntary work, student, etc.	68 (0.5)	35 (0.3)	103 (0.8)
All	6,728 (52.5)	6,092 (47.5)	12,820 (100.0)

TABLE 11.2 Current employment of mother by region

		Full-time housewife		Employed outside the home		Employed at home	Employed occasionally	Other	All N=100%
		No previous work	Gave up previous job	Full-time	Part-time				
English regions									
North	%	46.6	13.5	6.3	27.2	2.4	2.6	1.4	783
Yorkshire and Humberside	%	44.8	14.8	5.9	26.3	3.5	4.0	0.6	1,249
North West	%	40.0	14.1	7.7	31.3	3.6	2.2	1.1	1,672
East Midlands	%	43.1	13.4	5.6	26.4	6.6	4.3	0.6	863
West Midlands	%	46.8	11.5	7.0	26.0	4.2	3.7	0.7	1,388
East Anglia	%	44.8	10.6	3.5	25.4	5.9	9.2	0.6	3,494
South East	%	45.5	11.0	5.2	26.8	5.2	5.6	0.8	489
South West	%	44.0	10.7	3.6	28.2	5.9	6.6	1.1	957
England	%	44.5	12.3	5.8	27.4	4.6	4.6	0.9	10,895
Wales	%	50.2	11.4	5.1	24.9	3.8	4.4	0.3	731
Scotland	%	48.7	14.1	6.8	24.3	2.5	3.1	0.5	1,133
Great Britain	%	45.2	12.4	5.8	27.0	4.4	4.4	0.8	12,759

TABLE 12.1 Mother's occupational status by father's occupational status

Table includes all families in which both parents were in paid employment
Percentages are based on the grand total, N = 4,482

Mother's occupational status (social class)	Father's occupational status (social class)				
	I & II	IIINM	IIIM	IV & V	All
I & II	8.7	1.5	5.0	1.2	16.4
IIINM	8.5	3.7	13.6	4.0	29.7
IIIM	1.1	0.8	4.8	1.9	8.7
IV & V	6.1	2.9	25.2	10.9	45.2
All	24.6	8.9	48.5	18.0	100.0

Appendix 1

TABLE 12.2 Days on which mother worked weekends and during
the week

Percentages are based on the grand total, N = 4,629

Days worked	Weekdays:			
	None	1-4 days	5 days	All
Weekends:				
None	-	26.0	45.7	71.7
Saturday or Sunday	2.0	11.7	5.9	19.6
Saturday and Sunday	1.2	4.3	3.2	8.7
All	3.2	42.0	54.8	100.0

TABLE 13.1 Mother's attitudes towards sex equality and quality of life by whether employed or not

		Strongly agree	Agree	Cannot say	Dis- agree	Strongly disagree	Total N=100%	Chi square (4df)
Sex equality								
Women should have the same work opportunities as men	Housewife %	54.1	25.4	5.1	8.4	7.0	7,287	43.7
	Employee %	58.9	25.0	4.0	7.4	4.7	4,148	p < .001
Girls should accept the fact that they will marry and have children and not think about starting a career	Housewife %	5.3	4.7	4.1	15.7	70.1	7,287	17.4
	Employee %	5.1	4.6	3.0	14.3	73.1	4,145	p < .01
Girls are just as capable as boys of learning to be engineers	Housewife %	52.5	26.1	12.8	5.4	3.2	7,285	2.4
	Employee %	53.2	25.1	13.4	5.4	3.0	4,145	ns
Some equality in marriage is a good thing, but by and large the husband ought to have the main say-so in family matters	Housewife %	29.4	27.5	3.2	16.5	23.4	7,283	8.1
	Employee %	27.2	27.6	3.1	17.0	25.1	4,145	ns
Quality of life								
Women need something more from life than they can get by just looking after the home and children	Housewife %	43.3	41.8	4.3	6.4	4.2	7,286	320.8
	Employee %	59.4	33.3	2.7	2.9	1.7	4,144	p < .001
Mothers need a break from their children from time to time during the day	Housewife %	52.6	36.6	2.2	5.5	3.1	7,289	57.8
	Employee %	59.5	32.3	1.7	3.7	2.7	4,147	p < .001

335

TABLE 13.2 Mother's attitudes towards maternal employment by whether employed or not

			Strongly agree	Agree	Cannot say	Dis-agree	Strongly disagree	Total N=100%	Chi square (4df)
A mother's proper place is at home with her children	Housewife	%	42.2	32.3	6.1	13.6	5.8	7,270	935.2
	Employee	%	19.5	31.7	6.2	26.4	16.2	4,137	p < .001
There is nothing wrong with a mother going out to work if her children can be properly cared for by someone else	Housewife	%	30.5	36.1	5.1	15.1	13.2	7,293	710.3
	Employee	%	54.0	29.9	3.5	7.8	4.5	4,146	p < .001
A mother who leaves her children with someone else in order to go out to work is not fit to be a mother unless she needs the money for food and clothes	Housewife	%	15.5	18.5	14.4	23.2	28.4	7,272	622.6
	Employee	%	9.2	10.6	8.7	20.6	50.8	4,136	p < .001
A wife must sacrifice her right to go out to work once she has children	Housewife	%	18.8	22.1	7.3	25.8	26.0	7,272	559.6
	Employee	%	8.9	14.6	5.1	26.3	45.1	4,139	p < .001
The State should open more day nurseries so as to make it easier for mothers of young children to go out to work	Housewife	%	31.9	29.2	7.0	16.0	16.0	7,277	286.6
	Employee	%	44.7	29.9	5.5	12.0	8.0	4,141	p < .001

TABLE 13.3 Reasons why mother worked

All percentages are based on the grand total, N = 4,795 mothers in regular employment

Financial reasons	Social/career reasons			Family business	Other reason(s)	None of these reasons	All
	Social	Career/ enjoys work	Social and career/ enjoys work				
Financial –							
necessity	5.1	3.2	2.0	0.4	0.2	22.5	33.4
advantage	10.4	5.2	6.4	0.5	0.2	12.7	35.4
both	1.7	1.3	2.0	0.1	0.1	4.0	9.2
Financial reasons not mentioned	9.3	4.5	3.0	4.3	0.9	–	22.0
All	26.5	14.2	13.4	5.3	1.4	39.2	100.0

Notes

1 Working in family business was given priority over 'social', 'career' or 'other' reasons.

2 Social or career reasons were given priority over 'other' reasons.

Appendix 1

TABLE 13.4 Main reason why mother worked

	N	%
Financial necessity (e.g. contribution to housekeeping or rent, clothes, etc.)	1,519	36.2
Financial advantage (e.g. savings, holidays, household appliances, luxuries, car, to gain independence, etc.)	1,088	25.9
Social reasons (e.g. for company, making friends, relief of boredom, keep you young, etc.)	826	20.5
Career/enjoys the work	444	10.6
Family business	210	5.0
Other reason	73	1.7
All	4,196	100.0
Main reason not stated	630	
Total mothers in regular employment	4,826	

TABLE 13.5 Main reason why mother worked by selected social characteristics

Social characteristics		Main reason why mother worked						
		Financial necessity	Financial advantage	Social	Career/ enjoys job	Family business	Other	All N=100%
(a) Type of family								
Two-parent family	%	32.8	27.5	21.5	11.1	5.4	1.7	3,877
Single-parent – supported	%	73.2	11.9	6.5	4.2	1.2	3.0	168
lone	%	83.4	1.4	10.3	3.4	0.0	1.4	145
(b) Mother's educational qualification								
No qualifications	%	44.6	26.3	19.8	4.8	3.3	1.2	2,187
State Registered Nurse	%	18.5	17.7	21.0	33.9	5.6	3.2	124
Teacher's Certificate	%	16.4	13.3	14.8	45.3	4.7	5.5	128
Degree or higher qualifications	%	12.3	13.1	10.7	59.8	1.6	2.5	122
(c) Type of neighbourhood								
Poor	%	60.1	20.7	14.9	1.8	1.2	1.2	328
Average	%	43.0	27.5	20.1	5.7	2.4	1.4	2,123
Well-to-do	%	19.3	25.8	24.9	20.8	6.8	2.5	888
Rural	%	25.5	24.5	19.1	17.3	11.7	1.8	732
(d) Mother's ethnic group								
European – UK	%	34.5	26.4	21.3	11.0	5.1	1.7	3,896
West Indian	%	81.1	11.1	5.6	2.2	0.0	0.0	90
Asian	%	66.2	11.8	14.7	1.5	2.9	2.9	68
All	%	36.2	25.9	20.5	10.6	5.0	1.7	4,196

Appendix 1

TABLE 14.1   Current employment of mother and age of child
when mother started job by age child started
full-time placement

Sample: mothers with no children younger than the study
child

Current employment of mother and age of child when mother started job	Age child started attending full-time placement				
	<3 %	⩾3<4 %	⩾4<5 %	⩾5 %	All %
Age of child when mother started current job –					
< 3	45.4	27.5	17.6	17.3	18.6
⩾ 3 < 4	3.4	10.5	7.4	7.7	7.6
⩾ 4 < 5	10.1	18.3	18.8	11.8	16.7
Not employed outside the home at the time of the survey	41.1	43.7	56.2	63.2	57.1
All N = 100%	119	382	4,507	1,843	6,851

Overall Chi square = 145.3 (9 df)   p < .001

TABLE 14.2 Main caretaker of child whilst mother worked

Sample: mothers employed outside the home

(a) Child not attending nursery/infant school or playgroup full-time

Day care provided by -	N	%
Father	519	50.9
Mother at work	45	4.4
Adult relative	188	18.4
Older sibling	17	1.7
Paid childminder	31	3.1
Friend/neighbour	45	4.4
Part-time school or playgroup	140	13.7
Day nursery	35	3.4
All	1,020	100.0
Day care not known	12	
Total	1,032	

(b) Child attending nursery/infant school or playgroup full-time

After-school care provided by -	N	%
Father	957	33.3
Mother at work	77	2.7
Adult relative	322	11.2
Older sibling	77	2.7
Paid childminder	46	1.6
Friend/neighbour	62	2.2
School only	1,331	46.3
Total	2,872	100.0
After-school care not known	361	
Total	3,233	

TABLE 14.3 Main caretaker of child whilst mother at work by Social Index group

Sample: mothers employed outside the home with study child not attending a full-time educational placement

Main caretaker of child whilst mother at work	Social Index group					All
	Most advantaged	Advantaged	Average	Dis-advantaged	Most dis-advantaged	
	%	%	%	%	%	%
Father	51.8	54.2	49.8	48.8	50.4	50.9
Mother at work	4.8	4.6	5.0	2.5	4.1	4.4
Relative	9.6	15.4	22.1	25.6	22.3	20.1
Friend, neighbour, childminder	9.6	5.8	7.5	6.3	10.7	7.5
Day nursery	1.2	2.5	3.8	3.1	5.8	3.4
Part-time nursery school or playgroup	22.9	17.5	11.8	13.7	6.6	13.7
All N = 100%	83	240	416	160	121	1,020

Chi-square = 33.9 (20 df) p < .05

TABLE 14.4 Main caretaker of child whilst mother at work by
type of family

Sample: mothers employed outside the home with study child
not attending a full-time educational placement

Main caretaker of child whilst mother at work	Type of family			
	Two-parent family	Single-parent family		
		Supported	Lone	All
	%	%	%	%
Father	54.9	16.0	0.0	50.9
Mother at work	4.6	0.0	5.3	4.4
Relative	17.2	58.0	42.1	20.1
Friend, neighbour, childminder	7.3	2.0	18.4	7.5
Day nursery	2.4	12.0	18.4	3.4
Part-time nursery school or playgroup	13.6	12.0	15.8	13.6
All N = 100%	931	50	38	1,019

Chi-square = 28.8 (4 df) p < .001

Notes

1 Supported and lone single-parent mothers were grouped for
Chi-square test because of small expected frequencies in
some of these cells.

2 Day care by fathers was excluded for Chi-square test
because this form of care was unavailable to the majority
of single-parent mothers.

Appendix 1

TABLE 14.5 Main caretaker of child whilst mother at work by
hours per week mother works (preschool care)

Sample: mothers employed outside the home with study child
not attending a full-time educational placement

Main caretaker of child whilst mother at work	Hours per week mother works		All
	Full-time (> 30 hours)	Part-time (≤ 30 hours)	
	%	%	%
Father	28.6	55.7	51.3
Mother at work	2.5	4.6	4.3
Relative	34.8	17.3	20.1
Friend, neighbour, childminder	12.4	6.5	7.4
Day nursery	8.7	2.4	3.4
Part-time nursery school or playgroup	13.0	13.6	13.5
All N = 100%	161	848	1,009

Chi-square = 63.8 (5 df) p < .001

TABLE 14.6 Main caretaker of child whilst mother at work by
            hours per week mother works (after-school care)

Sample: mothers employed outside the home with study child
         attending a full-time educational placement

| Main caretaker of child whilst mother at work | Hours per week mother works | | All |
| | Full-time (> 30 hours) | Part-time (< 30 hours) | |
	%	%	%
Father	21.8	35.7	33.3
Mother at work	2.0	2.8	2.7
Relative	25.3	11.6	14.0
Friend, neighbour, childminder	9.7	2.5	3.7
School only	41.2	47.3	46.3
All N = 100%	495	2,332	2,827

Chi-square = 138.8 (4 df) p < .001

TABLE 15.1 Analysis of mother's employment and Social Index group by maternal depression

Mean maternal depression scores in cells (standard deviations)

Current employment of mother	Social Index group										
	Advantaged			Average			Disadvantaged			All	
	N	$\bar{X}_e$	$\bar{X}_o$	N	$\bar{X}_e$	$\bar{X}_o$	N	$\bar{X}_e$	$\bar{X}_o$	N	$\bar{X}_e$
Full-time housewife –											
no. previous work	2,146	-.20	-.21	1,800	.00	.00	1,429	.23	.27	5,375	-.01
gave up previous job	391	-.05	-.13	562	.15	.11	535	.38	.48	1,488	.14
Non-manual employment –											
full-time	173	-.28	-.23	129	-.08	-.13	70	.15	.17	372	-.09
part-time	748	-.26	-.22	463	-.06	-.06	164	.17	.05	1,375	-.07
Manual employment –											
full-time	34	-.13	.21	128	.07	.21	152	.30	.09	314	.06
part-time	389	-.21	-.05	782	-.01	-.05	640	.22	.16	1,811	-.02
Employed at home	251	-.16	-.16	227	-.02	-.03	43	.21	-.14	521	-.03
All	4,132	-.19	–	4,091	-.01	–	3,033	.24	–	11,256	.00

Analysis of variance: the effects of mother's employment and Social Index group are adjusted for the effects of type of family, number of children in the family, mother's educational qualifications, and type of neighbourhood given in Figure 15.6.

$\bar{X}_e$ Expected mean score derived from main effects (additive) analysis of variance (Figure 15.6).

$\bar{X}_o$ Observed mean score.

TABLE 16.1   Estimated size of cohort in 1975

Children born in England, Scotland and Wales and included in British Births survey		16,567

Non-surviving children –

Abortions	26
Stillbirths	208
Deaths before age five years	329

Total non-surviving children	563

Children in British Births survey surviving to age five years	16,004
Children born in England, Scotland and Wales during study week but excluded from British Births survey and assumed to have survived to age five years[1]	280
Estimated size of cohort at age five years[2]	16,284

Notes

1   See Chamberlain et al., 1975, p.6.

2   During the period 1970-5 there was a net outflow of immigrants from the British Isles (Central Statistical Office, 1978, Social Trends: 9, Table 1.12, p.38). Thus our estimated cohort size is likely to be a maximum.

Appendix 1

TABLE 16.2 Trace and interview rates

	N	%
Children interviewed -		
1975 survey - matched with birth data[1]	12,743	
- not matched with birth data	392	
- total	13,135	80.7
1977 survey	1,917	11.8
Children traced but not interviewed -		
Parents declined to take part	631	3.9
Interviewers failed to contact or information insufficiently complete	149	0.9
Reason for non-completion not known	46	0.3
Children not traced	406	2.5
Total estimated sample	16,284	100.0

Note

1 Includes 11 children born in Northern Ireland who were in British Births survey.

TABLE 17.1   Distribution of 1975 and 1977 samples by
standard region

Standard region	1975 sample		1977 sample	
	N	%	N	%
English regions				
North	799	6.1	98	5.1
Yorkshire and Humberside	1,280	9.8	180	9.4
North West	1,722	13.2	220	11.5
East Midlands	885	6.8	155	8.1
West Midlands	1,419	10.9	177	9.2
East Anglia	495	3.8	39	2.0
South East	3,582	27.4	626	32.7
South West	975	7.5	117	6.1
England	11,157	85.4	1,612	84.1
Wales	748	5.7	76	4.0
Scotland	1,166	8.9	229	11.9
All	13,071	100.0	1,917	100.0
Interviewed overseas	64		-	
Total	13,135		1,917	

Chi-square = 76.0 (9 df)   p < .001

Appendix 1

TABLE 17.2   Distribution of 1975 and 1977 samples by
             father's occupation (social class)

Father's occupation (social class)	1975 sample		1977 sample	
	N	%	N	%
I	843	6.9	125	7.4
II	2,405	19.6	376	22.1
IIINM	1,069	8.7	171	10.1
IIIM	5,726	46.7	708	41.7
IV	1,620	13.2	218	12.8
V	605	4.9	101 .	5.9
All	12,268	100.0	1,699	100.0
Not known	212	(1.6)	83	(4.3)
No father figure	655	(5.0)	135	(7.0)
Total	13,135	(100.0)	1,917	(100.0)

Note

Data for 1977 survey refer to situation at time of child's
fifth birthday.

Chi-square = 19.7 (5 df) $p < .01$

TABLE 17.3 Comparison of 1975 and 1977 samples in terms of selected social characteristics

Social characteristic	1975 sample		1977 sample		Chi square test
With natural mother	12,880/13,135	98.1%	1,762/1,917	91.9%	236.0 (1 df) p < .001
With natural father	11,937/13,135	90.9%	1,500/1,917	78.2%	277.4 (1 df) p < .001
Both parents of UK origin[1]	12,007/13,003	92.3%	1,582/1,884	84.0%	143.8 (1 df) p < .001
No household moves[2]	5,588/12,978	43.1%	491/1,857	26.4%	184.8 (1 df) p < .001
Child had been in care of the local authority[2]	264/10,496	2.5%	76/1,862	4.1%	13.9 (1 df) p < .001
Living in crowded accommodation (> 1.5 persons per room)	454/12,943	3.5%	45/1,904	2.4%	6.3 (1 df) p < .05
Had sole use of kitchen	12,814/13,102	97.8%	1,887/1,907	99.0%	10.4 (1 df) p < .01

Notes

1 Children with only one parent figure are classified according to the ethnic group of that parent.

2 Data for 1977 survey refer to period prior to study child's fifth birthday.

351

Appendix 1

TABLE 18.1 Classification of types of family

	N	%
Two-parent families –		
both natural parents	11,851	90.2
step-family (children living with one natural parent and a step-parent, adoptive parent or cohabitee of the natural parent)	357	2.7
adoptive family (child adopted by both parents)	96	0.7
One-parent families		
supported (children living with one natural parent plus at least one other adult in the household such as grandparents or others who may or may not be related. These include grandparents, uncles, aunts or adult siblings acting as parent figures to the child)	250	1.9
lone (children living with one natural parent and no other adult members of household)	505	3.8
Other families (children living with neither natural parent, e.g. with grandparents or foster parents)	62	0.5
Total	13,121	100.0

Note

Children living in residential institutions (N = 14) were excluded from this classification.

TABLE 18.2 Ethnic group of parents

Ethnic group	N	%
Both parents European (UK)	12,007	92.3
Both parents European (other)	179	1.4
Both parents West Indian	174	1.3
Both parents Asian (includes Indian, Pakistani and other Asian)	257	2.0
One parent European (UK) other parent not European (UK)	312	2.4
Other or unclear ethnic groups	74	0.6
All	13,003	100.0
In residential care	14	
Ethnic group not given	118	
Total	13,135	

Notes

1 Single parents were classified in categories 1 to 4 according to the ethnic group of the parent.

2 The ethnic group of the 'present parents' was requested but it is possible in some cases that the ethnic group of a (absent) natural parent was given. There is no information about the extent of this possible inconsistency.

Appendix 1

TABLE 18.3 Type of neighbourhood by classification of father's occupation (social class)

Type of neighbourhood		Classification of father's occupation (social class)					Not classified	Total	
		I & II	IIINM	IIIM	IV & V	All		N	%
Poor	%	9.0	3.8	53.1	34.1	100.0	137	1,037	8.2
Average	%	14.0	8.2	55.4	22.1	100.0	474	6,317	49.7
Well-to-do	%	50.1	12.2	30.8	6.9	100.0	104	2,954	23.2
Rural	%	35.8	7.2	42.0	15.0	100.0	112	2,403	18.9
All	%	26.5	8.6	46.8	18.1	100.0	827	12,711	100.0
Not known	%	26.8	11.2	44.3	17.7	100.0	40	424	
Total	%	26.5	8.7	46.7	18.1	100.0	876	13,135	

TABLE 18.4   Items comprising Social Index and system of
             weighted scores

Description of items comprising the Index	%	Weighted score
1. Classification of father's occupation (social class)		
Social class I	6.9	-1
Social classes II,IIINM & IIIM	75.0	0
Social class IV	13.2	1
Social class V	4.9	2
All	100.0	
(N)	(12,268)	
Not classified	867	0
Total	13,135	
2. Highest known qualification of either parent[1]		
Degree, Certificate of Education, State Registered Nurse	16.9	-2
'A' or 'O' levels or equivalent	28.6	-1
None of above qualifications	54.5	0
All	100.0	
(N)	(12,930)	
Not known	205	0
Total	13,135	
3. Type of neighbourhood		
Poor	8.2	1
Average	49.7	0
Well-to-do	23.2	-1
Rural	18.9	0
All	100.0	
(N)	(12,711)	
Not known	424	0
Total	13,135	

TABLE 18.4 (continued)

Description of items comprising the Index	%	Weighted score
4. Tenure of accommodation		
Owned or being bought	56.4	-1
Privately rented furnished	1.0	1
Other tenure	42.6	0
All	100.0	
(N)	(13,094)	
Not known	41	0
Total	13,135	
5. Persons per room ratio		
≤ 1.5 not crowded	96.5	0
> 1.5 ≤ 2.0 crowded	2.8	1
> 2.0 severely crowded	0.7	2
All	100.0	
(N)	(12,943)	
Not known	192	0
Total	13,135	
6. Availability of bathroom		
Bathroom available	97.5	0
No bathroom	2.5	1
All	100.0	
(N)	(12,929)	
Not known	206	0
Total	13,135	

TABLE 18.4   (continued)

Description of items comprising the Index	%	Weighted score
7. Type of accommodation		
Non-self-contained rooms	0.9	1
Other accommodation	99.1	0
All	100.0	
(N)	(13,097)	
Not known	38	0
Total	13,135	
8. Availability of car or van		
Car or van available	70.3	-1
Car or van not available	29.7	0
All	100.0	
(N)	(13,089)	
Not known	46	0
Total	13,135	

Note

1   This variable gives the educational qualification of the
parent with the highest qualification.   If there was only
one parent, that parent's educational qualifications
apply.

Appendix 1

TABLE 18.5 Social Index distribution

Social Index score	N	%
4	387	2.9
5	868	6.6
6	1,476	11.2
7	2,066	15.7
8	2,313	17.6
9	2,522	19.2
1o	2,o1o	15.3
11	854	6.5
12	420	3.2
13	136	1.o
14	44	o.3
15	2o	o.2
16	5	o.o
All	13,121	1oo.o
In residential care	14	
Total	13,135	

Mean   8.2

Standard deviation 2.o

TABLE 18.6   Number of missing Social Index items by Social
              Index score (grouped)

Social Index score (grouped)	Number of missing items					
	None		One		2 - 8	
	N	%	N	%	N	%
4 - 5	1,205	10.0	50	5.0	0	0.0
6 - 7	3,281	27.3	245	24.3	16	15.2
8 - 9	4,372	36.4	415	41.2	48	45.7
10	1,805	15.0	175	17.4	30	28.6
11 - 16	1,346	11.2	122	12.1	11	10.5
All	12,009	100.0	1,007	100.0	105	100.0

TABLE 18.7 Social Index (grouped) by classification of father's occupation (social class)

| Social Index group (Scores are given in brackets) | Classification of father's occupation (social class) | | | | | | | Not classified | Total |
	I %	II %	IIINM %	IIIM %	IV %	V %	All %	%	%
Most advantaged (4 & 5)	84.6	16.0	5.1	1.6	0.0	0.0	10.2	1.1	9.6
Advantaged (6 & 7)	14.4	55.5	48.6	24.3	4.1	0.0	28.0	12.5	27.0
Average (8 & 9)	1.1	24.9	39.6	52.2	33.2	4.3	37.4	29.6	36.8
Dis-advantaged (10)	0.0	2.8	5.2	16.8	31.1	12.1	13.5	41.0	15.3
Most dis-advantaged (11–16)	0.0	0.8	1.4	5.1	31.6	83.6	11.0	15.8	11.3
All	100.0	100.0	100.0	100.0	100.0	100.0	100.0	100.0	100.0
N	843	2,405	1,069	5,726	1,619	605	12,267	854	13,121
%	6.9	19.6	8.7	46.7	13.2	4.9	100.0		

Note

The 14 children in residential care are excluded from the table.

TABLE 19.1   Human Figure Drawing scoring scheme

The presence of any of the following features adds one point to the HFD score.

1. **Head:**   Any representation

2. **Eyes:**   Any representation

3. **Pupils:**   Distinct circles or dots within outlines of eyes

4. **Eyebrows or eyelashes:**   Either brows or lashes or both

5. **Nose:**   Any representation

6. **Nostrils:**   Dots or nostrils shown in addition to nose

7. **Mouth:**   Any representation

8. **Two lips:**   Two lips outlined and separated from each other: two rows of teeth only are not scored

9. **Ear:**   Any representation

10. **Hair:**   Any representation, or hat or cap covering head and hiding hair

11. **Neck:**   Definite 'stalk' separating head and body

12. **Body:**   Any representation, clear outline necessary

13. **Arms:**   Any representation

14. **Arms in two dimensions:**   Both arms represented by more than a single line

15. **Arms at an angle:**   One or both arms pointing downwards at an angle of 30° or more from horizontal position or arms raised appropriately for activity in which figure is engaged

16. **Arms correctly attached at shoulder:**   Arms firmly connected at shoulder with shoulder clearly evident

17. **Elbow:**   Distinct angle in arm;   rounded curve in arm not scored

18. **Hands:**   Differentiation from hands and fingers necessary such as widening of arm or demarcation from arm by sleeve or bracelet

361

TABLE 19.1 (continued)

19. Fingers: Any representation distinct from hands or arms; any number of fingers acceptable

20. Correct number of fingers: Five fingers on each hand or arm

21. Legs: Any representation; in case of female figures in long skirts this item is scored if distance between waist and feet is long enough to allow for legs to be present under the skirt

22. Legs in two dimensions: Both legs represented by more than single lines

23. Knee: Distinct angle in one or both legs (side view), or kneecap (front view); round curve in leg not scored

24. Feet: Any representation

25. Feet in two dimensions: Feet extending in one direction from heel (side view) and showing greater length than height, or feet drawn in perspective (front view)

26. Profile: Head drawn in profile even if rest of figure not entirely in profile

27. Clothing, one item or more: Items counted as clothing: trousers, shirt, skirt, blouse, dress (upper part of dress separated by belt scored as blouse), coat, hat, helmet, belt, tie, hair ribbon, necklace, watch, ring, bracelet, pipe, cigarette, umbrella, cane, gun, rake, shoes, wallet, briefcase, bat, gloves

28. Clothing, two or more items: Two or more items of clothing represented

29. Clothing, four or more items: Four or more items of clothing represented

30. Good proportions: Figure looks right, even if not entirely anatomically correct

TABLE 19.2 Human Figure Drawing score distribution

Score	N	%
1	22	O.2
2	18	O.1
3	69	O.5
4	215	1.7
5	341	2.7
6	631	4.9
7	971	7.6
8	1,288	1O.1
9	1,519	11.9
1O	1,581	12.4
11	1,563	12.2
12	1,372	1O.7
13	1,104	8.6
14	832	6.5
15	545	4.3
16	319	2.5
17	185	1.4
18	115	O.9
19	53	O.4
20	21	O.2
21	11	O.1
22	7	O.1
23	2	O.O
	12,784	1OO.O
Not scorable	139	
Not attempted	212	
Total	13,135	

Mean   1O.4

Standard deviation 3.1

Appendix 1

TABLE 19.3 Copying Designs score distribution

Score	N	%
0	78	0.6
1	375	2.9
2	1,357	10.4
3	2,267	17.4
4	2,143	16.4
5	2,100	16.1
6	1,743	13.4
7	1,561	12.0
8	1,404	10.8
	13,028	100.0
Not attempted	107	
Total	13,135	

Mean	4.7	
Standard deviation	2.0	

TABLE 19.4   Items comprising antisocial behaviour scale

Giving -

1. Individual items frequency distribution for total sample, N = 13,135

2. Results of principal components analysis

Item	Component loading	Component score co-efficient	Raw score	N	%
Is often disobedient	.67	.19			
Doesn't apply			0	3,950	30.1
Applies somewhat			1	7,797	59.4
Certainly applies			2	1,237	9.4
Not stated			-	151	1.1
Often destroys own or others' belongings	.60	.17			
Doesn't apply			0	9,998	76.1
Applies somewhat			1	2,437	18.6
Certainly applies			2	542	4.1
Not stated			-	158	1.2
Frequently fights with other children	.60	.17			
Doesn't apply			0	8,280	63.0
Applies somewhat			1	4,161	31.7
Certainly applies			2	550	4.2
Not stated			-	144	1.1
Irritable. Is quick to 'fly off the handle'	.60	.16			
Doesn't apply			0	7,044	53.6
Applies somewhat			1	4,447	33.9
Certainly applies			2	1,494	11.4
Not stated			-	150	1.1
Very restless. Often running up and down. Hardly ever still.	.58	.16			
Doesn't apply			0	4,040	30.8
Applies somewhat			1	5,193	39.5
Certainly applies			2	3,752	28.6
Not stated			-	150	1.1

TABLE 19.4 (continued)

Item	Component loading	Component score coefficient	Raw score	N	%
Has temper tantrums (that is, complete loss of temper with shouting, angry movements, etc.)	.58	.16			
Never			0	7,248	55.2
Less than once a month			1	2,265	17.2
At least once a month			2	1,223	9.3
At least once a week			3	1,588	12.1
Not stated			–	811	6.2
Cannot settle to anything for more than a few moments	.56	.16			
Doesn't apply			0	8,491	64.6
Applies somewhat			1	3,587	27.3
Certainly applies			2	905	6.9
Not stated			–	152	1.2
Often tells lies	.54	.15			
Doesn't apply			0	8,577	65.3
Applies somewhat			1	4,124	31.4
Certainly applies			2	290	2.2
Not stated			–	144	1.1
Is squirmy or fidgety	.54	.15			
Doesn't apply			0	7,317	55.7
Applies somewhat			1	4,083	31.1
Certainly applies			2	1,492	11.4
Not stated			–	243	1.9
Bullies other children	.53	.15			
Doesn't apply			0	10,984	83.6
Applies somewhat			1	1,821	13.9
Certainly applies			2	195	1.5
Not stated			–	135	1.0

TABLE 19.4 (continued)

Item	Component loading	Component score coefficient	Raw score	N	%
Sometimes takes things belonging to others	.49	.13			
Doesn't apply			0	10,315	78.5
Applies somewhat			1	2,420	18.4
Certainly applies			2	244	1.9
Not stated			–	156	1.2

Factor	Eigenvalue	Percentage of variance explained
1	3.6	33.0
2	1.2	11.3
3	1.0	9.4
4	0.8	7.6

Principal components analysis (Nie et al., 1975)

This table gives the component loading and component co-efficient for the first component obtained from an unrotated solution.

Appendix 1

TABLE 19.5 Items comprising neurotic behaviour scale

Giving -

1. Individual item frequency distributions for total sample, N = 13,135

2. Results of principal components analysis

Item	Component loading	Component score coefficient	Raw score	N	%
Often worried, worries about many things	.66	.32			
Doesn't apply			0	8,445	64.3
Applies somewhat			1	3,809	29.0
Certainly applies			2	712	5.4
Not stated			-	169	1.3
Often appears miserable, unhappy, tearful or distressed	.56	.27			
Doesn't apply			0	10,067	76.6
Applies somewhat			1	2,588	19.7
Certainly applies			2	328	2.5
Not stated			-	152	1.2
Tends to be fearful or afraid of new things or new situations	.54	.26			
Doesn't apply			0	8,312	63.3
Applies somewhat			1	3,816	29.1
Certainly applies			2	857	6.5
Not stated			-	150	1.1
Is fussy or over-particular	.50	.24			
Doesn't apply			0	7,719	58.8
Applies somewhat			1	4,047	30.8
Certainly applies			2	1,213	9.2
Not stated			-	156	1.2

TABLE 19.5   (continued)

Item	Component loading	Component score co-efficient	Raw score	N	%
Complains of stomach-ache or has vomited	.42	.20			
Never			0	5,153	39.2
Less than once a month			1	6,122	46.6
At least once a month			2	905	6.9
At least once a week			3	323	2.5
Not stated			–	632	4.8
Complains of headaches	.40	.20			
Never			0	8,105	61.7
Less than once a month			1	3,584	27.3
At least once a month			2	603	4.6
At least once a week			3	156	1.2
Not stated			–	687	5.2
Does child have any eating or appetite problems?	.40	.19			
None			0	8,299	63.2
Yes – mild			1	4,470	34.0
Yes – severe			2	270	2.1
Not stated			–	96	0.7
Tends to do things on his own – rather solitary	.39	.19			
Doesn't apply			0	7,123	54.2
Applies somewhat			1	4,642	35.3
Certainly applies			2	1,195	9.1
Not stated			–	175	1.3

TABLE 19.5 (continued)

	Com-ponent loading	Component score co-efficient	Raw score	N	%
Does your child have any sleeping difficulty?	.34	.17			
None			O	9,768	74.4
Yes - mild			1	3,081	23.5
Yes - severe			2	190	1.4
Not stated			-	96	0.7

Factor	Eigenvalue	Percentage of variance explained
1	2.1	22.9
2	1.2	13.3
3	1.0	11.2
4	0.9	10.2

<u>Principal components analysis</u> (Nie et al., 1975)

This table gives the component loading and component co-efficient for the first component obtained from an unrotated solution.

TABLE 19.6   Items comprising scale of maternal depression

Giving -

1. Individual item frequency distributions for total sample, N = 13,135

2. Results of principal components analysis

Item	Component loading	Component score co-efficient	Raw Score	N	%
Do you often feel miserable or depressed?	.64	.41			
No			0	8,605	65.5
Yes			1	4,273	32.5
Not stated			–	257	2.0
Does every little thing get on your nerves and wear you out?	.58	.34			
No			0	11,485	87.4
Yes			1	1,423	10.8
Not stated			–	227	1.7
Are you constantly keyed up and jittery?	.58	.34			
No			0	11,575	88.1
Yes			1	1,325	10.1
Not stated			–	235	1.8
Are you easily upset or irritated?	.54	.30			
No			0	7,445	56.7
Yes			1	5,460	41.6
Not stated			–	230	1.8
Do you feel tired most of the time?	.54	.29			
No			0	9,020	68.7
Yes			1	3,908	29.8
Not stated			–	207	1.6

TABLE 19.6 (continued)

Item	Component loading	Component score co-efficient	Raw score	N	%
Do you often get worried about things?	.52	.27			
No			0	5,698	43.4
Yes			1	7,213	54.9
Not stated			–	224	1.7
Does your heart often race like mad?	.51	.26			
No			0	11,115	84.6
Yes			1	1,819	13.8
Not stated			–	201	1.5
Do you often suddenly become scared for no good reason?	.49	.24			
No			0	11,514	87.7
Yes			1	1,423	10.8
Not stated			–	198	1.5
Do you often get into a violent rage?	.49	.24			
No			0	11,048	84.1
Yes			1	1,882	14.3
Not stated			–	205	1.6
Do people often annoy and irritate you?	.46	.21			
No			0	8,332	63.4
Yes			1	4,587	34.9
Not stated			–	216	1.6
Do you wear yourself out worrying about your health?	.46	.21			
No			0	12,105	92.2
Yes			1	843	6.4
Not stated			–	187	1.4

TABLE 19.6 (continued)

Item	Component loading	Component score coefficient	Raw score	N	%
Do you usually have great difficulty in falling asleep or staying asleep?	.41	.17			
No			0	11,138	84.8
Yes			1	1,815	13.8
Not stated			–	182	1.4
Do you often have bad headaches?	.38	.14			
No			0	8,908	67.8
Yes			1	4,018	30.6
Not stated			–	209	1.6
Are you scared to be alone when there are no friends near you?	.37	.14			
No			0	11,628	88.5
Yes			1	1,311	10.0
Not stated			–	196	1.5
Do you often have bad pains in your eyes?	.36	.13			
No			0	11,509	87.6
Yes			1	1,426	10.9
Not stated			–	200	1.5
Are you frightened of going out alone or of meeting people?	.35	.12			
No			0	11,774	89.6
Yes			1	1,164	8.9
Not stated			–	197	1.5
Do you wake unnecessarily early in the morning?	.35	.12			
No			0	11,349	86.4
Yes			1	1,603	12.2
Not stated			–	183	1.4

TABLE 19.6   (continued)

Item	Component loading	Component score coefficient	Raw score	N	%
Do you often suffer from an upset stomach?	.34	.12			
No			0	11,653	88.7
Yes			1	1,288	9.8
Not stated			–	194	1.5
Do you often have back-ache?	.32	.10			
No			0	8,614	65.6
Yes			1	4,346	33.1
Not stated			–	175	1.3
Is your appetite poor?	.31	.10			
No			0	12,115	92.2
Yes			1	834	6.3
Not stated			–	186	1.4
Have you at times had a twitching of the face, head or shoulders?	.29	.09			
No			0	12,222	93.0
Yes			1	729	5.6
Not stated			–	184	1.4
Have you ever had a nervous breakdown?	.28	.08			
No			0	12,339	93.9
Yes			1	590	4.5
Not stated			–	206	1.6
Do you suffer from indigestion?	.26	.07			
No			0	11,233	85.5
Yes			1	1,715	13.1
Not stated			–	187	1.4

TABLE 19.6   (continued)

Item	Component loading	Component score coefficient	Raw score	N	%
Are you troubled with rheumatism or fibrositis?	.17	.03			
No			0	11,291	86.0
Yes			1	1,631	12.4
Not stated			–	213	1.6

Factor	Eigenvalue	Percentage of variance explained
1	4.50	18.7
2	1.44	6.0
3	1.28	5.3
4	1.18	4.9
5	1.11	4.6
6	1.05	4.4
7	1.02	4.2
8	0.93	3.9

Principal components analysis (Nie et al., 1975)

This table gives the component loading and component score coefficient for the first component obtained from an unrotated solution.

TABLE 19.7 Age at testing by mean test scores

Age at testing	Mean test scores			Proportion of sample in age groups %
	HFD	Copying Designs	EPVT	
< 5y 0m	10.4	4.5	-.05	4.7
≥ 5y 0m < 5y 1m	10.4	4.6	-.03	66.1
≥ 5y 1m < 5y 2m	10.4	4.8	.06	20.9
≥ 5y 2m < 5y 3m	10.4	4.9	.14	3.6
≥ 5y 3m < 5y 4m	11.1	5.2	.12	1.6
≥ 5y 4m < 5y 5m	11.1	5.3	.05	0.9
≥ 5y 5m < 5y 6m	11.1	5.1	.02	0.8
≥ 5y 6m	11.6	6.1	.14	1.4
Overall mean	10.4	4.7	.00	100.0
Total N	12,546	12,818	12,011	12,818
One way analysis of variance (7 df) F	7.3	19.9	4.5	
Sig.	p < .001	p < .001	p < .001	
Departure from linear trend Sig.	p < .05	p < .05	n.s.	

TABLE 19.8 Test parameters and correlations between tests and assessments

Test or assessment	N	Mean	SD	Correlation matrix				
				Maternal depression	Neurotic behaviour	Antisocial behaviour	EPVT	Copying Designs
Human Figure Drawing	12,784	10.4	3.1	-.06 (12,597)	.02 (12,731)	-.12 (12,724)	.25 (12,023)	.40 (12,780)
Copying Designs	13,028	4.7	2.0	-.13 (12,830)	-.01 (12,972)	-.19 (12,965)	.34 (12,214)	
English Picture Vocabulary Test	12,234	0.0	1.0	-.17 (12,067)	-.04 (12,184)	-.18 (12,177)		
Antisocial behaviour score	13,059	0.0	1.0	.36 (12,915)	.31 (13,059)			
Neurotic behaviour score	13,066	0.0	1.0	.34 (12,922)				
Maternal depression score	12,923	0.0	1.0					

All correlations are significant at the p < .001 level except as follows:

Neurotic behaviour vs Human Figure Drawing p < .01
Neurotic behaviour vs Copying Designs   n.s.

TABLE 20.1 Percentage of variance in dependent variables explained by selected independent variables

Independent variables	df	Dependent variables Human Figure Drawing	Copying Designs	EPVT	Antisocial behaviour	Neurotic behaviour	Maternal depression
Child's sex	1	1.6	n.s.	1.2	2.3	0.2	n.s.
Social Index score	12	2.8	9.3	11.9	5.3	n.s.	7.5
Social Index group	4	2.5	8.8	11.1	4.9	0.1*	7.1
Social class	5	1.6	5.8	7.1	3.2	0.1*	4.0
Mother's educational qualifications	7	1.7	5.8	7.4	3.0	0.2*	5.0
Father's educational qualifications	7	1.7	6.4	7.5	2.4	n.s.	3.5
Type of neighbourhood	3	0.9	4.0	5.6	2.9	0.1**	4.0
Type of family	5	0.3	0.8	1.3	0.9	0.2	1.3
Total children	4	1.0	2.7	4.4	0.7	0.7	1.4
Number of children older than study child	4	0.4	1.4	2.1	0.1*	2.8	0.9
Number of children younger than study child	3	0.5	1.3	2.2	1.1	1.5	0.3
Mother's age (grouped)	5	0.2	0.9	2.1	2.3	0.9	1.2
Ethnic group	5	0.2	0.6	3.8	0.3	0.1*	0.5
Region	9	0.2	2.1	0.6	.0.5	0.7	0.4

All associations significant at the $p < .001$ level except where indicated:

** .01<p<.05. * .01<p<.05. n.s. $p > .05$

Child Health and Education in the Seventies

A national study in England, Wales and Scotland of all children born 5th—11th April 1970

Under the auspices of the University of Bristol
and the National Birthday Trust Fund

Department of Child Health Research Unit
University of Bristol
Bristol   BS2 8BH

Director: Professor Neville R. Butler, MD, FRCP, DCH

Tel. Bristol 27745/22041

Research team:
N. R. Butler
A. F. Osborn, BA
B. C. Howlett, BSc, FSS, MBCS
S. F. O. Dowling, BSc, MB, BS
M. C. Fraser, SRN, SCM, HV Tutor Cert.

In association with:
Area Health Authorities in England and Wales
Health Boards in Scotland

Co-sponsors:
Health Visitors' Association

CONFIDENTIAL

HOME INTERVIEW QUESTIONNAIRE

Health District Code   Child's Local Serial Number   Child's Central Survey Number

`1—5`

`6`

`0 4`
`7,8`

Details of child born 5th—11th April 1970
If twins use separate questionnaire for each.   Please use block capitals.

Full name of the Child .... Sex ....

`9—11`

Singleton or twin, specify .... Date of birth............ April 1970

Present home address in full ....

`12,13`

Address of child's present placement if living away from home. *Please specify if hospital, residential home, etc.*

`14—17`

Child's National Health Service Number ....

`18`

N.H.S. Doctor with whom child is registered. *If not registered, put NONE.*

Name ....

Full address of practice ....

`19,20`

Full home address of mother at time she gave birth to child.
If not known, put NOT KNOWN. If same home address as above, put AS ABOVE.

`21—24`

If born abroad, give approximate date child came to live in this country ....

Mother's maiden name ....
(These details are needed for matching purposes only)

Address of place of birth. *Please specify whether maternity hospital, G.P. unit, home, etc.*

....

....

NOTES

1.   Please read "Survey Notes and Information" in conjunction with this questionnaire.

2.   Throughout the questionnaire the study child is designated by the letter N.

3.   It is important that no question should remain unanswered without explanation.

Appendix 2

SECTION A FAMILY COMPOSITION

A.1 (a) People in the household

A household consists of a group of people who all live at the same address and who are all catered for by the same person.

List below **all** the members of this household. Include the study child, N, the present parents and others, e.g. relatives or lodgers, who are members of this household. Exclude any who are only at home for short periods; enter these in table **(b)** below.

Relationship to N (e.g. father, step-brother) or status in the household (e.g. lodger)	Surname	First name(s)	Sex	Date of birth
1. Study child—N				/ 4 / 70
2.				/ /
3.				/ /
4.				/ /
5.				/ /
6.				/ /
7.				/ /
8.				/ /
9.				/ /
10.				/ /

(b) List below any members of the family not included in the above table, for example, those who are only home for holidays or leave, and enquire or state from your own knowledge the reason for absence, for example at residential school, or working away.

Relationship to N	Surname	First name(s)	Sex	Date of birth	Reason for absence from home

A.2 (a) What is the relationship to N of the person now acting as his/her mother?

Relationship to N

Natural mother .1
Mother by legal adoption 2
Stepmother .3
Foster mother 4
Grandmother 5
Elder sister 6
Cohabitee of father 7
Other mother figure, specify 8
. . . .
No mother figure 9

(b) please give reason(s) for any past changes in N's situation, e.g. family changes, mother died, etc.

. . . .
. . . .
. . . .

(c) If N is not now living with natural mother, i.e. 2—9 ringed, please ask when this situation began.

Month   Year

Situation began . . . .

A.3 (a) What is the relationship to N of the person now acting as his/her father?

Relationship to N

Natural father .1
Father by legal adoption 2
Stepfather 3
Foster father .4
Grandfather 5
Elder brother .6
Cohabitee of mother 7
Other father figure, specify 8
. . . .
No father figure 9

(b) please give reason(s) for any past changes in N's situation, e.g. family changes, father died, etc.

. . . .
. . . .
. . . .

(c) If N is not now living with natural father, i.e. 2—9 ringed, please ask when this situation began.

Month   Year

Situation began . . . .

25—29
30—34

Except in Q's B.1 to B.4 and B.23 where information is specifically required about N's natural mother or father, the terms "father" or "present father" are used to denote the present father figure identified in Q. A.3(a). The terms "mother" or "present mother" are used to denote the present mother figure identified in Q. A.2(a).

SECTION B MEDICAL HISTORY AND PRESENT HEALTH

B.1   Enter obstetric details on the study child, N, and on all liveborn and stillborn children born subsequently to N's natural mother. Include also children no longer living with their natural mother. Record each member of twin pair separately. Exclude miscarriages. (Some children in this table will be included also in table A.1 on page opposite).

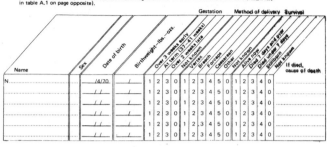

Name	Sex	Date of birth	Birthweight—lbs. —ozs.	Gestation				Method of delivery					Survival				If died, cause of death
N		/4/70	/	1 2 3 0	1	2 3 4 5 0		1 2 3 4 0									
....	/ /	/	1 2 3 0	1 2 3 4 5 0				1 2 3 4 0									
....	/ /	/	1 2 3 0	1 2 3 4 5 0				1 2 3 4 0									
....	/ /	/	1 2 3 0	1 2 3 4 5 0				1 2 3 4 0									
....	/ /	/	1 2 3 0	1 2 3 4 5 0				1 2 3 4 0									

B.2   How soon after N's birth did the mother first start to have regular contact with N, to hold and/or feed, not just look at?

Within 24 hours of birth 1

Between 25 and 48 hours after birth 2

On the third day or later, i.e. more than 48 hrs. after birth... 3   **(35)**

Not known 0

If on **third day or later**, how many days after N's birth did regular contact start? ⟶ ....   **(36,37)**

e.g. for third day enter ☐0☐3 , *if number of days not known enter* ☐9☐9

Please give reason(s) for delay in regular contact ....

....

B.3   After regular contact was established, was there any period of 24 hours or more during the first month of N's life when mother was not in normal contact with N, e.g. to hold and/or to feed?

No separation(s) of 24 hours or more 1

Mother and N out of contact for 24 hours or more 2   **(38)**

Cannot remember 3

Not known 0

If **separated**, give total duration of separation in completed days ⟶   **(39,40)**

e.g. for 2¼ days enter ☐0☐2 , *if number of days not known enter* ☐9☐9

Give reason(s) for separation(s) ....

....

B.4   Was N breast fed partly or wholly, even for a few days?

Yes —

for less than 1 month 1

for 1 month or more but less than 3 months 2

for 3 months or more 3

Yes but cannot remember for how long 4   **(41)**

No, was not breast fed at all 5

Not known 0

B.5   At what ages did N receive immunisation, against what diseases and where?

Enter everything given for each attendance, e.g. if on first attendance given triple and polio, ring 1, 2, 3, 4. If more than six attendances for immunisation please continue on back page.

Attendance	N's age in months	Diphtheria	Tetanus	Whooping cough	Poliomyelitis	Smallpox*	Measles	B.C.G.	Other	Not known	G.P.'s Surgery	Child Health Clinic	Other place	Not known
First att.		1	2	3	4	5	6	7	8	0	1	2	3	0
Second att.		1	2	3	4	5	6	7	8	0	1	2	3	0
Third att.		1	2	3	4	5	6	7	8	0	1	2	3	0
Fourth att.		1	2	3	4	5	6	7	8	0	1	2	3	0
Fifth att.		1	2	3	4	5	6	7	8	0	1	2	3	0
Sixth att.		1	2	3	4	5	6	7	8	0	1	2	3	0

*Please include smallpox vaccination, although now not recommended nationally.

B.6 Has N ever been seen at any of the following places for reasons specified, and if so at what ages, if known.

Ring all that apply in each row	Never seen	Seen at age:							Not known if ever seen
		48m+	36–47m	24–35m	12–23m	6–11m	under 6 mth	not known	
At–									
(a) Home by H.V. for any reason	1	2	3	4	5	6	7	8	0
(b) Child Health Clinic for any reason	1	2	3	4	5	6	7	8	0
(c) G.P. surgery or health centre for devel.screening	1	2	3	4	5	6	7	8	0
(d) Hospital birth follow-up clinic	1	2	3	4	5	6	7	8	0
(e) Assessment Centre or clinic for handicap	1	2	3	4	5	6	7	8	0

42–45

46–49

50,51

B.7 Has N ever been separated from his/her mother or mother substitute for one month or more?
Exclude N's hospital admissions and check these are detailed in B.9.

Yes 1
No 2   (52)
Not known 0

If **yes**, give total number of separations of one month or more, excluding N's hospital admission(s) ➞ (53,54)

e.g. if 2 separations enter [0][2] *if number of separations not known enter* [9][9]

Please give details below for all separations of **one month or over**. Exclude all N's hospital admissions.   *If more than three separations, continue on back page.*

	First	Second	Third
Age (years and months)			
Reason for separation			
Number of months (and weeks) separated			
Place of care of N?*			
Was the person looking after N known to him/her?			
Was N separated also from father?			

55–59

60–62

*Place of care: State if in child's own home, other's home, institutional placement, or specify if elsewhere.

B.8 Did the mother herself, as far as she can remember, ever spend more than a short time away from her parents as a child?   *Ring all that apply*

Yes –
fostered/in care 1
other reason(s), specify 2
.... (63)
No, never spent more than a short time away from parents 3
Not known 0

B.9 Has N ever been in hospital overnight or longer for any reason whatsoever? Exclude initial stay in maternity home/hospital.

Yes 1
No 2   (64)
Not known 0

If **yes**, give total number of hospital admissions overnight or longer ➞ (65,66)

Please give details below for every hospital admission.

If more than three admissions, continue on back page.

	First	Second	Third
Age (years and months)			
Diagnosis and nature of all special procedures, including operations			
Number of nights in hospital			
Name and address of hospital **in full**			
Type of ward and specify if children only admitted			

67–70

71–74

75

[0][5]

382

B.10 Has N ever attended a hospital outpatient department or any other specialist clinic?

Yes 1
No 2 (9)
Not known 0

If yes, please give details below for each condition or illness resulting in attendance(s) at out-patients or specialist clinic.

If more than three conditions or illnesses, continue on back page.

	First	Second	Third
Age at first attendance (years and months)			
Total number of attendances			
Diagnosis and treatment			
Name and address of department, hospital or clinic, in full.			

10—13

14—16

B.11 Please enquire or state from your own knowledge whether N has been seen by any of the following since the fourth birthday and/or previous to fourth birthday.

Ring all that apply in each row.

	Yes, after 4th b'day	Yes, before 4th b'day	No never	Not known	
Seen by a general practitioner* —					
at surgery/health centre	1	2	3	0	(17)
at home visit	1	2	3	0	(18)
Seen by dentist—					
for inspection, not therapy	1	2	3	0	(19)
for filling(s), extraction(s), etc.	1	2	3	0	(20)
Seen by doctor for routine medical exam.					
in nursery or school situation, specify	1	2	3	0	(21)
Seen by speech therapist—	1	2	3	0	(22)
age first seen...........yrs...........mths					
Seen by child guidance clinic	1	2	3	0	(23)
age first seen...........yrs...........mths					
Problem/diagnosis...........................					

*For medical reasons, not for development screening or immunisation.

B.12 Has N had any of the following in the past year and/or previous to past year?

Ring all that apply in each row.

	Yes, after 4th b'day	Yes, before 4th b'day	No never	Not known	
Operations					
(a) Tonsillectomy or T's & A's	1	2	3	0	(24)
(b) Adenoidectomy alone	1	2	3	0	(25)
(c) Circumcision	1	2	3	0	(26)
(d) Hernia operation	1	2	3	0	(27)
(e) Appendicectomy	1	2	3	0	(28)
(f) Any other operation, namely	1	2	3	0	(29)
....					
Medical Conditions					
(g) Eczema	1	2	3	0	(30)
(h) Hay fever or sneezing attacks	1	2	3	0	(31)
(i) Ear discharge (pus not wax)	1	2	3	0	(32)
(j) Repeated sore throats requiring medical attention	1	2	3	0	(33)
(k) Habitual snoring or mouth breathing	1	2	3	0	(34)
(l) Bronchitis	1	2	3	0	(35)
(m)Pneumonia	1	2	3	0	(36)
(n) Meningitis or encephalitis	1	2	3	0	(37)
(o) Hearing difficulty (suspected or confirmed)*	1	2	3	0	(38)
(p) Any vision problem (except squint) (suspected or confirmed)*	1	2	3	0	(39)

*If any suspected or confirmed hearing or eyesight problem, please give details below.

Appendix 2

B.13 Were there any of the following difficulties with N when he/she was a baby (i.e. under 6 months of age)?

		Yes	No	Not known	
(a)	Excessive crying	1	2	0	(40)
(b)	Frequent feeding problems	1	2	0	(41)
(c)	Frequent sleeping difficulty at night	1	2	0	(42)

B.14 Has N ever had an accident requiring medical advice or treatment?
Please include accidents in the road, home and elsewhere, accidental ingestion of medicines/poisons, burns/scalds, fractures, eye injuries, near-drowning, bad cuts and other injuries, with or without unconsciousness, and non-accidental injuries.

Ring all that apply.

Yes —

accidental swallowing of medicines or poisons	1
burn(s), scald(s)	2
road traffic accident(s)	3
Accident resulting in unconsciousness	4
other accidents	5
No accident	6
Not known	0

43,44

If **yes**, please state total number of accidents specified above ➡️ ..... (45,46)

e.g if 3 accidents enter 0 3

Please give details of every "accident"
Check that all "accidents" resulting in hospital admission or outpatient/casualty attendance are also included in B.9 and B.10 respectively. If more than four "accidents", continue on back page.

	First	Second	Third	Fourth	
Age (years and months)					
Where did it happen? (Road, home, school, etc.)					
What happened?*					
Description of "injuries" (e.g. burn/scald, fracture, head injury with unconsciousness, etc.)					47-49
Part(s) of body involved (head eyes, limbs, etc.)					50-53
Where treated? (G.P., Casualty, Inpatient)					
Treatment, including stitches, operation(s), plaster cast(s), traction, etc.					
Name and address of hospital **in full**, if attended or admitted					

*If ingestion of medicines/poisons, give name of substance.

B.15 Has N ever had one or more attacks or bouts in which he/she had wheezing on the chest, regardless of the cause?

Yes	1
No	2	(54)
Not known	0

If **yes**, please complete the following details.

(a) Age at first or only attack in which he/she wheezed on the chest: ....years .... mths

55-57

(b) How many attacks occurred:

(a) in first 12 months of life? ➡️ ..... (58,59)

(b) between first and fourth birthdays? ➡️ ..... (60,61)

(c) since fourth birthday? ➡️ ..... (62,63)

(c) Number of times ever admitted to hospital with any wheezing in the chest, whatever the cause ➡️ ..... (64,65)

(d) Please describe what the mother was told about the diagnosis in her own words ....

....

66

Check whether there have been any hospital admission(s) or out-patient attendance(s) for the above, if so, make sure they are included in B.9 and B.10 respectively.

384

B.16 Has N ever had any form of convulsion, fit, seizure or other turn in which consciousness was lost, or any part of the body made abnormal movements?

Yes 1

No, never 2   **(67)**

Not known 0

If yes,

(a) from health visitor's and mother's knowledge, and from records if possible, please give the most accurate diagnosis of the attack(s).

Ring all that apply

Epilepsy 1

Febrile convulsion(s) 2

Fainting, blackout(s) 3

Other diagnosis, namely 4

....

Not known 0   **68,69**

(b) please ask mother to describe the **first attack**

(i) form it took ....

....

(ii) how soon seen by G.P., or admitted, if at all ....

....

(c) please ask mother to describe **subsequent attack(s)**, if any.

(i) form they took if different from above ....

....

(ii) investigations, if any ....

(iii) medication and dates ....

....

(d) give number of convulsions, fits or seizures in each agegroup specified below.

	First four weeks	1–12 months	Over 1 yr under 2	Over 2 under 3	Over 3 under 4	Over 4 years
Number of attacks						

70–72

73–75

Check whether there have been any hospital admission(s) or out-patient attendance(s) for the above, if so, make sure they are included in B.9 and B.10 respectively.

B.17 Has N ever worn or been prescribed glasses?

Yes –

still has to wear them 1

but does not have to wear them now 2   **(76)**

No 3

Not known 0

B.18 Has N ever had a squint?

Yes –

now 1

in past but not now 2   **(77)**

No, never 3

Not known 0

If yes, what treatment was given?

Ring all that apply

Medical advice – "No treatment needed" 1

Patch over one eye 2

Glasses 3

Eye exercises 4   **77–78**

Operation 5

Treatment advised, but not known what 6

Never attended for advice or treatment 7

Not known 0

B.19 Has N ever had a stammer or stutter or any other difficulty with speech?

	Stammer or stutter	Other speech difficulty
Yes, at present—		
mild	1	1
severe	2	2
Yes, in past but not now	3	3
No	4	4
Not known	0	0

1–5

6

0 6
7,8

9,10

If ever difficulty in speech, other than stammer or stutter, give details

....

....

385

B.20 Do people outside N's household easily understand what he/she says?
If N's main language not English, ring 1.

N's main language not English 1
All or nearly all of N's speech is understood outside immediate family 2
Some of N's speech understood outside immediate family 3
Hardly any of N's speech understood outside immediate family 4 (11)
N's speech understood only by immediate family 5
Even immediate family have difficulty in understanding N's speech 6
Other answer, namely 7
Not known if others understand N. 0

B.21 From the health visitor's knowledge, observation and from records, has N ever been diagnosed as having any congenital abnormality or suspected congenital abnormality?

Ring all that apply

Yes —

Mongol 1
Spina bifida (meningomyelocele) 2
Hydrocephalus 3
Hare-lip 4
Cleft palate 5
Congenital heart condition (diagnosed) 6
Suspected congenital heart condition (murmur, etc.) 7 12-14
Skin naevus (portwine, strawberry, etc.) 8
Any other congenital abnormality, specify 9
....
No, none of the above 0

If yes, please describe abnormalities ....
....

B.22 From the health visitor's knowledge and observations, and where necessary from available records, does N have any physical or mental disability or handicap, or any other condition interfering with normal everyday life or which might be a problem at school?

Yes —
but no real handicap 1
mild handicap 2
severe handicap 3 15
No disability or handicap 4
Not known 0

If yes, (a) please give following details

Actual diagnosis ....
....

Effect on home or school life, if any 16
....

(b) indicate into which of the following categories the condition, handicap or disability falls

Ring all that apply

Visual defect 1
Hearing defect 2
Speech defect 3
Mental handicap or disability 4
Emotional problem 5
Motor/locomotor problem .... 6 17—19
Respiratory problem 7
Severe congenital condition 8
Severe acquired condition (e.g. malignancy) 9
Other condition, specify 0

B.23 Has N's natural mother or natural father or any brothers or sisters of N's ever had any of the following?

Ring all that apply in each column	Natural mother	Natural father	Sibling(s)
Asthma	1	1	1
Hayfever	2	2	2
Eczema	3	3	3
Late reader, i.e. not reading by 7 years	4	4	4
Poor reader or non-reader at present	5	5	5
Convulsion(s) or fit(s)	6	6	6
Bedwetting, after 5 years of age	7	7	7
Late in learning to speak	8	8	8
None of above	9	9	9
No siblings	—	—	10

20—22
23—25
26—28

SECTION C   TELEVISION VIEWING AND READING

C.1   Does N ever watch television at home?

Yes –

almost every day 1

occasionally 2   **(29)**

No, never 3

Not known 0

If N never watches TV proceed to C.6

C.2   Complete the following details of N's television viewing at home in the past seven days, by ringing all appropriate numbers for each day. Start with yesterday and go back day by day through the week.

Ring all that apply for each day.	Mon	Tue	Wed	Thur	Fri	Sat	Sun
Morning (e.g. before 1 pm)	1	1	1	1	1	1	1
Early afternoon (e.g. 1 pm—4 pm)	2	2	2	2	2	2	2
Late afternoon (e.g. 4 pm—6 pm)	3	3	3	3	3	3	3
Early evening (e.g. 6 pm—9 pm)	4	4	4	4	4	4	4
Late evening (e.g. after 9 pm)	5	5	5	5	5	5	5
Did not watch TV that day	6	6	6	6	6	6	6
Not known	0	0	0	0	0	0	0

30—33

34—37

38—41

42,43

C.3   Give total number of hours N watched each day in the past seven days

44—47

	Mon	Tue	Wed	Thur	Fri	Sat	Sun
Enter hours watched							

48—50

Enter **0** *for any day on which N watched TV under 1 hour or not at all. If not known on any day, enter* **NK**

Is this the usual amount of TV N watches?

Yes 1

No 2   **(51)**

Not known 0

If no, how many hours a day on average does he/she usually watch TV?........ ⟶ ....   **(52)**

If less than 1 hour a day enter **0**

C.4   What **types** of TV programmes does N watch at home?

Ring all that apply.

Children's programmes (e.g. Playschool, Sesame Street, etc.) 1

Cartoons 2

Thriller/dramatic programmes (e.g. cowboy, gangster, science fiction, war films, etc.) 3

Comedy programmes/series 4

Competition/quiz programmes (e.g. Double Your Money, Golden Shot, etc.) 5

Sport 6

News programmes 7

Documentary programmes (e.g. animal, travel films, etc.) 8

Other types of programmes, please give details 9

53—55

C.5   Which is N's favourite TV programme?

Specify title or series N likes best ....

56,57

C.6   Ring in column A all who have read to N at home at least once in the past 7 days. Ring in column B the one person who reads to N most often

	A	B
Mother	1	1
Father	2	2
Other adults, specify	3	3
Child(ren) 11 and over............................	4	4
Child(ren) under 11..................................	5	5
Nobody read to child	6	6
Not known	0	0

58—60

C.7   On how many days has N been read to at home in the past 7 days? ⟶ ....   **(61)**

If not read to in past 7 days enter **0** , *if not known enter* **9**

Is this the usual amount N is read to at home?

Yes 1

No 2   **(62)**

Not known 0

If no, how many days a week is he/she usually read to? ⟶ ....   **(63)**

Appendix 2

SECTION D NURSERY, PLAYGROUP AND SCHOOL EXPERIENCE

D.1 A. Ring in the **first** column **A** any school, playgroup, or nursery placements N attends at the **present** (or attended last term if at present on holiday).
If **currently** attending more than one, ring all he/she attends in column A.

B. Ring in the **second** column, **B** **all** other placements attended **previously for three months or longer**, that he/she has since stopped attending. *Ring all that apply in both columns*

	A Present placement(s)	B Previous placement(s)
Nursery school—		
Local Education Authority (free)	1	1
Private (fee charged)	2	2
Nursery class attached to infant/primary school—		
Local Education Authority (free)	3	3
Private (fee charged)	4	4
Normal school, full or part-time—		
Infant/primary school (L.E.A.)	5	5
Independent/private	6	6
Playgroup	7	7
Special day school, nursery or unit for physically or mentally handicapped children	8	8
Day nursery—		
Local Authority	9	9
Private	10	10
Creche, kindergarten	11	11
Mother and toddler club	12	12
Sunday school	13	13
Other placement, please specify	14	14
....		
Attends/attended none of these	15	15
Not known	0	0

If child has attended none of the above in the past or at the present proceed to D.10.

If child is attending, or has attended any of the above, please complete D.2 onwards.
Do not give further details of "mother and toddler club" or Sunday school.

D.2 Present placement — **A**

Name and address in full of the place N attends **at present** or, if on holiday, attended last term. (If child currently attends more than one place, please give details of the main one).

Designation of main place N attends now, i.e. as specified in D.1 A. ....

Name of place N attends now ....

Full postal address ....

....

Name of head teacher, supervisor, etc. ....

D.3 Previous placement — **B**

Name and address in full of place N has attended **previously** that he/she has since stopped attending.
(If the child has attended more than one place previously for three months or longer give details of **the one he/she left most recently**).

Designation of previous place N attended, i.e. as specified in D.1 B ....

Name of **previous** place N attended ....

Full postal address ....

....

Name of head teacher, supervisor, etc. ....

The following questions D.4 to D.8 refer to: **A**— *the present placement and* **B**— *the previous placement as identified above.*

D.4 Type of premises N attended for present and previous placements

	A Present placement	B Previous placement
Normal school or nursery premises	1	1
Village or community hall	2	2
Church hall	3	3
Private house	4	4
Nursery in factory/industrial premises	5	5
Other kind of premises, please specify	6	6
Not known	0	0

388

D.5 (a) At what age did N start attending:

	years	months
A – present placement?		
B – previous placement?		

(b) At what age did N stop attending the previous placement?

(c) What was the main reason he/she stopped attending the previous placement? ....

....

....

D.6 Days and periods of N's attendance

Ring the appropriate numbers under each day of the week to show whether N attended in the morning, afternoon or both. Enter in the last column the average length of a morning or afternoon session in hours.

		Mon	Tue	Wed	Thu	Fri	Sat	Sun	Hours attended per session
A – Present placement	Morning	1	2	3	4	5	6	7	.... hrs
	Afternoon	1	2	3	4	5	6	7	.... hrs
B – Previous placement	Morning	1	2	3	4	5	6	7	.... hrs
	Afternoon	1	2	3	4	5	6	7	.... hrs

D.7 Has the mother noticed any changes in N felt to be due to his/her attendance at present or previous placements?

	A Present placement	B Previous placement
Yes, change noticed	1	1
No, no change	2	2
Not attended long enough to say	3	3
Cannot say	4	4
Not known	0	0

If yes, what kind of changes have you noticed? *If only one or two are mentioned, ask, 'are there any other changes in him/her you have noticed?'*

A – Present placement ....

....

B – Previous placement ....

....

D.8 Has mother regularly taken part or helped in any way in the place(s) N attended? (e.g. looking after the children, helping with the administrative side or in other ways)

	A Present placement	B Previous placement
Yes–		
at least once a week	1	1
1–3 times a month	2	2
once or twice a term.....................................	3	3
less than once a term	4	4
No–		
Mother's help was not required	5	5
mother was busy doing other things...............	6	6
mother preferred not to take part	7	7
Child did not attend long enough to say	8	8
Other reply, please give details	9	9
....		
Not known	0	0

If mother has taken part, please describe what it was she did.

If only one or two things mentioned, ask 'were there any other things you did?'

A – Present placement ....

....

B – Previous placement ....

....

9—11

12—14

15—17

18,19

20—21

24—27

28—31

32—35

36,37

38,39

40,41

42,43

44

45

D.9 Have N's mother and/or father met the head teacher, supervisor or other staff from the **present placement** either **before** or **since** N started? (e.g. to discuss his/her settling down, N's school entry or anything else concerning N)

Ring all that apply in each column

	Before N started		Since N started	
	Mother	Father	Mother	Father
Yes, met staff to discuss N—				
at school, playgroup, etc.	1	1	1	1
at parents' home	2	2	2	2
elsewhere	3	3	3	3
No, never met staff	4	4	4	4
No mother figure/no father figure	5	5	5	5
N has no present placement	6	6	6	6
Not known	0	0	0	0

46—49

If **yes**, who initiated the meeting(s)?

Ring all that apply

Parents 1
Staff 2   (50)
Other reply, give details 3

....

Cannot say 0

D.10 If N is not **at present attending** infant/primary school (LEA or private) please give name and address of the school mother expects him/her to attend later.
If mother does not know which infant/primary school N is to attend, put NOT KNOWN.

(a) Name of infant/primary school ....

Full postal address ....

....

Name of head teacher ....

51

(b) When does the mother expect N to start attending this infant/primary school?

Summer term 1975 1
Autumn term (September) 1975 2   (52)
Other date, please specify 3

....

Cannot say 0

D.11 Irrespective of whether or not N attended, did the mother ever have his/her name down on a waiting list to go to a playgroup, nursery school or class, or day nursery?

Yes—   *Ring all that apply*

had name down on at least one waiting list for
nursery school/class or playgroup 1
had name down on waiting list for day nursery 2   (53)
No, name has never been on a waiting list 3
Cannot remember 0

D.12 Has N ever been regularly looked after during the day in **someone else's house**, for three months or longer? (For this purpose "regularly" is taken as two or more hours weekly)

Ring all that apply

Yes—

by a friend or neighbour 1
by paid child minder 2
by relative 3
by other person, please specify 4   54,55

....

No, never 5
Not known 0

If yes, give age in completed years N was first regularly looked after in someone else's house ⟶ .... ☐   (56)

If under one, enter ☐0☐ *, if 3¾ years enter* ☐3☐ *, if age not known enter* ☐9☐

SECTION E   EDUCATION AND OCCUPATION OF PARENTS

E.1   Educational or occupational qualifications of present parents   *Ring all that apply in both columns*

	Mother	Father
Qualifications in shorthand and/or typing, trade apprenticeships, or other vocational training, e.g. State Enrolled Nurse (SEN) or Enrolled Nurse (Scotland), hairdressing diploma, etc.	1	1
G.C.E. 'O' level, S.C.E. 'O' grade, Certificate of Secondary Education (CSE), City and Guilds Intermediate Technical Certificate, City and Guilds Final Craft Certificate	2	2
G.C.E. 'A' level, High School Certificate (HSC), Higher Grade of Scottish Leaving Certificate (SLC), Ordinary National Diploma/Certificate (OND, ONC), City and Guilds Final Technical Certificate, Higher Grade of Scottish Certificate of Education (SCE)	3	3
State Registered Nurse (SRN) or Registered Nurse (Scotland)	4	4
Certificate of Education (Teachers), Teaching Qualification (Primary/ Secondary Education in Scotland)..	5	5
Degree (e.g. BSc, BA, PhD), Higher National Diploma/Certificate (HND, HNC), Membership of Professional Institution (e.g. FCA, FRICS, MIMechE, MIEE, etc.) City and Guilds Full Technical Certificate	6	6
Other qualifications, please specify	7	7
....		
No qualifications	8	8
Not applicable, no mother or no father figure	9	9
Qualifications not known	0	0

☐☐ 57—59

☐☐ 60—62

E.2   At what age did the present parents leave school?

☐☐ 63,64

(a)   Age mother left school .... years

(b)   Age father left school .... years

☐☐ 65,66

E.3   How many completed years of **full-time** education did the present parents have **after** leaving school? (e.g. at college of education, at polytechnic, at university, etc.)   *If none, put NONE*

☐ 67

(a)   Mother, number of years .... years

(b)   Father, number of years .... years

☐ 68

E.4   Occupation of present father

E.4 to E.6 refer to the father or father substitute, including foster father, adoptive father, stepfather or any other father substitute.

If N has no father or substitute father now, please ring 8 in E.4 and proceed to E.8.

(a)   What is the father's actual job, occupation, trade or profession, or the last occupation if unemployed or retired? *Full and precise details of occupation are required. See "Survey Notes and Information".*

Actual job ....

☐ 69

(b)   What is the industry or business in which the father is engaged? *Give details of goods, materials or services. See "Survey Notes and Information".*

Type of industry ....

☐ 70

(c)   Father's employment status

☐ 1—5

Self-Employed

With 25 or more employees 1

With less than 25 employees 2

☐ 6

Without employees other than family workers 3

Employed

In managerial position 4

0 8
7,8

As foreman, supervisor, chargehand, etc. 5

Not in supervisory role 6

Other

Unemployed, sick, etc.

Please describe situation 7

....

No father figure 8

Not known, please explain situation 0

....

E.5 Do any of the following apply?

	Never or hardly ever	Sometimes	Often	Not known	
(a) Father away evenings until after N has gone to bed	1	2	3	0	(9)
(b) Father away most of Saturday and/or Sunday	1	2	3	0	(10)
(c) Father works away for long periods (i.e. a month or more at a time)	1	2	3	0	(11)
(d) Father works overnight	1	2	3	0	(12)
(e) Father works shifts	1	2	3	0	(13)

E.6 For how many weeks has the father been off work in the past 12 months, through illness or unemployment or for other reasons?

e.g. If off work 9½ weeks enter ⌷0⌷9⌷   if never off work enter ⌷0⌷0⌷   if not known enter ⌷9⌷9⌷

Number of weeks off work through:

(a) Illness or accident .... (14,15)

(b) Unemployment .... (16,17)

(c) Other reasons, give details .... (18,19)

....

E.7 When the present father left school, what was his own father's job?
See "Survey Notes and Information". If occupation not known put NOT KNOWN.

(a) Actual job ....

(b) Type of industry ....

E.8 When the present mother left school, what was her own father's job?
See "Survey Notes and Information". If occupation not known put NOT KNOWN.

(a) Actual job ....

(b) Type of industry ....

E.9 Does present mother have a job, either out of the home or at home, or is she a full-time housewife?

Mother works out of the home –

regularly: full-time or part-time employment, including evenings, overnight or weekends 1

occasionally: casual or freelance worker obtaining work on a day-to-day basis or seasonally, e.g. fruit picking, etc. 2

Mother works at home

regularly: family business, e.g. shop, farm, boarding house, clerical work for a self-employed husband, home industry i.e. working for a firm of manufacturers at home, etc. 3

occasionally: seasonal work done at home, e.g. holiday bed and breakfast business 4   (22)

Full-time housewife, no other kind of work 5

Other work situation, please give details 6

....

Not known 0

If mother works regularly at home or out of the home (i.e. ringed 1 or 3 in E.9) at the present time, please complete E.10 onwards.

If mother is now a full-time housewife or only works occasionally, (i.e. ringed 2, 4 or 5 in E.9) please proceed to E.17 on next page.

E.10 Describe mother's present job. *See "Survey Notes and Information".*

What is her actual job? (e.g. shop assistant, teacher, assembly line worker, typist, stitcher, etc.)

....

(b) What type of industry or business does she work in? (e.g. greengrocery, infant school, tobacco, insurance, glovemaking, etc.)

....

(c) What kind of position does mother occupy at work?

Managerial 1

As forewoman or supervisor, etc 2

Non-supervisory position 3

Works at home 4   (24)

Other, please specify 5

....

Cannot say/not known 0

(d) How many years has mother been doing this job? (Ignore short breaks for pregnancies or illness)

If 4½ years enter ⌷0⌷4⌷ . If under one year enter ⌷0⌷0⌷ , if not known enter ⌷9⌷9⌷

Number of years .... (25,26)

E.11 Please show in the table below the times (giving a.m. or p.m.) the mother started and finished work and the total hours worked each day last week. If not working last week, give details of the last week worked.

	Mon	Tues	Wed	Thurs	Fri	Sat	Sun
Time started							
Time finished							
Total hours worked*							

27—31

32—36

Include meal breaks as part of the working period. Enter 0 for any day not worked.

E.12 Does mother work these hours regularly every week?

37—40

Yes, every week the same 1

No, mother works a shift system 2

No set pattern of work, hours or days worked vary 3   (41)

Other reply, please give details 4

....

Cannot say 0

E.13 Please give average travelling time to and from work

(a) travelling to work .... hours .... mins

(b) returning home .... hours .... mins

42,43

If works at home put AT HOME

E.14 When mother is at work, is N usually looked after at home or away from home? (If N is sometimes looked after at home and sometimes away from home ring where he/she is mainly looked after).

Looked after at home 1

Looked after away from home 2   (44)

Varies 3

Cannot say 0

E.15 Who looks after N during mother's working hours? *Ring all that apply*

N's father 1

Mother at home 2

Accompanies mother to work 3

Adult relative e.g. grandparents, aunt, etc. 4

Older sibling 5

Paid childminder 6   45—48

Friend or neighbour (not paid) 7

Local authority day nursery 8

Day nursery run by an employer or private individual(s) 9

School, nursery school or class, or playgroup 10

Some other person or place, namely 11

....

Not known 0

If more than one, who mainly looks after N during mother's working hours?

....

49,50

E.16 Please ask the mother if she could say what are the main reasons she works. (If "for money" ask, "what is money mainly spent on?")   *Ring all that apply*

Financial necessity (e.g. contribution to housekeeping or rent, clothes, etc.) 1

Financial advantage (e.g. savings, holidays, household appliances, luxuries, car, to gain independence, etc.) 2

Social reasons (e.g. for company, making friends, relief of boredom, keep you young, etc.) 3   51,52

Career/enjoys the work 4

Other reasons, describe... 5

....

If more than one reason given, ask, "which of these is the most important reason", and write in

....

53

E.17 Has mother had a regular full-time or part-time job out of the home since the time of N's birth which she subsequently gave up?   *Ring all that apply*

Yes —

full-time job(s).. 1

part-time job(s)... 2

No, never had a job out of the home since N's birth 3   54

Other reply, give details.. 4

....

Not known.. 0

If yes, give total time worked since N's birth in completed years (exclude present job if any) ➞ ☐ (55)

If worked under one year enter 0

SECTION F   THE HOME AND SOCIAL ENVIRONMENT

F.1   What accommodation is occupied by this household?

Whole detached house or bungalow	1
Whole semi-detached house or bungalow	2
Whole terrace house (including end of terrace)	3
Flat/maisonette (self-contained)	4
Rooms (non self-contained flat)	5
Other, please give details	6

(56)

If Flat or Rooms, give the lowest floor on which rooms are situated

If on ground floor or basement, enter [0] [0]

Floor ⟶ (57,58)

F.2   Is the accommodation owned or rented by the household?

Owned outright	1
Being bought	2
Rented from Council	3
Privately rented — unfurnished	4
Privately rented — furnished or partly furnished	5
Tied to occupation of father	6
Other situation, please give details	7

(59)

F.3   Does the household have sole use of, share with another household, or lack any of the following amenities?

		Sole use	Shared use	None available	
(a)	Bathroom	1	2	3	(60)
(b)	Indoor lavatory	1	2	3	(61)
(c)	Outdoor lavatory	1	2	3	(62)
(d)	Hot water supply	1	2	3	(63)
(e)	Garden or yard	1	2	3	(64)
(f)	Kitchen	1	2	3	(65)

F.4   How large is the kitchen and is it used for living in (e.g. for having meals in)?

Less than 6 feet wide —	
Not used for living in	1
Used for living in	2
6 feet or more wide —	
Not used for living in	3
Used for living in	4
No kitchen	5
Not known	0

(66)

F.5   How many rooms are there within the accommodation? (Include all rooms except kitchen, bathroom, toilet, and any rooms used solely for business purposes. For complete definition see "Survey Notes and Information")

Number of rooms ⟶ (67,68)

F.6   Does N share a bedroom with others?

Yes	1
No	2
Not known	0

(69)

If yes, how many sleep in the same room ⟶ (70)

F.7   Does N share a bed with others?

No	1
Yes —	
with one other	2
with two others	3
with more than two others	4
Not known	0

(71)

F.8   Which of the following does the family have?

Ring all that apply

Refrigerator	1
Washing machine	2
Spin dryer	3
Colour T.V.	4
Black and White T.V.	5
Van or car	6
Telephone	7
None of the above	8

72—74

1—5

6

09
7,8

F.9 In the past seven days has anyone helped mother at all with any of the following? (Include father, members of the household, friends, neighbours, relatives and paid help).

Ring all that apply in each row

		Yes father	Yes others	No	Not known	
(a)	Housework/shopping	1	2	3	0	(9)
(b)	Looking after N for part of the day while mother shops, attends appointments, does housework, etc.	1	2	3	0	(10)
(c)	Babysitting in the evening	1	2	3	0	(11)
(d)	Putting N to bed	1	2	3	0	(12)
(e)	Taking N to school/nursery/playgroup, etc.	1	2	3	0	(13)

F.10 In the past 7 days has N done any of the following with others or by him/herself:

Ring all that apply in each row.

		Yes with adult(s)	Yes with child(ren)	Yes by self	No	Not known	
(a)	been to a friend's or relative's house	1	2	3	4	0	(14)
(b)	been to a park, recreation ground, adventure playground	1	2	3	4	0	(15)
(c)	been on a bus or train	1	2	3	4	0	(16)
(d)	been to the shops, launderette, etc.	1	2	3	4	0	(17)

F.11 Indicate to which of the following broad ethnic categories N and the present parents belong.

	N	Mother	Father
European (U.K.)	1	1	1
European (other)	2	2	2
West Indian	3	3	3
Indian/Pakistani	4	4	4
Other Asian	5	5	5
African	6	6	6
Other, specify	7	7	7
Not known	0	0	0

(18—20)

F.12 What language is mainly used with N in the home?

English 1
Other language, namely 2 (21)
Not known 0

F.13 How many times has N moved since birth?
If no moves enter [0][0] . *If not known enter* [9][9]

Number of moves ➡ [ ][ ] (22,23)

F.14 Has N ever been in any of the following situations?

Ring all that apply in both columns
"In care"* (voluntary or statutory) in —

	Now	In the past but not now
fosterparents' home	1	1
assessment centre	2	2
family group home	3	3
children's home	4	4
In "Part III" accommodation	5	5
In homeless family unit	6	6
None of the above	7	7
Not known if any of above	0	0

(24—27)

*For each "in care" situation please give the following details:

Name & address of home, centre, etc., if known	Local Authority or Voluntary Society	Age when first entered this situation	Length of stay	Reason N in care

F.15 From your knowledge and anything you have learned from the interview, has anyone in the household since N's birth had contact with any statutory or voluntary social work or welfare organisations? (For example, Social Services or Social Security Departments, Probation Service, etc.)

Yes 1
No 2 (28)
Not known 0

If yes, give details ....

395

SECTION G FAMILY HEALTH AND SMOKING

G.1 Has anyone in N's household since N's birth had any severe or prolonged illness (medical, surgical or psychiatric) or any handicap or disability?

Ring all that apply

Yes—

mother	1	
father	2	
other adult in household	3	
child in household (excluding N)	4	29,30
No, none	5	
Not known	0	

If **yes**, please give the following details for each member of the household concerned.

Relationship to N	
Diagnosis or nature of condition	
Date of onset	
Duration of condition (years and months)	
Outcome (i.e. recovered, died, condition still present)	
In what way, if any, has condition caused any interference with N's everyday care?	

G.2 (a) Do either N's mother or father smoke at all at present?
(Cigarette smoking is defined as smoking an average of one or more cigarettes a day)

Ring all that apply in both columns	Mother	Father
No, is non-smoker	1	1
Yes —		
smokes cigarettes	2	2
smokes pipe or cigars	3	3
Not known if smokes	0	0

31,32

If smokes cigarettes, how many are smoked per day on average?

If not known how many, enter [9][9] Average number smoked: Mother ⟶ (33,34)

Father ⟶ (35,36)

(b) Irrespective of whether or not N's mother or father smoke at present, for how many years since N's birth have they smoked cigarettes, if at all?

During the period since N's birth —	Mother	Father
Smoked all the time	1	1
Smoked for more than 3 years	2	2
Smoked for between 1 and 3 years	3	3
Smoked for less than 1 year	4	4
Smoked but not know for how long	5	5
Non-smoker all the time	6	6
Not known if smoked at all	0	0

37,38

From interviewer's and mother's knowledge or any other source, has N ever previously had any special test(s) of progress in connection with a follow-up of the British Births Survey or any other study of child development?

No	1
Yes	2
Not known	0

If **yes**, please complete details below.

Age(s) of N	Name of study, if known	Where tested and by whom

39

Relationship of informant to N

Mother	1	
Father	2	(40)
Other, specify	3	

END OF INTERVIEW

Please thank the mother for her help in this confidential enquiry. When doing so, please mention that the study will be continued in the nurseries, playgroups, hospitals and other places already attended by the children taking part. We will also record the results of screening tests and medical examinations undergone by the children to complement the information that the mother has so kindly given.

If there are any further points the mother would care to add concerning N or the survey, we would be grateful if these could be noted on the back page.

SECTION H   TO BE COMPLETED AFTER THE INTERVIEW IS OVER

Please complete H.1 to H.5 from your knowledge and any impression you have gained during the interview.

H.1 Please ring the descriptions which you feel best characterise the home and relationship of family with neighbours.

(a) Furniture/equipment in home	(b) Tidiness of home	(c) Relationship of family with neighbours
Luxurious 1	Over-tidy 1	Very good terms 1
Well equipped 2	Very tidy 2	Good terms...................2
Adequate 3	Average.........................3	Satisfactory.................3
Low standard...............4	Untidy..........................4	Don'tmix.......................4
Very low standard 5	Chaotic 5	Bad terms......................5
Can't assess 0	Can't assess...................0	Can't assess...................0

`41—43`

H.2 In order to get some impression of the kind of district N lives in, please ring which one of the following descriptions best characterises the district.

In this district, houses are closely packed together and many are in poor state of repair. Multi-occupation is a common feature, and most families have low incomes   1

This district consists largely of council houses and flats or less expensive privately owned houses, for example, older terrace houses. Multi-occupation is unusual and families have average incomes. Include 'new towns' here   2

In this district houses are well spaced and the majority are well maintained. Multi-occupation is rare and most families have higher than average incomes...   3   **(44)**

This district is part of a small market town, rural community or village. Some families may lack basic amenities but others may be fairly well-to-do. It is mainly characterised by the fact that well-to-do and poorer families live fairly close together in the community   4

If none of these descriptions seem to characterise the district N lives in, please describe in your own words what it is like: 5

....

H.3 From the health visitor's knowledge and observations of the child, and where necessary from available records, what is N's intellectual development considered to be?

Normal or above average	1
Slightly backward	2
Definitely backward	3 **(45)**
Other situation, please describe	4
....	
Insufficient information	0

If at all backward in intellectual development, give any relevant diagnosis and details of assessment procedure(s) or investigations, if any.

....

....

H.4 How well do you know this family?

Very well...	1
Fairly well..	2
Slightly	3 **(46)**
Never in contact before this interview	4
Other situation, please describe.................................	5
....	

H.5 Were there any interruptions, distractions or other problems which made interviewing difficult?

No, no difficulty	1
Yes, slight difficulty	2 **(47)**
Yes, considerable difficulty.......................................	3

If yes, please describe any difficulty

....

H.6 What procedure was adopted for the completion of the Maternal Self-completion Questionnaire?

Questionnaire left with mother and collected after completion	1
Mother completed it without help during the home interview	2
Mother completed it with some help from the interviewer................................	3 **(48)**
Interviewer read out all the questions for mother to respond	4
Other procedure, ...	5

If 3, 4 or 5 ringed, please give reason(s), e.g. mother couldn't read, etc. ....

....

Date of interview .... [49-51]

Name of Health Visitor conducting the interview: ....

Employing Area Health Authority/Health Board ....

Health District, if applicable .... [52-55]

Please note below:

(i)   any other relevant information which you feel has not already been brought out in the
       interview form,

(ii)   any comments or observations by the General Practitioner, if he so wishes,

(iii) any further details about questions if insufficient space earlier in questionnaire.

H.7   Please indicate degree of completeness of the documents.

	Fully completed	Partly completed	Not completed	If not fully completed, give reason(s)
Home Interview Questionnaire	1	2	3	
Maternal Self-completion Questionnaire	1	2	3	
Test Booklet	1	2	3	

We are most grateful for the time you have given. Thank you for your help.

398

Appendix 3 Maternal Self-completion Questionnaire

Child Health and Education in the Seventies

A national study in England, Wales and Scotland of all children born 5th—11th April 1970

Under the auspices of the University of Bristol
and the National Birthday Trust Fund

Department of Child Health Research Unit
University of Bristol
Bristol   BS2 8BH

Director: Professor Neville R. Butler, MD, FRCP, DCH

Tel. Bristol 26491/27745

Health District Code   Child's Local Serial Number

Child's Central Survey Number   **CONFIDENTIAL**

MATERNAL SELF-COMPLETION QUESTIONNAIRE

Full Name of the Child ....   **Sex** ....

Address .... Date of birth.............. April 1970

....

To the Mother:

This questionnaire is part of a survey into the health and education of 5 year old children. In this form we are asking about the behaviour of your child, your own health and your opinions on a number of subjects. We hope that you will be able to find time to complete the form and that you will find it of interest. We would be grateful to have any remarks you may care to make about the questions in this form and you will find space for this on the last page. All information will be treated in the strictest confidence.

If you should have any difficulty in filling in any part of the form, the Health Visitor will be pleased to advise you.

Please leave blank

1-5

SECTION 1   Child's Behaviour

Please put a cross in the box by the answer which best describes which is true about your child's behaviour.

The following examples will help you to see what is required.

6-8

Example 1

PLEASE SAY IF:

	Never in the last 12 months	Less than once a month	At least once a month	At least once a week
Child has dizzy spells	☐	☒	☐	☐
Child complains of aching back or limbs	☐	☐	☐	☒

The crosses in these boxes mean that this child has dizzy spells less than once a month, and complains of aching back or limbs at least once a week.

Example 2

DOES CHILD HAVE ANY DIFFICULTY DRESSING?

NO   ☐

YES   ☒ ——————— IF YES, is this with:

Shoes .... ☐

Socks .... ☒

Pants .... ☐

Shirts/dresses etc... ☐

Buttons .... ☒

Zips .... ☐

The crosses in these boxes mean that this child has difficulty in dressing, and socks and buttons are the main problems.

PLEASE TURN OVER THE PAGE AND ANSWER THE QUESTIONS

399

Appendix 3

PLEASE ANSWER EVERY QUESTION

1. Below is a list of minor health problems which most children have at some time. Please tell us how often each of these happens with your child by putting a cross in the box which best describes this.

	Never in the last 12 months	Less than once a month	At least once a month	At least once a week
Complains of headaches	☐	☐	☐	☐
Complains of stomach-ache or has vomited	☐	☐	☐	☐
Complains of biliousness	☐	☐	☐	☐
Has temper tantrums (that is, complete loss of temper with shouting, angry movements, etc.)	☐	☐	☐	☐

Most children go through "difficult" stages. Please show by putting a cross in the correct boxes whether or not your child has any of the following difficulties **at the present time.** Please answer every question.

2. **DOES YOUR CHILD HAVE ANY SLEEPING DIFFICULTY?**

NO ☐

YES – MILD ☐

YES – SEVERE ☐ ——— IF YES, which of the following difficulties does he/she have?

getting off to sleep .... ☐

waking during the night .... ☐

waking early in the morning .... ☐

nightmares or night terrors .... ☐

sleepwalking .... ☐

Please describe any sleeping difficulties, including those above:

....

3. **DOES CHILD EVER WET THE BED AT NIGHTS?**

NO ☐ ——— IF NO, at what age did he/she become dry at night? ....

YES ☐ ——— IF YES, is it:

very occasionally (less than once a week) .... ☐

occasionally (at least once a week) .... ☐

most nights .... ☐

every night .... ☐

4. **DOES CHILD EVER WET HIS/HER PANTS IN THE DAYTIME?**

NO ☐

YES ☐ ——— IF YES, is it:

very occasionally (less than once a week) .... ☐

occasionally (at least once a week).................. ☐

most days .... ☐

every day .... ☐

5. **DOES CHILD EVER SOIL OR MAKE A MESS IN HIS/HER PANTS?**

NO ☐

YES ☐ ——— IF YES, is it:

very occasionally (less than once a week) .... ☐

occasionally (at least once a week) .... ☐

most days .... ☐

every day .... ☐

400

6. DOES CHILD HAVE ANY EATING OR APPETITE PROBLEMS?

NO ☐

YES – MILD ☐
YES – SEVERE ☐ ——— IF YES, is it:

not eating enough .... ☐

over-eating for more than the occasional meal. ☐

faddiness .... ☐

·Please describe any other eating problem:

....

☐ 19,20

7. DOES CHILD ATTEND SCHOOL, NURSERY SCHOOL, PLAYGROUP OR ANYTHING LIKE THAT?

NO ☐

YES ☐ ——— IF YES, has he/she had tears on arrival

NO .... ☐

YES, once or twice a week .... ☐

YES, every day .... ☐

☐ 21

8. Below is a series of descriptions of behaviour often shown by children. After each statement are three columns — "Doesn't apply", "Applies somewhat", and "Certainly applies". If your child definitely shows the behaviour described by the statement put a cross in the box under "Certainly applies". If he/she shows the behaviour described by the statement but to a lesser degree or less often, place a cross under "Applies somewhat". If, **as far as you are aware,** your child does not show the behaviour, place a cross under "Doesn't apply".

Please put **one** cross against **each** statement.

	Doesn't apply	Applies somewhat	Certainly applies
Very restless. Often running about or jumping up and down. Hardly ever still	☐	☐	☐
Is squirmy or fidgety	☐	☐	☐
Often destroys own or others' belongings	☐	☐	☐
Frequently fights with other children	☐	☐	☐
Not much liked by other children	☐	☐	☐
Often worried, worries about many things	☐	☐	☐
Tends to do things on his own — rather solitary	☐	☐	☐
Irritable. Is quick to "fly off the handle".	☐	☐	☐
Often appears miserable, unhappy, tearful or distressed	☐	☐	☐
Sometimes takes things belonging to others	☐	☐	☐
Has twitches, mannerisms or tics of the face or body	☐	☐	☐
Frequently sucks thumb or finger	☐	☐	☐
Frequently bites nails or fingers	☐	☐	☐
Is often disobedient	☐	☐	☐
Cannot settle to anything for more than a few moments	☐	☐	☐
Tends to be fearful or afraid of new things or new situations	☐	☐	☐
Is fussy or over particular	☐	☐	☐
Often tells lies	☐	☐	☐
Bullies other children	☐	☐	☐

22-25

26-29

30-33

34-37

38-40

401

Appendix 3

Many mothers find caring for their children difficult if their own health is not very good. Listed below are a number of common symptoms that mothers often describe to doctors. We would like you to say if these happen to you by putting a ring round Yes or No as in the examples given.

Here are two EXAMPLES:

Do your hands often tremble? .... Yes (No)

Are you worried about travelling long distances?................................. (Yes) No

This means my hands do not tremble but I am worried about travelling long distances.

PLEASE RING THE CORRECT ANSWER TO EACH OF THE FOLLOWING:

Do you often have back-ache? .... Yes   No

Do you feel tired most of the time? .... Yes   No

Do you often feel miserable or depressed? .... Yes   No

Do you often have bad headaches? .... Yes   No

	41-44

Do you often get worried about things? .... Yes   No

Do you usually have great difficulty in falling asleep or staying asleep? .... Yes   No

Do you usually wake unnecessarily early in the morning?......................... Yes   No

Do you wear yourself out worrying about your health?............................ Yes   No

	45-48

Do you often get into a violent rage? .... Yes   No

Do people often annoy and irritate you?... Yes   No

Have you at times had a twitching of the face, head or shoulders? .... Yes   No

Do you often suddenly become scared for no good reason? .... Yes   No

	49-52

Are you scared to be alone when there are no friends near you? .... Yes   No

Are you easily upset or irritated? .... Yes   No

Are you frightened of going out alone or of meeting people?...................... Yes   No

Are you constantly keyed up and jittery?.. Yes   No

	53-56

Do you suffer from indigestion? .... Yes   No

Do you often suffer from an upset stomach?....................................... Yes   No

Is your appetite poor?.. Yes   No

Does every little thing get on your nerves and wear you out? .... Yes   No

	57-60

Does your heart often race like mad?... Yes   No

Do you often have bad pains in your eyes?... Yes   No

Are you troubled with rheumatism or fibrositis?................................... Yes   No

Have you ever had a nervous breakdown? .... Yes   No

	61-64

Do you have any other health problems worrying you?............................. Yes   No

IF YES, please describe in your own words:

....

....

....

....

....

....

	65-68

SECTION 3 Opinions

This section asks for your opinion about a wide range of subjects. Please give your own opinions and do not worry about what others may think. There are no "correct" answers to the questions. We expect you will agree with some statements and disagree with others.

If you strongly agree, ring the 'A'

If you mildly agree, ring the 'a'

If you mildly disagree, ring the 'd'

If you strongly disagree, ring the 'D'

If you cannot say whether you agree or disagree with a statement, for instance when it "depends on circumstances", ring the 'X'

Please try to answer every one, but if you do not understand a statement leave it out.

These three examples should help you to see how to answer the questions.

Example 1

	Strongly agree	Mildly agree	Cannot say	Mildly disagree	Strongly disagree
People are not very co-operative these days	A	a	X	d	(D)

This means I strongly disagree with this statement

Example 2

	Strongly agree	Mildly agree	Cannot say	Mildly disagree	Strongly disagree
If people were not so selfish the world would be a happier place	A	(a)	X	d	D

This means I mildly agree with this statement

Example 3

	Strongly agree	Mildly agree	Cannot say	Mildly disagree	Strongly disagree
No marriage is complete without children	(A)	a	X	d	D

This means I strongly agree with this statement

PLEASE ANSWER EVERY QUESTION

	Strongly agree	Mildly agree	Cannot say	Mildly disagree	Strongly disagree
1. Women need something more from life than they can get by just looking after the home and children	A	a	X	d	D
2. Such activities as painting and playing should take second place to teaching reading and arithmetic in infant schools	A	a	X	d	D
3. Girls should accept the fact that they will marry and have children and not think about starting a career	A	a	X	d	D
4. Strictly disciplined children rarely grow up to be the best adults	A	a	X	d	D
5. Young children who never see children's T.V. miss a lot which is of value	A	a	X	d	D
6. It's best not to visit children under five in hospital because it is too upsetting for the child	A	a	X	d	D
7. Women should have the same work opportunities as men	A	a	X	d	D
8. If a child is often allowed to have his own way while he is young he will be uncontrollable later	A	a	X	d	D

		Strongly agree	Mildly agree	Cannot say	Mildly disagree	Strongly disagree		*Please leave blank*
9.	A person that does not let others stand in his way is to be admired	A	a	X	d	D		
10.	Things should be made easier for unmarried mothers	A	a	X	d	D		
11.	Increases in vandalism and delinquency are largely due to the fact that children nowadays lack strict discipline	A	a	X	d	D		
12.	Children should not be allowed to talk at the meal table	A	a	X	d	D		17-20
13.	Children under five should always accept what their parents say as being true	A	a	X	d	D		
14.	Mothers need a break from their children from time to time during the day	A	a	X	d	D		
15.	T.V. is a useful way of keeping the children amused	A	a	X	d	D		
16.	It is unreasonable to expect hospitals to upset their routine by allowing unlimited visiting in children's wards	A	a	X	d	D		21-24
17.	Parents should treat young children as equals	A	a	X	d	D		
18.	Young children pick up a lot of bad habits from T.V.	A	a	X	d	D		
19.	One of the things parents must do is sort out their children's quarrels for them and decide who is right and wrong	A	a	X	d	D		
20.	Some equality in marriage is a good thing, but by and large the husband ought to have the main say-so in family matters	A	a	X	d	D		25-28
21.	Nothing is worse than a person who does not feel a great love, gratitude, and respect for his parents	A	a	X	d	D		
22.	Unquestioning obedience is not a good thing in a young child	A	a	X	d	D		
23.	The State should open more day nurseries so as to make it easier for mothers of young children to go out to work	A	a	X	d	D		
24.	The trouble with hospital specialists is that they never have time to explain all their patients would like to know	A	a	X	d	D		29-32
25.	People should be satisfied with their lot in this world and not struggle to get more	A	a	X	d	D		
26.	A mother who always gives in to her young child's demands for attention will spoil him	A	a	X	d	D		

404

		Strongly agree	Mildly agree	Cannot say	Mildly disagree	Strongly disagree

Please leave blank

27. There is nothing wrong with a mother going out to work if her children can be properly cared for by someone else

    A   a   X   d   D

28. Teaching 5 year old children obedience and respect for authority is not as important as all that

    A   a   X   d   D

    `33-36`

29. If pre-school children would pay more attention to what they are told instead of just having their own ideas they would learn more quickly

    A   a   X   d   D

30. A mother who leaves her children with someone else in order to go out to work is not fit to be a mother unless she needs the money for food and clothes

    A   a   X   d   D

31. A child should not be allowed to talk back to his parents

    A   a   X   d   D

32. There are many things a 5 year old child must do with no explanation from his parents

    A   a   X   d   D

    `37-40`

33. A young child must be allowed to be himself even if this means going against his parents' wishes

    A   a   X   d   D

34. Parents must face the fact that teenagers have different morals to their own when they were that age and must put up with it

    A   a   X   d   D

35. It is not surprising if educational standards are falling when children have so much freedom in school nowadays

    A   a   X   d   D

36. A wife must sacrifice her right to go out to work once she has children

    A   a   X   d   D

    `41-44`

37. A mother should accept that her children are sometimes too busy to do as she asks.

    A   a   X   d   D

38. You cannot expect a child under five to understand how another person feels

    A   a   X   d   D

39. A well brought up child is one who does not have to be told twice to do something

    A   a   X   d   D

40. A mother's proper place is at home with her children

    A   a   X   d   D

    `45-48`

41. Children under five should never be allowed to watch adult T.V.

    A   a   X   d   D

42. Children who get upset whilst in hospital soon get over it afterwards

    A   a   X   d   D

43. Girls are just as capable as boys of learning to be engineers

    A   a   X   d   D

    `49-51`

The last few questions on this page are to give us some idea about how you got on with the form.

1. Did you have any difficulty in understanding any of the questions?

    NO, no difficulties .... ☐

    YES, some questions were difficult.................................... ☐

    YES, many questions were difficult .... ☐

    IF YES, please say which questions were difficult and why

    ....

    ....

    ....

2. Did you have any difficulty in making up your mind about any questions?

    NO, no difficulty.. ☐

    YES, some difficulty .... ☐

    YES, a lot of difficulty .... ☐

    IF YES, please say which questions and why

    ....

    ....

    ....

3. Who answered this form?

    Mother alone .... ☐

    Father alone .... ☐

    Mother and father together .... ☐

4. How long did it take to complete?

    .... minutes

5. Any other comments about the form:

    ....

    ....

    ....

    ....

    ....

    ....

THANK YOU VERY MUCH FOR ALL YOUR HELP

Child Health and Education in the Seventies

A national study in England, Wales and Scotland of all children born 5th—11th April 1970

Under the auspices of the University of Bristol
and the National Birthday Trust Fund

Director:Professor Neville R. Butler, MD, FRCP, DCH

Department of Child Health Research Unit
University of Bristol
Bristol   BS2 8BH

Tel Bristol 27745/22041

CONFIDENTIAL

DEVELOPMENTAL HISTORY SCHEDULE

Health District Code   Child's Local Serial Number   Child's Central Survey Number

Full Name of the Child .... **Sex** ....

Address .... **Date of birth** .... **April 1970**

....

If moved into present Health Authority/Board since birth, please give:

(a)   name of previous A.H.A./L.H.A., or Health Board ....

(b)   age (approx. in years and months) of N when moved to present

A.H.A./L.H.A./Health Board ....

Notes for Completion of Schedule

1. Aims

   The purpose of this Schedule is to obtain data on the utilisation by the study child of child health clinics, health visiting facilities, developmental screening tests and other important aspects of the community health services. As parental recall of past events is often incomplete, reference to pre-school child health records is also essential as a means of confirming and supplementing information obtained by the Health Visitor in the home interview.

2. Person(s) Completing Schedule

   Ideally the Health Visitor who is carrying out the home interview should also complete this schedule. Some of the information may require access to records usually held centrally, such as in Area or District Offices or in Health Boards (Scotland), e.g. special handicap records, centrally held registers. The personnel used and arrangements made for completion will doubtless be decided by the Area or District officer responsible according to local contingency.

3. Records Required

   (a) The following basic types of records are essential for the main part of this schedule.

   (i) Records used by health visitor to record health visiting, e.g. Home Visiting records, Consultation Record Cards and, where available, Family Records. These will be referred to as H.V. records,

   (ii) Records used in Child Health Clinics or Child Welfare Clinics by doctors to record developmental screening and other health care, e.g. MCW 46. These will be referred to as C.H.C. records.

   (b) Some questions require reference to other sources, in addition to the above basic records — for children for whom there may be letters or reports indicating past hospital outpatient attendances or inpatient care, children who are on observation or other registers, children who have been assessed for special educational treatment and other children who have handicaps or disabilities. In some instances, this information will be available in H.V.'s or C.H.C. records, but arrangements will probably be necessary for this to be supplemented from records or information held centrally.

   (c) Records about developmental screening are needed for question 4. The majority of general developmental check-ups and specific screening tests will be recorded on records used by doctors in Child Health Clinics and on H.V. records. Additional information about any developmental check-ups at G.P. practices or health centres would be valuable, and may be readily available to health visitors attached to G.P. practices. Developmental check-ups are sometimes carried out elsewhere, e.g. at hospital birth follow-up clinics, and vision and hearing are often screened during routine medical examination at day nursery, nursery and infant school. This information would be appreciated if it is readily available.

1—5

6

0 1
7,8

9—12

13

14,15

407

2

4. Developmental Screening & Assessment

Developmental screening in Q.4 refers to check-ups usually routinely performed on all pre-school children to identify those who may be developmentally delayed or have a suspected vision or hearing defect.

Developmental assessment in Q.5 refers to a much more detailed examination of development, which is usually only performed on children who have already been identified as having a possible delay or defect in hearing, vision or other aspect of development.

What to include as Developmental Screening in Q.4 Part I

(a) Any record of a routine general developmental examination or a check-up of overall developmental progress.

This term does not refer to an isolated single screening test, though specific screening tests may often be included in the general observations and examination made of the child's developmental achievements. General developmental examinations or check-ups of overall developmental progress are usually carried out at or near prescribed ages in C.H.C., home or G.P.'s practices by doctor or health visitor. The result is often entered on C.H.C. or H.V. records under several headings of 'developmental' function e.g. hearing and language, posture and locomotion, vision, social behaviour, or may be entered in the form of observations of individual developmental achievements of the child, e.g. sitting, smiling, saying single words, etc. If neither of these forms of recording are present in the notes, but it is definitely indicated that a general developmental check-up was made, this should be included. Please include also any record you may have of a general medical examination or check-up carried out by a doctor at nursery or infant school.

(b) Any record of tests for vision, hearing or squint.

Vision and hearing may be tested on their own or as part of a general developmental examination or check-up of overall developmental progress. They are routine clinical procedures used for testing these special functions, e.g. routine testing of hearing by rattle, paper etc. by H.V. at 7—9 months, screening of vision by Stycar 5-letter test at age 3 years. If the details of the type of test used are not clear but the records indicate that vision, hearing or both have been checked, such entries should be included as vision or hearing tests.

Any record that there has been a check-up for a squint should be entered separately as "examination for squint" and not be entered as a vision test in section b of the table in Q.4. Include as "examination for squint" any occasion where records indicate a specific test was made, e.g. cover test or light reflection test, or where the records indicate only if a squint was, or was not, evident in the course of a general examination. Records of any such test(s) for vision, hearing or squint carried out at nursery or infant school should also be included.

(c) Please exclude from Q.4 Part I any remarks or observations of developmental progress made at times **other than** the developmental screening examinations and tests described above. Details of these should be entered in Q.4 Part II.

5. General Notes

(a) Every question should be answered.

(b) Please base your answers only on information which is contained in the record form(s), registers etc. There is space provided below each question for you to add any information known to you from other sources.

(c) If you have any difficulty in interpreting or reading the relevant entry on records, ring code marked "records unclear" and give details in the space for "comments" at the end of the question.

(d) If you do not have the relevant record(s) at all when answering a question, please ring code marked "No records".

(e) Allowance should be made for the fact that the format of every question inevitably cannot correspond with all the different recording systems in use throughout the country. Space is therefore provided at the end of each question for comments, and for supplying extra data such as:

(i)   additional information known to you but not on the records;

(ii)   details of any difficulties with obtaining or interpreting the data on the relevant record;

(iii) other observations, e.g. where the information given on records is considered not to reflect a true picture of the actual events.

(f) Some abbreviations are used in this schedule, e.g.

Study Child	N
Health Visitor records	H.V. records
Child Health Clinic records used by doctor ...	C.H.C. records
Local Health Authority	L.H.A.
Area Health Authority	A.H.A.
Phenylketonuria	P.K.U.
Question	Q

(g) Further details about C.H.E.S. and on the completion of questions are given in "Survey Notes and Information".

ALL INFORMATION RECORDED ON THIS SCHEDULE WILL BE TREATED AS STRICTLY CONFIDENTIAL IN ACCORDANCE WITH MEDICAL RESEARCH COUNCIL REGULATIONS AND NO CHILD WILL BE IDENTIFIED OR REFERRED TO IN ANY REPORT BY NAME.

3

1. Do the Health Visitor's records or child health clinic records indicate that N has ever had for any reason whatsoever — .

	Yes	No	Records unclear	No records	
(a) any home visit from H.V.?	1	2	3	0	(16)
(b) any attendance at C.H.C.?	1	2	3	0	(17)

If yes to either of above, please give further details:

	First H.V. home visit*	First C.H.C. attendance	
(c) Give date of first H.V. visit* and first C.H.C. attendance for any reason whatever.	.../.../...	.../.../...	18—22 / 23—27

(d) Give the total number of visits from H.V. and N's C.H.C. attendances for any reason whatsoever, in each time-period specified below.

If none, enter NONE.

	Child's age in months	Time period	Total number of H.V. home visits *	Total number of C.H.C. attendances	
First	0—5	Apr. 1970 — Sep. 1970			28—31
year	6—11	Oct. 1970 — Mar. 1971			
Second	12—17	Apr. 1971 — Sep. 1971			32—35
year	18—23	Oct. 1971 — Mar. 1972			
Third	24—29	Apr. 1972 — Sep. 1972			36—39
year	30—35	Oct. 1972 — Mar. 1973			
Fourth year	36—47	Apr. 1973 — Mar. 1974			40—43
Fifth year	48+	Since April 1974			44—47
		Total since birth			

* *Exclude any visit where no access gained to home and note such visits in "comments" below.*

Comments, e.g. Notes unclear, records absent, extra information, etc.

....

2. Please state if H.V. or C.H.C. records indicate that N's history contains any risk factors — either as a complication or condition which occurred during the perinatal period (pregnancy, labour, or postnatal in first week), or as a genetic, social or environmental factor.
Include the following type of entries as risk factors.

(i) Any entry of a condition of N in space specially provided on the H.V. or C.H.C. record form for risk (or similarly named) factors, or any entry of a condition specified on the H.V. or C.H.C. record as reasons for inclusion in at risk/observation register.
(ii) Any condition which, though not directly labelled as a risk-factor in the above records, is implied to be a risk factor by virtue of being printed in a check-list of abnormal conditions on the H.V. or C.H.C. record form. One example of such a list is on the front page of C.H.C. record MCW 46.

Include all above conditions, irrespective of whether N's name was actually placed on a Register or not.

Is there any risk factor recorded:

	Yes	No	Record Unclear	No records	
(a) on H.V. records?	1	2	3	0	(48)
(b) on C.H.C. records?	1	2	3	0	(49)

If yes to (a) or (b), ring any condition(s) listed below which correspond to risk-factor(s) reported in N's records. Ring risk factor(s) reported from H.V. records separately from C.H.C. records. If any risk factor(s) reported in N's records do not correspond exactly or nearly exactly to any condition listed below, ring the category 'other risk factor' and specify the nature of the risk-factor in the space provided.
Where "combined" record used, with both H.V. and C.H.C. doctor's entries, ring both columns and note "combined record" in comments below.

Ring all that apply in each column	H.V. record	C.H.C. record	*Ring all that apply in each column*	H.V. record	C.H.C. record	
Pregnancy/Delivery			First week of N's life			50—52
Rubella in first 4 mths	1	1	Low birthweight	1	1	
Twin pregnancy	2	2	Birth asphyxia	2	2	53—56
Rh or ABO incompatibility	3	3	Jaundice	3	3	
Hypertension, toxaemia	4	4	Convulsions	4	4	57—59
Any pregnancy bleeding	5	5	Any cong. abnorm.	5	5	
Psychiatric illness	6	6	Resp. distress	6	6	
Diabetes	7	7	Other risk factor(s)	7	7	60—63
Gestation under 36/37 wks	8	8	specify....................			
Postmaturity (42 wks+)	9	9	....			
Breech	10	10	Social or Genetic			64—66
Prolonged/diffic. labour	11	11	Social or environmental			
Foetal distress	12	12	risk factor(s), specify	1	1	
Other risk factor in pregnancy/labour, specify	13	13	.... Genetic risk factor(s),			67—69
....			specify	2	2	

Comments, e.g. Notes unclear, records absent, extra information etc.

....
....

Appendix 4

Please refer to notes 3(c) and 4(a–c) at the beginning of this schedule concerning Q.s 3–4.

3. Do the records specified below contain any indication that the following have been done?

Is there a record of:	Yes	No	Records unclear	No Records	If yes, specify
From H.V. or C.H.C. records only					
(a) N's birthweight?	1	2	3	4	. . . . . lbs . . . . oz
					or . . . . gm
(b) N's gestational maturity?	1	2	3	4	. . . . wks
(c) Any congenital defect in N?	1	2	3	4	specify . . . .
					. . . .
From H.V., C.H.C. & any other records					
(d) Any screening for P.K.U.?	1	2	3	4	
(e) Any screening for CDH (hip)?	1	2	3	4	
(f) Any screening for hearing?	1	2	3	4	
(g) Any screening for squint?	1	2	3	4	
(h) Any screening for vision?	1	2	3	4	
(i) Any gen. devlp. check-up(s)?	1	2	3	4	

If yes to (f), (g), (h) or (i), please ensure that each test or check-up is entered in Q.4.

Comments, Notes unclear, records absent, extra information, etc.

....

4. Part I

Please complete table below for each occasion N received developmental screening (exclude P.K.U./hip tests) — either a general developmental examination or check-up or a screening test of hearing, vision or squint, (see notes on page 2). The following examples illustrate what is required (see table below).

Example A. If it was noted on the H.V.'s record that on 15th November 1970, the H.V. carried out a routine test of hearing at N's home, the entry should be as in Example A.

Example B. If on 8th January 1971 it was recorded by the doctor at the C.H.C. at a nine-month developmental examina-tion that the child had turned right and left to the sound of rattle, paper, spoken voice, had visually followed rolling balls and that his general development was tested, with normal co-ordination, motor and social development, the entry should be as in Example B.

Note that only the fact that N was tested is to be entered in the answer to this question; details of any referral for assess-ment or for further investigations for suspected delay or abnormality should be recorded in Q.5.

Notes for completion of section (b) in table below.
Whenever records indicate that a routine general developmental check-up or examination was made, ring 1. If a hearing test, a vision test and/or an examination for squint was included as part of this general developmental check-up, ring 2, 3 and/or 4 as appropriate. If a comprehensive developmental scale, e.g. Denver or Griffiths, was used, ring 1, 2 and 3 even though individual components may not be specified; please name any such scale used in "comments" below the table. Ring 2, 3 and/or 4 in section (b) if screening for hearing, vision and/or squint was done on occasion(s) separate from a general developmental check-up.
In answering section (c) below, give the main person responsible if more than one person carried out tests or made observations on any one occasion.

	Examples		Times screened or given check-up									
	A	B	1st	2nd	3rd	4th	5th	6th	7th	8th	9th	10th
(a) When "screened"?												
Day	15	8	–	–	–	–	–	–	–	–	–	–
Month	11	1	–	–	–	–	–	–	–	–	–	–
Year	70	71	–	–	–	–	–	–	–	–	–	–
(b) What was done?												
Ring all that apply												
Genl. devel. check-up	1	①	1	1	1	1	1	1	1	1	1	1
Hearing test	②	②	2	2	2	2	2	2	2	2	2	2
Vision test	3	③	3	3	3	3	3	3	3	3	3	3
Exam. for squint	4	4	4	4	4	4	4	4	4	4	4	4
(c) Who screened N?												
Doctor	1	①	1	1	1	1	1	1	1	1	1	1
Health visitor	②	2	2	2	2	2	2	2	2	2	2	2
Other or uncertain	3	3	3	3	3	3	3	3	3	3	3	3
Not known who	0	0	0	0	0	0	0	0	0	0	0	0
(d) Where screened?												
Child Health Clinic	1	①	1	1	1	1	1	1	1	1	1	1
G.P.'s practice	2	2	2	2	2	2	2	2	2	2	2	2
N's home	③	3	3	3	3	3	3	3	3	3	3	3
Nursery/Infant school	4	4	4	4	4	4	4	4	4	4	4	4
Hospital birth follow-up clinic	5	5	5	5	5	5	5	5	5	5	5	5
Other or uncertain	6	6	6	6	6	6	6	6	6	6	6	6

Comments, e.g. Notes unclear, records absent, extra information, etc.

....

....

5

Part II

Please enter below the details of any observations of developmental progress which have been made at times other than on the occasions of routine developmental screening examinations or tests, described in Part I. If not known by whom or where observed put NOT KNOWN. If more space required, please continue on back page of schedule.

Date Day Mth Yr	Who observed N? H.V. or Dr.	Where observed C.H.C./home/ G.P.'s etc.	Summary of observations recorded
.../.../...			
.../.../...			
.../.../...			
.../.../...			

5. Is there any information on available records, reports or letters that N has ever been seen for assessment (see note 4 on second page) or for further tests, as a result of a (suspected) defect in hearing or vision or any other developmental problem? Include assessments in special assessment/handicap centres as well as hospital OP/IP situation.
If assessed as result of developmental screening mentioned in Q.4 ring code 2.
If referred from other source or if not known who referred N, ring code 3.

| | | Yes, referred: | | Records | |
Recorded to have been seen for:	No	after develop. test (Q.4)	from other source	unclear whether assessed	No records	
(a) specialist hearing assessment or further hearing tests ...		1	2	3	4	0	(9)
(b) specialist visual assessment or further eye tests		1	2	3	4	0	(10)
(c) specialist or further assessment for any other developmental problem.*		1	2	3	4	0	(11)

*e.g. delay in motor, intellectual, mental, language, social or emotional development.

If yes ringed to (a), (b) or (c), please give details below for each referral.
If records indicate more than three, please continue on back page.

Date	Problem for which referred, diagnosis if recorded, and any further details	Name and address in full of hospital, clinic, or assessment centre
.../.../....		
.../.../....		
.../.../....		

Comments, e.g. Notes unclear, records absent, extra information, etc.

6. Is there any information on available records, reports or letters that N has ever:

	Yes	No	Records unclear	No records	
(a) attended hospital outpatients or special(ist) clinic?	1	2	3	0	(15)
(b) been admitted to hospital?	1	2	3	0	(16)
(c) been in-care, fostered, or in other residential placement?	1	2	3	0	(17)

If yes ringed to (a), (b) or (c), please give any recorded details below for each condition for which seen at hospital or admitted, and for any occasion fostered or in care or other residential placement.
If records indicate more than three, please continue on back page.

Date	Hosp. OP/IP or placement	Details of illness and diagnosis or reason for placement	Name and address in full of hospital or placement
.../.../....			
.../.../....			
.../.../....			

Comments, e.g. Notes unclear, records absent, extra information, etc.

411

6

7. Has N ever had any injury considered or suspected to be "non-accidental"?

Yes, has had suspected or confirmed condition of this type	1
No, but has been considered to be "at risk" of this	2 (21)
No, never	3
Not known	0

Comments:..
....
....

8. Has N's name ever been included on a Register of any sort?
A register is a means of identifying children with special needs or those who require follow-up. It is usually kept in the form of a list, card index, master file or on a computer.
In answering this question, reference should be made, where possible, to information contained in the register concerned in addition to details from C.H.C. or H.V. records or reports.

Yes —	
on one register	1
on more than one register	2 (22)
No, never on any register	3
Not known	0

If yes, was it because N is/was considered to be:

Ring all that apply

"At risk"/in need of observation, for medical reasons?	1
"At risk"/in need of observation, for social reasons?	2
Handicapped?	3
Other situation, specify	4
Reason not known	0

Please give details below from each register on which N's name has ever been placed.
If insufficient space, please continue on back page.

	First Register	Second Register
(a) Give name by which register known ...		
(b) Who "keeps" register? *		
(c) Reasons in detail why N included on this register		
(d) Date first put on register		
(e) If taken off, give date		

23,24

* Indicate if "peripheral" register, e.g. initiated by and confined in use to a particular clinic; or if a "central" register, e.g. initiated and kept by L.H.A./Area/District or Board.

Comments, e.g. Notes unclear, records absent, extra information, etc.

....
....

9. Has a decision ever been reached by a Local Education Authority that N is in need of 'special educational treatment'?

No —	
and not likely to be required	1
but a decision pending	2 (25)
Yes —	
but waiting for a place	3
and receiving special educational treatment	4
Not known	0

If yes, or if a decision is pending, into which category does child fall?

Ring all that apply in both columns

Blind	1	Severely E.S.N. (Eng. & Wales)	7
Partially sighted	2	Epileptic	8
Deaf	3	Maladjusted	9
Partially hearing	4	Physically handicapped	10
Mentally handicapped (Scotland)	5	Speech defect	11
Educationally subnormal (Eng. & Wales)	6	Delicate (Eng. & Wales)	12

26-29

Comments, e.g. Notes unclear, records absent, extra information, etc.

....
....

7

10. In summary, is there any indication from records and reports available to you that N has now or has had in the past any developmental problem, or any disability or any handicapping condition — physical, mental or emotional, irrespective of whether condition is mentioned elsewhere in this questionnaire?

Ring all that apply

Yes —
    currently   1
    in past   2
No   3
Not known   0

If yes, list each developmental problem, disability or handicapping condition in N:

(i) ....

(ii) ....

(iii) ....

(iv) ....

Comments, e.g. Notes unclear, extra information, etc.

....

| 30,31 |

11. Is there any period in N's life for which it is known that either main H.V. records or C.H.C. records have been destroyed or lost or are unobtainable for any other reason, resulting in the present H.V. or C.H.C. records being incomplete for that period of N's life?

	H.V. records	C.H.C. records
No — no records known to be missing	1	1
Yes —		
records known missing for part of N's life	2	2
records known missing for all of N's life	3	3
Other answer, specify	4	4

32—35

36—39

If 2 or 3 ringed in either column, give further details below.

(a) Approximate time period to which missing records relate. Please give dates.
From ..../..../.... ..../..../....
To ..../..../.... ..../..../....

40—43

(b) Please give reason why record(s) not available.

Destroyed, lost, etc., i.e. no longer exists	1	1
Record(s) elsewhere or in transit, i.e. exists but not available	2	2
Other reason, specify	3	3
Reason not known	0	0

44—47

Comments, e.g. Extra information etc.

....

12. Have any of the following records been used for the completion of this schedule?

Ring all that apply

Records of any developmental screening in G.P.'s surgery/health centre 1
Handicap record(s), e.g. 2 HP, 4 HP, specify 2
Medical records of nursery school/class or infant school 3
Medical records of day nursery or other day-care 4
Medical records of residential nursery or other residential care 5
Other record(s) or source(s) of information, namely 6

Comments, e.g. Notes unclear, records absent, extra information, etc.

....

48 49

50—53

Name(s) of person(s) completing this Schedule ....

Professional status ....

54—57

Employing Area Health Authority/Health Board ....

Date of completion of Schedule .... / .... / 1975.

58—61

413

Appendix 4

Please use this page to give further details of any questions if insufficient space in the questionnaire.

Please write in your own words a short account of the impression you have gained from the records of this child's health and health care in the first five years and also whether there are any environmental, social or family factors which you consider to be important.

THANK YOU VERY MUCH FOR ALL YOUR HELP

Appendix 5 Test Booklet

Child Health and Education in the Seventies

A national study in England, Wales and Scotland of all children born 5th—11th April 1970

Under the auspices of the University of Bristol
and the National Birthday Trust Fund

Director: Professor Neville R. Butler, MD, FRCP, DCH

Department of Child Health Research Unit
University of Bristol
Bristol   BS2 8BH

Tel Bristol 27745/22041

TEST BOOKLET

Health District Code   Child's Local Serial Number   Child's Central Survey Number

Full Name of the Child .... **Sex** ....

Address .... **Date of birth** .... April 1970

....

Introduction

To complete the tests in this booklet the following are needed:

> A pencil for the child's use
> The English Picture Vocabulary Test Series of Plates
> Word card for Reading Test
> A tape measure.

Tests and measurements to be completed:

A   Copying Designs Test
B   Human Figure Drawing (Draw-a-Man Test)
C   English Picture Vocabulary Test (Survey Version)
D   Profile Test
E   Reading Test
F   Measurements of child's height and head circumference.

Please read the instructions for each test carefully before going to the interview.

It is useful to try out the tests with another child to familiarise yourself with the procedures beforehand.

The tests can easily be done in the child's own home and it is recommended that they are done in the order given. They need not be administered in one continuous session; for example, the Human Figure Drawing and Copying Designs Test could be done by the child before the interview with the mother or in a break during it and the other tests afterwards.

Put the child at his/her ease in the usual way before starting any test. While you will obviously show the child that you are interested in his/her response in general, be **very** careful not to influence his/her responses in any way.

If a child refuses any test, go on with the others and return to any refused later.

415

Appendix 5

A. Copying Designs Test

1. Ask the child to copy the designs on the next two pages as carefully as possible.

2. Fold the book back so that the child can see only one page at a time.

3. Point to each design in turn and say "see if you can make one just like this—here" and point to the space beside the design.

4. Two attempts should be made at each design.

DO NOT GIVE THE CHILD ANY MORE HELP THAN THESE INSTRUCTIONS ALLOW.

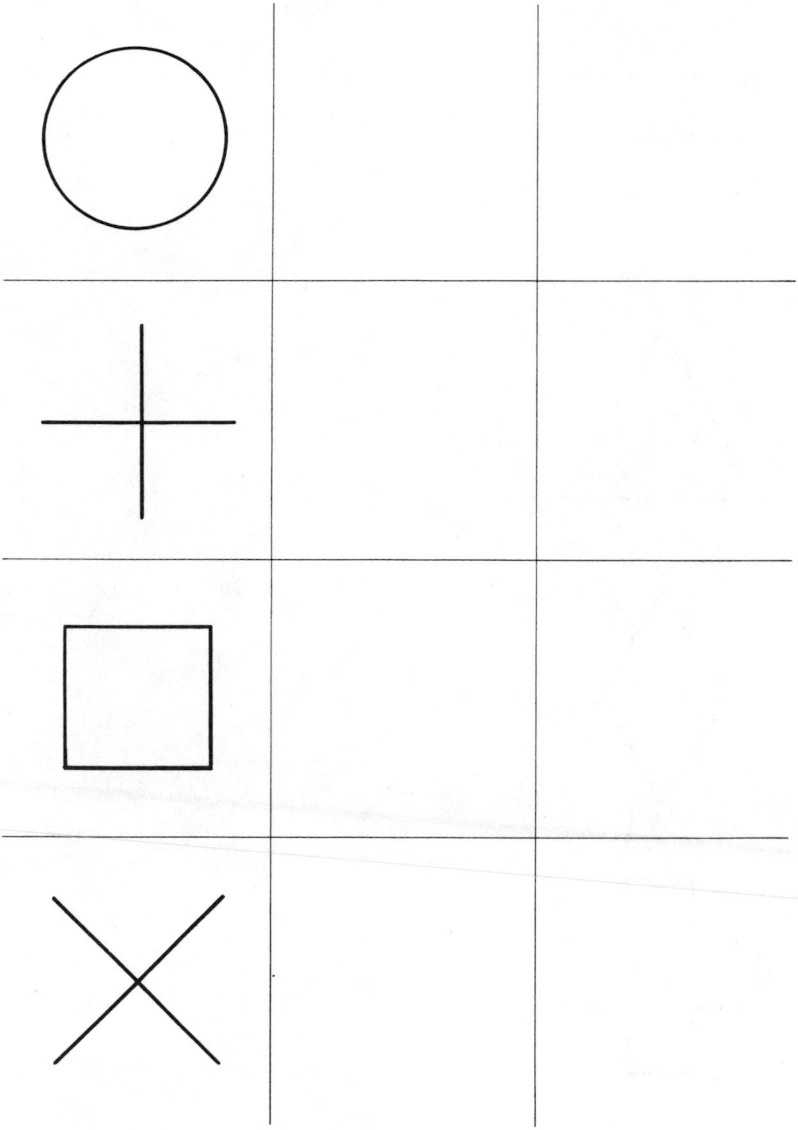

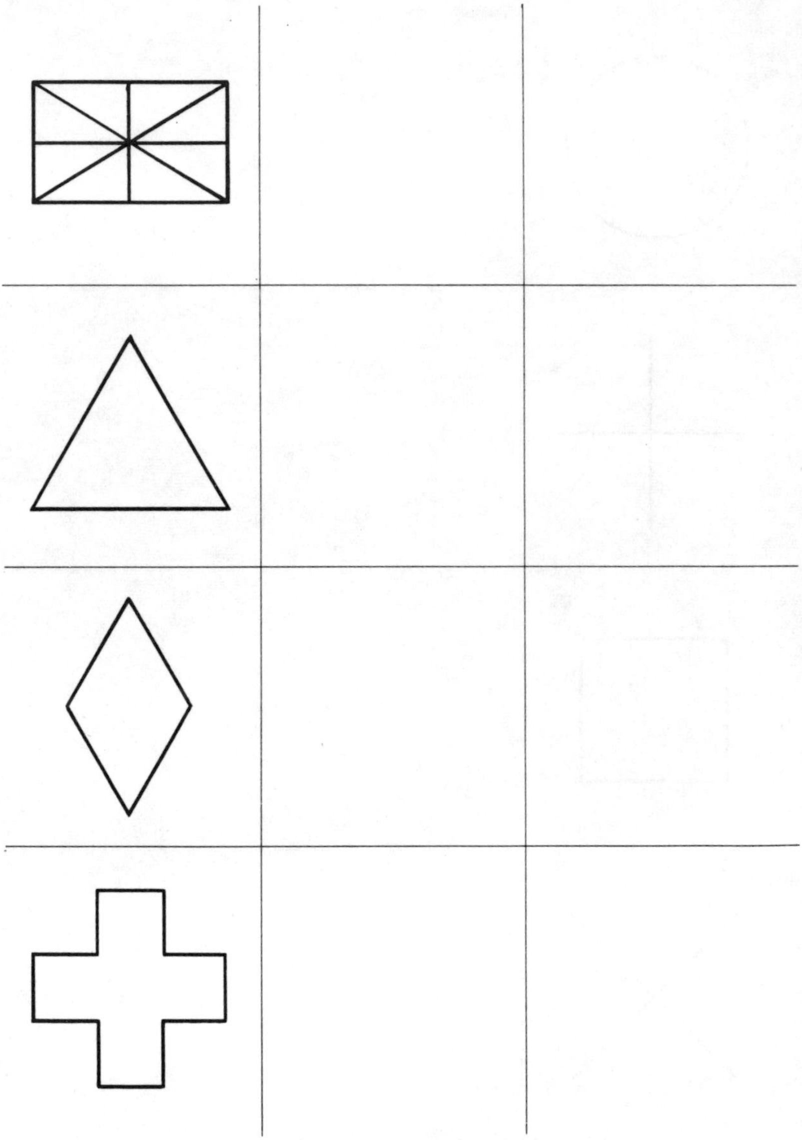

B. Human Figure Drawing (Draw-a-Man Test)

1. Ask the child to "make a picture of a man or lady" on the page opposite this one. Terms such as "daddy", "mummy", "boy", "girl", etc. may be used in place of "man" or "lady" if the child responds better to these.

2. Ask him/her to make the best picture he/she can and to draw a **whole person**, not just a face or head.

3. When the child stops drawing ask if it is finished and allow him/her to make any additions he/she wants to. Be careful, however, not to **suggest** additions.

4. When the drawing is finished, ask the child what it is and note what he/she says at the bottom of the page.

5. Then ask the child to make another picture on the next page of a person the opposite sex to the first. Note what the child says·it is at the bottom.

6. If it is not clear, ask the child to say what the various parts of the drawings are and label them. Do this by asking, "What's this?" and pointing but **do not ask questions such as** "Where's his arm?, legs?, eyes?" etc.

DO NOT GIVE THE CHILD ANY MORE HELP THAN THESE INSTRUCTIONS ALLOW.

Appendix 5

C. English Picture Vocabulary Test
(Survey Version)

The Test

Each page of the "English Picture Vocabulary Test Series of Plates" (E.P.V.T. booklet) contains four different pictures numbered 1, 2, 3, 4, one of which is a picture of a test word to be found on the score sheet for this test. The object of the test is for the child to identify the pictures, which correspond to the test words. The test words become harder as the test progresses. Do not attempt the test with non-English-speaking children.

Introducing the Test

1. Show the child the first page (P) of pictures in the E.P.V.T. booklet and read the instructions opposite page P keeping as close as possible to natural speech. The child should **point** to the picture corresponding to the test word "**ball**".

2. If the child points to a different (i.e. incorrect) picture, ask him /her again to find the picture of "**ball**". If a wrong picture is again picked out, go over the procedure again until the child understands what to do but do not show him/her the right answer.

3. If the child is shy or physically handicapped and refuses or is unable to point, you should point to each picture in turn yourself, asking, "Is it this one?" and establish a signal, e.g. nodding, for the child to select a picture. Be careful not to pause longer over the right picture than over the others, or the child will guess.

Practice Words

The next three pages in the E.P.V.T. booklet (A, B and C) are for practicing the test. Using the procedure established in introducing the test, make sure the child understands what to do by going through these in the same way using the test words spoon, chair and car, as shown on the score sheet.

If the child persists in pointing to the picture in the same **position** on each page, e.g. always picture 1, go over the practice words again, saying, "Which is the picture of −?" pointing to each of the pictures on the page until the child understands.

Things to avoid when doing the Test

1. Do not say anything other than the test word for each page given on the score sheet.

2. Do not give alternative words in place of the test words, e.g. hen in place of chicken, even if you think this is the word the child normally uses.

3. Do not use "a", "an" or "the" with the words and do not use plurals unless this is given on the score sheet (e.g. 24, tweezers but 27, binocular).

4. Do not give clues or tell the child if he/she is right or wrong. If child asks directly about this, say, "You are getting on fine" or something like this.

Conducting the Test

After the first four pages described above, the child should understand what to do and be given no more help whatsoever. The following procedure should then be adhered to closely.

1. Show a page and say the single test word printed on the score sheet for that page, e.g. 'drum'. Do not say anything else but 'drum' for the first page, 'time' for the second page, and so on. The test word for each page may, however, be given more than once and, if there is a different local pronunciation, this can be used as well as the standard version.

2. If the child points to the **correct** picture put the number of that picture in the **left-hand** box by the test word on the score sheet.

3. If the child points to the **wrong** picture put the number of the picture chosen by the child in the **right-hand** box by the test word on the score sheet.

4. If the child says he does not know the answer encourage him/her by asking, "Which do you think fits the word best?". If he/she still refuses to pick a picture, **draw a line** through both boxes for that word on the score sheet and continue with the test. Such refusals count as errors for the purpose of this test.

5. Continue with the subsequent pages of pictures in the same way.

6. After page 27, turn the book around to continue page 28 onward.

When to stop Testing

Stop testing when the child makes **five consecutive errors**. This will be when there are five consecutive entries in the right-hand column.

Below is an **example** of a test which was stopped at word 30.

15	4 ☐	goat	29	☐ ☐	barber
16	4 ☐	peeping	30	☐ 1	wasp
17	3 ☐	temperature	31	☐ ☐	yawning
18	☐ 1	signal	32	☐ ☐	captain
19	2 ☐	river	33	☐ ☐	trunk
20	☐ 4	badge	34	☐ ☐	argument
21	2 ☐	hook	35	☐ ☐	coin
22	2 ☐	whale	36	☐ ☐	hive
23	☐ 1	acrobat	37	☐ ☐	chemist
24	1 ☐	tweezers	38	☐ ☐	funnel
25	3 ☐	submarine	39	☐ ☐	insect
26	☐ 3	balancing	40	☐ ☐	cutlery
27	☐☐	binocular	41	☐ ☐	shears
28	☐ 1	ornament	42	☐ ☐	exhausted

After the Test

If the child has persisted during the **test** in pointing to the same picture **position** on each page, indicate this by answering the separate question about this at the bottom of the score sheet.

This is a picture of ....

This is a picture of ....

Appendix 5

Introductory word (Page P)   P ☐ ☐ ball

Practice words (Pages A, B & C)   A ☐ ☐ spoon
                                              B ☐ ☐ chair
                                              C ☐ ☐ car

Test words (Pages 1 to 56)

1 ☐ ☐ drum	15 ☐ ☐ goat	29 ☐ ☐ barber	43 ☐ ☐ sole
2 ☐ ☐ time	16 ☐ ☐ peeping	30 ☐ ☐ wasp	44 ☐ ☐ walrus
3 ☐ ☐ fence	17 ☐ ☐ temperature	31 ☐ ☐ yawning	45 ☐ ☐ weapon
4 ☐ ☐ skiing	18 ☐ ☐ signal	32 ☐ ☐ captain	46 ☐ ☐ sentry
5 ☐ ☐ chicken	19 ☐ ☐ river	33 ☐ ☐ trunk	47 ☐ ☐ wailing
6 ☐ ☐ climbing	20 ☐ ☐ badge	34 ☐ ☐ argument	48 ☐ ☐ globe
7 ☐ ☐ leaf	21 ☐ ☐ hook	35 ☐ ☐ coin	49 ☐ ☐ valve
8 ☐ ☐ digging	22 ☐ ☐ whale	36 ☐ ☐ hive	50 ☐ ☐ plumage
9 ☐ ☐ teacher	23 ☐ ☐ acrobat	37 ☐ ☐ chemist	51 ☐ ☐ assistance
10 ☐ ☐ sewing	24 ☐ ☐ tweezers	38 ☐ ☐ funnel	52 ☐ ☐ carpenter
11 ☐ ☐ nest	25 ☐ ☐ submarine	39 ☐ ☐ insect	53 ☐ ☐ destruction
12 ☐ ☐ arrow	26 ☐ ☐ balancing	40 ☐ ☐ cutlery	54 ☐ ☐ spire
13 ☐ ☐ parachute	27 ☐ ☐ binocular	41 ☐ ☐ shears	55 ☐ ☐ reel
14 ☐ ☐ cobweb	28 ☐ ☐ ornament	42 ☐ ☐ exhausted	56 ☐ ☐ coast

Did the child persist during the test in pointing
to the same picture position on each page?

*Please
ring*

Yes 1
No 2

*The instructions and method of scoring for this test have been produced as a result of trials and are not exactly
as described by M. A. Brimer and Lloyd M. Dunn.*

D. Profile Test

1. The object of this test is for the child to complete the profile drawn on the page opposite

2. Make sure that the child understands what the drawing is by introducing it in the following way and answer the question at the foot of this page.*

   (a) Point to the profile and say,

      "**What do you think this is?**". The child should show that he/she understands what it is by replying "a head", "a face", "a man", etc.

   If the child does **not** show that he/she understands what it is, ask,

   (b) "**Can you see what this is?**" and follow with your finger the left side of the outline of the profile from forehead to the chin.

   If profile is still not recognised, say,

   (c) "**Look, this is a face, isn't it?**" and trace around the left side of the profile with your finger as before.

3. As soon as the child recognises what the drawing is, or you have explained it, say, "**Do you think you could finish it for me? Draw everything that is missing in it**".

4. When the child stops drawing, ask if it is finished and allow him/her to make any additions he/she wants to. Be careful, however, not to **suggest** additions. If it is not clear, ask the child to say what the various parts of the drawing are and label them, ear, eye, mouth, etc. Do this by asking, "What's this?", and pointing.

   DO NOT GIVE THE CHILD ANY MORE HELP THAN THESE INSTRUCTIONS ALLOW

---

*At what stage in introducing the profile did the child show he/she recognised what the drawing is?

	Please ring
stage (a)	1
stage (b)	2
stage (c)	3

The Profile Test is being used with the permission of the author Alex F. Kalverboer, Department of Developmental Neurology, University Hospital, Groningen, The Netherlands, and the publishers Switz and Zeitlinger, Heereweg 374B, Lisse, The Netherlands.

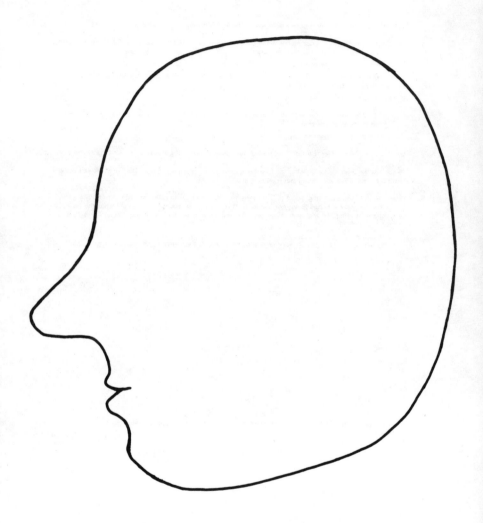

E.   Reading Test

Ask the mother if she thinks the child has begun to read at all.

No, child can read nothing or has not tried 1
Yes, child can read – some letters 2
– some words 3
– simple sentences 4
Cannot say if child can read 5
Other reply, give details... 6
....

If **no**, or the child reads letters only, omit reading test.

Administering the reading test

If mother says the child **can** read some words or sentences, show the **word-card** to the child and ask if he/she would read out as many of the words as he/she can. Point to the first word and say, "See if you can say this one". If child responds, say, "Now try these others", and run your finger from word to word across the first five words at the top of the card. If the child misses a word out, point to that word on the word-card and say, "Can you tell me this one?" and record the response. Then continue with the second and subsequent rows in the same way.

How to record responses on score sheet below

Put a **tick** ☑ in the box against each word the child reads **correctly**.

Put a **cross** ☒ if read **incorrectly** or response is unintelligible or for any other response, e.g. child says "Don't know".

Leave box blank if no response.

Where there is an irregularity of speech or articulation, e.g. "tee" for "tree", or "fink" for "think", count as correct if it is clearly an attempt to say the word in question.

When to stop Testing

The child should continue the test until he/she makes **five consecutive mistakes,** or refuses to continue.

DO NOT GIVE THE CHILD ANY MORE HELP THAN THESE INSTRUCTIONS ALLOW.

Reading Test Score Sheet

☐tree	☐little	☐milk	☐egg	☐book
☐school	☐sit	☐frog	☐playing	☐bun
☐flower	☐road	☐clock	☐train	☐light
☐picture	☐think	☐summer	☐people	☐something
☐dream	☐downstairs	☐biscuit	☐shepherd	☐thirsty
☐crowd	☐sandwich	☐beginning	☐postage	☐island
☐saucer	☐angel	☐ceiling	☐appeared	☐gnome
☐canary	☐attractive	☐imagine	☐nephew	☐gradually
☐smoulder	☐applaud	☐disposal	☐nourished	☐diseased
☐university	☐orchestra	☐knowledge	☐audience	☐situated

The test words from the Schonell Reading Test are reproduced by permission of the publishers, Oliver and Boyd, Edinburgh. The instructions and method of scoring for this test are not exactly as described by the author F. Schonell.

Appendix 5

F. Child's Measurements

Give in inches and parts of inches or in centimetres:

(a) Height (without shoes) .... inches

.... cms.

(b) Head circumference   .... inches

........:.. cms.

Measure around forehead and occiput recording maximum circumference as accurately as possible.

Test Conditions

1. Where were tests carried out?

Child's own home 1

Other place, specify............................. 2

....

2. How readily did the child respond to the tests?

If child was not asked to try a test, ring the 4 against the relevant test(s) and explain why any test was not given.

	Normal response	Slow response (e.g. Shy)	Child refused	Test not given	If not tested, give reason
Copying Designs Test	1	2	3	4	
Human Figure Drawing (Draw-a-Man)	1	2	3	4	
English Picture Vocabulary Test (Survey Version)	1	2	3	4	
Profile Test	1	2	3	4	
Reading Test	1	2	3	4	

3. Were there any distractions, interruptions or other disturbances when the child was being tested?

Ring all that apply

Yes—

remarks made about child's performance 1

child was encouraged to respond 2

other children were noisy or interrupted 3

other noise or distraction, e.g. T.V./radio on............................... 4

No, test conditions reasonable 5

Other situation, please describe 6

....

4. Date of testing ....

5. Name of interviewer ....

6. Area Health Authority/Health Board ....

7. District ....

428

References

Askham, J., 1969, Delineation of the lowest social class, *Journal of Biosocial Science*, 1, 327-35.

Atkins, E., Cherry, N.M., Douglas, J.W.B., Kiernan, K.E. and Wadsworth, M.E.J., 1980, The 1946 British birth survey: an account of the origins, progress and results of the National Survey of Health and Development, in Mednick, S.A. and Baest, A.E. (eds), *An Empirical Basis for Primary Prevention: Prospective Longitudinal Research in Europe*, London: Oxford University Press.

Backett, K.C., 1982, *Mothers and Fathers, A study of the Development and Negotiation of Parental Behaviour*, London: Macmillan.

Banfield, F., 1978, 1971 Census: voluntary survey on income, *Population Trends*, 12, 18-21.

Barnes, J.H. and Lucas, H., 1974, Positive discrimination in education: individuals, groups and institutions, in T. Leggatt (ed.), *Sociological Theory and Survey Research*, London: Social Science Research Council-Sage.

Beckman, L. and Houser, B.B., 1979, The more you have, the more you do; the relationship between wife's employment, sex-role attitudes and household behaviour, *Psychology of Women Quarterly*, 4 (2), 160-74.

Bereiter, C. and Engelmann, S., 1966, *Teaching Disadvantaged Children in the Pre-school*, New Jersey: Prentice-Hall.

Bernstein, B., 1961, Social class and linguistic development: a theory of social learning, in Halsey, A.H., Floud, J., and Anderson, C.A., (eds), *Education, Economy and Society*, New York: Free Press.

Bernstein, B., 1970a, Education cannot compensate for society in *New Society*, 15, 344-7.

Bernstein, B., 1970b, A critique of the concept of 'compensatory education', in Rubinstein, D., and Stoneman, C., (eds), *Education for Democracy*, Harmondsworth: Penguin.

Berthoud, R., 1976, *The Disadvantages of Inequality*, London: Macdonald & Janes.

Berthoud, R. and Brown, J.C., 1981, *Poverty and the Development of*

429

References

Anti-poverty Policy in the United Kingdom, a report to the Commission of the European Communities, London: Heinemann Educational.

Bibby, D.M. and Thomas, R.F.M., 1980, Government policy on day nurseries for children of hospital staff, Social Policy and Administration, 14 (2), 115-23.

Black Report, 1980, Inequalities in Health, A report of a Research Working Group chaired by Sir Douglas Black, London: Department of Health and Social Security.

Blackstone, T.A.V., 1971, A Fair Start, London: Allen Lane.

Bone, M., 1977, Preschool Children and the Need for Day-Care, OPCS Social Survey, London: HMSO.

Bowlby, J., 1951, Maternal Care and Mental Health, Bulletin of the World Health Organisation, 3 (3).

Bradley, M., 1982, Coordination of Services for Children Under Five, Windsor: NFER-Nelson.

Brimer, M.A., and Dunn, L.M., 1962, English Picture Vocabulary Test, Bristol: Education Evaluation Enterprises.

Brodman, K., Erdmann, A.J., Lorge, I., Gershenson, C.P., Wolff, H.G. and Broadbent, T.H., 1952, The Cornell Medical Index Health Questionnaire IV: The recognition of emotional disturbances in a general hospital, Journal of Clinical Psychology, 8, 289-93.

Brown, G. and Harris, T., 1978, Social Origins of Depression, London: Tavistock Publications.

Bruner, J., 1980, Under Five in Britain, London: Grant McIntyre.

Bryant, B., Harris, M. and Newton, D., 1980, Children and Minders, London: Grant McIntyre.

Burgoyne, J. and Clarke, D., 1981, Parenting in step families, in Chester, R., Digory, P., and Southerland, M.B., (eds), Changing Patterns of Child-Bearing and Child Rearing, Proceedings of the 17th Annual Symposium of the Eugenics Society (1980), London: Academic Press.

Burnell, I. and Wadsworth, J., 1981, Children in One-parent Families, The effects on children of changing family status at birth to age five, Interim report, Department of Child Health, University of Bristol.

Butler, D. and Sloman, A., 1980, British Political Facts, 1900-1979, 5th edition, London: Macmillan.

Butler, N.R. and Bonham, D.G., 1963, Perinatal Mortality, London: E & S Livingstone.

Central Policy Review Staff, 1978, Services for Young Children with Working Mothers, London: HMSO.

Central Statistical Office, 1975, Social commentary: social class, Social Trends, 6, 10-32.

Chamberlain, R. and Davey, A., 1975, Physical growth in twins, post-mature and small-for-dates children, Archives of Disease in Childhood, 50, 437-42.

Chamberlain, R. and Davey, A., 1976, Cross-sectional study of developmental test items in children aged 94 to 97 weeks: report of the

430

British Births Child Study, *Developmental Medicine and Child Neurology*, 18, 54-70.

Chamberlain, G., Philipp, E., Howlett, B. and Masters, K., 1978, *British Births 1970, Volume 2: Obstetric Care*, London: Heinemann.

Chamberlain, R., Chamberlain, G., Howlett, B. and Claireaux, A., 1975, *British Births 1970, Volume 1: the First Week of Life*, London: Heinemann.

Chazan, M., Laing, A. and Jackson, S., 1971, *Just Before School*, Schools Council Research and Development Project in Compensatory Education, Oxford: Basil Blackwell.

Clarke, A.M. and Clarke, A.D.B., (eds), 1976, *Early Experience: Myth and Evidence*, London: Open Books.

Coffield, F., Robinson, P. and Sarsby, J., 1980, *A Cycle of Deprivation: A Case Study of Four Families*, London: Heinemann Educational.

Committee on One-Parent Families, 1974, *Report of the Committee*, (Finer Report), Volumes 1 and 2, London: HMSO.

Cox, A., Rutter, M., Yule, B. and Quinton, D., 1977, Bias resulting from missing information, *British Journal of Preventive and Social Medicine*, 31, 131-6.

David, M.E., 1978, The family education couple: towards an analysis of the William Tyndale dispute, in Littlejohn, G., Smart, B., Wakeford, J., and Yuval-Davis, N. (eds), *Power and the State*, London: Croom Helm.

David, M.E., 1982, Day care policies and parenting, *Journal of Social Policy*, 11 (1), 81-92.

Davie, R., Butler, N.R. and Goldstein, 1972, *From Birth to Seven, a report of the National Child Development Study*, London: Longman.

Department of Education and Science, 1972, *Education: A Framework for Expansion*, London: HMSO.

Department of Health and Social Security, 1982, *Health and Personal Social Services Statistics for England*, London: HMSO.

Department of Health and Social Security and Department of Education and Science, 1976, *Low Cost Day Provision for the Under-fives*, Papers from a conference held at the Civil Service College, Sunningdale Park, 9-10 Jan., 1976.

Department of Health and Social Security and Department of Education and Science, 1978, Joint Circular: *Coordination of Services for Children Under Five*.

Douglas, J.W.B., 1964, *The Home and the School*, London: MacGibbon & Kee.

Douglas, J.W.B., 1976, The use and abuse of national cohorts, in Shipman, M. (ed.), *The Organisation and Impact of Social Research*, London: Routledge & Kegan Paul, pp. 3-21.

Douglas, J.W.B. and Blomfield, J.M., 1948, *Maternity in Great Britain*, London: Oxford University Press.

Douglas, J.W.B. and Blomfield, J.M., 1958, *Children Under Five*, London: Allen & Unwin.

Douglas, J.W.B. and Ross, J.M., 1965, The later educational progress and emotional adjustment of children who went to nursery schools or classes, *Educational Research*, 7 (2), 73-80.

Elias, P. and Main, B., 1982, *Women's Working Lives, evidence from the National Training Survey*, University of Warwick: Institute for Employment Research.

Equal Opportunities Commission, 1978, *I Want to Work, but What About the Kids?*, Manchester: Equal Opportunities Commission.

Equal Opportunities Commission, 1982, *Women and Government Statistics: Towards Better Statistics*, Manchester: Equal Opportunities Commission.

Evans, R. and Sparrow, M., 1975, Trends in the assessment of early childhood development, *Child: Care Health and Development*, 1, 127-41.

Eyken, van der, W., 1977, *The Pre-School Years*, Fourth edition, Harmondsworth: Penguin.

Eyken, van der, W., 1978, The politics of day care, *Where*, 137, April 1978, 102-5.

Eyken, van der, W., 1982, *The Education of Three-to-Eight-year-olds in Europe in the Eighties*, Windsor: NFER-Nelson.

Farel, A.M., 1980, Effects of preferred maternal roles, maternal employment, and sociodemographic status on school adjustment and competence, *Child Development*, 51 (4), 1179-86.

Ferri, E., 1976, *Growing up in a One-parent Family*, Windsor: NFER.

Ferri, E., Birchall, D., Gingell, V. and Gipps, C., 1981, *Combined Nursery Centres, A New Approach to Education and Day Care*, London: Macmillan.

Festinger, L., 1957, *A Theory of Cognitive Dissonance*, Evanston, Ill.: Row, Peterson.

Fonda, N. and Moss, P. (eds), 1976, *Mothers in Employment*, Uxbridge: Brunel University Management Programme.

Gales, K.E. and Marks, P.H., 1974, Twentieth-century trends in the work of women in England and Wales, *Journal of the Royal Statistical Society Archives*, 137, 60-74.

Gallaway, L.E., 1969, The effect of geographical labor mobility on income: a brief comment, *Journal of Human Resources*, 4, 103-9.

Garland, C. and White, S., 1980, *Children and Day Nurseries, Management and practice in nine London day nurseries*, London: Grant McIntyre.

Gibson, C., 1974, Divorce and social class in England and Wales, *British Journal of Sociology*, 25, 79-93.

Gold, D. and Andres, D., 1978, Developmental comparison between ten-year-old children with employed and nonemployed mothers, *Child Development*, 49 (1), 75-84.

Goldstein, H., 1968, Longitudinal studies and the measurement of change, *The Statistician*, 18 (2), 93-117.

Goldthorpe, J.H., 1980, *Social Mobility and Class Structure in Modern Britain*, Oxford: Clarendon Press.

Goodenough, F., 1926, *Measurement of Intelligence By Drawings*,

New York: Harcourt, Brace & World.

Gowler, D. and Legge, K., 1982, Dual-worker families, in Rapoport, R.N., Fogarty, M.P., and Rapoport, R., (eds.), *Families in Britain*, London: Routledge & Kegan Paul, pp. 138-58.

Halsey, A.H., 1972, *Educational Priority*, Volume 1, London: HMSO.

Halsey, A.H., 1980, Education can compensate, *New Society*, 172-3.

Halsey, A.H., Heath, A.F. and Ridge, J.M., 1980, *Origins and Destinations. Family, Class and Education in Modern Britain*, Oxford: Clarendon Press.

Harris, D.B., 1963, *Children's Drawings as Measures of Intellectual Maturity*, New York: Harcourt, Brace & World.

Hoffman, L.W. and Nye, F.I., 1974, *Working Mothers, An Evaluative Review of the Consequences for Wife, Husband and Child*, San Francisco: Jossey-Bass.

Holman, R., 1978, *Poverty: Explanations of Social Deprivation*, London: Martin Robertson.

Holmans, A.E., 1978, Housing tenure in England and Wales, *Social Trends*, 9, 10-19.

Holmstrom, L.L., 1972, *The Two Career Family*, Cambridge, Mass.: Schenkman.

Hood, C., Oppé, T.E., Pless, I.B. and Apte, E., 1970, *Children of West Indian Immigrants, a study of one-year-olds in Paddington*, London: Institute of Race Relations.

Hughes, M., Mayall, B., Moss, P., Perry, J., Petrie, P. and Pinkerton, G., 1980, *Nurseries Now*, Harmondsworth: Penguin.

Hunt, A., 1968, *Survey of Women's Employment*, Volumes 1 and 2, Government Social Survey, London: HMSO.

Hunt, A., Fox, J. and Morgan, M., 1973, *Families and their Needs*, London: HMSO.

Hurstfield, J., 1978, *The Part-time Trap, Part-time workers in Britain today*, London: Low Pay Unit.

Jackson, B. and S., 1979, *Childminder, A Study in Action Research*, London: Routledge & Kegan Paul.

Kingsley, S. and McEwan, J., 1978, Social Classes for women of differing marital status, *Journal of Biosocial Science*, 10 (4), 353-9.

Kohn, M.L., 1969, *Class and Conformity, a study in values*, Homewood, Ill.: Dorsey Press.

Koppitz, E.M., 1968, *Psychological Evaluation of Children's Human Figure Drawings*, New York: Grune & Stratton.

Lambert, L. and Streather, J., 1980, *Children in Changing Families. A study of the circumstances and development by 11 years of illegitimate and of adopted children*, London: Macmillan.

Lazar, E. and Darlington, R.B. (eds), 1978, *Lasting Effects After Pre-school, A report of the Consortium for Longitudinal Studies*, New York: Cornell University.

Leete, R., 1978, One Parent Families: numbers and characteristics, *Population Trends*, 13, 4-9.

Leete, R., 1979, Changing patterns of family formation and dissolution in England and Wales, 1964-76, *Studies on Medical and Population Subjects*, 39, OPCS, London: HMSO.

Leigh, A., 1980, Policy research and reviewing services for under fives, *Social Policy and Administration*, 14 (2), 151-63.

Long, L.H., 1978, Women's labor force participation and the residential mobility of families, in Stromberg, A.H., and Harkness, S. (eds), *Women Working*, Palo Alto: Mayfield, pp. 226-38.

Marsh, A., 1979, *Women and Shiftwork, A report prepared by the Office of Population Censuses and Surveys for the Equal Opportunities Commission*, London: HMSO.

Mayall, B. and Petrie, P., 1977, *Minder, Mother and Child*, London: University of London Institute of Education.

Ministry of Health and Ministry of Education, 1945, *Joint Circular* (Nos. 221 and 75), 14 December 1945.

Moss, P., 1978, *Alternative Models of Group Child-Care for Pre-School Children with Working Parents*, Manchester: Equal Opportunities Commission.

Moss, P. and Plewis, I., 1977, Mental distress in mothers of pre-school children, *Psychological Medicine*, 7, 641-52.

Moss, P., Tizzard, J. and Crook, J., 1973, Families and their needs, *New Society*, 23, 638-40.

National Board for Prices and Incomes, 1970, *Hours of Work, Overtime and Shiftwork*, Report no. 161, HMSO Cmnd 4554.

National Council for One Parent Families, 1980, *Annual Report and Accounts, 1979-80*, London: NCOPF.

Newson, J. & E., 1970, *Four Years Old in an Urban Community*, Harmondsworth: Penguin.

Newson, J. & E., 1978, *Seven Years Old in the Home Environment*, Harmondsworth: Penguin.

Nie, N.H., Hull, C.H., Jenkins, J.G., Steinbrenner, K. and Bent, D.H., 1975, *Statistical Package for the Social Sciences*, Second Edition, New York: McGraw-Hill.

Oakley, A., 1974, *The Sociology of Housework*, Bath: Pitman Press.

Oakley, A., 1976, *Housewife*, Harmondsworth: Penguin.

Oakley, A., 1981, *Subject Women*, Oxford: Martin Robertson.

Office of Population Censuses and Surveys, 1970, *Classification of Occupation*, London: HMSO.

Organisation for Economic Cooperation and Development, 1979, *Equal Opportunities For Women*, Paris: OECD.

Osborn, A.F., 1981, Under-fives in school in England and Wales, 1971-9, *Educational Research*, 23 (2), 96-103.

Osborn, A.F. and Carpenter, A.P., 1980, A rating of neighbourhood types, *Clearing House for Local Authority Social Services Research*, 3, 1-37, Birmingham: University of Birmingham.

Osborn, A.F. and Morris, T.C., 1979, The rationale for a composite index of social class and its evaluation, *British Journal of Sociology*, 30 (1), 39-60.

Osborn, A.F., Morris, T.C. and Butler, N.R., 1979, *Regional Study of*

Children Born 5-11 April 1970, Final report for the Social Science Research Council, Ref. HR 3145.

Osborn, A.F. and Morris, A.C., 1982, Fathers and child care, *Early Child Development and Care*, 8 (4), 279-307.

Palmer, R., 1971, *Starting School*, London: University of London Press.

Parry, M. and Archer, H., 1974, *Pre-school Education*, London: Macmillan.

Plowden Report, 1967, *Children and their Primary Schools*, Central advisory council for education (England), Volumes I and II, London: HMSO.

Pollack, M., 1972, *Today's Three-Year Olds in London*, London: Heinemann.

Preschool Playgroups Association, 1978, *Facts and Figures*, London: PPA.

Pringle, M.K., 1980a, *The Needs of Children, a personal perspective*, 2nd Edition, London: Hutchinson.

Pringle, M.K. (ed.), 1980b, *A Fairer Future for Children*, London: Macmillan.

Pringle, M.K., Butler, N.R. and Davie, R., 1966, *11,000 Seven-year olds*, London: Longmans.

Rapoport, R. and R., 1971, *Dual-Career Families*, Harmondsworth: Penguin.

Reid, I., 1981, *Social Class Differences in Britain*, Second edition, London: Grant McIntyre.

Richman, N., 1976, Depression in mothers of preschool children, *Journal of Child Psychology and Psychiatry*, 17, 75-8.

Richman, N., 1978, Depression in mothers of young children, *Journal of the Royal Society of Medicine*, 71, 489-93.

Rodmell, S. and Smart, L., 1982, *Pregnant at Work, The experiences of women*, The Open University and Kensington, Chelsea and Westminster Area Health Authority, London.

Rossi, A.S., 1977, A biosocial perspective on parenting, *Daedalus*, 106 (2), 1-31.

Rowbotham, S., 1973, *Women's Consciousness, Man's World*, Harmondsworth: Penguin.

Rutter, M., 1972, *Maternal Deprivation Reassessed*, Harmondsworth: Penguin.

Rutter, M. and Madge, N., 1976, *Cycles of Disadvantage, A review of research*, London: Heinemann.

Rutter, M., Tizard, J. and Whitmore, K., 1970, *Education, Health and Behaviour*, London: Longman.

Rutter, M., Tizard, J., Yule, W., Graham, P. and Whitmore, K., 1976, Isle of Wight Studies, 1964-1974, *Psychological Medicine*, 6, 313-32.

Scheffe, H.A., 1959, *The Analysis of Variance*, New York: Wiley.

Scott, L.H., 1981, Measuring intelligence with the Goodenough-Harris drawing test, *Psychological Bulletin*, 89 (3), 483-505.

Scottish Education Department, 1982, *Statistical Bulletin*, Edinburgh: SED.

Shimmin, S., McNally, J. and Liff, S., 1981, Pressures on women

References

engaged in factory work, *Department of Employment Gazette*, 89, 344-9.

Simpson, R., 1978, *Day Care for School Age Children*, Manchester: Equal Opportunities Commission.

Smith, G. and James, T., 1977, The effects of preschool education, some American and British evidence, in Halsey, A.H., (ed.), *Heredity and Environment*, London: Methuen.

Stevenson, J. and Ellis, C., 1975, Which three-year olds attend preschool facilities?, *Child: Care, Health and Development*, 1, 397-411.

Strober, M.H. and Weinberg, C.B., 1980, Strategies used by working and non-working wives to reduce time pressures, *Journal of Consumer Research*, 6 (4), 338-48.

Stromberg, A.H. and Harkness, S. (eds), 1978, *Women Working, Theories and facts in perspective*, Palo Alto, California: Mayfield.

Study Commission on the Family, 1983, *Families in the Future*, London: Study Commission on the Family.

Sylva, K., Roy, C. and Painter, M., 1980, *Child Watching at Playgroup and Nursery School*, London: Grant McIntyre.

Tizard, B., 1974, *Pre-School Education in Great Britain, a research review*, London: Social Science Research Council.

Tizard, J., Moss, P. and Perry, J., 1976, *All Our Children*, London: Temple Smith/New Society.

Toland, S., 1979, Changes in living standards since the 1950's, *Social Trends*, 10, 13-38.

Townsend, P., 1979, *Poverty in the United Kingdom*, Harmondsworth: Penguin.

Turner, I., 1977, *Pre-school Playgroups Research and Evaluation Project*, Report submitted to Govt. of Northern Ireland, Department of Health and Social Services.

Wadsworth, J., Taylor, B., Osborn, A. and Butler, N., 1983, Teenage mothering: child development at five years, *Journal of Child Psychology and Psychiatry* (in press).

Watt, I., 1980, Linkages between industrial radicalism and the domestic role among working women, *Sociological Review*, 28 (1), 55-74.

Weber, C.U., Foster, P.W. and Weikart, D.P., 1978, *An Economic Analysis of the Ypsilanti Perry Preschool project*, Monographs of the High/Scope Educational Research Foundation, number 5, Michigan.

Wedge, P. and Prosser, H., 1973, *Born to Fail?*, London: Arrow Books.

Welsh Office, 1980, *Health and Personal Social Services Statistics for Wales*, Cardiff: HMSO.

Wilmott, P. and Young, M., 1960, *Family and Class in a London Suburb*, London: Routledge & Kegan Paul.

Wilson, H. and Herbert, G.W., 1978, *Parents and Children in the Inner City*, London: Routledge & Kegan Paul.

Wolfe, D., 1971, *The Uses of Talent*, Princeton: Princeton University Press.

Young, M. and Willmott, P., 1975, *The Symmetrical Family*,
    Harmondsworth: Penguin.
Yudkin, S. and Holme, A., 1963, *Working Mothers and Their Children*,
    London: Michael Joseph.

Name index

General index

housing, 15-16; and maternal employment, 171-3, 210; and maternal involvement in pre-school institutions, 128; and occupational status, 193-4; and preschool education, 115-16; rationale, 6-9; and reason for maternal employment, 217, 221-3; by region and country, 18-20; scoring method, 276-8; and type of family, 49-53; and unsocial hours of work, 197-201; *see also* social class; social inequality

social inequality, 5-22; *see also* social class; Social Index

socioeconomic status, *see* social class; Social Index

step-families, *see* family, type of; parent loss

telephone ownership, 17, 47
television ownership, 16, 47
tenure, *see* housing tenure
testing, child's age at, 286
tests: relationship between, 286-7; scoring the, 281-2

vocabulary, *see* English Picture Vocabulary Test

washing machine ownership, 17, 47